MW00788843

The Idea of Indian Literature

FLASHPOINTS

The FlashPoints series is devoted to books that consider literature beyond strictly national and disciplinary frameworks and that are distinguished both by their historical grounding and by their theoretical and conceptual strength. Our books engage theory without losing touch with history and work historically without falling into uncritical positivism. FlashPoints aims for a broad audience within the humanities and the social sciences concerned with moments of cultural emergence and transformation. In a Benjaminian mode, FlashPoints is interested in how literature contributes to forming new constellations of culture and history and in how such formations function critically and politically in the present. Series titles are available online at http://escholarship.org/uc/flashpoints.

SERIES EDITORS: Ali Behdad (Comparative Literature and English, UCLA), Editor Emeritus; Judith Butler (Rhetoric and Comparative Literature, UC Berkeley), Editor Emerita; Michelle Clayton (Hispanic Studies and Comparative Literature, Brown University); Edward Dimendberg (Film and Media Studies, Visual Studies, and European Languages and Studies, UC Irvine), Founding Editor; Catherine Gallagher (English, UC Berkeley), Editor Emerita; Nouri Gana (Comparative Literature and Near Eastern Languages and Cultures, UCLA); Susan Gillman (Literature, UC Santa Cruz), Coordinator; Jody Greene (Literature, UC Santa Cruz); Richard Terdiman (Literature, UC Santa Cruz), Founding Editor

A complete list of titles begins on page 275.

The Idea of Indian Literature

Gender, Genre, and Comparative Method

Preetha Mani

NORTHWESTERN UNIVERSITY PRESS | EVANSTON, ILLINOIS

Northwestern University Press
www.nupress.northwestern.edu

Printed in the United States of America

10 9 8 7 6 5 4 3 2 1

Library of Congress Cataloging-in-Publication Data

Names: Mani, Preetha, author.
Title: The idea of Indian literature : gender, genre, and comparative method / Preetha Mani.
Other titles: FlashPoints (Evanston, Ill.)
Description: Evanston, Illinoia : Northwestern University Press, 2022. | Series: FlashPoints | Includes bibliographical references and index.
Identifiers: LCCN 2022006348 | ISBN 9780810144996 (paperback) | ISBN 9780810145009 (cloth) | ISBN 9780810145016 (ebook)
Subjects: LCSH: Indic literature—20th century—History and criticism. | Short stories, Hindi—History and criticism. | Short stories, Tamil—History and criticism. | Women in literature.
Classification: LCC PK5423 .M36 2022 | DDC 891.471—dc23/eng/20220215
LC record available at https://lccn.loc.gov/2022006348

Contents

Acknowledgments

"Gripping my pen with all my might was the only way I felt I could keep hold of the reigns over my character. Still, they slipped out of my hands like always," says the narrator of Mannu Bhandari's short story "Maiṃ Hār Gaī" (I lost, 1955) as she struggles to mold her protagonist to fit her plot. This is how it sometimes seems when writing a first book. So, I am extremely fortunate to have received the generosity and support—both scholarly and personal—of so many people while undertaking this project. From the very beginning, Vasudha Dalmia and George Hart have been steadfast in their confidence in me, even before I knew what my scholarship would become. This book owes immensely to the questions they have stimulated, care for language they have instilled, and fields of study they have ardently built. I am indebted to Kausalya Hart, Usha Jain, Mrs. Jayanthi, Mrs. Soundra Kohila, Neelam ji, Dr. Bharathy Rajulu, Swami ji, and Vidhu ji—my Hindi and Tamil language teachers without whose good will, dedication, and patience this work would not have been possible. Nancy Bauer and Jonathan Strong helped me to hear the writerly voice that set me on my path. The librarians at the Institut Français de Pondichéry (IFP), Hindi Sahitya Sammelan, Roja Muthiah Research Library (RMRL), and Sahitya Akademi happily opened their archives, so full of treasures. R. Narenthiran at the IFP and G. Sundar at RMRL went to especially great lengths to help me locate issues of old journals. My heartfelt thanks to them all.

Conversations over continents and years enabled this book to grow. To map the meandering discussions about Tamil literature and everything else that I have had with Kannan M. of the IFP would be to chart new constellations. He and Anupama have housed, nourished, and loved me unconditionally. Francesca Orsini welcomed me into her vibrant world of scholarly investigation, gently prodding me to look more closely and question more openheartedly. Her warmth and inquisitiveness, depth and breadth of scholarship, and strong sense of commitment to friends, colleagues, and students inspire my approach to literature. Dilip Kumar in Chennai willingly shared his trove of stories and books. Lakshmi Holmstrom sparked my interest in Tamil literature and helped me to navigate the trials and pleasures of translation. I miss her quiet tenderness, constant reflectiveness, and fierce devotion to exploring the inner lives of Tamil women. I was too late to meet most of the writers I examine in this book and so hold all the more dearly to the long chats I had with Rajendra Yadav in Darya Ganj and Mannu Bhandari in Hauz Khas. I hope this book captures some of the world of which they were a part. Laura Brueck has been a more stalwart advocate, thoughtful reader, and fun-loving friend than I could have ever hoped for. Rahul Parson and Greg Goulding set off on the long road with me and steadfastly accompanied me the whole way—always with compassion and at times from miles away. Kamal Kapadia and Matthias Fripp made me their family and held my hand through many ups and downs. So many others provided crucial input: A. R. Venkatachalapathy, Lalit Batra, Allison Busch, C. S. Lakshmi, Sharad Chari, Supriya Chaudhuri, Supriya Chotani, Jennifer Clare, Frank Cody, Whitney Cox, Aparna Dharwadker, Vinay Dharwadker, Jennifer Dubrow, E. Annamalai, Sascha Ebeling, Swarnavel Eswaran, Toral Gajarawala, Corin Golding, Nikhil Govind, Charu Gupta, Hans Harder, Udaya Kumar, David Lunn, Carlos Mena, Farina Mir, Pritipuspa Mishra, Sujata Mody, Janaki Nair, Costas Nakassis, Shobna Nijhawan, Geeta Patel, Robert Phillips, Alok Rai, Sara Rai, Bhavani Raman, Pritpal Randhawa, S. Shankar, Kumkum Sangari, Simona Sawhney, Rena Searle, Taylor Sherman, Snehal Shingavi, Neelam Srivastava, Rajeswari Sunder Rajan, Ashwini Tambe, Torsten Tschacher, V. Arasu, and V. Geetha. I am eternally grateful to each and every one.

Friends and colleagues at Rutgers have given me rich intellectual sustenance and cheery camaraderie. I have depended on Sylvia Chan-Malik, Chie Ikeya, Suzy Kim, Christian Lammerts, and Rick Lee in more ways than I thought could be possible. My debts to Chie and Christian strain the imagination. Jessica Birkenholtz, Anjali Nerlekar, and Meheli Sen read many portions of this book with utmost care and enthusiasm, providing me with the encouragement and wise perspective I needed to push through. They sustained me otherwise, too, with food, drink, and merriment when I needed these the most. It is rare, I think, to find such a kindred spirit as I have found in Anjali. She is a cornerstone in myriad ways. Ousseina Alidou, Charles Haberl, Alamin Mazrui, Jorge Marcone, Andrew Parker, Samah Selim, Janet Walker, and Rebecca Walkowitz have been compassionate mentors, fierce advocates, and intellectual role models whose footsteps I endeavor to follow. My colleagues in African, Middle Eastern, and South Asian Languages and Literatures (AMESALL) have extended me great kindness, making the department feel like home. I am especially lucky for the friendship and sincere advice of Karen Bishop, Indrani Chatterjee, Andrew Goldstone, Sumit Guha, Dorothy Hodgson, David Hughes, Sneha Khaund, Efe Khayyat, Triveni Kuchi, Mazen Labban, Mukti Lakhi Mangharam, Melanie McDermott, Nida Sajid, Laura Schneider, and Rick Schroeder. Hudson McFann swooped in at the last minute with selflessness and grace to help tie up loose ends. To all, my deepest gratitude.

This project benefited from faculty fellowships at the Rutgers Institute for Research on Women in 2013–14 and the Rutgers Center for Cultural Analysis in 2019–20. I am also grateful for feedback from the participants of the "Indian Literature as Comparative Literature" workshops at Rutgers in 2013 and the IFP in 2014, the "Literary Sentiments" conferences at Heidelberg in 2016 and Northwestern in 2017, the "Hindi/Urdu Arts and Literature" conferences at Princeton in 2015 and 2018, and the Chicago Tamil Forum in 2019. Many of this book's arguments were presented at the Fredrich Schlegel Graduate School of Literary Studies, Nehru Memorial Museum and Library, Northwestern University, Penn State University, Postcolonial Print Cultures Network, School of Oriental and African Studies, University of California, Berkeley, University of California, Davis, University of Texas at Austin, and Yale University. This book was made possible due to generous financial support from the American Council of Learned Societies, American Institute for Indian Studies, Andrew W. Mellon Foundation, Rutgers Center for Cultural Analysis, Rutgers Global, Rutgers Institute for Research on Women, and Rutgers Research Council. It is my pleasure and privilege to thank them here.

At Northwestern University Press, Susan Gilman's support of this project has been constant and unflagging. I am immensely grateful for her faith in my work and her sage counsel. I thank Gianna Mosser, Trevor Perri, Maia Rigas, Patrick Samuel, and Faith Wilson Stein for so graciously guiding me through the publishing process. Portions of chapters 2, 3, and 5 appeared in *South Asia: Journal of South Asian Studies*, *Comparative Literature*, and *Comparative Studies of South Asia, Africa, and the Middle East*. I appreciate their permission to reprint this material here. I also extend sincere thanks to Ashok Maheshwari of Rajkamal Prakashan and the uncredited artist of the January 1963 issue of *Naī Kahāniyāṁ* for use of their image on my book cover.

My greatest debt is to my family, a debt in the face of which words flounder. Venk, Usha, Priya, and Sunita Mani may have puzzled to understand my scholarship, but this never stopped them from wholeheartedly tending to everything else in my life so that I could continue the work I was doing. Nancy and Lory Ghertner have lavished me with love and nurtured me unceasingly. Zoë Ghertner has been my sister and Robin Ghertner and Kenny Warren my brothers. Steven Baldi is a steady fellow. Gina, Arjan, Gabriel, and Jaimal Ghertner and Lee Baldi give me so much glee. Ameya Mani Ghertner arrived, and Zubin Mani Ghertner followed soon after, making this project a more wonderous adventure than I anticipated, infusing my writing with the possibilities of worlds I am yet to imagine. Apart from me, only Asher Ghertner knows what has gone into composing this book. He has lived with it as long as I have, listened to every idea, read every draft, and believed in it when I have faltered. This book is for him and for our shared, wide-open future.

Note on Translation and Transliteration

All translations from Hindi and Tamil in this book are mine. Some passages have been translated before, and some have not. I use my own translations because, as many have argued before me, translation is an intimate and profound act of interpretation. It is the primary means through which I have learned from the thinkers I discuss in this book.

In transliterating Hindi and Tamil words, I have followed the American Library Association–Library of Congress (ALA-LC) standards for romanization. Exceptions to this are place names, caste names, and personal names. For all of these, I have retained their popular spellings in Roman letters without diacritics.

The Idea of Indian Literature

INTRODUCTION

The Idea of Indian Literature

The idea of an Indian literature, though fairly old, is yet to emerge as a distinct literary concept.

—Sisir Kumar Das, "The Idea of an Indian Literature"

In 1981 Sujit Mukherjee—writer, editor, translator, cricketer, and scholar of comparative literature in India—published *The Idea of an Indian Literature*, a compilation of English-language essays by various thinkers on the subject. The volume discloses how Indian literature arose as a new preoccupation in the nineteenth century, particularly among Orientalists and precisely when Indian languages entered into sustained interaction with English. Rather than accomplishing its self-proclaimed task to uncover "the underlying concept" of Indian literature, the volume documents how Indian literature remained an ambiguous, contested, and shifting category—with persistently troubled ties to English—throughout the nineteenth and twentieth centuries.[1]

For the scholars that Mukherjee excerpts, the primary conundrum is that the very term "Indian literature" undermines the triangulation of language, literature, and nation that the eighteenth-century philological revolution in Europe had put in place.[2] Whereas individual literatures mapped onto distinct language communities in Anglo-European traditions, the multilingual makeup of the subcontinent meant that Indian literature could not be linked to just one language: "I cannot say that [my lectures] are to treat the history of 'Indian literature'; for then I should have to consider the whole body of

Indian languages," German Indologist Albrecht Weber reflects in the 1852 piece with which Mukherjee's anthology begins.[3] To resolve this dilemma, Weber turns to Sanskrit as the Indian literature par excellence. Others in the volume, such as linguists Robert Caldwell and George Grierson, conceptualize Indian literature around the shared life of the living vernaculars. Still others, like philosopher and nationalist Sri Aurobindo and founder of Indian sociology Dhurjati Prasad Mukerji, emphasize the connecting motif of Hindu spirituality. Mukherjee himself concludes that Indian literature, a field yet to be realized, depends solely on the "bold and imaginative speculation" that it even exists.[4] The idea of Indian literature, it thus would seem, is the idea of Indian literature's possibility at all.

This book contends that the idea of Indian literature is constituted by the irresolvable question of language's relationship to literature—rather than by specific concepts, texts, or languages. This idea is therefore indeterminate, propositional, and presented through a multitude of mismatched desires that aspire to bypass language, while conjoining literature and nation. The idea of Indian literature was spurred by nineteenth-century processes of vernacularization, which produced new relationships among Indian languages and between them and English. It arose from the paradox that a single literature could be written in multiple, distinct languages.

The Idea of Indian Literature explores the persistence of this paradox through an examination of how Hindi writers based in North India and Tamil writers based in Madras (now Chennai) used the short story to give purchase to the idea of Indian literature between the 1930s and 1960s, both in conversation and in conflict with English. Hindi, with its contentious history of Hinduization and opposition to Urdu and English, has long embodied questions of national belonging.[5] Tamil, by contrast, epitomizes the anti-Brahmin and secessionist propensities of the region.[6] For the writers I discuss in this book, the idea of Indian literature served as a means of contesting the fraught linguistic divisions that twentieth-century Hindi and Tamil ethnolinguistic movements sought to sediment. It offered a platform for their efforts to make the boundaries of language more malleable and to create understandings of community based on literary, rather than linguistic, norms.

At the same time, I examine how, at critical junctures in the late colonial and early postcolonial periods, Hindi and Tamil writers produced new, nonaligning conceptions of Indian literature precisely when debates over national language were renewed. For them, the question of language simultaneously raised the question of literature, and literature became a means for tackling—and sometimes bracketing—language. While the possibility of

Hindi becoming the national language seemed imminent to many by the 1930s, it also positioned Hindi and Tamil writers unequally vis-à-vis the nation and forced them to grapple with the schism between language and literature in divergent ways. For this reason, even as Hindi and Tamil writers jointly imagined a pan-Indian literature, their speculations about what it could mean were profoundly shaped by questions of identity and belonging that were unique to the Hindi- and Tamil-speaking regions. This book's comparison of these writers reveals how Indian literature could be neither one nor many.[7]

The paradox of Indian literature extends into contemporary Indian literary studies, which—as Aijaz Ahmad famously observed three decades ago—pivots around the problem of comparative methodology.[8] How can a pan-Indian literature also account for the singularities of the many subcontinental languages? Some scholars have developed aggregative models of Indian literature that confer circumscribed regional literary histories with parallel and equal status.[9] Others have postulated frameworks for highlighting literary commonalities and interactions across linguistic spheres.[10] More recent scholarship elaborates paradigms of degreed cultural autonomy, co-constitution and cross-fertilization, and multilingualism as a "structuring and generative principle."[11] All these approaches have advanced important insights for understanding the complex, multilingual makeup of Indian literary fields and for productively problematizing the notion of Indian literature itself.

Nonetheless, the idea of Indian literature endures, and the tension between the monolingual disposition of regional language movements, on one hand, and diverse multilingual histories and networks, on the other, remains its formative feature. This is precisely the tension that a comparison of Hindi and Tamil literature presents. Although well read in two or more languages—and often translating prolifically between them—the Hindi and Tamil writers I discuss in this book consciously invested in promoting the development of their respective literary fields. Their commitment to working primarily in Hindi and Tamil necessarily, if also contrarily, linked their writing with regionalist positions. It placed these writers at a tangent to nationalist and internationalist politics aimed at superseding ethnolinguistic difference, even as they viewed themselves as contributors to subcontinental and global literary circulations. This contradictory position, *The Idea of Indian Literature* shows, was a consequence of evolving processes of vernacularization. This book argues that Indian literature was an idea that Hindi and Tamil writers could wield to productively challenge the condition of vernacularity to which their literatures had been assigned and in reaction to which regional and national language politics had emerged.

THE VERNACULAR

Examining the rise of regional-language literary cultures in South Asia, Sheldon Pollock links vernacularization to specific political shifts occurring at the beginning of the second millennium. Vernacularization, in his view, is defined by the appropriation of cosmopolitan Sanskrit literary conventions to impart less-traveled regional languages with a literariness that they had previously been denied.[12] Emphasizing its democratizing impulse to elevate the language of commoners into the language of the public sphere, Christian Novetzke further identifies vernacularization as a demarcated time period spanning the fifth to the seventeenth centuries.[13] Alexander Beecroft extends this periodization to worldwide literary developments that together constitute what he calls a "vernacular literary ecology," a global ecology characterized by the standardization and subsequent literarization of vernacular languages based on genre or the history of literary custom—rather than their identification with territories, peoples, or cultures that an ensuing national literary ecology later established.[14] In all these scholars' views, vernacularization precedes the emergence of nation-states, entails a symbiotic relationship between cosmopolitan languages and vernaculars, and signals the conscious choice of intellectual elites to construct geographically narrow audiences for their work.

Conversely, scholars working in the early modern, colonial, and postcolonial periods have approached the concept of the vernacular through a critical, rather than historical, lens. Pointing to South Asia's multilingual history where several cosmopolitan languages mingled and sometimes served purposes contradictory to their universal ambitions, Francesca Orsini replaces the "vernacular" with the "local" to acknowledge the wider networks and significant geographies that writers engage and envision.[15] S. Shankar calls for a relational approach that understands the vernacular contextually, through the terms that exist in relation to it, and as a synonym for the culturally autonomous.[16] Partha Chatterjee links the vernacular to spaces of history writing beyond English and the colonial modern, while Toral Gajarawala dissociates the concept from language altogether to focus on shared citational practices and social grammars.[17] These recent discussions observe that, even when the term itself is disputed, the "vernacular" plays a "supplementary" role,[18] functions as "a name under which to gather overlooked archives in overlooked languages,"[19] and offers a potential arena for examining "protest, non-conformity, utopia and dystopia."[20]

I summarize these differing approaches to the vernacular to highlight a distinct rift between scholars of premodern literatures and those working on later eras: whereas the former understand the category as revolutionary and complementary to the cosmopolitan, the latter seek to qualify, repudiate, or reverse its inferior and provincialized status.[21] Bracketing my own position on these debates for a moment, I want to suggest that this scholarly schism is a consequence of a new vernacularization, which can be traced to the nineteenth century and which positioned Indian languages in vexed relation to one another and to English.[22] The study of Indian literatures in the periods leading up to, during, and following colonization necessarily contends with the entrenched linguistic hierarchies established over the course of this time. These hierarchies actively shape the currency that the vernacular carries in contemporary linguistic activism and literary production. Understanding how colonial-era dynamics instigated a different politics of language in South Asia—rather than perpetuating an older one—allows us to better articulate the stakes of claiming the vernacular as a scholarly position. It also helps to explain why vernacularization could democratize the premodern public sphere,[23] while conversely obscuring caste hierarchies within the private sphere in colonial and postcolonial times.[24]

A NEW VERNACULARIZATION

A rich body of scholarship has offered insight into the sea change in India's linguistic landscape that occurred during the nineteenth and early twentieth centuries. Drawing on this work, I reframe these transformations as a new vernacularization, taking place vis-à-vis English rather than Sanskrit or Persian. My argument is that colonial-era vernacularization should not be viewed as an extension or deepening of the premodern linguistic hierarchies that Pollock and Beecroft outline. English did not succeed Sanskrit and Persian to become the imperial language of the modern era. Nor did Indian regional languages then straightforwardly appropriate English literary conventions to supersede its aesthetic and political power. Rather, colonial-era vernacularization positioned English as *the* paradigmatic vernacular, while simultaneously supplying it with exceptional cultural and economic capital. This contradictory process created dynamics of both affiliation and antagonism between English and Indian languages. Twentieth-century moments of heightened linguistic tension shifted these dynamics, each time reconfiguring the multilingual landscape of the subcontinent. To view these linguistic and literary changes as evidence of new processes of vernacularization is to call attention to the distinctly colonial associations between Indian languages and English and their formative role in shaping subcontinental triangulations of language, literature, and nation. These associations underscore the unique monolingualizing and nationalizing consequences of the philological revolution in colonialized contexts, like India, in contrast to Europe.[25]

Lisa Mitchell has characterized the nineteenth-century transformation of Indian multilingualism as a shift from a task-based view of language—in which different languages function more like different registers "specific to particular tasks and contexts"—to an identity-based view of language that links languages to the cultural identities of their speakers.[26] "By the early twentieth century," she writes, "it was increasingly believed that someone literate should be capable of doing everything that needed to be done within a single language."[27] While this change parallels the European rise of monolinguistic nationalisms that both Yasemin Yildiz and Alexander Beecroft describe, it was also unique in that it occurred simultaneously with the emergence of the concept of the vernacular itself. The term "vernacular" only came into parlance in South Asia in the nineteenth century.[28] Orientalists such as William Jones, John Gilchrist, and George Grierson were among the first to use the term to describe Indian languages and to gloss it with the Indian word *bhāshā*.[29] Prior to this moment, *bhāshā* (language)—used interchangeably with *deśabhāshā* (language of place)—referenced a range of regional languages that possessed poetic traditions distinct from supra-regional literatures such as Sanskrit and Persian.[30] However, colonial efforts to learn and classify Indian languages—influenced greatly by Gottfried von Herder's view that languages possess unique biological and cultural characteristics—prompted an equation of *bhāshā* with the living tongues of the various Indian regions vis-à-vis the reified classicism of Sanskrit.[31] This new understanding of the vernacular, though spurred by Indological curiosity and concerns about good governance and religious conversion, was by no means one-sided. A rising Indian intellectual class critically shaped ideas of the vernacular through their production of grammars, dictionaries, and language surveys, as well as through their involvement in regional language training, publishing, and scholarship.[32]

These activities were central to the institution, in mid-nineteenth-century India, of what Bhavani Raman has called the Anglo-vernacular regime, which initiated the standardization of Indian languages through deeper interaction with English.[33] Multiple transformations—in education, publishing, and policy making—helped to consolidate this regime through the development of new genres, vocabularies, syntaxes, and styles of orthography and prose. Sisir Kumar Das and E. Annamalai have observed how print conventions used for English introduced new forms of punctuation, paragraph breaks, syntax, and spacing between words into Tamil and Bengali.[34] Raman shows how English conventions oriented Tamil grammar toward the colloquial by emphasizing accuracy in the transcription and translation of sermons and oratory. This new grammar replaced existing Tamil poetic conventions that prioritized rote memory.[35] Mitchell uncovers similar shifts in Telugu, which reorganized lexicons around etymology instead of literary usage.[36] Vasudha Dalmia and Alok Rai outline new publishing ventures, political debates, and educational policies that fashioned Hindi as a modern and accessible language comparable to English and in contrast to the aristocratic outlook of Urdu.[37] Sudipta Kaviraj traces syntactic and semantic changes through which notions of Western science imparted Bengali with modern sensibilities and rationalities.[38] And Sitamshu Yashaschandra documents how British textbook-style education spurred new Gujarati styles and genres focused on individual experience.[39] These are just a few examples of how new processes of vernacularization took shape across Indian languages.[40] In each of these cases, English served as the preeminent model to be emulated—the perfect vernacular, synonymous with the spoken language of its people and the cultural and territorial breadth of its nation.[41]

At the core of this colonial-era vernacularization lay a deep anxiety about the diglossic nature of Indian languages. Diglossia distinguished Indian languages from the perceived fluidity between written and spoken forms of English and posed an obstacle to colonial efforts to know and control Indian populations.[42] Orientalists, administrators, and missionaries consequently construed existing literary traditions, which consisted mainly of poetry, as antiquated and removed from everyday life. Prose served as a means for language reform. As Sascha Ebeling has argued in the case of Tamil, poetry "was deemed too difficult and artificial," while prose could convey "'useful or substantial knowledge,' and 'sounder and more elevated sentiments.' In short, a new 'vernacular literature' had to be created."[43] Among both the colonial and indigenous elite, a bias toward linguistic realism quickly overshadowed older poetic conventions based on devotional tropes, word play and alliteration, interlinguistic paronomasia, and creative adaptation.[44] Meenakshi Mukherjee cautions us to remember that English linguistic and literary models did not supersede Indian writers' complex engagement with precolonial genres and literary traditions.[45] Nonetheless, she also chronicles a distinctive change in emphasis in Indian literary fields during the nineteenth century from poetry to prose through which realism became "the highest mode of perception . . . and a good word from the English press the highest conceivable reward."[46] The development of literary prose was a primary aim of colonial-era vernacularization because it effectively diminished diglossia by bringing Indian written forms closer to spoken language.[47]

As several scholars have pointed out, Thomas Macaulay's infamous 1835 "Minute on Indian Education"—which called for "a class of persons, Indian in blood and colour, but English in taste"[48]—epitomizes the privileged position that English occupied in this process.[49] British education policies sedimented a clear linguistic division by promoting English at the level of higher education and Indian vernaculars at the primary and secondary levels. This division made English education available to a small minority of upwardly mobile, upper-caste Indians aspiring to work in government, while relegating vernacular language education to middling castes and professional classes in mofussil areas.[50] At the same time, however, English and Indian vernaculars were viewed as equally important mediums for the dissemination of European knowledge. As Ulka Anjaria notes, "*both* English and the vernaculars were the site of the consolidation of colonial power."[51] Most, if not all, nineteenth-century Indian writers were educated in English and moved effortlessly between English and regional languages, understanding their labors as part of a renaissance in Indian vernaculars.[52] Their experiments evidence how practices of education and the material realities of print brought English and Indian languages into syntactic, semantic, aesthetic, and ideological relations of co-constitution, which operated on both visible and subcutaneous levels.[53] For instance, early Indian novels bring to light an array of multidirectional crossovers in vocabulary, phrasing, tropes, and genres between English and Indian languages.[54] In addition, almost all late nineteenth- and early twentieth-century vernacular publications integrated English within their covers. Title pages, prefaces, magazine and newspaper articles, and advertisements partially or fully written in English abutted vernacular text; Roman script popped up mid-sentence in vernacular fiction, criticism, and journalism; and passages in vernacular works that were quoted from English texts sometimes went untranslated. These examples demonstrate more than just physical proximity and linguistic interchangeability between English and Indian languages. More crucially, they reveal that Indian writers presumed multilingual readers who could move between these languages and also that these writers were comfortable addressing multiple readership communities that possessed varied linguistic groundings. While linguistic nationalisms would create distinct boundaries between Indian languages and English by the late colonial era, they remained relatively contiguous throughout the nineteenth century.

What I am here describing as a new nineteenth-century vernacularization thus entailed several components. First, it began a longer process of reconfiguring multilingualism along the axis of cultural identity wherein Indian languages became envisioned as equal and parallel yet underdeveloped in comparison to English. Second, it established new educational institutions, language policies, and print practices and generated new literary styles and genres—all of which led to a deep and irrevocable imbrication of English and Indian languages, literatures, and readerships. Third, it was motivated by a desire to reduce linguistic diglossia by bringing older, seemingly inaccessible literary forms closer to spoken language. Fourth, and relatedly, colonial-era vernacularization tackled the problem of diglossia primarily through the medium of literature by developing prose and discrediting poetry, thereby installing linguistic realism as the privileged marker of literary modernity. The idea of Indian literature emerged in the twentieth century as a fortuitous result and creative response to the changing language dynamics spurred by these processes.

THE HETEROLINGUAL TURN

While colonial-era vernacularization initiated the reconfiguration of multilingualism around cultural identity in the nineteenth century, regional linguistic nationalisms did not become full-fledged until the 1920s, when the national language question came to the fore. In the North, the recognition in 1900 of Devanagari alongside Nastaliq as an official script of the court constituted a pivotal moment in the development of Hindi nationalism.[55] Yet, no sense of Hindi as a standardized language distinct from Urdu existed even in the 1910s.[56] Mahavir Prasad Dwivedi's editorship of the Hindi journal *Sarasvatī* from 1903 to 1920—through which Dwivedi carefully crafted the spelling, punctuation, vocabulary, and genres now associated with *Khaṛī Bolī* (equated today with modern standard Hindi)—provided an avenue for expressions of Hindi language devotion to emerge.[57] The crescendo of Tamil nationalism follows a similar chronology with Maraimalai Adigal's launch of the Pure Tamil Movement (Taṉi Tamiḻ Iyakkam) in 1916 and Mahatma Gandhi's establishment of the opposing South India Society for the Propagation of Hindi (Dakshiṇa Bhārat Hindī Pracār Sabhā) in Madras in 1918.[58] The Indian National Congress—the leading political party of the Indian Independence Movement—officially declared its support for Hindustani as the lingua franca of India in 1925, propelling language debates theretofore internal to North Indian politics into the national arena. Only in the 1930s did Tamil language-devotion organizations and conferences and anti-Hindi protests arise in the South and, meanwhile, political discussions about Hindustani as a national compromise between Hindi and Urdu take center stage in the North.[59]

These heated contestations around language mark the completion of a shift, which had begun in the nineteenth century, from task-based multilingualism to identity-based multilingualism—with Indian languages now recognizably separate and tied to distinct regional communities and territories. The rise of the national language question therefore represents a turning point in colonial-era vernacularization, a moment when free-flowing interactions among Indian languages, and between them and English, had become thoroughly politicized and deeply constrained. This is evident in the work of Indian intellectuals such as Bengali writer Rabindranath Tagore and Hindi writer Dhanpat Rai Srivastava "Premchand." Both favored the cultivation of regional languages while simultaneously expressing astonishment that Indians from different regions could not understand one another. Attending a Women's Indian Association gathering in Madras in 1934, Tagore confessed that he could not follow the address, which was delivered in Tamil (though translated into English). "It is most unfortunate that they who belonged to the same country are separated by different languages," he reported to *The Hindu* afterward. He admonished South Indians for using "too much English to the detriment of vernaculars" while emphasizing his own commitment to speaking Bengali whenever possible.[60] These comments are remarkable because they divulge Tagore's view of Tamil speakers as outsiders and his desire for a common national language, even as he ardently encouraged linguistic regionalism.

Premchand—who was well versed in and moved between Hindi, Urdu, and English throughout his career—held a similar stance.[61] Despite his multilingual background, Premchand's writings document his increasing investment in Hindi and ambition to install it as the national language. He articulated a firmly anticolonial position, arguing that "the most insulting, most extensive, most unyielding component of our subjugation is the supremacy of English."[62] He further stressed, "The foundation of a nation is its national language."[63] In Premchand's view, Hindi was the most suitable language for operating on a national scale because it was the most widely understood and possessed an affinity to both Urdu and Sanskrit—the latter being, to his mind, the ur-language of most Indian languages.[64] In the early 1930s he began to track the progress of the South India Society for the Propagation of Hindi and report on the number of students advancing through the society's Hindi-training programs.[65] He also toured the South—traveling from Madras to Mysore to Bangalore—to promote Hindi and observe its progress in the Tamil- and Kannada-speaking regions.[66] At the same time, however, Premchand delimited the scope of Hindi by clearly demarcating its boundaries from Urdu, linking the two languages to different religions, scripts, and literary histories.

Premchand articulated this contradictory position explicitly in "Rāshṭrābhāshā Hindī aura Uskī Samasyāeṁ" (The national language Hindi and its problems), a speech he delivered at the December 1934 graduation ceremony of the South India Society for the Propagation of Hindi. Premchand began the address by pinpointing a change in political perspective that made the creation of a national language a viable possibility. The same Indian intellectuals who had earlier put their energies into English, he noted, were now deliberately choosing Hindi for the good of the nation. Premchand also presented an inclusive understanding of Hindi as a language open to diverse vocabularies, speakers, and influences. He pleaded for more commitment to Hindi across the regions so that it could gain depth, breadth, and status. "I dream of the day when the national language has fully occupied the place of English . . . when—from Madras and Mysore, Dhaka and Pune—excellent books written in the national language shall come out in all locations," he exclaimed.[67]

While praising the broad reach of the Hindi language, however, Premchand restricted the trajectory of its literary history. He lamented that the Hindi canon was still impoverished compared to other Indian literatures. In his view, its premodern texts were mired in the indulgent, love-stricken tones of erotic poetry, and the Hindi novel still lacked aesthetic merit. Nonetheless, Premchand asserted that modern Hindi had achieved what Urdu could not: a complete break with the past.[68] On this positive note, Premchand concluded by giving the society's graduates an overview of important Hindi literary developments, deliberately juxtaposing Hindi authors and texts with their Urdu counterparts. In his narrative, Premchand designated Urdu in Nastaliq as the language and literature of the Urdu-speaking community, narrowly defined. He projected Hindi in Nagari, by contrast, as the future language and literature of the independent Indian nation.[69]

Premchand's speech highlights a shift in the role of language choice in colonial-era vernacularization, which was incited by the national language question. Nineteenth-century writings across regional languages illustrate what might be considered a less restricted multilingualism—characterized by Indian writers' comparatively uninhibited movements between English and Indian languages, use of diverse and nonstandardized vocabularies, and embrace of English as a model for developing Indian languages.[70] By the 1930s, however, many regional writings had taken on a decidedly anti-English position, albeit to varying degrees.[71] The entrenchment of regional language movements, momentum of Indian nationalism, and apparent imminence of independence led to circumstances in which the vernacular—now binarily opposed to English—seemed the only viable option to many.[72] Premchand's passionate rejection of English exemplifies this knotty linguistic situation.

In the late colonial era, the compulsory nature of the vernacular legitimized linguistic regionalism while simultaneously requiring allegiance to Hindi as an all-India language. These competing conditions of vernacularity established an incompatibility between regionalist and nationalist commitments that continues to this day. Premchand's address expresses this incompatibility as a mismatch between Hindi language and literature, by framing Hindi as an expansive language, while restricting its literature to an established, exclusively Hindi canon.[73] In this way, the speech articulates a change in the relationship of language to literature that nineteenth-century vernacularization had established—wherein literature had served as a means for aligning written language with spoken forms. By the 1930s, regional language movements had established well-defined protocols for what constituted vernacular literatures, reifying them by distinguishing literary language from other language uses. Heir to this fraught history of vernacularization, Premchand spoke from a perspective of literary regionalism, despite advocating for linguistic diversity and breadth.[74]

Following his address at the society's graduation, Premchand published in February 1935 an account about his sojourn in the South. In the piece Premchand noted his unfamiliarity with South Indian customs and foods, conveying his sense of the region's foreignness. He also voiced his dismay at the lack of financial and institutional support for Hindi, which seemed precarious, especially in Tamil-speaking areas.[75] "Hindi or Hindustani is like a foreign language in the South. . . . Neither could [people] speak Hindi, nor could they easily understand a Hindi speech," he bemoaned.[76] While these reflections are not unusual in and of themselves, I find them surprising in light of the address that Premchand gave to Tamil students of Hindi just a few months earlier. What must have led him to address an uncomprehending audience in rather formal Hindi? Why would he have dwelled on Hindi-Urdu language debates and literary histories that were mostly obscure to his addressees?

These strange new conditions of incomprehension were, I suggest, a consequence of the national language question. The potential of an all-India language reshaped Indian multilingualism around what Naoki Sakai—examining Japanese cultural nationalism—has called "heterolingual address." Observing that "'addressing' is anterior to 'communicating,'" Sakai defines heterolingual address as speech or texts directed to not only speakers of the addresser's language but speakers of other languages as well.[77] In heterolingual address, the "we" that comprises the community of listeners or readers is a nonaggregate one for which "neither reciprocal apprehension nor transparent communication [is] guaranteed."[78] Misunderstanding and complete lack of comprehension are both possible outcomes of heterolingual address. Nevertheless, the vocative "we" of heterolingual address imagines a community formed by the act of address itself, rather than any preexisting commonality. Sakai offers heterolingual address as an alternative to the monolingual disposition of the nation, which constructs addressers and addressees as members of a homogenous language society. However, in multilingual India, unlike Japan, linguistic homogeneity was both contentious and arguably impossible. Late-colonial efforts to install a national language therefore generated circumstances in which lack of communication was the norm. The fundamental point of heterolingual interactions like Premchand's speech was, I believe, to summon a national community into existence through the act of address—not to foster reciprocal exchange and understanding.

This new moment of linguistic opacity precipitated an unprecedented investment in the idea of Indian literature as a means of uniting Indian regions. Premchand, for example, argued vociferously for the development of a pan-Indian corpus and formation of all-India literary societies and institutions alongside his appeals for making Hindi the national language.[79] "Indian literature [*bhāratīya sāhitya*] is that which contains the full aesthetic essence of each region's literary wealth. Everyone should be able to see the soul of their nation through this literature," he proclaimed.[80] While such an entity—as Premchand and others were fully aware—did not yet exist, the very idea of Indian literature now enabled writers to more intimately feel the presence of readerships beyond their own linguistic spheres. In this way, it fostered a new dialogism rooted in Indian multilingualism. Mikhail Bakhtin defines the dialogic nature of language as the inherently anticipatory orientation of all discourse toward the responses of others.[81] In late-colonial India, Indian literature represented an ideational horizon that directed Indian writers' utterances toward prospective addressees from other language communities, not just their own. To such readers and listeners, these utterances were intelligible because of their significance as Indian literature, beyond the semantic meanings they conveyed.

The second stage of colonial-era vernacularization was thus characterized by the relative estrangement of Indian languages from one another, their opposition to English, and their congregation around the idea of Indian literature as the promise of their cultural unification. In this context of deepened linguistic isolationism, the English term "vernacular" became highly contested, leading the Government of India to dispense with it in all official publications and correspondence in 1939.[82] Late-colonial vernacularization was, in this way, marked by anticolonial resistance to the stigma that the vernacular had garnered during the early twentieth century. Indian writers, including the ones I examine in this book, began to demand the linguistic and literary recognition that they understood other world languages to enjoy. They had always read extensively in, translated voraciously from, and creatively innovated on multiple languages. In this moment, however, these activities became the primary means through which they rejected vernacularity by dialogically engaging with readership communities both known and unknown, comprehending and uncomprehending.

PARALLEL AND SEPARATE WORLDS

These late-colonial shifts in the trajectory of vernacularization gave rise to the idea of Indian literature as an arena that could facilitate the congregation of the subcontinent's many, distinct languages. Writers consequently began to approach literature as separate from language, viewing it as a utopian realm that promised to insert cosmopolitan perspectives into linguistic regionalisms. Following independence in 1947, fervent battles over the installation of a national language and the formation of linguistic states enhanced this separation.[83] Hindi and Tamil writers, for example, deliberately distanced themselves from the violent language debates taking place in their regions by using literature to articulate sensibilities of interconnection between region, nation, and world. They replaced what they saw as the provincial politics of language with a more globally oriented discourse of aesthetics. At the same time, they remained committed to enriching their respective languages and literatures.

Compare, for example, passages from two literary treatises written during the postindependence period that exemplify this desire to detach literature from narrow language politics. The first is from Hindi writer Rajendra Yadav's long essay "Ek Duniyā Samānāntar" (A parallel world), published in 1966. The essay represents a synthesis of ideas generated over nearly a decade of discussions between prominent Hindi writers across North India about the role of literature in expressing and shaping postindependence life. It ambitiously declared a new task for Hindi literature to dissociate individuals from the colonial past and reintegrate them into society through an aesthetics of discontentment, disillusionment, and uncertainty.[84]

To accomplish this, Yadav argued that the writer bore the unique responsibility of delinking art from reality:

> A literary work . . . is an independent creation parallel [*samānāntar*] to this world . . . that is inspired by and functions according to the rules and conventions of its own structure and assembly. . . . The task of constructing an aesthetic world [*kalā-jagat*] lies in the hands of those tangled, complex, unanalyzable aspects of the artistic personality that creates it, in those moments of creative tension—when the keen, piercing vision of genius penetrates material objects and touches upon their essential nature. And the artist—shaking off all influence [*prabhāv*] and acculturation [*saṃskāra*]—outlines nature and materiality from a novel perspective and unexamined angle and in an unfamiliar form. . . . No longer an imitation [*pratikṛti*] or representation [*pratinidhi*] of nature . . . art becomes an entirely new creation.[85]

This passage articulates the emphasis that Yadav and his contemporaries placed on the requisite independence of art—its evocation of, and existence within, a universe separate from day-to-day life. This position resonated with nationally and internationally circulating discussions about the autonomy of modernist art and literature with which Yadav was undoubtedly aware.[86] At the same time, his understanding of literature as a parallel world is striking for its complete erasure of the messy politics of Hindi regionalism. At a moment of acute contention around Hindi as the national language, language politics are here nowhere to be found. Nonetheless, as I elaborate in chapters 3 and 4, specters of these debates can be read into Yadav's sheer refusal to acknowledge them and his corresponding insistence on the independence of the literary realm.[87] By independence, he means independence from not only existing Hindi literary norms but also embattled linguistic ones.

During the same period, Yadav's contemporary C. S. Chellappa published a series of essays in his little magazine *Eḻuttu*, which he later anthologized in his now iconic work of Tamil criticism *Tamiḻ Ciṟukatai Piṟakkiṟatu* (The birth of the Tamil short story). Chellappa had established *Eḻuttu* in 1959 as a venue for highlighting what he believed to constitute "high literary" (*ilakkiya taramāṉa*) Tamil works. *Eḻuttu* featured older Tamil writers and debuted new ones, placing them on the path of canonicity. The essays comprising Chellappa's *Tamiḻ Ciṟukatai Piṟakkiṟatu*—written between 1964 and 1969—were part of this endeavor, and together they formed a tract on the history, significance, and function of the Tamil short story in postindependence society. In it, Chellappa underscored literature's profound impact on, and potential for transforming, individual comportment. Literature, he argued, created "an expansive space" for emotion, taking readers "to a separate world [*taṉi ulakam*]—a place of ecstasy . . . made possible by a great writer."[88] This aesthetic world, according to Chellappa, freed individuals from politics and allowed them to explore their deeper natures.

Like Yadav's *duniyā samānāntar* (parallel world), Chellappa's *taṉi ulakam* (separate world) emerged in an environment of extreme linguistic antagonism. Following independence, anti-Brahmin and anti-Hindi sentiments had led Pure Tamil and Dravidian activists to demand not only the excision of "foreign" vocabularies and forms from Tamil but also the secession of the Tamil region from the Indian nation. Chellappa's response—similar to Yadav's—was to stake a claim to literature as a domain outside this impassioned ethnolinguistic nationalism and to bestow the writer with the duty of fostering it. Drifting through an eclectic range of references to Tamil, South Asian, and international writers alike, Chellappa's treatise undermined positions that sought to narrow the scope of Tamil or establish a one-to-one relation between Tamil literature and language. He presented a broad-minded approach to aesthetics that could refine and possibly redefine the Tamil linguistic field.

What led Yadav and Chellappa—who were embedded in differing regional dynamics, focused on distinct literary spheres, and oblivious to each other's endeavors—to adhere to a common conceptualization of literature in this moment? Why would both have remained silent on the national language question? It may seem obvious to answer that Yadav and Chellappa were citing the same literary references and networks—both national and global—to counteract provincializing tendencies within their respective regions during a high point of postcolonial internationalization. Still, I want to dwell on the conclusions we might draw about such a condition, which enabled their literary approaches to align despite an environment in which a Hindi writer could know about "Ezra Pound or T. S. Eliot . . . while knowing . . . nothing about . . . writers in . . . Tamil"—as S. Radhakrishnan, vice president of the Sahitya Akademi (India's National Academy of Letters), put it in 1957.[89] Yadav's and Chellappa's shared insistence that literature be approached separately from language politics marks, I suggest, yet another turn in the trajectory of vernacularization. Literature now *had* to be understood separately from linguistic regionalisms if it were to represent the national caliber of India on the world stage.

In the immediate postindependence moment, language politics reoriented India's multilingual landscape around what Sudipta Kaviraj has identified as a cultural bilingualism that privileged English, giving secondary status to regional languages. As the preferred medium of elite discourse, English now occupied the apex of the Indian linguistic pyramid. Regional languages associated with the mother tongues of the home took residence on a middle stratum, and the countless dialects of popular discourse and the masses became permanently relegated to the bottom rung.[90] At the same time, Hindi and Tamil writers' efforts to build literary worlds independent of the politics of language—while simultaneously insisting on the use of regional languages over English—constitute the presence of powerful contestation to this top-down linguistic model. Their aesthetic worldviews were part of a project to elevate regional languages to stand on par with English and reflect a distinctly postcolonial desire to shed regional languages of the vernacular status that colonialism had conferred on them. Their impulse to move beyond the vernacular was symptomatic of political decolonization; their interest in texts from elsewhere indexed their worldly aspirations; and their commitment to their regional literatures marked their differing cultural formations.

I am not arguing, however, that ideas of vernacularity or processes of vernacularization disappeared with independence. As the persistence of arguments against the dominance of English attests, Indian languages still inhabit a subordinate position in several regards.[91] Rather, I am suggesting that the postcolonial condition prompted a shift in how Hindi and Tamil writers approached the problem of the vernacular, just as the national language question had done two decades earlier. It led them to seek possibilities for living in the aftermath of the vernacular—to ask what it would take to carve out a sanctioned space for their work in the wider world. This placed them in the contradictory position of advocating for literatures that they knew might never travel, while nonetheless envisioning those literatures as linked into national and global circuits of literary exchange. Postindependence Hindi and Tamil writers dialogically engaged with their respective language communities, as well as national and international readers whom they would likely never encounter, let alone understand.[92] This dialogism was facilitated by the idea of Indian literature, which postulated that worldly cosmopolitanisms could be located in regionally specific and untranslated affiliations.

NOVEL, SHORT STORY, POETRY

Because the kind of anonymous affiliation that Hindi and Tamil writers shared with readers beyond their regions was dialogic across languages, it signals a different model of community than the deep, horizontal comradeship that Benedict Anderson characterized as the basis of the "imagined community" of the nation. Anderson argued that print capitalism's ability to standardize and diffuse notions of language and culture across territorial expanses was fundamental to the eighteenth- and nineteenth-century transformation of European vernaculars into national languages. Print created a feeling of temporal simultaneity among disaggregated individuals residing within a region, recruiting them to jointly "think the nation."[93] The novel played a central role in this process because of its realistic portrayal of typical characters and settings, which were linked by a "succession of plurals." By descriptively placing the recognizable interiors of homes in contiguous relation with familiar exterior surroundings—such as "hospitals, prisons, remote villages, monasteries, Indians, [and] Negroes"—the novel, Anderson argued, generated a sense of sociological solidity among readers who were otherwise unknown to one another and the author.[94] It furthermore synchronized readers across geographical space by routing them onto the chronological tracks of clocked, calendrical time. Anderson viewed the novel as the paragon of the book form—"the first modern-style mass-produced industrial commodity"—and thus the principal vehicle of print capitalism. In this schema, other genres derived their significance insofar as they replicated the novel's evocation of contemporaneity and fraternity among readers. The newspaper, for example, was "merely an 'extreme form,'" a kind of "one-day best-seller" that reassured readers of the "imagined world visibly rooted in everyday life" that was represented preeminently in the novel.[95]

Anderson's interpretation of the novel aligns with a general scholarly understanding of the genre as *the* symbolic form of modernity. As Fredric Jameson observes, the European novel played a "significant role in what can be called a properly bourgeois revolution whereby populations whose life habits were formed by other, now archaic modes of production [were] effectively reprogrammed for life and work in the new world of market capitalism."[96] Scholars similarly understand the Indian novel as the primary genre through which the negotiation of colonial modernity and cultivation of Indian national consciousness occurred.[97] In European and Indian accounts alike, the novel is recognized for enacting a shift from fabulous to mundane settings, heroic to ordinary characters, elevated to heteroglossic representations of language, and epic to biographical time—thereby giving expression to new nationalist, capitalist, and individualist modes of existence. Scholars gather these narrative transformations under the umbrella of realism, through which the novel evokes the "freshness of some unexpected 'real'" by undermining and demystifying "preexisting inherited traditional or sacred narrative paradigms."[98]

Rather than understand realism as a generic feature of the novel—as these scholars have done—I want to conceptualize it as a rhetorical mode that moved across forms of print during the period when the novel emerged.[99] Doing so allows us to understand how the novel worked in concert with other genres within broader spheres of print culture to articulate experiences of modernity and shape notions of community. Consider, for example, Anderson's oft-cited interpretation of José Rizal's 1887 novel *Noli Me Tangere* in which Anderson stresses that the narrator's descriptions of Filipino life effectively imagine a national community because of the author's tone: "While Rizal has not the faintest idea of his readers' individual identities, he writes to them with an ironical intimacy, as though their relationships with each other are not in the smallest degree problematic."[100] Instead of its formal, thematic, stylistic, or narratological features, Anderson here calls attention to the rhetorical means through which Rizal's novel positions the author and characters in relation to readers to enlist them in a modern sense of "oneness" conditioned by the act of reading itself. While metonymic detailing may constitute a particularly novelistic feature for Anderson, his focus on Rizal's tone points to the currency of a new, realist strategy of address, which could imbue readers with a sense of collective belonging.

Recognizing this form of address required a type of readerly training that was undertaken by the expansive terrain covered by print—a terrain that extended into readers' lives through multiple genres and rhetorical devices. Without the armature of print culture, the imaginary potential of the novel for constructing a sense of community could only have been limited. In his explication of *Semarang Hitam*, an Indonesian novel by Marco Kartodikromo, published serially in 1924, Anderson writes: "Marco's [use of] 'our young man,' [for the unnamed hero] not least in its novelty, *means* a young man who belongs to the collective body of readers *Indonesian*, and thus, implicitly, an embryonic Indonesian 'imagined community.'"[101] This reading does not establish *how* the novel constructs "our young man" as a member of the Indonesian collective; it *presumes* an already existing community to which readers may ascribe the young man's belonging instead. In this way, Anderson's account of *Semarang Hitam* presupposes the existence of an imagined nation rather than demonstrating the primacy of the novel in constituting it. This slippage in argument provides a window for considering how the novel may not have done this constituting alone.

By the late nineteenth century, the novel was perhaps an extreme among many circulating forms of print, and the emergence of Indian novels substantiates this claim. For example, Supriya Chaudhuri has shown in the case of Bengal that, as early as the 1820s, books were complemented by a range of other printed matter being churned out by active independent presses and distributed through vibrant book markets. In this environment, "literary journals serialized new fiction."[102] Most early Bengali novels were therefore enclosed in a midst of other genres when presented to readers. Sascha Ebeling has shown that serialization was similarly the norm for many Tamil novels, and Vasudha Dalmia has chronicled how the Hindi novel arose in dialogue with several genres, which writers were concurrently developing in North Indian newspapers, magazines, and journals.[103] Tagore's autobiographical account of the "breathless anticipation with which instalments of [Bankim's novel] *Brishabriksha* were awaited (as they appeared serially in the journal *Bangadarshan* from its first issue in 1872)" is also instructive.[104] This observation underscores how readers' understandings of early Indian novels were keenly shaped by the medium of the periodical and the material experiences linked with it—of anticipating it in advance, going out to buy it or waiting for it to be delivered, flipping through its pages, perusing its pictures and advertisements, skipping eagerly to and devouring its fiction, discussing its essays and opinions with family and friends. Moreover, the debates, reviews, letters, and opinions surrounding the serialized segments of novels guided readers in how they should understand and respond to fiction, differentiate between genres, and view their readerly encounters in relation to those of other readers.

The emplacement of the novel within magazines and periodicals suggests that the paratexts surrounding it were as consequential as its form and content for enabling this genre to fabricate modern life. Gérard Genette defines paratexts as "those liminal devices and conventions, both within the book and outside it, that form part of the complex mediation between book, author, publisher, and reader."[105] Although Genette developed this understanding with an eye toward the book, extending his framework to the wider realm of print offers a useful vocabulary for thinking about how new nineteenth-century genres developed in conversation with one another. In the periodical, essays, reviews, op-eds, short stories, novels, plays, journalism, letters, personal reflections, and advertisements all functioned as paratexts to one another, shaping the meanings that each produced. The novel therefore existed along a continuum of prose genres rather than as a self-enclosed form.

For this reason, the novel operated in concert with the short story—and not as a countergenre, as Mary Louise Pratt has argued—to develop written prose forms over poetry, which was fundamental to the colonial-era vernacularization processes I described above. Pratt's well-known essay "The Short Story: The Long and the Short of It" seeks to deconstruct the prevailing bias in Western criticism toward the novel and against the short story, which, she writes, was "neither logical nor an empirical necessity, but rather a fact of literary history."[106] Pratt emphasizes how literary theory came to view the short story's brevity as a marker of its inferiority. Beginning in the twentieth century, North American, English, and Russian critics valorized the novel for representing the totality of life, documenting national culture, epitomizing high artistry, and modernizing epic traditions. By contrast, they derided the short story for its journalistic and crafts-like nature and focus on fragmentary experience, singular emotions, marginal characters, and folk culture. Pratt's interest is to intervene in structuralist understandings of genre by establishing that the hierarchical relationship of the novel to the short story was accidental rather than inherent to the genres themselves. Perhaps for this reason, she fails to ask *why* the novel achieved such an elevated position in Western literary criticism—despite her thorough discourse analysis of the language that critics used to place it on top.

The concern and care that Hindi and Tamil writers directed toward the short story between the 1930s and 1960s compels me to ask this question, however—even if I have no resolute answer. The short story proliferated contemporaneously in India, North America, and Europe beginning in the late nineteenth century, and in all three locations it was deeply rooted in the dynamics of periodical culture and mass circulation.[107] Yet, at the very same moment that Hindi writer Premchand and his Tamil counterpart Cho. Vrithachalam "Pudumaippittan" gave preeminence to the short story in the late colonial era, literary theorists in the West—such as Bakhtin, Georg Lukács, and Erich Auerbach—turned to the novel to interrogate the crisis of European modernity.[108] Could the multilingual colonial environment of India—which was profoundly shaped by the particularities of linguistic vernacularization—have spurred Hindi and Tamil writers' increased interest in this form?[109] The simultaneous and interconnected emergence of novels and short stories in nineteenth-century periodicals problematizes any easy polarization of the two genres. At the same time, Premchand's and Pudumaippittan's preference for the short story above the novel compels us to recognize the key role that the short story played in articulating critiques of modernization and mass culture—which many writers felt were not possible in the novel during the late colonial era.[110] In chapter 2 I illustrate how Premchand's and Pudumaippittan's efforts to build the modern Hindi and Tamil canons combined with their lifelong involvement in print culture to cultivate the short story as an emblem of high literature. The corollary point

I want to make here is that, in this moment, the short story became the primary means through which they sought to separate literature from the politics of language as they attempted to work around the national language question.[111] This is evidenced by their extended discussions about the short story's ability to convey literature's connection to the deeper truths of life—which were aesthetic, rather than linguistic, at their core.

The operating literary distinction that colonial-era vernacularization processes established was between prose and poetry—not the novel and the short story. The diminishment of the novel in the 1930s was not, therefore, a simple reversal of the novel/short story hierarchy that Pratt identifies in the West. Rather, it was rooted in colonial-era uses of literature to navigate the Indian multilingual landscape and the centrality of print in these processes. The colonial bias against poetry—which located its roots in archaic tradition, rote convention, aristocratic indulgence, and erotic spiritualism—led to its troubled renewal in the nineteenth century. For example, Hindi writers applied to poetry the themes of realism, nationalism, social reform, and modern subjectivity and the English- and Sanskrit-inflected styles of language that they were concurrently exploring in prose—ultimately divorcing poetry from existing conventions for verse.[112] While Hindi *Chāyāvād* (neo-Romantic) poetry of the 1920s and 1930s provocatively returned to the themes of devotion and desire that earlier writers had critiqued, it constructed an entirely new poetic lens, which, according to Lucy Rosenstein, translated "the desire for political independence . . . into a quest for individual freedom."[113] The almost immediate critique of poetic individualism that arose in response persisted into the postindependence period, despite the free-verse innovations of *prayogvād* (experimentalism) in the 1940s and *nayī kavitā* (new poetry) in the 1950s. In the case of Tamil, the rediscovery of ancient *Caṅkam* poetry in the late nineteenth and early twentieth centuries fed directly into the rise of Tamil ethnolinguistic nationalism.[114] For this reason, despite their deep admiration of Subramania Bharati's inventive Tamil poems of the early twentieth century, leading writers of the 1930s turned to the short story to enact a break with the Tamil past. Tamil poetry would not become the focus of literary criticism again until the 1960s, when Chellappa began to publish upcoming poets and theorize a new genre of Tamil *putukkavitai* (new poetry).[115]

I raise these examples to underscore how poetry was conceived of as existing in contentious relation to prose—wherein the norms being developed for prose helped to delink poetry from its association with past traditions—and not to suggest that it was an inferior medium, subordinate to the short story or novel. My argument is that recognizing how Hindi and Tamil writers navigated a literary terrain shaped by colonial-era vernacularization leads to a more complex picture of the interrelations between genres within broader spheres of print culture. To understand Hindi and Tamil writers' elevation of the short story above the novel, and their coinciding depreciation of poetry, requires a multiscalar lens that views these perspectives in dialogue with literary debates occurring concurrently on different planes, from the global to the local.[116] Placing their work in relation to short-story writers across the world—such as Anton Chekhov, Maxim Gorky, Ernest Hemingway, O. Henry, Henry James, Guy de Maupassant, Frank O'Connor, Edgar Allan Poe, and Leo Tolstoy—Hindi and Tamil writers added their voices to the international debates on the short story and novel that Pratt cites. Conceiving of their literary endeavors as part of national struggle, they positioned the short story as an anticolonial, and later postcolonial, rejoinder. Immersed in the contradictory pulls of region and nation, they used the short story to deprovincialize the outlooks of their fellow regional-language speakers. And, active in local literary coteries, they composed the short story as a playful riposte to their everyday encounters. These various scales of literary conversation structured the dialogic nature of Hindi and Tamil writers' work, cutting across the ideal comradeship characteristic of Anderson's imagined nation.

GENDER AND GENRE

The Hindi and Tamil writers I examine in this book—including, most prominently, in Hindi, Mannu Bhandari, Premchand, Mohan Rakesh, Kamleshwar Prasad Saxena "Kamleshwar," and Yadav and, in Tamil, Chellappa, R. Chudamani, D. Jayakanthan, Pudumaippittan, and Ka. Naa. Subramanyam—viewed the short story as a historical record of the present and the primary medium for understanding human experience and individual desire. Due to its accessibility through low-cost print—and its translatability across many cultural and educational backgrounds—they employed this genre, above others, to articulate new expressions of individuality and community in late-colonial and early-postcolonial India. They considered autobiography as too personal, the novel too protracted, and poetry too abstract. For these reasons, these writers turned to the short story to develop a literary politics aimed at transforming modern gender relations. They wielded new literary formations of gender to revolutionize the parameters of the genre, while simultaneously manipulating the short story's formal features to creatively reconfigure popular feminine tropes linked to notions of modernity and tradition. This allowed them to join the social and aesthetic functions of the short story to the realignment of interpersonal relationships.

Aamir Mufti has observed a related intersection of gender and genre in the work of Urdu writer Sa'adat Hasan Manto. Examining Manto's short-story depictions of prostitutes in the late-colonial era, Mufti argues that the "excessive and improperly sexual figure of the courtesan or prostitute" embodies the "trouble that 'Muslim' represents for nationalist discourse." He views Manto's prostitute as the degraded heir of the Mughal-era courtesan culture that colonialism displaced in the late nineteenth century and as a foil to the "domesticated and desexualized figure of the mother" that symbolizes the nation.[117] Mufti further contends that Manto compounds the prostitute's marginalization by portraying this figure in the minor genre of the short story. This double minoritization—of gender and genre—reflects, for Mufti, the forsaken place of Urdu and Islam within a national culture that privileges Hindi and Hinduism. "Urdu is perhaps unique among the major literatures of South Asia in its emphasis on the short story. . . . In Urdu the hierarchical relationship of novel to short story that one would expect of any major narrative tradition is reversed," he writes.[118] In Mufti's reading, Manto's representations of gender come together with his uses of genre to counter the normative filiations of Indian national belonging with the "unique resources of affect, attachment, and freedom" made available in fragmentary representations of brothel life.[119]

Mufti rightly highlights Manto's exceptionality as a writer, whose portrayals of gender relations through the desires of marginalized men and women were inventive and unprecedented.[120] He also identifies Manto's representations of the prostitute as an important response to ongoing critiques of prostitution and its connection to Muslim culture.[121] But I would argue that Mufti's presumption of the Urdu short story's minor position derives from the preeminence given to the novel within Western literary criticism—and not in relation to other South Asian literatures.[122] The imbricated history of the novel and short story outlined above compels us to read Manto's short stories through a comparative and multiscalar lens that places his work in the context of South Asian—and broader colonial and postcolonial—short story writing across languages. The Hindi and Tamil short stories that I examine in this book offer just two examples of how the short story thrived—and played a central role in periodical culture—across most Indian literary fields by the 1930s. They also speak to how Indian writers understood their short stories in dialogic relation to fiction and criticism from around the subcontinent and world. Viewing Manto's stories as part of this broader conversation helps to locate his work within the print networks in which he participated throughout his life. It also helps to underscore Manto's literary contributions to the larger sphere of story production, despite the increasing minoritization of Urdu and Islam in Indian nationalist discourse.

Mufti also overlooks the looming presence of the prostitute figure in late-colonial prose across Indian languages—in relation to which I propose that Manto's depictions be understood. In the 1910s and 1920s, linguistic nationalisms across the subcontinent took root in popular culture by conflating the mother figure with mother tongue and mother nation—largely in the medium of poetry. This is exemplified, for example, by Subramania Bharati's Tamil verses about *Tamiḻ tāy* (Mother Tamil) and Mathili Sharan Gupt's Hindi poems referencing *Bhārat mātā* (Mother India).[123] Such representations were mostly absent, however, in regional language prose. One reason for this, I believe, was the distance that writers sought to create between their literary endeavors and regional-language politics, especially in the 1930s. Another reason was the intimate connection of prose to social-reform debates that had been raging since the nineteenth century.

The literary focus of prose therefore fell on questions of how to define and control feminine desire, which were embodied by feminine figures broadly classifiable under the rubric of the suffering Indian woman. Literary representations of the widow, prostitute, virgin, and good wife challenged the limits of patriarchal guardianship and governance. These figures held principal roles in almost all early Indian novels, articulating deep social anxieties about women's independence and agency.[124] Tagore's well-known protagonist Binodini in his novel *Chokher Bali* (A grain of sand in the eye), serialized between 1901 and 1904, provides a quintessential example. Educated and beautiful, but widowed at a young age, Binodini becomes the mistress of her best friend's husband. A later change of heart leads her to seek his friend's hand in marriage. Ultimately, she renounces both men to follow a proper Hindu widow's path of piety and asceticism. Binodini's trajectory thus traverses the entire range of feminine tropes mentioned above—from innocent virgin to prostituting vamp to prospective good wife to asexual widow. Her story reflects the ways in which the modern freedoms accorded to the Indian woman threatened to bring her too close to the prostitute, who possessed full control of her agency, desire, and familial and economic relations. While Binodini's ability to nurture conveys her potential as a mother, this is not her primary feature. The driving impulse of the novel is a concern with Binodini's desires and the inability of the men around her to contain them.

Premchand's Urdu novel *Bāzār-e-Ḥusn* (The marketplace of beauty) and its Hindi version *Sevāsadan* (The orphanage) together provide another important example.[125] The protagonist Suman—who leaves her husband to work in the brothel—turns, in the end, like Binodini, toward a life of service. In her comparison of the Hindi and Urdu texts, Anita Anantharam argues that slight changes in vocabulary—and additions and omissions of content—construct a focus on women's freedom in the Urdu novel, whereas the Hindi version expresses a moralizing sentiment about women's chastity and devotion.[126] This difference reveals that when the prostitute figure crossed over languages, she articulated different responses to the same questions about female desire and agency—responses that were shaped by the specific concerns of various readership communities. It also shows how the association of the prostitute with Urdu and Muslim culture cast a shadow over representations of this figure in all Indian languages, not just in Urdu. Manto's prostitutes were part of pan-Indian literary discussions about female sexuality and autonomy, and the ways that his representations pushed the boundaries of these discussions are one reason they are so remarkable.

Gender and genre cannot be understood entirely independently of one another, but neither do their functions fully align. This is why I view Manto's work along the same continuum as Tagore's and Premchand's novels, while also insisting on the singularity of his short story uses. In later chapters I demonstrate how the short story, rather than the novel, enabled Hindi and Tamil writers to do different things with representations of gender—such as retain, rather than resolve, the enigma of feminine desire, thereby reconfiguring heterosexual relations. I also argue that their citations of popular feminine tropes pushed the short story form toward more modernist modes of rhetorical style. The relationship of gender to genre that I offer in this book is one of content to form, wherein the pressures that content places on form, and form on content, help to mold the aesthetic characteristics constituting different understandings of literariness. In this framework, gender and genre function as intersecting aesthetic nodes around which the idea of Indian literature starts to crystalize.

COMPARATIVE METHOD

To explore the idea of Indian literature is to explore the changing dynamics between language and literature in the subcontinent. This requires embracing the paradox that the idea of Indian literature is real and persists, even though what this idea entails will always be vague, evolving, contested, and multiple. Because the idea of Indian literature emerged through colonial-era processes of vernacularization—offering writers a new dialogic horizon toward which they could orient their literary visions—it can only be approached comparatively. This means viewing regional and national literary spheres in the subcontinent as co-constitutional formations composed of mutually constellated fabrics, rather than as overlapping spheres of literary knowledge within the larger field of Indian literature. These formations have been, and continue to be, consolidated through processes of canonization that fix their seemingly rigid boundaries of inclusion and exclusion.

The following chapters investigate these processes by placing Hindi and Tamil fiction in conversation with each other and with the metaliterary discourses surrounding them—including criticism, literary history, and autobiography—which were written in Hindi, Tamil, and Indian English. They combine close readings of texts with attention to the geographically specific social, historical, and literary historical processes in which they emerged to consider how Hindi and Tamil short stories worked in concert with metaliterary discourses to theorize aesthetic and linguistic affiliations. The short stories I examine in this book distill Hindi and Tamil theories of literature into the language of fiction. They operate in tandem with other genres—both literary and metaliterary—to map the intersecting legacies and compulsions that shaped the audiences Hindi and Tamil writers sought to address and the worldviews they imagined literature could produce by navigating of the idea of Indian literature.

Chapter 1 outlines the worlding approach I employ throughout the book to consider the imbricated notions of Hindi, Tamil, and Indian literature. It argues for a focus on how writers and texts perform literary acts of "worlding"—the strategies, aims, and discourses they use to construct criteria for literary value—rather than defining, as contemporary scholarship has done, which texts belong in regional, national, and world literature canons. Exploring the prominent Progressive Writers' Association circles in London and North India and the *Maṇikkoṭi* writers' circle in Madras, the chapter demonstrates how writers mobilized different understandings of translation to identify certain texts as literary while excluding others. In each case, theorizing translation was an important metaliterary activity through which writers considered the problems of implementing a national language in their different locations. Translation therefore became a central question for late colonial–era writers as they contemplated definitions of Indian literature that could accommodate the Hindi, Tamil, and English readerships they envisioned. These definitions would undergird their approaches to gender and genre and theorizations of literary purpose throughout the late-colonial and early-postcolonial eras.

Chapter 2 examines the formal possibilities opened up by genre. Capitalizing on the short story's popularity and extensive reach through periodicals, Hindi and Tamil writers turned to this genre—rather than the novel or poetry—to theorize the relationship between literature and society in late-colonial India. They used the short story's brevity to compress their portrayals of well-known female types—including the widow, prostitute, virgin, and good wife—into singular emotional events. This allowed Hindi and Tamil writers to reference wider debates about tradition and modernity that these female types evoked without taking the social reformist positions to which they were linked. The short story thereby allowed writers in both contexts to dislodge their portrayals of the Indian woman from existing gender norms, creating a shift from social realism to modernist realism.

Chapter 3 investigates the aesthetic affiliations constituted through modernist realism. It elaborates how Hindi, Tamil, and Indian English writers—prompted by a postindependence mandate to suppress the legacy of colonial violence—produced new literary histories to synthesize realist and modernist trends into an overarching postcolonial modernist-realist mode. Aspiring to fulfill the postindependence Indian state's aspiration to forge "unity in diversity," this mode used literary history to promote diverse postcolonial literary projects for local audiences. Mobilizing geographically specific rhetorical devices and literary techniques, modernist realism sought to articulate a shared Indian middle-class ethos, fraught with both anguish and hope.

Chapter 4 considers reconfigurations of heterosexuality through short-story representations of feminine desire. By focusing on the apprehensions surrounding the new woman's desires, postindependence Hindi and Tamil writers located the problem of feminine desire above religious and caste contentions. Hindi writers subsumed the injuries of Partition—which loomed large in the North Indian cultural imaginary—beneath the inscrutability of the new woman's wants, the anguish of unrequited love, and the inadequacy of masculine agency. Tamil writers, by contrast, masked the fault lines of South Indian caste hierarchy by articulating the Brahmin woman's desires for reform as a broader appeal for cultural modernization. In both cases, the new woman's ambitions became a horizon for realigning communal and caste questions along the axis of heterosexual relations.

Chapter 5 probes new authorizations of feminine desire that women short story writers brought to bear on the postindependence Hindi, Tamil, and Indian literary fields. Entering into the male-dominated sphere of "literary" writing for the first time, these writers used the same modernist-realist frameworks as their male contemporaries to develop an idiomatically inflected language of entitlement. Through this language, writers authorized themselves to portray female characters who had as much desire for sexual expression, economic independence, and human equality as their male partners. By engaging with women's rights and freedoms in literary terms, women writers inaugurated a new literary humanist tradition of women's writing across the Hindi, Tamil, and Indian literary fields.

In each of these chapters, *The Idea of Indian Literature* advances an approach for exploring diverse, nonaligning understandings of literary value; for undertaking comparisons that hold both similarities and differences in view; and for examining metaliterary discourses alongside properly "literary" ones to imagine how fiction also operates as theory. Through this approach, I conceive of Hindi, Tamil, and Indian literature as partial, incomplete, and unstable expressions of region, nation, and world—literary geographies that are inextricable from one another and from the local, regional, national, and global readerships that they envision. Co-constituted and co-constituting, the idea of Indian literature lends us a view of comparative literature as a field composed by the multifarious literary others that it perpetually and persistently endeavors to gather under its auspices.

CHAPTER 1

Comparative Worldings

The Case of Indian Literatures

INDIAN LITERATURE AND TRANSLATABILITY

A new concept of Indian literature emerged in the 1930s. It was a utopian idea that attributed a coherence to Indian literature on the grounds of perfect translatability between the various Indian languages. Such translatability would reveal shared values and goals for India's future, uniting the Indian people through a common vision.

This idea of Indian literature was an implicit corollary to the concept of a national language. If a single language were to be instituted across the multilingual Indian nation, then it had to be one in which other Indian languages and literatures could be easily and truthfully expressed. The implementation of an overarching Indian language across the regions went hand in hand with the creation of a pan-Indian literary canon made up of internally translatable texts.[1]

As India reeled toward independence, the language question produced distinct political coteries. Orthodox Hindi nationalists advocated for a Sanskrit-derived Hindi, which aligned with their vision of the nation's Hindu character. Conversely, the Indian National Congress (INC)—the leading political party led by Gandhi and Jawaharlal Nehru—supported the use of Urdu-inflected Hindustani. The INC argued that Hindustani was a composite language, inclusive of both Hindus and Muslims, and closer to the colloquial language used widely in North India.[2] These views faced staunch opposition from Tamil nationalists in South India who characterized Hindi and Hindustani—between which they saw no real difference—as utterly foreign. From their point of view, only the Tamil language could hold sway over the ethnically Dravidian, Tamil-speaking region.[3]

On the literary front, writers formed associations and collectives to emphasize literary progressiveness and catholicity above orthodox positions on language. Prominent among these were the All-India Progressive Writers' Association (PWA) in London and Hindi-speaking North India and the *Maṇikkoṭi* writers' circle in Madras. The writers in these circles debated the issue of translation, purpose of literature, and possibility of creating a pan-Indian corpus. Taking inspiration from North American, Russian, European, and South Asian thinkers past and present, they viewed their efforts as part of "Indian" and "world" literary production and built positions that placed world literature at the forefront of anti-imperialist and anti-fascist struggle.

These groups, however, used different criteria to define literariness, each based on their particular stances on the national language question. Correspondingly, each group also formulated a different understanding of Indian literature and how it fit within the world literary canon. In the essays and memoirs that I examine below, Indian English writers in London, Hindi writers in North India, and Tamil writers in Madras used the concept of world literature as a tool for outlining their approach to translation and defining the purpose of literature. How they conceptualized literariness within their respective contexts was central to how they determined the broader political project of Indian literature and the role of translation in circulating it within world literary space. To consider the translatability of Indian literature in this moment is therefore also to interrogate the status and nature of world literature.

Through a juxtaposition of the Indian English, Hindi, and Tamil literary spheres, this chapter argues for a focus on how writers and texts perform acts of "worlding," rather than defining, as contemporary scholarship has done, which texts belong in the global literary canon. As I will show, such acts mobilize "world literature" to define certain texts as "literary," while simultaneously concealing other existing literary processes and social relations. Exploring how prominent writing circles in London, North India, and Madras "worlded" Indian literature brings to light not only that the national language question engendered multiple politics of literary translation but also that a theory of translation underpins any conception of world literature. What a comparative worlding approach offers, then, is attention to the political stakes in framing relations between region, nation, and world. More specifically, it shows how processes of worlding—whether at the scale of the regional, national, or global—elevate some texts and exclude others from the category of the "literary." The midcentury vision of a perfectly translatable Indian literature was therefore tenuous and incomplete and masked a range of communal, caste, and linguistic tensions across the subcontinent.

I begin this chapter with a discussion of how the idea of Indian literature as a canon of internally translatable texts has become the established paradigm within institutional spaces, such as the Sahitya Akademi (India's National Academy of Letters), as well as academic scholarship, particularly postcolonial studies. This ideal, I show, mirrors contemporary conceptions of world literature, which also attribute a central role to translation in shaping the global literary canon. In contrast to the narrow understandings of literary value that these models advance, I outline a methodology for examining worlding processes that shifts attention to how literary spheres establish contextually specific norms and standards for literariness. The final sections of the chapter return to the late-colonial period, during which PWA writers in London and North India and *Maṇikkoṭi* writers in Madras grappled with the national language question and its assumption of perfect translatability. The unique approaches to translation and Indian literature that these writers formulated in response to the national language debate illustrate multiple and varied acts of worlding, offering alternative avenues through which to understand the categories of Indian and world literature.

INDIAN LITERATURE/WORLD LITERATURE

Disputes over India's national language only heightened following independence, spurring Prime Minister Nehru to establish the Sahitya Akademi in 1954. The Akademi took a multipronged approach to the language question, including the promotion of Hindi and the use of the Devanagari script, an emphasis on the shared cultural roots of all Indian languages, and the creation of institutional venues for dialogue among various Indian literatures. Translation was an essential tool for each of these ventures and part of the Sahitya Akademi's central mission.[4] As S. Radhakrishnan—first vice president of India and of the Akademi—wrote in his 1962 essay "A Writer's Role in National Integration," the "Sahitya Akademi is doing its best as far as linguistic controversies are concerned. It is bringing writers together, bringing the peoples together by its translations."[5] The Sahitya Akademi was one of the key institutions responsible for reinforcing the thesis of translatability among Indian languages during the postindependence period.

Yet, a number of articles addressing the function and practice of translation in *Indian Literature*, the Akademi's literary journal, expressed an anxiety about whether this translatability was attainable. During the 1950s and 1960s, the journal's contributors repeatedly stressed the need for increased translations, better translations, and more open-minded approaches to translation.[6] For example, discussing Indian publishing trends in 1962, C. R. Banerji mourned that "the number of translations from one modern Indian language to another is discouraging."[7] He concluded that "Indian publications are quite inadequate for nation-building purposes. . . . We do not have a sufficient number of authors, [and] translators."[8] Similarly, Nehru—who served as the Akademi's first president—inaugurated a debate in *Indian Literature*, in 1963, on "Creative Writing in the Present Crisis" in which he appealed to writers to accept translation:

> To think that a language is crushed or suppressed by another language, is not quite correct. It is enriched by another language. So also our languages will be enriched the more they get into touch with each other and it is the Sahitya Akademi's function to get them into touch with each other and to some extent get them into touch with foreign languages too, by translations.[9]

From the Sahitya Akademi's perspective, translation lay at the heart of creating Indian literature. Until unmitigated translation between Indian languages could be achieved, Indian literature would remain an incomplete canon.[10]

Consistently beyond reach, translatability remains the ideal literary paradigm—not only of the Sahitya Akademi but also of contemporary scholarship on Indian literature and postcolonial studies. For example, discussing the difficulties of positing "a *theoretical* unity or coherence of an 'Indian' literature,"[11] Aijaz Ahmad noted in the 1990s that the "machinery of translations for the circulation of literary works within the various literary communities is poorly developed."[12] In Ahmad's view, translation provides a central way to recoup Indian multilingualism, without which "no solid scholarship of an 'Indian Literature' is possible."[13] Meenakshi Mukherjee—who worried that English was eclipsing other Indian literatures—observed in 2000 that translation was "a major conduit for cultural transmission within the country for nearly a century [that in recent years] seems to have declined to make way for . . . the translation of Indian fiction into English."[14] More recently, in 2009, Christi Merrill, drawing on the work of G. N. Devy, has argued for an approach to Indian literature inspired by the "translating consciousness" of Indians, who constantly negotiate multilingual contexts. Built upon *anuvād* (acts of "telling in turn") rather than exact replication, a translating consciousness is "an approach . . . that might serve as a model for challenging us to rethink the ways we demarcate difference in the rhetoric of nationalist-minded or even globalized identitarian politics."[15]

Implicit in the idealization of translatability proffered by postcolonial studies and national literary bodies is what might be called an aggregative model of Indian literature. In this model Indian literature is fashioned through the summative assembling of (translated) texts, as if to add richness and resolution to the picture of what Indian literature is. The Sahitya Akademi's valorization of translation, coupled with the expanding range of translation endeavors undertaken by prominent Indian publishing houses—such as Katha, Harper Collins India, and Penguin India—have strengthened this model, continuing its application into the present.[16] Encyclopedic studies, like the magisterial histories of Indian literature orchestrated by Sisir Kumar Das and K. M. George, complement this aggregative project by collecting "adjacent but discrete histories of India's major language-literatures."[17] These studies list literary trends and canonical texts from major Indian languages, making them intelligible to one another and to readers in the English language. As such, we might think of Das's and George's literary histories as acts of translation in themselves.

Ahmad, Mukherjee, and Merrill all underscore how translation is a key site through which modern Indian literature is constructed, and they see it as a way to undermine linguistic divisiveness and monolingual tendencies. At the same time, I also want to call attention to how translatability establishes the very terms on which Indian literature is constructed. I do not wish to downplay the significance of translation. Rather, I want to note the very different theories of translation that undergirded Indian English, Hindi, and Tamil definitions of literariness. As I demonstrate below, the political stakes of defining Indian literature rested in how PWA and *Maṇikkoṭi* writers theorized and practiced translation.

The thesis of translatability, despite its utopian intent of fostering linguistic diversity, reinforces the privileged position of the English language in the Indian literary sphere. It perpetuates a form of what Yasemin Yildiz has called "the monolingual paradigm," which emerged in the late eighteenth century.[18] "According to this paradigm," Yildiz argues, "individuals and social formations are imagined to possess one 'true' language only, their 'mother tongue,' and through this possession to be organically linked to an exclusive, clearly demarcated ethnicity, culture, and nation."[19] The idea of

Indian literature is slightly different because it is built on the premise that, although individuals possess different "regional" mother tongues that are not English, they share a common linguistic and civilizational background.[20] Nonetheless, the translatability thesis upholds a monolingual paradigm because it proposes that all Indian literatures are discrete, yet uniformly substitutable for one another. Together, they form a culturally bounded entity, which offers an original and authentic contribution to the world republic of letters. Indian multilingualism, to use Yildiz's language, "has been and continues to be refracted through the monolingual paradigm," which presumes the possibility of a unified linguistic frame.[21] The Sahitya Akademi's and Indian publishing market's activities show that translation is largely unidirectional, moving from other Indian languages into English. English serves as a language of unification, linking regional Indian languages to the nation and world, just as Nehru had envisioned.[22]

Understood from this perspective, Indian literature is analogous to world literature: both fields are created through the aggregation of translations, mainly into English. David Damrosch's oft-quoted definition of world literature as "all literary works that circulate beyond the culture of origin, either in translation or in their original language"[23] and as "writing that gains in translation" summarizes the translatability thesis of world literature most explicitly.[24] This thesis holds translation as both promise and proof of the literary value that world literary texts possess.[25] The difference between Indian literature and world literature, then, is only a question of how that literary value is defined. The literariness of a world literary text lies in the vaguely defined "beauties of its language, its form, and its themes."[26] In the case of Indian writings, by contrast, it coheres around what Ahmad defines as "Indianness"—a "High Textuality of the Brahminical kind" that elevates the shared "civilizational moorings and cultural ethos" of Indian languages and literatures.[27]

Of course, all theories of literature are aggregative, accumulating texts according to (or in opposition to) the continually evolving standards of various local, regional, national, and global canons. All theories of literature are in this sense exclusive, creating center-periphery dynamics in which some texts participate and others necessarily do not. Consequently, the question of which texts to include within the canons of Indian and world literature will always be contested, underdeveloped, or incomplete. Considering the case of modern Indian literatures, my impulse is *not* to (re)define the criteria by which texts enter world literary space but, instead, to prioritize a methodological approach that accounts for "worlding"—that is, practices through which texts acquire literariness within one or multiple literary spheres.

WORLDING LITERATURE

I use "worlding" to refer to the process of making texts intelligible "*as* literature" to specifically defined readerships.[28] Writers, critics, scholars, publishers, and academic and literary institutions—as well as texts in and of themselves—all participate in the worlding of literatures. They world individually and in concert, envisioning imagined readerships and establishing standards for literariness accordingly. Asking how the worlding of a literature or text occurs—rather than which texts comprise world literature within a global literary system—allows us to disclose the norms determining what counts as the "beauties" of a text's language, form, and themes, which most scholars of world literature take for granted. As the case of Indian literatures will show, ideas of literary value arise out of the social, historical, political, and literary constraints and requirements of a specific cultural context, while also engaging with globally circulating literary and political discourses. How Indian literatures imagine the relationship between texts and these wider discourses are constitutive acts of worlding because they frame how texts are positioned and received.

Not surprisingly, scholars have conceptualized the notion of worlding literature before, so let me clarify how I use this term differently, with reference to Djelal Kadir's and Pheng Cheah's recent elaborations of the concept. Kadir and Cheah focus on the idea of worlding, while other scholars have offered frameworks for expanding or pluralizing the notion of a literary "world."[29] My own methodological focus centers on *processes* of worlding because I am interested in critically deconstructing the boundaries of inclusion and exclusion that literary worlds preserve—the boundaries that worlding processes create. In addition, taking worlding processes into consideration enables us to see how texts that, at first glance, seem narrowly directed toward specific readership communities might be engaged in conversations unfolding on different geographical scales—in this way, working within and helping to envision multiple literary worlds. The uses of "world literature" that the Hindi, Tamil, and Indian English writers in this chapter employ evidence how they directed their writing toward regional language audiences, while simultaneously calling on and responding to broader circulating notions of Indian and world literature.

Apposite to my argument is Kadir's observation that North American and Western European scholars themselves have produced the elite, narrowly defined canon of world literature. Noting that "world" is actually a verb, he writes, "[W]e, who do the worlding arrogate to ourselves not only the verb's agency but the world itself. . . . The universality of whatever may be deemed universal by the various accommodations of world literature . . . does not reside in the world or in literature. . . . [It] is merely a function of the universalizing impulse in the cultural optic and subject agency of those doing the worlding."[30] For Kadir, the concept of "worlding" characterizes the critical activities that literary comparatists perform.

I use the term, however, to describe all acts of defining literariness, not just those undertaken by Western scholars. Driven by universalizing impulses, these acts are diverse, context specific, and fundamental to all literatures. In my view, the world literature that Kadir describes emerges as the result of just one among many sets of worlding practices. Acts of worlding establish every literature—not just world literature—*as literature* because they articulate the criteria by which texts should be judged vis-à-vis regional, national, and global circulations.[31] Charting processes of worlding therefore requires a multiscalar approach that exposes more than our own scholarly biases and the formal, rhetorical, and thematic dynamics of texts. It also demands attention to the literary criticism, literary historical debates, and institutional spaces surrounding texts—what might be called the "metaliterary" discourses alongside which properly "literary" texts develop. These discourses shape the literary worlds of which texts are a part.

Whereas Kadir uses the concept of worlding for scholarly self-reflection, Cheah employs it to contemplate why literature matters. He argues that world literature enables us to redefine the world—by which he means our present, common world. World literature "worlds" because it opens our world, shapes it, "actualizes or brings something into actuality . . . compel[ling] us to see our humanity, and . . . mov[ing] us to action because it allows us to see that we can actualize our potentialities."[32] Cheah presents worlding as a corrective to existing one-world literary system models that misread the potentialities of globalization and valorize the circulation of texts, production of cultural capital, and power of symbolic form.[33] Yet he replaces these models with a one-world system model of his own. Cheah conceives of worlding as a unifying temporal and normative force that precedes and exceeds the human subject, "giv[ing] rise to the totality of meaningful relations that is the ontological condition for the production of values and norms."[34]

For Cheah, literature is the privileged site of worlding because it lays bare human beings' intrinsic connection to others, a connection established through language and discourse. Drawing from Martin Heidegger's views on poetry and art, Cheah understands literature as the nonthematic, symbolic dimension of discourse that exceeds grammar and phonemics to express the "total meaningfulness of the logos or setting up of a world."[35] By this definition, not all writing has the capacity to world, and, by extension, not all literature is "world literature."[36] In short, world literature is literature that—through self-reflective narrative and formal instability—plainly articulates Cheah's particular phenomenological account of the world in the era of globalization, an account that he formulates through readings of Karl Marx, Heidegger, Hannah Arendt, and Jacques Derrida.

Curiously absent from Cheah's understanding of world literature, however, is the violence inherent to processes of worlding. Heidegger—who was the first to theorize the concept of worlding—points to this violence in his 1936 essay "The Origin of the Work of Art" when he describes worlding as simultaneously disclosure and concealment. For Heidegger, when a great work of art illuminates a world (or a particular set of relations), it also conceals all other possible truths (or worlds), which are blocked or obscured by the artwork's horizon of disclosure. He uses "earth," in contrast to "world," to signify all that is forcefully concealed in any given instance of worlding. Heidegger aestheticizes the concept of "earth," like "world," using it to encapsulate feelings of awe and reverence for the mysteriousness and incomprehensibility of what every act of worlding conceals—affective responses that he believed great works of art necessarily inspire in their beholders.[37]

In the 1980s Gayatri Spivak brought the immanent violence of Heidegger's concept of worlding to the fore when she redeployed the term to articulate a critique of imperialism. She argued that the worlding of a world is an act of epistemic violence—violence inflicted through the production of knowledge. Worlding, in her view, is the process of inscribing imperial discourse on colonized space through cultural representations. In Spivak's famous example, the British soldier Birch worlds the world of the native simply by traversing the Indian countryside on horseback, thereby obliging the native to see Birch as Master and himself as Other. This act places the native within a colonial grid of intelligibility, concealing all preexisting sets of relations. In Spivak's "necessarily false analogy" with Heidegger's concept of worlding, "earth" is the colonized space that imperialist discourse brutally effaces as it establishes a new set of power relations.[38]

Whereas Spivak is interested in the violence intrinsic to the constitution and representation of "Third World" subjects, I use the term worlding to refer to the inherent violence of literary processes of canonization. What stands out in critical formulations of world literature and the more emergent literary politics of worlding is that only certain texts are visible from a global perspective, just as only certain texts come into view if one were to take the region, for example, as one's analytical starting point. If the aim of literary scholarship is—as Cheah argues—to understand literature's causality in the world, then I would further add that the scope of literary study needs to be broad enough, and its methods rigorous enough, to enable scholarly engagement with diverse literary processes around the globe.

By considering practices of worlding within the Indian English, Hindi, and Tamil literary spheres, I offer a methodology for approaching texts on their own terms, situating them within their respective literary spheres, and also showing how they engage ideas of world literature. Attending to processes of worlding literature—rather than the canon of world literature—exposes the ways in which texts simultaneously participate in literary conversation on multiple levels, from the global to the local. This method therefore exposes how "world" and "literature" are components of myriad, continually evolving canonizing processes that sometimes converge and sometimes diverge. In elaborating this methodology, I show that while Indian English writers in London constructed an idea of Indian literature that accords with the contemporary understanding of world literature as a global literary system, Hindi writers in North India and Tamil writers in Madras did not. Engaging with world literature in nonaligning ways, these writers addressed readerships that were deeply tied to their specific language communities and sociopolitical contexts. At the same time, they viewed themselves as participants in national and international conversations about the meanings and aims of Indian and world literature. But, while the work of London PWA writers has gained visibility in contemporary discussions of world literature, that of Hindi and Tamil writers remains largely ignored. The rest of this chapter explores how late-colonial Indian English, Hindi, and Tamil writers theorized differing criteria for determining the value of literature. Accordingly, they formulated distinct understandings of Indian and world literature, all of which produced enduring aesthetic norms and standards in postindependence India.

INDIAN LITERATURE ON THE WORLD STAGE

A forceful act of worlding, the first concerted articulation of a coordinated pan-Indian literature comprised of many languages took shape in London in the mid-1930s. Responding to the rise of fascism in Europe and continued imperialist oppression in India and beyond, Indian writers—most of them students living in London—convened the Indian Progressive Writers' Association the PWA and drafted a manifesto for Indian literature.[39] The manifesto, fashioned primarily by Mulk Raj Anand and Sajjad Zaheer, was written in November 1935 and published in the British journal *Left Review* in February 1936.[40] Anand also sent the manifesto to India, where Dhanpat Rai Srivastava "Premchand" translated it into Hindi and published it in his journal *Haṃs* in January 1936. The manifesto was presented at the first All-India PWA meeting in Lucknow in April 1936, and it became the founding document of a new "progressive" Indian literature, aimed at chronicling contemporary Indian experiences and envisioning social change.[41]

The London PWA manifesto was clearly leftist in its language and aims.[42] I quote the manifesto at length, numbering each sentence for later reference:

> [1] Radical changes are taking place in Indian society. . . . [2] The spirit of reaction . . . though moribund and doomed to ultimate decay, is still operative and is making desperate efforts to prolong itself. [3] It is the duty of Indian writers to give expression to the changes taking place in Indian life and to assist the spirit of progress in the country. [4] Indian literature, since the breakdown of Classical culture, has had the fatal tendency to escape from the actualities of life. [5] It has tried to find a refuge from reality in spiritualism and idealism. [6] The result has been that it has produced a rigid formalism and a banal and perverse ideology. [7] Witness the mystical devotional obsession of literature, its furtive and sentimental attitude towards sex, its emotional exhibitionism and its almost total lack of rationality. [8] Such literature was produced particularly during the last two centuries, one of the most unhappy periods of our history, a period of disintegrating feudalism and of acute misery and degradation for the Indian people as a whole. [9] It is the object of our association to rescue literature and other arts from the priestly, academic and decadent classes in whose hands they have degenerated so long; to bring the arts into the closest touch with the people; and to make them vital organs which will register the actualities of life, as well as lead us to the future. [10] While claiming to be the inheritors of the best traditions of Indian civilization, we shall criticize ruthlessly, in all its political, economic and cultural aspects, the spirit of reaction in our country; and we shall foster through interpretive and creative work (with both native and foreign resources) everything that will lead our country to the new life for which it is striving. [11] We believe that the new literature of India must deal with the basic problems of our existence today—the problems of hunger and poverty, social backwardness and political subjugation. . . .

> [12] With the above aims in view, the following resolutions have been adopted:
>
> 1. The establishment of organisations of writers to correspond to the various linguistic zones of India; the coordination of these organisations by holding conferences, publishing of magazines, pamphlets, etc. . . .
>
> 3. To produce and to translate literature of a progressive nature of a high technical standard. . . .
>
> 4. To strive for the acceptance of a common language (Hindustani) and a common script (Indo-Roman) for India. . . .
>
> 6. To fight for the right of free expression of thought and opinion.[43]

Creating a place for Indian writing in world literary space, illuminating its cohesiveness as a national literature among others, and demonstrating its rational and socialist modernity were the primary objectives of the manifesto. It availed world literary (what it called "foreign") resources for "foster[ing] . . . everything that will lead our country to the new life for which it is striving" (sentence 10), creating a new idea of a unified Indian literature in the process. It is in this sense that the manifesto used "world literature" to *world* Indian literature—that is, to make Indian literature comprehensible *as literature* to global readers united against capitalism, fascism, and imperialism by defining the social-realist standards that constituted "progressive" Indian literary texts.

In their autobiographical accounts, Anand and Zaheer mention a wide range of socialist-leaning thinkers whose writing they admired—Marx, Lenin, George Bernard Shaw, H. G. Wells, John Galsworthy, Ralph Fox, E. M. Forster, Romain Rolland, André Gide, André Malraux, Maxim Gorky, and Louis Aragon. Even more than these influences, however, what stands out in the manifesto are the resonances it shares with the critiques of capitalism, fascism, imperialism, and literary modernism that were articulated at the August 1934 Soviet Writers' Congress in Moscow and the June 1935 International Congress of Writers for the Defense of Culture in Paris.[44] Neither Anand nor Zaheer attended the Soviet Writers' Congress. However, both men were exposed to socialist realism at the Paris Congress—if not earlier—through their association with writers such as Gorky, who had presided over the Soviet Writers' Congress and also helped to sponsor the Paris Congress.[45] Both Anand and Zaheer recall the significance of the Paris Congress in their memoirs, underscoring that "it was the first occasion when the writers of almost every civilised nation had collected together at one place for consultation amongst themselves."[46] They viewed the Paris Congress as a pivotal moment in the creation of a new world literary space organized around cultural freedom and political emancipation.

The PWA manifesto's emphases on the social decay caused by spiritualism and idealism, the disintegration and degradation generated by feudal culture, the mystical devotionalism and irrationality of earlier forms of Indian literature, and the problem of political subjugation all fit neatly with the rhetoric expounded at the Soviet Writers' Congress. For example, Maxim Gorky linked spiritualism and idealism to how the church used religious mythology to control the toiling masses.[47] A. A. Zhdanov—articulating the need for a new socialist-realist literature—similarly connected the decadence of existing bourgeois literature with capitalist disintegration and decay: "Characteristic of the decadence and decay of bourgeois culture [and literature] are the orgies of mysticism and superstition."[48] To counter such disintegration, Karl Radek called for an international proletarian literature grounded in materialism that would serve as a "shield" in the "defense of colonial peoples against barbarism" and that would be a "literature of struggle against fascist obscurantism and mysticism" that was capable of "teach[ing] the masses of the people in all countries how to fight for . . . human reason."[49]

In the Soviet Writers' Congress speeches, socialist realism emerged as a new thesis to overcome capitalist decay, which was manifest in fascism and imperialism. It marked a "split in world literature" between the reactionary and decadent literature of the bourgeoisie and the new and revolutionary literature of the proletariat.[50] Socialist realism remedied the shortsightedness of modernist individualism, depicting not only "reality as it is, but [also] . . . whither it is moving."[51]

Speeches at the Paris Congress echoed this position, offering further language that would be taken up by London PWA writers. For instance, André Gide—perhaps the most dominant literary figure at the assembly—stressed that "it is from foundations in the solid ground, from the life of the people, that a literature derives vigour and rejuvenation."[52] Gide specifically argued against symbolism and the "undue love of form," which he considered indicative of Western literature's penchant for abstraction above concrete descriptions of human struggle. According to Gide, moving beyond the stage of capitalism toward communism required a new "literature of opposition . . . aimed at the emancipation of the mind."[53]

The London PWA writers' manifesto shares more than a close resemblance to these speeches. As Ahmed Ali pronounced in his address at the Lucknow All-India PWA conference, "[B]ecause our society is torn between two disintegrating forces, feudalism and capitalism . . . the social structure is riddled with restlessness and decay. We do not have the progress which were [*sic*] present in Europe . . . between the decay of feudalism and the gradual rise of capitalism."[54] The PWA manifesto attributed the entrenched spiritualist and idealist tendencies and reactionary impulses of Indian literature to feudal cultural and imperialist subjugation. It folded Indian cultural history into a Marxist-Leninist narrative, wherein the Indian past (sentence 8) was situated within the world-historical past and the new progressive literature facilitated India's transformation from a feudal, colonized state to a free, socialist one.

Like the speeches at the Soviet Writers' Congress and Paris Congress, the London PWA manifesto also reflects a vexed relationship to literary modernism—particularly the form of modernism that PWA writers had encountered in Bloomsbury in the 1920s and 1930s. Anand, for instance, recounts suppressing the literary inspiration he drew from romanticism, naturalism, and Indian literary trends—from the ancient epics to contemporary Urdu poetry—fearing disapproval from figures such as T. S. Eliot and Virginia and Leonard Woolf. He describes nervously fidgeting in response to their flippant and deeply racist opinions about Indian literature and culture—which, in several instances, had provided the fodder for the Bloomsbury writers' modernist experiments. Anand also highlights his acute unease with the classicist formalism underlying their perspectives.[55]

Such experiences help to explain the London PWA writers' preference for social realism and the manifesto's firm rejection of "rigid formalism" and its associated "banal and perverse ideology" (sentence 6) that had led to Indian literature's desire "to escape from the actualities of life" (sentence 5). Citing Gorky's critique of modernist individualism—its creation of a "unique, mystical, and incomprehensible god, set up for the sole purpose of justifying . . . the right of the individual to absolute rule"[56]—Anand underscored the PWA manifesto's intention to shift "the standards of criticism which we naively adopted under the influence of the subjective, idealist, individualist bourgeois point of view . . . to what is called social realism."[57] From a social-realist perspective, the "individual is the correlative of the community," whereas, in modernist thought, "the individualist is the very opposite of community, the eccentric."[58] For London PWA writers, bourgeois literature's elevation of form over content and its preference for the individual over society were antithetical to efforts across the world to tie literature to social and political change.

Fighting for "the free expression of thought and opinion" (resolution 6), the London PWA manifesto saw progressive Indian writing as a part of the growing field of proletarian world literature. Drawing from "native and foreign resources" (sentence 10), the manifesto sought to correct imperialist characterizations of Indian culture and tradition and to allow Indians a voice in international discussions about culture and politics.[59] As Zaheer observed, the London PWA sought "to represent Indian literature in the West and to interpret for India the thoughts of Western writers and the social problems which were profoundly influencing Western literature."[60] And, as Anand proclaimed, "The task of building up a national culture out of the debris of the past, so that it takes root in the realities of the present, is the only way in which we will take our place among those writers of the world who are facing with us the bitterest struggle in history."[61] The London manifesto positioned Indian literature within a global capitalist framework—through which it became recognizable to the West and conversant in Western literary texts and trends. This was how PWA writers *worlded* Indian literature, establishing new "progressive" norms for this national corpus and rendering it intelligible on the world stage.[62]

A specific notion of translatability undergirded this act of worlding. Aiming "to produce and to translate a literature of a progressive nature" (resolution 3), the manifesto proposed that all progressive literatures—both native and foreign—were mutually intelligible and translatable. This idea of translatability allowed the London PWA writers to call for a pan-Indian literature—"for the acceptance of a common language (Hindustani) and a common script (Indo-Roman) for India" (resolution 4)—even though the manifesto was written in English, the only language shared among the English, Bengali, Hindi, and Urdu writers who drafted it.[63] Nehru—an early advocate of the PWA's objectives—would later propagate the same notion of translatability through the Sahitya Akademi and its aim to "get [Indian languages] into touch with each other and . . . with foreign languages too, by translations."[64] Basing their idea of Indian literature on the thesis of translatability, the London PWA writers defined and presented Indian literature in English, the contradictoriness of this move for establishing a national literature distinct from the language of imperialism notwithstanding.

HINDI LITERATURE AS INDIAN LITERATURE

Premchand's Hindi translation of the London PWA manifesto in *Haṃs* reveals a fundamentally different vision for Indian literature. The London writers worlded Indian literature by making it legible to and interchangeable with other progressive world literatures. In doing this, they took the translatability of Indian literature as a given. Premchand, by contrast, was more focused on preparing Hindi literature to represent the newly emerging nation. Consequently, he expressed greater ambivalence about translation, viewing it as subordinate to the creation of original literary works (*maulik racnā*), which would bolster the Hindi canon, making it worthy of national recognition and pride. Premchand—perhaps the most widely read Hindi writer, both in his time and ours—introduced the Progressive Writers' Movement to Hindi writers. Subsidiary to questions of global progressivism and how individual works gain recognition as world literature, Premchand saw the construction of a national literature as the task of progressive writers. His thinking on literature—while certainly in dialogue with pan-Indian and worldwide debates on the function of literature—therefore developed along tangential lines, which were directed toward a Hindi readership. In his writings, worlding was the process of positioning Hindi literature as Indian literature—a corpus of original texts that stood apart from other world literatures. For this reason, Premchand's worlding efforts do not fully align with the prevailing scholarly characterization of his work as belonging to the field of proletarian world literature, a field represented most prominently in South Asia by the PWA.[65]

Carlo Coppola, in his comparison of the London PWA manifesto and Premchand's Hindi translation of it, argues that the London manifesto used language that was "more direct and uncompromising" in its leftist call for social change. Coppola views the *Haṃs* manifesto, by contrast, as "watered down," "vague and pallid," and attempting to "set all things Indian in the foreground."[66] Put in the context of Premchand's other writings on national language and literature, however, Premchand was clearly struggling to define a new concept—"progressive literature"—in terms that he thought would appeal to the particular Hindi-speaking, Hindu readership he sought to address. This effort materialized from the very outset of his translation. Alongside his excitement about the creation of the PWA, Premchand's introductory remarks also suggested his distance from the London PWA writers' views:[67]

> I was truly pleased to learn that among our well-educated and wise youth, too, a keen desire has been born to bring a new energy and awareness to literature. The Indian Progressive Writers' Association in London was established with this very aim, and seeing the manifesto it has sent, I am hopeful that if this association stays committed to its new path, a new era for literature will dawn. I present a few lines of that manifesto here to convey its intent.[68]

Premchand was encouraged that the younger generation was showing an interest in literature similar to his own. But he avoided calling his rendering a "translation," perhaps sidestepping the question of its representational authenticity. His prefatory remarks were simultaneously open-minded and reserved in tone. He asked readers to explore and consider—rather than to endorse unequivocally—the London manifesto's claims and objectives.

In Premchand's rendering, the London PWA's critiques of capitalism, fascism, imperialism, and literary modernism disappeared. He removed the references to "the spirit of reaction . . . moribund and doomed to decay" (sentences 2 and 10) and indexed an Indian, rather than Marxist world-historical, past:

> Indian literature, after ancient civilization was destroyed, fled from the realities of life and took refuge in asceticism [*upāsanā*] and devotion [*bhakti*]. The result was that it became spiritless and dull in form as well as meaning. And today, devotion and asceticism have become abundant in our literature. Sentimentality is on display, while thought and intellect have, in a way, been exiled. This type of literature was produced particularly during the last two centuries, which are a shameful period in our history. It is the aim of this association to take our literature and other arts out of the control of priests, pandits, and the conservative [*apragatiśīl*] classes, to bring them in closer contact with the people, and to bring life and reality into them, through which we can illuminate our future.[69]

Lacking the London manifesto's specific allusions to capitalist degeneration, Premchand's interpretation of the decline of Indian literature here recalls the literary historical framing of Hindi literature that his contemporary Ramchandra Shukla had popularized during this period—and with which Premchand's Hindi readers were abundantly familiar. Shukla's framing therefore constituted an important metaliterary discourse that, in tandem with Premchand's own writings, made Premchand's translation of the PWA manifesto intelligible to Hindi readers. Shukla's literary history helped to *world* Premchand's manifesto not via Hindi literature's translatability into English or European progressivism, but rather through renewing its connection to ancient Indian traditions of truth-telling.

Shukla was a preeminent critic and literary historian, head of the Hindi department at Benares Hindu University, and closely involved with the activities of the Hindī Nāgarī Pracāriṇī Sabhā (Society for the Promotion of the Nagari Script). His influential *Hindī Sāhitya kā Itihās* (The history of Hindi literature), published in 1929, was largely responsible for producing the still prevailing nationalist narrative of Hindi literature. For Shukla, Hindi literature had "a glorious, martial beginning with the *rāsos* in Rajasthan, had come to a cultural and literary climax with Surdas and Tulsidas during the Bhakti period, the flame being kept alive even in the dark age of Muslim occupation . . . declined into unhealthy and useless eroticism during the *rīti* period and started ascending again along a reformist path in the nineteenth century."[70] In Shukla's view, Hindi literature—a distinctly Hindu literary tradition—arose despite and in contradistinction to Persian and Urdu literature and Islamic culture more broadly. His account therefore marginalized the influences of fifteenth-century outcaste Muslim poet Kabir and of the *rīti* (high style) poetry of Mughal courts, both of which emblemized the degradation against which Hindi literature struggled to persevere.[71] It also critiqued Western religion for deviating from the paths of rationalism and ethical responsibility, which Shukla believed formed the foundations of the Hindi canon.[72]

Premchand's discussions of Hindi and Indian literature align with Shukla's efforts to detach modern Hindi from the declining literary merit of the previous era. He described this wayward medieval literary turn in essays such as "The Art of the Short Story," as well as in his inaugural address at the first All-India PWA conference, held just two months after the publication, in *Haṃs*, of Premchand's translation of the London manifesto. According to Premchand, the "magical adventures [*tilismātī kahāniyāṁ*], ghost stories [*bhūt-pret kī kathā*], and romances [*prem-viyog ke ākhyān*]" of the previous era were solely for entertainment.[73] To counter this escapism, Premchand called for contemporary Indian literature to draw from ancient ideals, while also staying grounded in present-day truths. Indian literature could thus define itself as a national tradition distinct from the false idealism of the medieval past and the gross realism of the Western present. Differing starkly from the London manifesto, Premchand expressed a need for Indian literature to move away from contemporary Western literary trends:

> [European] realists [*yathārthvādī*] maintain that nowhere in the world do the fruits of good and evil seem apparent; rather, the effects of bad deeds are often good and those of good deeds, bad. The idealist [*ādarśvādī*] says, what's the value of realistically showing reality when we already see it with our own eyes? For a while, we must maintain a distance from [both] these contemptible [literary] approaches, or the primary aim [*uddeśya*]

> of literature will disappear. This [aim] holds literature not just as a mirror, but also as a lamp, the task of which is to spread light. The ancient literature of India does, indeed, support idealism [*ādarśvād*]. We, too, must nurture a respect for ideals [*ādarś*]. Yes, reality [*yathārth*] must be intermingled with it so that we don't stray too far from the truth.[74]

Premchand saw the ancient Indian past as a golden era and its literature as exemplary of the type of idealism from which Indian literature must draw inspiration.[75] This historical narrative informed Premchand's denunciation of devotion, asceticism, and sentimentality, which pervaded the literature of the "shameful" past two centuries. It also motivated his appeal for a new literature in closer contact with the people. Therefore, Premchand's Hindi rendering of the London manifesto contained no opprobrium of "spiritualism and idealism." Similarly, in Premchand's version, the London manifesto's acerbic critique of literary modernism—its "rigid formalism" and its "banal and perverse ideology" (sentence 6)—read instead as an indictment of medieval Indian literature's detachment from people's everyday struggles and its lack of commitment to social change. Premchand transformed the London manifesto's capitalist critique of the "decadent" bourgeoisie into a charge against the culturally "conservative" Indian classes—the educated elite who continued to extol older, entertainment-oriented literary forms.[76]

Premchand also removed the London manifesto's embrace of "foreign resources" and added a new sentence to define the meaning of "progressive" in its place:

> While protecting the traditions [*paramparā*] of Indian civilization, we will mercilessly criticize our nation's degrading inclinations and with critical and creative works we will accumulate all those things which will help us reach our goal. We believe that the new literature of India must connect with the basic facts of our present life, and those are the questions of our daily bread, our poverty, our social degeneracy, and our political subjugation. . . . Everything that leads us towards inactivity, idleness, and superstition is base; and everything that instills in us a critical mentality, that encourages us to test even our dearest traditions on the touchstone of our intellect, that makes us industrious, and that brings us the strength of unity—all this we understand as progressive [*pragatiśīl*].[77]

It is possible to interpret this passage, like Coppola does, as Premchand's attempt to be "as all-inclusive [of different viewpoints] as possible" and more focused on "things Indian" than that of the London manifesto.[78] Indeed, Premchand's definition of progressive writing offers a tempered counterpoise to the London manifesto's critique of religion by pointing out that traditions need to be tested, not summarily disbanded. But I interpret Premchand's rendering as a reflection of his own anxieties about the contentious status of Hindi vis-à-vis English and Urdu, as well as Hindi's tenuous capacity to serve as a national language and literature. Premchand left out the allusion to "foreign resources" and defined progressive literature in general terms because he was interested in expanding the Hindi canon to take on a new pan-Indian representational role.

Premchand's ambivalence toward translation provides insight into his position on building Hindi into a national literature. Premchand began his writing career in Urdu and later moved fluidly between Urdu and Hindi. In many instances, he produced Hindi translations of his own Urdu texts and vice versa.[79] He also translated from Urdu and European languages—via English—into Hindi, including works by Ratan Nath Dhar Sarshar, Leo Tolstoy, Anatole France, Charles Dickens, Oscar Wilde, John Galsworthy, George Eliot, Guy de Maupassant, Maurice Maeterlinck, and Hendrik van Loon. Premchand dedicated large portions of his journal *Haṃs* to Hindi translations of writing from European and other Indian languages, stressing that translations enabled Hindi literature to expand its scope.[80] Yet, despite his investment in translation, Premchand cautioned against relying too much on translation into Hindi:

> It is not an objectionable thing to fill one's treasury with the jewels of some other language. Translations from other languages continue to occur in the richest languages. But what kind of language is it that contains everything in translation and nothing of its own? . . . Our aim is to make Hindi the national language [*rāshṭra bhāshā*]. Can it attain the status of a national language through translations?[81]

He also highlighted the secondary nature of translation:

> One who has the capacity for original writing would not translate, nor would he ever wish to acquire fame through translation. Sure, I translated a lot from English into Urdu at the beginning of my literary career. The reason is that, at the time, I was inca-

> pable of producing original works. All those translations have died away because they didn't have the power to survive.[82]

Translation, Premchand argued, harmed the growth of contemporary Hindi fiction.[83]

Premchand's desire to bolster the Hindi canon surfaced most clearly in his polemics against English's threat to Hindi literature. He resisted Nehru's appeals to accept the influential role of English in national life, arguing that the queen's English "had made beggars" of Indian languages and caused educated Indians to abandon their mother tongues.[84] Premchand also denied Nehru's suggestion that all Indian languages were equal, and he qualified Nehru's call for Indian involvement in international literary organizations:

> To get involved in international organizations, we will have to take recourse to a national language. We cannot enter into the international arena on the strength of our regional [*prāntīya*] languages. It's a mistake to dream that all our regional languages can be equal to the world's developed languages. A nation can stand before international organizations only in one language. Of course, regional languages may be presented to the world through English translations; but . . . the honor that [a translated work] acquires is that of the individual [author]. And the book's original language doesn't gain any prestige. Today the international recognition that some Russian, Swedish, and French books have is not because they were printed in English translation. Rather, it's because they were read in their original language and appreciated. . . . If we are to acquire a place in world literature [*saṃsār-sāhitya*], then we will have to establish a national language and participate in world literary culture [*saṃsār sāhitya-samāj*] on its basis. . . . It is impossible that India's twelve main languages will ever be equal to the world's mature languages.[85]

Whereas the London PWA manifesto viewed free literary exchange among Indian languages and between Indian and European languages as central to its objectives, Premchand called for strengthening Hindi on its own terms. In his view, Hindi needed to be established as a national literature before it could be recognized globally.

Premchand's intimate knowledge of Urdu literary culture contributed to his apprehensiveness about the deficiencies of Hindi as a national language.

In his comparison of Premchand's Hindi novel *Sevāsadan* (The orphanage) with its Urdu version *Bāzār-e-Ḥusn* (The marketplace of beauty), Snehal Shingavi has observed that *Sevāsadan* is far more concerned with the detrimental effects of translation on Hindi literature than its Urdu counterpart.[86] Shingavi argues that *Sevāsadan* is "about rescuing Hindi fiction from the supposed decadence of Urdu institutions . . . as well as the actual power and prominence of the Urdu literary scene and the seductions of other languages."[87] Premchand's resistance toward Urdu literary culture echoes his denunciation of the medieval past and erasure of "foreign" literary influences in his version of the London manifesto. To Premchand, "foreign" stood for anything outside Hindi literature, including Urdu, other Indian languages, and all European languages.

In light of Premchand's efforts to develop the Hindi canon, it makes sense that he would insert such a broad definition of progressive literature into his version of the manifesto. Premchand was conscious of the fact that Hindi was a young literature, with very few "original" works of its own. Still, he was deeply committed to developing Hindi into a cultural vehicle for unifying the Indian nation, and he encouraged a wide range of new Hindi literary production. Narrowly defining progressive literature within the Marxist framework proposed by the London manifesto would have proved too contentious for many Hindi writers and impeded the accomplishment of this goal.

In an attempt to link the London PWA writers' proposal to the specific demands of the Hindi context, Premchand concluded with several remarks of his own. He pushed back against making Indo-Roman the national script, arguing instead that Devanagari be "utilized equally by all Indian languages."[88] The London PWA writers viewed the adoption of Hindustani in the Indo-Roman script as the least contentious, most inclusionary solution to the national language question. They saw no problems with producing Indian literature in multiple languages, later to be translated into Hindustani. Premchand's objections to foreign languages and his commitment to building Hindi as a distinguished national canon prevented him from fully accepting this perspective. He argued for a diverse form of Hindi—which drew from Sanskrit, as well as Farsi, Arabic, and even English—but he also promoted Hindi as *the* national language and literature.[89] Propagating the Devanagari script was part of this project.

Premchand also suggested that the London PWA's most effective role in developing a national Indian literature—perhaps even more than creating progressive writing—was in translating Hindi works into English. This, he professed, "would be a true service to both literature and the nation."[90] If producing original Hindi works was the first step in building the national canon, then English translations complemented this endeavor by making Hindi internationally accessible and renowned.

Lastly, Premchand appealed to members of the Hindi Writers' Association (Hindī Lekhak Saṅgh) to consider the London PWA's proposal for creating progressive Indian literature. "The [Hindi] Writers' Association's aims converge a great deal with those of this association," he wrote, "and there is no reason that the two cannot cooperate."[91] Premchand offered the London manifesto as a starting point to consider the aims and objectives of a new Indian literature. But he considered it the task of Hindi writers to envision and implement this literature on a pan-Indian scale.

The idea that Indian literature is Hindi literature underlay Premchand's rendering of the London PWA manifesto. In this translation, as well as in his other writings, Premchand *worlded* Hindi by advocating it as the ideal instrument to unify the Indian people and to represent their cultural heritage. Despite tapping into conversations about world literature that were unfolding on both the global and national scales, Premchand minimized world literature's role in developing the Hindi field by conceptualizing it as an arena to be confronted after Hindi became established as a national canon. Translatability, in his view, endangered Hindi literature's distinctness, while the ancient Indian past imbued it with moral fortitude and cultural authenticity.

UNTRANSLATABILITY IN TAMIL AND INDIAN LITERATURE

Comparable to the PWA writers in London and Premchand in North India, the Tamil writers who converged around the literary magazine *Maṇikkoṭi* in Madras were responsible for creating a new idea of Indian literature in the 1930s. They were familiar with and often translated Premchand's fiction—alongside the work of numerous other Indian and international writers—in their magazine. However, they engaged neither with Premchand's ideas for developing a national literature nor with the literary standards that the PWA outlined for establishing a pan-Indian progressive corpus.[92] The *Maṇikkoṭi* writers—known for inaugurating a new tradition of Tamil modernism—put forth an alternative understanding of Indian literature, one that welcomed foreignness and untranslatability into the process of developing Tamil literature. They used translation to connect Tamil literature to the Indian and world literary canons and, in doing so, *worlded* Tamil literature. Translation, they believed, was crucial to opening Tamil literature to outside influences in the face of growing ethnolinguistic nationalism in the region.

The founding editors of *Maṇikkoṭi* underscored the magazine's intentions to attract a literarily inclined Tamil readership.[93] As B. S. Ramaiah, who was involved with *Maṇikkoṭi* from its inception and transformed it into a premier venue for short story writing, recounted in his memoir:

> Even though *Maṇikkoṭi* was a weekly and then a short story bimonthly, it wasn't just a Tamil magazine. It was a movement [*iyakkam*] . . . launched with the intention of inciting a new awakening in social and political life within the hearts of the people and elevating their literary taste [*ilakkiya cuvai*].[94]

Ramaiah described the establishment of *Maṇikkoṭi* as a response to Dravidianism that sought to reclaim Tamil (Dravidian) language and culture from Sanskritic (Aryan, Brahmin) dominance, which had come from the north. The magazine took a decisively "art for art's sake" stance to combat what *Maṇikkoṭi* writers saw as the corrosive effects of Dravidianist rhetoric, which threatened the pursuit of national independence.

Ramaiah pointed specifically to the political divisiveness of the Self-Respect Movement (Cuyamariyātai Iyakkam), which, for him, encapsulated the most detrimental effects of Dravidianism. Founded in 1925 by E. V. Ramasamy Naicker "Periyar" the movement sought to eradicate the entrenched gender, caste, and religious norms associated with Brahminical Hinduism. According to Ramaiah, *Maṇikkoṭi* emphasized the oneness of Indians against colonial rule, in contrast to the Self-Respect Movement's comprador position, which "hindered the national independence movement with its unpatriotic force [*aṉṉiya ātikkam*]."[95] While Ramaiah had no objections to the movement's efforts to abolish caste hierarchies, he viewed it as corrupted by the skewed influence of its non-Brahmin leadership, which used the logic of Dravidianism to gain influence within the colonial administration. Because Periyar's writing and speeches were imbued with Dravidianist rhetoric, they were, according to Ramaiah, poor in aesthetic taste and quality as well as antagonistic to the cultural and political unity of the Indian people.

In addition, Ramaiah and other *Maṇikkoṭi* writers positioned themselves against Maraimalai Adigal's Pure Tamil Movement (Taṉi Tamiḻ Iyakkam). The Pure Tamil Movement, launched in 1916, "proposed that Brahman power in Tamilnadu would be subverted if Tamilians stopped using Sanskrit words in Tamil writing and speech."[96] Adigal's neo-Saivite glorification of Tamil history departed from Periyar's atheistic and rationalist vision of Dravidian solidarity. Still, the two political ideologies converged insofar as they pitted Dravidian ethnicity against the dominance of North Indian Sanskritic culture and the imposition of Hindi as the national language.[97] The Pure Tamil Movement placed particular value on ancient Tamil literature, which emblemized the autonomy and distinction of Tamil culture and language.[98]

In his memoir Ramaiah expressed deep frustration with the Pure Tamil pundits and university professors who refused to acknowledge the innovations of modern Tamil writers.[99] Similarly, Pudumaippittan—perhaps the most widely read of the *Maṇikkoṭi* writers today—cautioned against the Pure Tamil Movement's narrow vision of Tamil. In a 1934 essay published in *Kānti* (*Gandhi*)—a magazine that soon thereafter merged with *Maṇikkoṭi*[100]—he lashed out against the Pure Tamil Movement's classicism:

> About the Tamil language—"Why don't you use the term 'Pure Tamil'?" some might growl. . . . Tamil once held prestige . . . [and] they fear it will now fade away. They worry that Goddess Tamil might have an intercaste marriage. So they try to hide her behind a screen of isolation as if she were a young maiden to protect her with virtuous backbiting from the arrows of discord. . . . Tamil is not an insolvent language. The addition of new words is not going to destroy her essential form. For her to receive new words is the same as conquering new countries and attaining storehouses of new artistic treasures. . . . Creating aesthetically pleasing prose requires great practice in several languages and a strong interest in their best qualities. The pundits cannot help is in this matter even a little.[101]

In contrast to their characterization of the Pure Tamil Movement's linguistic and literary extremism, *Maṇikkoṭi* writers valorized a modern prose style that reflected everyday Tamil speech and embraced the incorporation of diverse vocabularies, dialects, and literary influences.[102]

Maṇikkoṭi writers lionized the work of Tamil poet Subramania Bharati, viewing it as exemplary of the type of literary innovation they aspired to produce. Bharati was an activist and social reformist who was deeply involved in the Indian Independence movement. To *Maṇikkoṭi* writers, his poetry represented an unprecedented renaissance in Tamil literature. Bharati's patriotic themes awakened nationalist sentiment in readers, while his creative uses of language and form kindled artistic inspiration. His poetry thus gave Tamil literature both national and international standing. As the well-known *Maṇikkoṭi* writer Na. Piccamurti stated: "Expanding the subjects appropriate to poetry and elevating . . . poetic sentiment; bringing poetry into the hearts of contemporary Tamilians and connecting it to world progress; transforming poetic style—Bharati's service to Tamil literature included all of this and more."[103] Tamil scholars and Pure Tamil activists criticized Bharati's nationalist stance and unrestrained use of Sanskrit and English vocabulary. *Maṇikkoṭi* writers, conversely, praised what Sumathi Ramaswamy has characterized as Bharati's "Indianist" literary outlook, which provided the first crucial step in demonstrating Tamil literature's place within the broader Indian canon. In their view, Bharati's work exemplified the uniqueness of Tamil language and literature, while simultaneously expressing national oneness and cultural unity.[104]

Not surprisingly, the *Maṇikkoṭi* writers' opposition to the Self-Respect and Pure Tamil movements' exclusionary and polemical uses of Tamil shaped their position on the national language question. Following a meeting of the Akhil Bhārtīya Sāhitya Parishad (All-India Society for Indian Literature), held in Madras in March 1937, *Maṇikkoṭi* ran a series of opinion pieces under a new column called "Yātrā Mārkkam" (The journey's path). The series debated whether Hindi and the Devanagari script should be implemented nationally.[105] The first piece was published under the pseudonym "Batasari."[106] It quoted from Lady Lokasundari Raman's welcome address at the meeting during which she articulated the impossibility of using the same script for all Indian languages.[107] Batasari argued that a language's uniqueness, deeply linked to its script, could not be replicated in any other language—that it was a mistake to think that Tamil's subtle nuances could be expressed in any other language.[108]

Others concurred with Batasari's insistence on the singularity of language and its deep connection to context. For example, reviewing R. K. Narayan's *The Bachelor of Arts* (1937), Pudumaippittan questioned Narayan's choice to write the novel in English, stating that "the thoughts fused with the flesh and blood of a region's people can only be expressed through the intimacy of their own language."[109] A few issues later, he argued that, while literary characters share general human attributes, every character is also formed by the unique circumstances into which he or she is born.[110] Several *Maṇikkoṭi* writers switched from English to Tamil for this very reason, and their prolific publishing endeavors in Tamil demonstrated their ardent commitment to building it into a prominent constituent of the Indian canon, placing it on par with other world literatures. Simultaneously giving expression to Tamil modernity and Indian unity, *Maṇikkoṭi* "produced the life energy and force that . . . was linked in style with the world literature movement [*ulaka ilakkiya iyakkam*]."[111]

Thus, *Maṇikkoṭi* writers' dedication to Tamil did not translate into a resistance to installing Hindi as the national language. In the October 1937 issue of *Maṇikkoṭi*, Batasari spoke out against the Pure Tamil Movement's position on Hindi: "Pure Tamil folks ask, 'why make [the Hindi language] the rule of law?'. . . . [But] don't we need a common language for the progress of the nation? . . . Without a common language, we cannot come together to form an independent country."[112] In the same vein, Ramaiah—writing under the pseudonym "Vyasan"—stressed that the colonial imposition of English across the subcontinent was different from attempts to implement Hindi on a national scale. Responding to the one dissenting voice in the series by "Dasiketan," Ramaiah argued:

> One needs farsightedness to fully understand [the idea of] "Hindi as a common language" [*Hindi potu pāṣai*]. One must have an open mind and high ambitions and desires for the future of the nation's people. Our friends must consider the imperialist rule of this country over our people and the condition of our country under its dominance. . . . If we build our foundation on the insistence that children must only learn their mother tongues in schools, what is to become [of our future]?[113]

In line with their nationalist leanings, the *Maṇikkoṭi* writers saw the acceptance of Hindi as integral to national progress.

Having established their generally pro-Hindi position, the *Maṇikkoṭi* writers soon transformed their debate over national language into an exploration of the differences between literary translation and literary adaptation. The two issues were linked, since welcoming a new language into the Tamil region also meant welcoming new literary influences. In general, the *Maṇikkoṭi* writers supported translation over adaptation. In the same article in which he argued for the necessity of Hindi, Batasari critiqued a recent Tamil adaptation (*taḻuval*) of a French story, in which the characters' names had been changed to Tamil ones: "If it's a story from another country, aren't the names of that country also important? . . . Can they [the characters] simply become Tamilians? . . . Writing in adaptation is, therefore, a false life."[114] Defining the difference between translation and adaptation, Pudumaippittan pressed the matter even further:

> Translation [*moḻi peyarppu*]: to translate a story means that to the best of our ability, to the very extent that the flexibility of our language allows, we present the product of a particular

> foreign country [*aṉṉiya nāṭu*] without jeopardizing its essence [*cāram*].
>
> Adaptation: This is to take the main events of a narrative from a particular foreign country—more or less as they are—and to concoct a story out of them without necessarily retaining all the original's literary qualities. . . . This is simply theft.
>
> Those who argue that a story must be adapted belong to one party. Their contention is that Tamil people will never enjoy reading about foreign codes of behavior because they can never understand them. If that were true, then we shouldn't even bother thinking about stories from foreign lands.[115]

From Pudumaippittan's perspective, adaptation meant closing Tamil off from the rest of the nation and world.

Offering a final word on the translation-adaptation debate in the December 1937 issue, Ramaiah argued that adaptation was an isolationist practice that cut Tamil off from the world literature movement.[116] He shared an adapted story, in which an American narrative about race discrimination was rewritten as a Tamil story about caste prejudice. Ramaiah concluded that such literary transcreations sheltered Tamilians from various struggles around the world, keeping Tamilians in a cage. They reflected the weakness of the translator—not the Tamil language—to expose himself creatively to foreign cultures and influences. Translation, by contrast, provided the necessary means for Tamil literature to grow, facilitating artistic innovations in style, content, and form.[117]

The translation-adaptation debate illustrates how *Maṇikkoṭi* writers used translation to undermine Tamil ethnolinguistic nationalism. Through translation, they welcomed new concepts and uses of language into Tamil literature, even as they insisted on the contextually specific nature of languages and cultures. Exploring foreign ideas and ways of life and using their unfamiliarity to bend the Tamil language, the *Maṇikkoṭi* writers sought to bring Tamil literature into conversation with the rest of the nation and the world. For them, grappling with the untranslatability of foreign concepts confirmed Tamil literature's modernity and place within both Indian and world literature.

Arguing against the "translatability assumption" of world literature—its "reflexive endorsement of cultural equivalence and substitutability"—Emily Apter has recently called for a focus on untranslatability, which requires close reading, philological and historical awareness, and deep knowledge of multiple languages. She invokes "untranslatability as a deflationary gesture toward the expansionism and gargantuan scale of world literary endeavors."[118] Apter's emphasis on the untranslatable—through which she seeks to foster a humanistic intervention into the "possessive collectivism" of world literature[119]—valorizes an understanding of literariness that is based on moments of "militant intransigence . . . non-sense that becomes strangely accessible through the sheer force of grammar."[120] I would argue, alternatively, that how writers grapple with issues of translatability is essential to how they define aesthetic value—and, relatedly, how they understand the category of world literature—in different literary contexts. An in-depth examination of the Indian English, Hindi, and Tamil literary spheres discloses the variability of ideas of translatability and the complex role of social and historical circumstances in their construction—not, as Apter argues, the universal aesthetic (and ethical) value of untranslatability.

The London PWA writers viewed translatability as a requisite for establishing a nationally and internationally recognizable progressive Indian canon. Premchand, by contrast, warned against translation, emphasizing instead the importance of untranslatability for creating an original Hindi corpus. Diverging from both these approaches, the *Maṇikkoṭi* writers used translation to *world* Tamil literature by inviting other languages and literatures to defamiliarize Tamil and elevate Tamil readers' aesthetic discernment above Dravidianist political rhetoric. In the *Maṇikkoṭi* worldview, Indian literature was comprised of multiple literatures, which were linguistically and culturally distinct but still connected to the progress of the Indian nation. Untranslatability opened regional literatures to their strange yet familial others, providing the means through which this national literature took shape.

COMPARATIVE WORLDINGS

The diverse understandings of Indian and world literature that I have examined here find no place in current approaches to world literature, which sustain world literature as an exclusive and Eurocentric category. Aamir Mufti has recently argued along these lines, noting how "throughout its history, world literature . . . has functioned as a *plane of equivalence*, a set of categorical grids and networks that seek, first of all, to render legible *as literature* a vast and heterogeneous range of practices of writing from across the world and across the millennia."[121] For Mufti, "literature" is an idea that became globally available through Enlightenment-era intellectual and literary practices, and he uses it interchangeably with "world literature" to mark a new "*border regime*, a system for the regulation of movement" of literary texts.[122] "Literature," in Mufti's view, is inseparable from the emergence of nationalism, modern bourgeois society, and English as *the* global literary vernacular. Mufti's key intervention is to show that the categories of national and world literature are mutually constitutive. The transnational, "borderless world" that theorists of world literature imagine remains deeply rooted in "modern Orientalism . . . the cultural system that for the first time articulated a concept of the world as an assemblage of 'nations' with distinct expressive traditions."[123] In Mufti's analysis, the case of Indian literature, in particular, epitomizes how Orientalist processes of extraction invented national literature for the purpose of creating world literature: "India may be said to have made, in the form of its ancient Sanskritic culture, a distinct *national* contribution" to establishing world literary space.[124]

Such analyses are useful for disclosing the power dynamics inherent in the "one-world literary system." However, the prevalent scholarly emphasis on this global system—even in those works, such as Mufti's, that critique it—conceals and renders irrelevant all those literary processes that fall beyond its purview. From a "one-world literary system" perspective, world literature is the only way to understand literature. Equating Indian literature with national literature, this approach offers no pathways for exploring the multilingual and dialogic relations that constitute both Indian literature and world literature as shifting, utopian, and indeterminate ideas. The multiple contestations over the idea of Indian literature—and uses of the idea of world literature—that I have explored here compel us to understand literature as something more than a singular discursive formation that was consolidated in post-Enlightenment Europe and that continues to prescribe *the* authoritative criteria for literary recognition and inclusion. They ask us to consider how literary processes of worlding may have different comparative coordinates, genealogies, and aims.

In the 1930s, Indian English, Hindi, and Tamil writers mobilized Indian literature as a discursive project with distinct power dynamics and political effects. In each of these cases, differing criteria for literariness put in place their own regulations for the movement of literary texts. Indian English writers understood Indian literature through an international progressivist lens that was shaped by Marxism and modernism. For Premchand, however, this standard was inadequate. He viewed Indian literature as modern Hindi literature, which combined realistic depictions of contemporary Indian experience with idealistic lessons that drew from the ancient Indian past. Premchand's literary philosophy of idealistic realism (*ādarśommukhī yathārthvād*)—which I elaborate in the next chapter—took shape most forcefully in his short story writing and deeply influenced postindependence Hindi *nayī kahānī* (new story) writers. In stark contrast to the views of both Indian English and Hindi writers, Tamil *Maṇikkoṭi* writers defined literary value as innovation in the use of modern Tamil. For them, literary experimentation with foreign sources established the foundation for a national Indian literature and evidenced Tamil literature's place within world literary space. As I show in the following chapter, the *Maṇikkoṭi* approach to literariness—articulated most powerfully in Pudumaippittan's short stories and essays—established a literary politics of estrangement and loneliness (*nampikkai vaṟaṭci*) that would later shape the short stories of postindependence *Eḻuttu* writers.

To understand the function of literature—the preeminent concern of the writers considered in this book—is to understand the multiple border regimes that constitute the idea of Indian literature and how they never quite cohere into a singular literary system. A focus on processes of worlding discloses how ideas of literary value are not necessarily bound to the totalizing ontological worldview that current theorizations of worlding present. Attending to the question of how literature is constituted as a field of power, a comparative analysis of worlding reveals alternative standards for literary value, ones that are not based on translatability, the English language, and the novel form—the major premises on which contemporary understandings of world literature have been built.

CHAPTER 2

Citations of Sympathy

How the Hindi and Tamil Short Story Gained Preeminence

A GENRE OF TRUTH

The short story epitomized the deepest emotional experiences of the individual, concisely conveying life's profound truths. This at least was the idea that Premchand and Pudumaippittan—considered the doyens of the Hindi and Tamil short story, respectively—put forth in the late colonial era.[1] Both writers praised the short story for its capacity to inspire individual reflection and social transformation.

Certainly, their position was pragmatic. As committed fiction writers, editors, and journalists, Premchand and Pudumaippittan recognized how periodicals could create new readerships. They also understood the centrality of the short story within the journal medium. The short story sold magazines. "Without short stories, no magazine is interesting," Premchand declared in a 1926 special issue of the popular magazine *Cāṅd* that celebrated the genre.[2] Ordinary and accessible, the short story had the unique ability to reach audiences across class and caste barriers, providing readers with important insights into common issues and mundane experiences.[3]

Pragmatic reasons such as these may have led Premchand and Pudumaippittan to focus their energies on the genre. Still, this does not explain why these writers viewed the short story as intimately connected to "life's truths." Did the short story have a special access to truth? Were the truths this genre offered distinct from the insights that emerged in other literary forms? Did the short story address the dynamics of the late-colonial Hindi and Tamil contexts more accurately than other genres, or did it expose these dynamics in a different light? What, in short, was the social function of the short story?

This chapter explores how the short story became the primary genre through which Premchand and Pudumaippittan theorized the relationship between literature and society. Translation, as I demonstrated in the previous chapter, enabled these two writers to define the meanings of Hindi and Tamil literature in relation to the canons of Indian and world literature. The short story, I show in this chapter, allowed them to encapsulate these meanings into its compressed form. Prolific writers across multiple genres, Premchand and Pudumaippittan developed the short story in conversation with other forms—especially the novel—to make a case for the short story's distinct position within their respective literary fields. This genre, they argued, most effectively articulated their visions for how the Hindi and Tamil communities should evolve as India's independence became more possible.

In particular, Premchand and Pudumaippittan used the genre to reconsider popular representations of the Indian woman—a figure highly charged in nationalist debates about community identity. The Indian woman had already become a contested site in the battle between tradition and modernity in nineteenth-century Indian novels.[4] Meenakshi Mukherjee has observed that the European novel's typical man-woman romantic relationship could not be easily rendered in early Indian novels because of rigid social structures and restrictive marriage conventions. Instead of individual desire and free will, Indian novels sought to "reconcile two sets of values—one obtained by reading an alien literature and the other available in life."[5] Widows, prostitutes, virgins, and goodwives conveyed social reformist anxieties—surrounding issues such as education, property inheritance, child marriage, widow remarriage, women's reproductive health, and women's rights to adoption and divorce—allowing Indian novelists to explore the national and regional identities that these types collectively represented. The suffering female figure was a constitutive component of colonial-era Hindi and Tamil literature, and it featured prominently in Premchand's and Pudumaippittan's short stories.

This chapter argues that the brevity of the short story enabled Premchand's and Pudumaippittan's depictions of the Indian woman to reference debates about tradition and modernity without evoking the social reformist positions that this figure embodied in contemporary novels and poetry. Counter to both the novel's protracted descriptions of character and setting, and poetry's lyrical emphasis on spirituality and desire, the short story compressed colonial-era female types into singular emotional events. Using thumbnail sketches of female characters demanded by the form, Premchand's and Pudumaippittan's short stories articulated "truth" through emotional insight rather than novelistic didacticism or poetic ecstasy. The formal constraints of the short story dislodged Premchand's and Pudumaippittan's female characters from conventional gender norms, allowing these figures to express Premchand's and Pudumaippittan's understandings of truth through affect and tone. At the same time, their representations of gender pushed back against the formal requirements of the short story, prompting a transformation in colonial-era Hindi and Tamil prose from a social-realist concern with social reform to a modernist emphasis on individual turmoil.

The first sections of this chapter show how Premchand and Pudumaippittan theorized the function of literature based on their distinct aesthetic traditions and sociopolitical contexts. Premchand formulated what he called idealistic realism (*ādarśommukhī yathārthvād*)—the integration of material conditions with cultural ideals surrounding propriety, kinship, and social structure—in the context of North Indian discussions about Hindi as the national language, Hindu and Muslim forms of community, and national independence. Pudumaippittan, by contrast, theorized a notion of disillusionment (*nampikkai vaṟaṭci*)—which he viewed as necessary to the development of the self—to dissociate literature from ideological debates surrounding language, culture, and marriage in colonial Tamil Nadu. These theorizations were powerful acts of worlding, which scholars have since interpreted through the lenses of anticolonial resistance, modernist critique, and proletarian solidarity.[6] Yet, they were also deeply engaged in regional political contestation.

In the following section I illustrate how the short story's brevity gave form to the two writers' divergent understandings of literary purpose by focusing on female characters whose traits had to be presumed based on recognizable female types rather than extended character development. This focus allowed Premchand and Pudumaippittan to unmoor their portrayals of the Indian woman from existing gender roles, thereby dissolving the tradition-bound notions of the Hindi and Tamil communities that this figure represented. In the final part of the chapter, I trace this unmooring through Premchand's and Pudumaippittan's short stories. A comparison of the two writers' work makes visible how the Hindi and Tamil short story gained literary import through the citation of locally circulating representations of the Indian woman. Premchand's and Pudumaippittan's citational and iterative uses of gender and genre enabled their short stories to produce enduring aesthetic positions that were intelligible to multiple readerships across regional, national, and global scales.

LITERARY BLISS

Scholars almost exclusively turn to Premchand's "Sahitya kā Uddeśya" (The aim of literature)—his address at the 1936 inaugural meeting of the All-India PWA in Lucknow—to analyze his theory of realism and its connection to social justice. Viewing the speech in light of the PWA's vision to create a new, "progressive" Indian literature, scholars understand it as an expression of what Priyamvada Gopal has called the PWA's "critical realism," that is, "a philosophy that brings together an affective sense of justice, fairness and harmony with an understanding of all that violates that sense."[7] But Premchand acted as an observer and translator of London PWA discussions rather than a principal interlocutor.[8] Delivered just six months before his death and before the PWA became fully established in the subcontinent, "Sahitya kā Uddeśya" drew heavily from Premchand's earlier writings, reiterating ideas he had developed elsewhere—sometimes verbatim. The speech encapsulates the literary historical view that Premchand carefully developed over his prolific career, rather than the PWA's more rigorously Marxist approach.[9]

In the address Premchand defined literature as "the criticism of life" and that "which expresses a truth, whose language is mature, refined, and beautiful, and which has the quality of impacting the heart and mind."[10] Its primary aim, he proclaimed, was the cultural formation of the mind (*man kā saṃskār*).[11] This literary perspective centered on the elevated position Premchand awarded to writers:

> Defending and advocating for the oppressed, suffering, and deprived—whether they be individuals or groups—is the writer's duty. He presents his claims in their court and may consider his efforts successful if he awakens its instincts for justice and beauty. . . . The court's change of heart [*hṙday-parivartan*] only occurs when [the writer] refuses to turn away from the truth [*satya*]. . . . He writes stories, but with attention to reality [*vāstavikata*]; he creates images, but those which are alive and emotionally generative—he observes human nature with a keen eye, studies psychology, and tries to have characters who

> behave in every condition and circumstance as if they were men made of flesh and blood; due to his natural sympathy [*sahaj sahānubhūti*] and a love of beauty, the writer accesses the subtlest arenas of life, which man is incapable of reaching because of his own humanity.[12]

Premchand understood writers to possess greater sympathetic connections, more acute observational skills, and more sophisticated aesthetic sensibilities than ordinary individuals. These traits enabled them to critique life, disclose truth, and "rouse our thoughts and feelings," thereby cultivating minds.[13]

The above passage is often cited as proof of Premchand's social realism, wherein literature realistically portrays social inequalities and injustices to inspire a "change of heart" in readers.[14] Although Premchand famously claimed that "literature is a reflection [*pratibimb*] of its age," he did not—contrary to common understandings—advocate documentary realism.[15] Instead he used this phrase to throw light on what he viewed as the preceding era's moral decline and his belief that literature should present an idealistic outlook. Premchand insisted that literature should portray life as it should be—rather than how it was—to shape a more perfect society.[16] The aim of literature, he suggested in a three-part essay on "Kahānī Kalā" (The art of the short story), published in 1934, is "not just as a mirror, but also as a lamp, the task of which is to spread light."[17] Critiquing European realism for its pleasure-oriented approach to literature, Premchand argued that integrating realism with idealism (which was grounded in ancient Indian values) better served readers. He highlighted literature's role in fostering moral and aesthetic sensibilities rather than exposing bitter reality. The writer committed himself or herself to imagining a more utopian future: "As soon as we pick up the pen, a great responsibility falls upon us. . . . A writer must be an idealist."[18]

When read as an echo of the PWA's literary politics—"to register the actualities of life"—Premchand's "Sahitya kā Uddeśya" might be understood as advocating mimesis rooted in lifelike descriptions of character.[19] Considering Premchand's larger oeuvre, however, a different view of character development emerges—one in which character elaboration belonged to a broader literary project of enlightening readers. Truth and reality, in this worldview, were interchangeable terms referencing the "psychological secret" (*manovaijñānik rahasya*) of man's existence.[20] Referred to in the speech above as "the subtlest arenas of life," this was the secret of man's changing mental states (*mānsik avasthā*) and emotions (*bhāv*). Man's emotional life comprised the realm on which Premchand believed that literature was focused.[21]

Within this literary framework, psychological reality was not synonymous with external reality. Rather, it comprised an ulterior reality that was constructed to illicit emotional responses in readers whose real-life interpersonal relationships were uninspiring. For this reason, "it would be a mistake to understand that the short story is a realistic picture [*yathārth citra*] of life," Premchand argued, elucidating that "an uncultured being cannot draw as close to a subtle mind as he can to a fictional character."[22] Within Premchand's literary framework, character descriptions were often exaggerated to better illuminate the secrets of the mind.[23] Characters were portrayed with pure hearts and simple natures to "lift us to some enchanting place."[24]

The purest emotional state (*bhāv*), Premchand repeatedly argued, was *ānand* (bliss). This was the underlying disposition that literature sought to uncover:

> Man engages in a lifelong search for bliss [*ānand*]. Some find happiness in jewels and wealth, some in the completeness of family, some in having a huge mansion, and some in sensual pleasure; but the bliss of literature is greater than this kind of happiness, more divine. Its basis is beauty and truth. In fact, true bliss is synonymous with beauty and truth, and the aim of literature is to portray such bliss, begetting it [in readers].[25]

If the basis of literature was emotion, Premchand argued, then *ānand* was the most foundational emotional state because it enabled readers to sympathize with one another.[26] Premchand's philosophy of idealistic realism (*ādarśommukhi yathārthvād*)—which he defined as "the incorporation of reality and ideals"—was tilted toward idealism.[27] Realist character description, when employed, served to inspire *ānand*, the greatest of all ideals.

Premchand's elaboration of *ānand* was a reframing of *rasa*, an aesthetic framework created at dawn of the first millennium to systematize mood and emotion in Sanskrit drama. *Rasa* theory described eight emotions (*bhāv*), of which the erotic sentiment (*śṛṅgāra*) helped to reproduce the poet's experiences of intense emotion in audience members.[28] Devotional (*bhakti*) literature in the medieval era drew from classical erotic tropes to describe the passionate relationship between the devotee and the divine. Twentieth-century Hindi writers, however, critiqued erotic literary depictions for their focus on sensuality and individual desire. "There was," Charu Gupta writes of this new literary trend, "a growing fear of romance, of sexual and bodily pleasure: these were seen as a transgression of the ideals of the nation."[29] Influential Hindi littérateur Mahavir Prasad Dwivedi, for example, railed against the erotic depictions of heroines in the *rīti* (high style) poetry of the Mughal court—denouncing them for centering on women's bodies and sexual desire outside the marital fold.[30] Similarly, eminent literary scholar Ramchandra Shukla saw the erotic sentiment in *bhakti* literature as detrimental to literature's ability to create *lok maṅgal* (public good and welfare).[31] Dwivedi and Shukla also opposed 1920s and 1930s *Chāyāvād* poetry—often characterized as Hindi Neo-Romanticism—for using erotic sentiments to advance individuality and freedom.[32] By contrast, they promoted the role of the writer, whose literary expertise and moral vision enabled the social advancement of the national community.

Premchand expressed a similar literary outlook. His essays drew from the terminology of *rasa*, but he reworked the emphasis in Hindi aesthetics on *śṛṅgāra bhāv* (erotic emotion) to highlight the writer's responsibility to instill rational "feelings of loyalty, truthfulness, sympathy, and love of justice and equality" in readers.[33] He singled out poetry and novels influenced by *bhakti* literature and the Persian *dāstān* tradition of storytelling, both of which focused on passion and fantasy, asking:

> Can a literature limited to topics of erotic disposition [*śṛṅgāra manobhāv*] and the pain of separation and hopelessness that arise from it . . . fulfill our intellectual and emotional needs? Erotic emotion is only one part of life, and a literature that is focused largely on it cannot be a thing of honor for its community or era, nor can it be a standard for taste.[34]

Premchand believed that poets of the previous era were "tainted with individualism [*vyaktivād*]" and idealized the "satisfaction of desire," promoting decadence, division, and enmity, when they should be advocating for love of humanity and knowledge of truth.[35]

He also critiqued *Chāyāvād* poets, viewing their work—like Dwivedi and Shukla—as escapist and superficial. For instance, Premchand's "Abhilāshā" (Desire), published in 1928, contrasts a lower-class wife's experience of domestic abuse and deprivation with an upper-class wife's desire to rekindle the love she felt for her husband when they were briefly separated. The short story ends with a quote from a poem written by the well-known *Chāyāvād* poet Mahadevi Varma that evokes the erotic sentiment Premchand denounced: "A lover's renunciations are strange / And her worlds of pain lonely, / Where have you disappeared, / Having stolen my love like gold."[36]

Juxtaposed with the lower-class wife's struggles, the upper-class wife's sentimental evocation of these lines parodies the longing between lovers so significant in *Chāyāvād* poetry, making them appear frivolous. How true can such romantic yearning be, the story asks, in light of the gender inequalities women face in everyday life?

As my discussion of Premchand's uses of world literature and his work in translation in the previous chapter makes clear, Premchand was familiar with and drew from multiple European and South Asian worldviews. At the same time, his understanding of idealistic realism was shaped by broader metaliterary discussions about *rasa* that were circulating in North India during his time. In the late nineteenth century, Bharatendu Harischandra—known as the father of Hindi literature—had already renewed conventional *rasa* categories, adding *ānand* as a new aesthetic effect that he defined as "the pleasure derived from good literature."[37] Following Harischandra's lead, Dwivedi viewed *ānand* as the aesthetic experience derived from "useful literature" in the early twentieth century.[38] Premchand's interest in *ānand* emerged within this larger milieu of reworking *rasa*, which was part of an effort to rescue classical Sanskrit aesthetics from the literary historical narrative of medieval decline that Dwivedi and Shukla had popularized. For Dwivedi and Shukla, as Simona Sawhney has argued was true for many writers of the period, "the linguistic and literary lineage of Sanskrit became significant as a means of distinguishing Hindi from Urdu and thus presenting a genealogy of 'Indian' poetry that emphasized both a linguistic and spiritual community."[39] Premchand's emphasis on *ānand* as the preeminent literary sentiment assisted with this nationalist project—perhaps unintentionally—because it reinforced a Hindu literary history as the basis of Hindi literature.

This is not to argue, therefore, that Premchand deliberately sought to alienate Urdu from Hindi like Dwivedi and Shukla, both of whom held an antagonistic attitude toward Islamic culture. Premchand was deeply aware of Urdu literary debates, and his Urdu writings evince a keen familiarity with the tastes and demands of Urdu readers.[40] At the same time, Premchand's Hindi writings bring to light the centrality of contemporary Hindi discourses in shaping his efforts to build Hindi as a national literature. Premchand followed the *rasa* terminology that Dwivedi and Shukla used, but he also innovated upon the literary sentiment of *ānand*. Loosely based on *rasa*'s theory of emotional transference from artist to audience, this modern emotion encapsulated Premchand's particular literary humanist position: "Only when [a writer's] characters are so alive and attractive that the reader can put himself in their place may he attain bliss [*ānand*]. If a writer does not inspire such sympathy [*sahānubhūti*] in the reader, then he has failed in his aim [*uddeśya*]," he wrote.[41] If Premchand's emphasis on *ānand* aligned with Dwivedi's and Shukla's nationalist project, it also added an element of political materialism to their elevation of the lofty critic. This element affiliated Premchand's idealistic realism with social-realist literary endeavors unfolding elsewhere, while simultaneously addressing the particular vocabularies of late-colonial Hindi literary debate.

AN AESTHETICS OF ISOLATION

Pudumaippittan also located emotional truth at the heart of the literary endeavor. His literary approach, however, was markedly different. In Premchand's framework of idealistic realism, *ānand* inspired culturally specific ideals of human connection in readers. Premchand insisted that isolating oneself from society caused both mental affliction and social degeneration. This perspective was linked to Premchand's lifelong project to assemble a Hindi readership around a shared sense of Indian culture and community. He believed that individualism was detrimental because it detracted readers from blissful social cohesion. For Pudumaippittan, by contrast, *taṉimai* (loneliness or isolation) formed the core literary sentiment, possessing similar transformative social qualities to Premchand's *ānand*. At the same time, Pudumaippittan's *taṉimai* was based on a fundamentally different understanding of community, one which was critical of alliances based on language, culture, and ideology.

Pudumaippittan wrote that *uṇarcci* (emotion, sentiment, sensibility) was literature's "life force" (*jīvanāḍi*), the basic element underlying its form (*amaippu*) and creative power.[42] Emotion was the hidden truth that literature unveiled. In his 1934 essay "Ilakkiyattiṉ Irakaciyam" (The secret of literature), Pudumaippittan expanded on the interconnectedness of literature and emotion:

> What is the place of literature in life? . . . Literature is the elaboration of the self [*uḷḷam*], the awakening of the self, its blossoming. A writer examines life with all its complexities and problems, subtleties, and twists. These produce an emotion [*uṇarcci*] deep within him. Literature is the very thing that governs over that stream of emotion. It could be the name of a flower that [the writer] doesn't know, a detested political scheme, or the severity of human cruelty that catches his attention. No matter. As soon as he notices some particular aspect of life, his heart and

> mind become troubled. Literature is the representation of this arousal of emotion. . . . The pulse of literature is emotion. . . . The sheer truth [*uṇmai*] of emotion leads to a new consciousness [*viḻippu*]; [this] truth is the very secret [*rakaciyam*] of life.[43]

Arising from the writer's everyday life, emotion inspired creative production. Fiction transferred writers' own emotional experiences to readers, kindling a transformation of selfhood within them. In Pudumaippittan's view, *uṇarcci* enabled readers to heighten their aesthetic sensibilities for encountering the world in new, unconventional ways. Literature was the truth of life, the primary basis of human knowledge and community belonging.

Pudumaippittan furthermore maintained that *uṇarcci* could only emerge in a state of *taṉimai*—isolation or loneliness. In a 1946 essay tracing man's social development, he meditated on the relationship between the individual and society, pointing out a contradiction between them: "Man precedes society. . . . [T]he individual [*taṉimaṉitaṉ*] who tries to see the truth is an exception; he is life's sacrificial lamb." He viewed tradition and religion as narrow and "society [*camūkam*] [as] a constraint to the gathering of men."[44] In a 1934 essay Pudumaippittan argued against the popular understanding that unity required a consensus around social issues.[45] Rather, he believed that isolation was necessary to discover new truths. In this formulation writers were perhaps the loneliest individuals of all. They alone accessed the emptiness (*veṟuppu*) of everyday modern experience and saw "the truths of the world and secrets of life in a different light."[46] The writer's eyes, according to Pudumaippittan, were the very "eyes of emotion."[47]

Pudumaippittan viewed *taṉimai* as a thoroughly literary sentiment. It offered a capacious notion of interiority that encompassed a range of meanings—including a Lukácsian notion of the hero's inward search for meaning, as well as the more overdetermined godly force propelling the inner life of the individual, which had been widely theorized in the medieval Tamil poetic tradition.[48] Twelfth-century Tamil poet Kamban provided the original example. Analyzing Kamban's work, Pudumaippittan argued that the poet carefully "create[d] a web of emotion" through descriptions of his heroine's torment during the sleepless nights she spent awaiting her lover.[49] Kamban's language, style, and imagery awakened the young woman's feelings of desolation in readers. Whether by Kamban, John Milton, or modern writers in Tamil (among other languages), authentic literature expressed such loneliness. For Pudumaippittan, the purpose of literature was to create the feeling of *taṉimai*, through which readers could develop an aesthetic sense of truth.

Taṉimai belonged to a worldview that Lakshmi Holmstrom and A. R. Venkatachalapathy have identified as Pudumaippittan's *nampikkai vaṟaṭci* ("a drying up of hope or belief"), the principal concept guiding his writing. Often translated as "pessimism," Holmstrom explains that *nampikkai vaṟaṭci* "can also mean skepticism or agnosticism, a this-worldly and questioning position in [Pudumaippittan's] exploration of myths, beliefs and practices."[50] Venkatachalapathy further notes that "while [Pudumaippittan] is deeply, in fact, violently critical of the existing social order, he also doubts every emancipatory project."[51] Alongside these understandings, I would highlight another dimension of Pudumaippittan's literary approach, namely the profound disillusionment with existing norms and beliefs in his writing, in particular those regarding interpersonal relationships. As I argue in the sections below, understanding *nampikkai vaṟaṭci* as a sense of disenchantment with contemporary social reformist framings of chastity, love, and marriage enables us to see Pudumaippittan's short stories recasting prevailing gender norms, grounding them in a literary—rather than social or political—sensibility.

Pudumaippittan himself coined the phrase to distance himself from the gatekeepers of Tamil literature who dictated which topics were appropriate to literary expression. In a 1942 essay describing his relationship to his writing, Pudumaippittan asked:

> Isn't literature supposed to arouse mental agitation [*maṉa avacam*]? . . . It's nothing but an outright contradiction of experience to . . . encounter people like Raman the store clerk, Sitammal the cinema actress, and Brahmanayakam the ever-bargainer and never give their lives any place [in literature]. . . . There is nothing inferior in writing about the practices and affairs of daily life. . . . In literature, artistry lies precisely in the pulses of life. . . . But, we might ask whether a general drying up of hope or belief [*nampikkai vaṟaṭci*] in my stories gives legitimacy to a literature focused on unfavorable human characteristics? It is not about the "poisonous" nature of contrariness, despite what the mature-minded folks who believe this say.[52]

In this passage—and throughout the essay—Pudumaippittan expressed frustration with his contemporaries, many of whom wanted to censor "obscene" literary depictions of underworld characters. He also responded to the egocentric critics who called his expressions of disillusionment harmful, implying that their criticisms were personal rather than substantive critiques of his literary project. Pudumaippittan posed the literary worth of *nampikkai vaṟaṭci* as an ironic rhetorical question, concluding that the very madness (*pittam*) of his work comprised its creativity and originality. This act was a deliberate play on Pudumaippittan's pseudonym, which meant "one who is mad or crazy (*pittaṉ*) for the new (*putumai*)."

Who were the critics to whom Pudumaippittan was responding? He left them unnamed in the essay cited above. In other pieces, however, Pudumaippittan targeted many individuals against whom he defined his work: "popular" writers producing entertainment-oriented fiction; activists focused on cleansing Tamil of Sanskrit and English influences; social reformers using literature to convey moral lessons; and scholars arguing against deviations from traditional Tamil literary conventions and themes.[53] In the preface to his 1943 short story collection, Pudumaippittan proclaimed that his stories were meant neither to teach lessons nor to envision future realities.[54] Elsewhere, he joked about the nonchalance with which he produced his most well-known stories, conjuring them immediately upon request or in response to a friendly challenge.[55] Through such remarks, Pudumaippittan dissociated his writing from pedagogic or moralistic projects. He claimed madness as a mantle, rejecting predominant Tamil literary methods and cultural and political ideologies.

Despite championing the depiction of quotidian characters and affairs, Pudumaippittan neither endorsed nor rejected literary realism. He used poetry as a proxy for all literature, distinguishing between inner and outer reality: "Poetry is truth born of man's emotions . . . . Whether man's inner self is part of the *yatārtta* (realistic) world, or separate from it, is anyone's guess. It emerges from inner experience, in the grip of the rush of emotions. That is what poetry is."[56] Glossing the Tamil word *yatārtta* with the English word "realistic" (printed in Roman script), he singled out the European-influenced realist trend in Tamil literature, which he sought to dismantle by emphasizing emotion. In Pudumaippittan's view, each writer's unique inner experience created his or her writerly style (*naṭai*). To substantiate this point, Pudumaippittan engaged in literary experiments with fellow writers, who compared the differences among short stories they wrote about the same event.[57] Each individual's distinct creative energy meant that no two writers could narrate the same experience in the same way. A writer's depiction of reality could thus be truthful, despite its diverging from external circumstances.

This emphasis on inner truth did not coincide with Premchand's understanding that true literature evoked *ānand*. Pudumaippittan eschewed commitment to either realism or idealism, exalting the lonely individual who existed apart from society, unfettered by its constraints. Whereas Premchand viewed literature as the quintessential avenue for thinking through social reform issues, Pudumaippittan denied literature any connection to political squabbles. In this sense, Pudumaippittan's position aligned with the separation of politics and art typically associated with European modernist thought.[58] He argued—with other writers who converged around the little magazine *Maṇikkoṭi*—that literature provided intuitive insight into the enigmatic nature of life.[59] Literature therefore was built on, but also elevated above, everyday experience. It articulated the truth of solitude, suffering, and despair by giving form to the imaginative worlds produced by these experiences.

Pudumaippittan advanced a literary approach of *nampikkai vaṟaṭci* (disillusionment) in the context of widespread debates on Tamil language and identity, marriage and conjugality, and the national struggle for independence. As I demonstrated in chapter 1, he opposed Tamil ethnolinguistic nationalism and its vision of an unadulterated Tamil past. He also stood at odds with Indian nationalist and Tamil Self-Respect politics, which produced contrasting understandings of heterosexual relationships. The former focused on marriage reform to modernize the nation, and the latter focused on intercaste marriage to promote social equality.[60] A newly emerging genre of popular Tamil fiction—which depicted arranged marriage through the lenses of family romance and drama—provided another counterpoint to Pudumaippittan's work. All these views, his philosophy of *nampikkai vaṟaṭci* contended, produced overwrought ideals. Pudumaippittan viewed Kamban's work as an expression of *taṉmai*—an emotional state which, until that point, had connoted misery in Tamil literature—and placed the poet at the head of a literary lineage that included both Tamil and Western writers. These interpretations were meant to shock.[61] His worldview of disillusionment implored Tamil readers to connect through shared emotion and aesthetic enlightenment rather than communal values, traditions, or ideals.

PARADIGMATIC TITLES AND OVERDETERMINED TYPES

Although Premchand and Pudumaippittan had diverging perspectives on which emotion literature should convey, they both agreed that literature should produce emotional experiences in readers. For this reason, their literary philosophies led to a similar elevation of the short story form. The two writers considered the short story to be an exceptional medium for disclosing literary truth because of its narrowed thematic focus and compact portrayals of character. The short story's brevity enabled the genre to provide readers with unencumbered access to emotional insight.

"The short story is a window on life," Pudumaippittan wrote in a 1935 piece, succinctly capturing the understanding of the short story that both writers shared.[62] The short story offered a careful but partial view, one that required whittling down plot and sifting out unnecessary description. Its ambitions were linguistic precision and affective depth, not thematic scope. The short story possessed a singular artistic unity, which was structured around emotion and event. "All other matters are contained within a single event," Premchand clarified—an event which homed in on "some psychological truth."[63] The short story was a tight-knit genre, its totality based on the strength of focus rather than its expansiveness or heteroglossia.[64] In developing this view, Premchand and Pudumaippittan drew from and dialogued with short story writing from around the subcontinent and world, which they voraciously read and translated.[65] At the same time, their position was based on their personal experiences with the genre as career writers and editors, their inheritance of colonial-era contestations around literature and language, and their keen participation in Hindi and Tamil literary debates of their time.

To clarify their views on the short story, both writers juxtaposed the short story with the novel.[66] Though most English-language scholarship focuses on Premchand's novels, a great deal of his thinking was related to the short story. He wrote almost three hundred short stories and about fifteen novels over his lifetime and was known equally for his work in both genres.[67] Premchand's essays on the short story convey that he believed it to be both more accessible and more developed in Hindi than the novel.[68] His essays on the novel, by contrast, focused on training writers to produce better novels, disclosing his anxieties about the quality of Hindi novels in comparison to novels in Urdu and other languages.[69] Premchand argued that, unlike the short story, the novel comprised an aggregate of various characters and events that need not be related. In addition, novelists complemented detailed descriptions of character, plot, and setting with their own philosophical or pedagogical explanations. The short story, however, contained no room for authorial intervention. It provided a more direct means to enlightenment for readers of all classes:

> In a novel demonstrate with as much force as your pen has the strength to do so, argue about politics, take up ten or twenty pages to describe some assembly; these are not flaws! . . . [But]

> not a single sentence or even a word should be there that doesn't illuminate the short story's aim. . . . People who have money read novels, and those who have money also have time. The short story is written for ordinary people, who have neither money nor time. . . . A short story is that note in a *dhrupad* performance through which the singer, at the very beginning of the gathering, displays his entire brilliance. In one moment he satisfies the soul with such sweetness that couldn't come about even if one listened to his singing all night.[70]

Pudumaippittan viewed the relationship between the short story and the novel similarly. Over his lifetime, he published around one hundred short stories and a novella, and he also left behind an unfinished novel. But, although Pudumaippittan admired several poets—particularly, Kamban, Subramania Bharati, and Kanakasabai Subburathinam "Bharatidasan"—he wrote very few poems himself. I suspect that Pudumaippittan, like other *Maṇikkoṭi* writers, invested primarily in the short story because this genre represented a departure from existing Tamil literary traditions. They associated the Tamil novel with social reformist agendas and viewed Tamil poetry as the primary medium of Dravidian and Pure Tamil activists.

In his essays on the short story, Pudumaippittan explained that "the difference between [the short story] and the novel is that the novel attempts to depict life exactly as it is, with its various difficulties and turbulences. The short story handles one small event or individual matter."[71] While the novel was a "large mirror reflecting life" and meandered through time periods, characters, and themes, the short story scrutinized a single instance, expertly omitting all else.[72] Writers who interjected moralistic lessons into their fiction, Pudumaippittan further argued, failed to create artful stories that encouraged the development of aesthetic sensibilities.[73]

If the novel portrayed life comprehensively, through authorial interpolation, then the short story conveyed human truths through momentary emotional insight. Such insight, moreover, addressed a more fundamental reality than did the novel. "The short story constructs and reveals life's many subtleties through words," wrote Pudumaippittan. For this reason, he praised a new generation of short story writers who "stood at the limits of the imagination and folded ideas [into their fiction], which had [otherwise] been trapped within words and refused expression."[74] Premchand likewise attributed a higher truth to the short story, insofar as it depicted more profound human experience than the novel's diffusion of the details of daily life:

> It would be a mistake to understand that the short story is a realist portrayal of life. . . . Art is not simply a name for the imitation of reality. If art manifests, so does reality, but [art] is not reality. Its uniqueness is precisely that it appears as reality even though it is not. . . . The secret of art is delusion, but it is a delusion over which lies the veil of reality.[75]

Both writers contended that reality in the short story was the reality of inner truth, a deeply aesthetic truth that did not necessarily correspond with—to use Pudumaippittan's words—"life exactly as it is."

These writers argued that formal coherence—rather than realistic description—dictated the parameters of the short story genre. They recognized what Charles May has described as the short story's structure of pattern and repetition, which constructs the "immaterial reality of the inner world" and highlights "an experience . . . directly and emotionally created and encountered."[76] May traces the development of the short story in the West and locates the genre's pattern in Western writers' uses of language and symbolism. The recurrence of words and images within a story imparts it with ineffable, metaphoric meaning.[77] But in Premchand's and Pudumaippittan's cases, patterns of words and symbols sometimes operated within individual stories, but more often these patterns were reiterations of words and images from texts outside them. The repetition was in essence a citation of representations already in circulation, particularly those related to the ideal Indian woman. Premchand's and Pudumaippittan's citations of overdetermined female types, as I argue below, made emotional insight in their stories possible.

Formally, these citations could be found in the reverberations between Premchand's and Pudumaippittan's short story titles and their female characters. In the novel, the title is what Gerard Genette calls a "paratext." Separated from the novel's content by a page break, the title imposes thematic unity from beyond, designating the novel's primary subject matter and articulating the author's, translator's, editor's, or publisher's own interpretation of the work.[78] Short story titles work differently. Published in journals and magazines, they—like poems or book chapters—adjoin the text, function as the first line of the text, and relay meaning through their constant conversation with the narrative.[79] Many of Premchand's and Pudumaippittan's short story titles referenced well-known objects, figures, or images. They served as launching points for shaping alternative perspectives on their stories. They brought signs already burdened with meaning into these writers' stories to explore, parody, or critique those meanings, changing them as a result.

Premchand's and Pudumaippittan's short story oeuvres are full of paradigmatic titles. In Premchand's case, consider, for example, some of his most famous stories that identified specific feminine types: "Veśyā" (The prostitute), "Satī" (The good wife), "Baṛe Ghar kī Beṭī" (A well-bred daughter), "Swāminī" (Mistress of the house), "Saut" (The cowife), "Beṭoṃvālī Vidhvā" (The widow with sons), "Ekṭres" (The actress), and "Būṛhī Kākī" (The old aunt). Other titles—for instance, "Rahasya" (The secret) and "Abhīlāshā" (Desire)—recalled the widely debated enigma of female desire. Still others—like "Kafan" (The shroud), "Ṭhakur kā Kuāṁ" (The landlord's well), and "Dūdh kā Dām" (The price of milk)—highlighted objects saturated with social and cultural significance.[80] Each of these titles invited readers to draw on their familiarity with particular characters, themes, and symbols, while also inviting readers to reconsider what they thought they knew.

Pudumaippittan's titles operated in similar fashion. Take, for instance, stories such as "Poṉṉakaram" (The golden city), "Akalyai" (Ahalya), "Oppantam" (The contract), "Āṇmai" (Manliness), "Vaḻi" (A way out), and "Kōpālayyaṅkāriṉ Maṉaivi" (Gopal Iyengar's wife).[81] Though not all these titles are evocative of female types per se, each employs a stereotype or motif linked with contemporary conceptions of gender. For example, Pudumaippittan's "Poṉṉakaram" refers to the city of Madurai where Kannaki—the unjustly wronged heroine of the ancient Tamil epic *Cilappatikāram*—was honored as a goddess and presiding deity.[82] To a Tamil reader, Pudumappittan's ironic use of this title becomes evident immediately after discovering the story's plot. "Poṉṉakaram" follows Ammalu, the wife of a useless drunkard, who slips off with a stranger to earn a few rupees for her family. "'Chastity, chastity!' you keep saying. Well, this, sir, is the golden city!" the narrator concludes.[83] Contrasting Ammalu's transgression of wifely chastity with the ancient heroine Kannaki's virtuous devotion to her husband, Pudumaippittan's story addresses the sexual anxieties associated with city living and exposes the impracticalities of upholding traditional expectations of wifely behavior in such a setting. The story's title and its depictions of Ammalu work with—as well as against—one another to topple the utopian ideals of gendered propriety prevalent in the rapidly urbanizing Tamil context of Pudumaippittan's time.

Like "Poṉṉakaram," Pudumaippittan's "Akalyai"—which I discuss further below—contrasts ancient and modern ideals of gender through an unusual account of the despair and isolation felt by the ideal wife Ahalya, whose story is recounted in the ancient epic *Rāmāyaṇa* (circa the second century CE). At odds with social reformist positions on marriage, "Oppantam" compares the dowry contract with the business "contract" arranged between philanderers and prostitutes. "Āṇmai" exposes the character weakness of a young man and the mental derangement of his lover as the two try to break away from the conventions of arranged marriage. "Vaḻi" delves into a widow's despair as she contemplates suicide now that the practice of *satī* (widow immolation) has been banned. And, lastly, "Kōpālayyaṅkāriṉ Maṉaivi" portrays a Brahmin man's failed efforts to defy caste conventions by marrying a low-caste woman. Pudumaippittan begins the story with a note referencing the characters Gopal Iyengar and Meenakshi, who were featured in his literary predecessor Bharati's novella *Cantirikaiyiṉ Katai* (The story of Chandrika). He fashions his portrayal as an ironic rewriting of this iconic intercaste couple. All these story titles use recognizably gendered tropes and symbols to destabilize existing social reformist paradigms.

Premchand's and Pudumaippittan's female short story characters are brilliant in their allusion to already circulating types, rather than in their precise or extensive character development. These characters are, for this reason, neither flat nor round. In his 1927 book *Aspects of the Novel*, E. M. Forster defined the concepts of flatness and roundness in a way that has now become commonplace. He designated flat characters as "types" or "caricatures" that are "constructed round a single idea or quality."[84] They are familiar and predictable, while round characters are more nuanced and extend from the pages of a novel into the reader's own reality.[85] Both flat and round characters are, according to Forster, principal features of a successful novel. Their delineation helps to meet the requirements of the genre—such as plot, theme, and mood—as well as to satisfy readers' tastes.

Unlike the novel, the formal aspects of the short story hinge on brevity, a property that does not permit flat or round characters to fully surface. Since short story characters are circumscribed within a single moment, they remain at a tangent to the chronological rootedness that the novel affords its protagonists. Lukács argued that the novel's development of characters in historical time undergirds the "typicality" of literary types—their ability to synthesize idiosyncratic individual experience with broader historical processes to expose the social whole. For this reason, Lukács was pessimistic about the short story. He believed that it lacked the same utopian potential as the novel, which could reconcile individual interiority with external reality. The short story, for Lukács, was not properly historical.[86] Yet, Premchand's and Pudumaippittan's short stories bring to light that the historicity of the genre lay in its citation of recognized character types—its ability to call types into existence without lending them narrative space. This is what their short story titles enabled the two writers to accomplish.

CITATIONS OF SYMPATHY

The citation of female types allowed Premchand's and Pudumaippittan's stories to prioritize affect. Citation replaced protracted descriptions of character with familiar descriptors, allowing female characters to quickly and concisely evoke current understandings of Indian womanhood. In this way citation cleared a path for Premchand's and Pudumaippittan's female characters to facilitate the unfolding of the short story's emotional event.

Female short story characters alluded to existing feminine ideals, which were associated with women's suffering. Dipesh Chakrabarty has argued that, beginning in the nineteenth century, the widow became the model subject of suffering. Produced by individual and collective experiences, the widow embodied the modern self's struggle to negotiate individual desire within traditional kinship structures. Furthermore, "to build an archive of the widow's interiority, to see her self as deep and stratified . . . required the development of a set of observational techniques for studying and describing human psychology. This was a role performed primarily by the novel."[87] By transforming the widow's heterosexual romantic desires into a transcendent spiritual love, the novel trained readers to enter into what Toral Gajarawala has called the "circle of readerly sympathy."[88] The novel's sublimation of feminine desire allowed readers to feel compassion for female characters. Premchand's and Pudumaippittan's short stories evidence a fundamental difference between the novel and the short story. The short story referenced female suffering—rather than chronicling it—stirring readerly sympathy without sublimating feminine desire. If the aim of literature was to generate human connection, as both Premchand and Pudumaippittan maintained, then the short story's citation of female suffering was the most direct means for achieving this end.

Let me turn to Premchand's short story "Mis Padmā" (Miss Padma) to elaborate this argument. Published at the end of Premchand's life, the story cites current discourses about the new woman. Even before readers fully enter the narrative, the "Miss" in the title announces the stereotype of a single, westernized woman who is both sexually available and socially at risk. In the opening paragraph the narrator constructs a portrait of the protagonist using few words: Miss Padma is a successful lawyer, independent and promiscuous. Instantly, she evokes the interwar modern girl, whom Priti Ramamurthy has shown to be "cheeky, cosmopolitan, and seductive," "racially ambiguous and religiously hybrid," urban, professionalized, sometimes androgynous, always autonomous, and—by the mid-1930s—heavily critiqued by the Indian nationalist movement.[89] Intelligent, beautiful, and confident, Padma is a modern girl in every way.

"Miss Padma did not detest sensual pleasure," the narrator tells us. "What she hated was dependency and turning marriage into the main business of life. Why shouldn't she remain free and enjoy sex if she could?"[90] Padma's belief in free love and gender equality recalls many westernized women who preceded her—women who emerged in the social reform debates, film, and literature of the period and in Premchand's stories more specifically. For example, characters such as Jenny in Premchand's "Unmād" (The crazed, 1931) or Padma in "Do Sakhiyāṁ" (Two friends, 1928) embody tensions between tradition and modernity.[91] Described as the mistress of the house, an uninspired mother, and her lover's whore, Padma invites a juxtaposition with the many different feminine types featured in Premchand's work, even if her story is unique. Among Premchand's stories, two particular characters—the eponymous Miss Padma of Premchand's Urdu version of the story and Miss Malti of his Hindi novel *Godān* (The gift of a cow)—compel close comparison. All appearing near the end of Premchand's life, Malti and the two Padmas share uncanny resemblances.[92] I view them as revisions of one another, worked and reworked over the writer's career. They are citations that reveal the craftwork of form.

The Hindi "Mis Padmā" is often read as a cautionary tale that depicts detrimental effects of westernization, particularly for Indian women.[93] Padma's downfall is precipitated by the incompatibility of her independence with her heartfelt desire to find a faithful companion. Part 1 describes Padma's compact with her lover Prasad to live together as a free but committed couple. Part 2 recounts Prasad's laziness, drunkenness, and predilection for comfort and luxury—all encouraged by Padma's unquestioning adoration and financial support. In part 3, Prasad robs Padma of her savings and runs off with his young student, abandoning Padma with their newborn child. The narrative is pithy and the conclusion poignant:

> A month went by. Padma stood at the gate of her bungalow with her child in her arms. By now, her anger had turned into bitter despair. Sometimes she felt compassion toward the child, sometimes love, and sometimes hatred. As she looked toward the road, a European lady walked by with her husband, pushing her baby in a stroller. She watched the lucky couple longingly and her eyes filled with tears.[94]

Appearing extemporaneously, the European lady might be dismissed as a metonymic detail had she emerged in the setting of a novel. The bounded nature of the short story, however, accords her great symbolic weight. Here she embodies all that Padma cannot attain: one on hand, modern womanhood shaped by freedom of choice and, on the other, satisfied motherhood supported by spousal companionship. Discussing this ending, Susmita Roye has argued that rather than pit Western against Indian womanhood, "the [European] memsahib is seen to embody the values of *strīdharma* [wifely duty and devotion]. . . . This indicates that Premchand extols ideal womanhood, as represented by good wifehood and motherhood, be it Indian or European."[95] In Roye's understanding, the European woman expresses Premchand's penchant for traditional conjugality—though not necessarily his anticolonial views.

I view the story, instead, as an exploration of what types of Indian womanhood were imaginable in late-colonial North India. The impossibility of being European overshadows Padma's fate, exposing the dismal prognosis for Indian women's independence and free will. If Padma's citation of the licentious, westernized modern girl casts her as less than ideal, her tears undo any binary interpretation of the ideal feminine type. Rather, they implore a sympathetic response that makes outright rejection of Padma's character difficult. In the final instance, Padma's despair—drenched through and through with longing for love and companionship—achieves affective resonance.

This interpretation becomes even sharper when it is juxtaposed with Premchand's Urdu rendition of the same story.[96] Twice the length of his Hindi version—including back stories and additional characters—the Urdu "Mis Padmā" is sprawling in structure, but its citational force is weaker. Nowhere is Padma a "Miss," except in the title. The Urdu rendition reads as an experiment with character development within the formal confines of the short story genre. Padma's sister Ratna is estranged from her husband Jhilla, and she criticizes marriage for enslaving her. Ratna is portrayed as misguided for marrying for love and silly for expecting her husband to give her more than she gives him. Padma is also depicted as flirtatious and flighty, the success of her law practice based on her seductive ways rather than on her intelligence or skill. The girls' father is dead, and the two condemn their mother for observing the conventions of a devout widow, honoring a useless and heartless man.

Padma earns her fame by arguing Ratna's marital separation case in court. In a strange twist, however, she soon develops a relationship with Jhilla, and the two begin living together out of wedlock. Like the Hindi Padma, the Urdu Padma falls for the gallivanting Jhilla and is heartbroken when he disappears just before their child's birth. A week later, when she learns that Jhilla has withdrawn all her savings, Padma angrily barges into his private study. She curses Jhilla and smashes his things before he suddenly reappears with her money in hand. Criticizing the fickleness of her love, he professes the sanctity of his marriage to Ratna and takes leave. The story concludes: "Padma stood like a statue. Jhilla walked away—like a prisoner who had been released."[97] The final focus thus falls on Jhilla, who teaches the two sisters a lesson in the strength of marriage as an institution. Set against the story's lengthy character descriptions and complex plot, Jhilla's righteousness—not Padma's pain—dominates the story's mood.

Malti of Premchand's *Godān* is the two Padmas' novelistic doppelgänger, the type whom they cite. Upon first meeting, Malti is juxtaposed with her friend Khanna's homely wife:

> The one wearing a homespun sari looking very serious and thoughtful was Mr. Khanna's wife Kamini. The other woman dressed in high heels and bursting with laughter was Miss Malti. She had studied medicine in England and was now practicing, often visiting the estates of large landholders. She was a veritable image of the new age. An extrovert with tender, bright cheeks; lacking any trace of hesitation or doubt; skilled in applying make-up; quick-witted; and an expert in male psychology, she understood the essence of life to be merriment and pleasure and was a master in charm and entertainment. Instead of a soul, she possessed spectacle; instead of a heart, flattery. She held strong restraint over her emotions, which had extinguished her longing and desire.[98]

In addition to the narrator's deep observations of her character, Malti receives an extended backstory. The eldest daughter of a spendthrift invalid father, she oversees her two younger sisters' education and cares for her devoted—albeit gullible—mother. Malti's circumstances may have forced her into a modern lifestyle, but her intelligence and strength of character have enabled her to succeed.

A significant portion of the novel is structured around Miss Malti's relationship to Mr. Mehta, a bachelor philosopher who idealizes Indian women for their sacrifice and devotion. In multiple monologic passages, Mehta romanticizes marriage as the highest form of selflessness and truest test of character. Despite her independent nature, Malti grows fond of Mehta, but she overcomes her feelings when he fails to reciprocate her love. In a gesture of generosity, she brings Mehta to live with her and begins to manage his affairs. Over time, Mehta becomes attracted to Malti's honorable nature and compassion, and, in one of the final scenes in the novel, he proposes. Malti responds:

> "No, Mehta, I've been thinking about this question for months, and I've decided that, ultimately, there's more happiness in being friends than in becoming husband and wife. You love me, I believe that, and I'm confident that you would protect me with your life if the occasion arose. . . . I love you too, I believe in you, and there's no sacrifice I wouldn't make for you. . . . What more do we need for our fulfillment, for the evolution of our souls? Could we approach the infinite by creating our own little household, shutting our souls in a little cage, and restricting all our joys and sorrows to each other? . . . The day our hearts become engrossed in desire and we get chained down, in that very moment the breadth of our humanity will shrink. . . . Follow your path with increased enthusiasm and force, using your learning and intellect and enlightened humanity, and I will follow behind you. . . . If your heart should spring toward worldliness, I will still restrain my own so that I may redirect you." . . . Though separate, the two were bound in close embrace. Tears streamed from their eyes.[99]

Malti's speech documents the sublimation of her desire—her turn toward spiritual rather than physical love—granting her the status of a feminine type. Her suffering for the sake of others ennobles her, despite her independence and modernity. In this way, Malti's well-reasoned stance on love reconciles modern existence with the ideals of Indian womanhood to recruit readers' sympathy. This is how the novel's idealistic realism works.

As citations of Malti, the two Padmas reference readerly sympathy and the ideals of womanhood with which it is associated. Without achieving the sublimation of feminine desire, however, they fail to produce sympathy on their own terms. Whereas Malti possesses the totality of a type, the Padmas bear the weight of affect instead. Both—but especially the Hindi Padma, since she is so pared down—become figures of emotion. They symbolize something inexpressible, unattainable, immanently relatable, yet also unnerving and troubling. Premchand's idealistic realism (*ādarśommukhī yathārthvād*) is perfectly—though differently—realized in the short story as the ideals of Indian womanhood confront the realities of feminine desire, producing a tense emotional event. Momentarily, the world becomes tangible through Padma's eyes, her wistful longing crying out for human connection—the fundamental aim of Premchand's aesthetic bliss (*ānand*).

DISSOLUTION OF THE FEMININE TYPE

Miss Padma is a trope more than a type. She is a metaphor that exceeds caricature. She parodies the modern girl type—to use Linda Hutcheon's words, "revising, replaying, inverting, and 'trans-contexualizing'" the many versions of herself.[100] Through parody, Padma unsettles gender norms, signaling the looming dissolution of the ideal Indian woman. As I show in the following chapters, this was a project that postcolonial Hindi and Tamil writers would soon complete.

Pudumaippittan's stories illustrate the dissolution of the female type more starkly than Premchand's—perhaps because Pudumaippittan was deliberately iconoclastic. Premchand maintained some type of social reformist outlook throughout his career. Miss Padma is still legible within this framework, her tears suggesting both female culpability and the futility of feminine desire. Pudumaippittan, by contrast, took issue with all named or stated ideologies and traditions. His stories—very much a part of this spirit—portray the question of female culpability as tangential, when present at all.

Pudumaippittan's two retellings of the Ahalya episode from the *Rāmayāṇa* encapsulate the arc of his experimentation with gender norms. The two Ahalyas are explicit citations of the feminine ideals embodied by Ahalya, ideal wife of the sage Gautama. In the epic version, when lusty Indra visits Ahalya in the dead of night disguised as her husband, Ahalya—though she "knew it was Indra of the Thousand Eyes"—sleeps with him, "excited, curious about the king of gods."[101] Enraged when he discovers what has happened, Gautama curses Ahalya to become a stone until King Rama's foot should brush it as he walks past. Many years later, Rama releases Ahalya from her curse, and cleansed of her blemished past, she reunites with her husband.

Pudumaippittan's first retelling of "Akalyai" (Ahalya) was published in *Maṇikkoṭi*, in 1934, at the beginning of his career. This was the first in a series of Ahalya rewritings, which were part of a wider debate about the relationship of fiction to literary convention and cultural tradition.[102] The *Maṇikkoṭi* writers' turn to myth was related to their concomitant experiments with narrating "real life" events.[103] They believed that reenvisioning their own experiences and exploring canonical stories would challenge the breadth of their creativity and imagination. Pudumaippittan's "Akalyai" launched this exercise by imagining the conditions under which Ahalya, who was "the epitome of womanhood," would fall for another man.[104]

"Akalyai" drew on several existing versions of the Ahalya episode, which revised the *Rāmayāṇa* story to portray Ahalya as an innocent victim of Indra's wiles rather than a knowing participant.[105] Pudumaippittan's retelling was unusual, however, because it focused on Ahalya's psychological state. In his story, Ahalya is a devoted—but also desiring—wife. One evening she waits patiently for Gautama to finish his textual recitations:

> For a while, Gautama doesn't even notice she's there, he's so engrossed in the text. He laughs with a glance full of tenderness, "What is it, Ahalya? Getting late? Time to bathe? I'll be there soon. There's only a little more of this text left to read." She puts down her basket and gathers his head into her chest. She brushes her lips across his forehead and just stands there. "See you." She picks up the basket and walks toward the river. In her heart, a trace of disappointment—if she hadn't had to wait so long, she might have been able to enjoy being with her husband for a little and to take him to the river. She's not angry with him though.[106]

In Pudumaippittan's version, Gautama and Ahalya share a passionate relationship. For Gautama, though, the relationship is less important than his ascetic duties. Gautama is serious, focused, equanimous. Conversely, Ahalya longs to frolic with her husband and savor his physical intimacy, even if she suppresses these desires.

When Ahalya discovers Indra spying on her as she bathes, she stares him down and rushes away. Gautama consoles his distraught wife and puts the incident behind him. Ahalya's mind, however, "is in turmoil, as if she has committed some great, unacceptable sin"—as if she might fail to restrain her physical response to Indra, despite her wifely devotion.[107] This is an intuition that foreshadows her impending rape. More significantly, it reflects a deep anxiety found in most of the late colonial-era Ahalya retellings—that no matter how disciplined and pure women's minds may be, their bodies cannot be fully controlled.

When Gautama rises for his morning ablutions, Indra sneaks into their bedroom. Ahalya lies dreaming of her husband. Indra "looks at the feeble woman, asleep, her clothes disheveled. An animal's lust is fulfilled today. Ahalya doesn't wake from her half-dream state. She embraces Indra thinking it's her husband. In a way, this is the victory of nature."[108] Corporeal desire, the narrator suggests, cannot be suppressed. Gautama furthers this idea in his response to Indra's insidious actions:

> "Dearest Ahalya, how could your body have become an unfeeling stone at such a moment?" he says, stroking her hair.
>
> In his mind, tranquility.
>
> A new truth:
>
> "Emotion can turn even a god into an animal. But chastity lies in the purity of the mind. What can a poor woman do if her body becomes polluted in such circumstances?"
>
> Silence.
>
> "Leave Indra!" says Gautama. Even now, the calmness of his mind is clear.
>
> And Ahalya?
>
> The irrevocable, apocalyptic event that had taken place within her stands opposed to her husband's peace.[109]

The story ends with this somber image of Ahalya's emotional turmoil. Its truth is the trauma of rape, not Gautama's rationalization. Ahalya's distressing personal experience distances her from Gautama. It creates a condition of inner isolation.

Pudumaippittan's second retelling of the Ahalya episode focused on this isolation, depicting it as an integral component of Ahalya's identity. I read the story as the third in a trilogy of stories featuring specter-like women that Pudumaippittan published consecutively, in 1943, in the magazine *Kalaimakaḷ*. In the first story the eponymous Kanchanai appears at the doorstep of a writer and his pregnant wife. She offers her services in exchange for room and board. Instantly, the writer's wife takes pity and befriends Kanchanai, but the writer himself cannot shake the feeling that Kanchanai poses a threat.[110] Is she a ghost or a human? A wife, a widow, a prostitute? Similarly, Chellammal—the eponymous character of the second story—is dead in the opening scene. The rest of the narrative flashes back to her slow deterioration through the eyes of her husband, who structured his entire life around Chellammal's illness.[111] Chellammal is an empty vessel around which gathers profound sadness and inertia. Both stories leave the question of female identity unanswered, offering Kanchanai and Chellammal as dubious citations of the ideal female type.

The protagonist of third story in the 1943 trilogy—Pudumaippittan's Ahalya—follows in a similar vein. She interrogates the female type, disputing the feasibility of its existence in contemporary times. Titled "Cāpa

Vimōcaṉam" (Deliverance from the curse), the story begins with a caveat: "For those familiar with the *Rāmāyaṇa*, this story may seem incomprehensible, distasteful even. I haven't bothered about this."[112] At the outset the story seeks to unsettle readers. Ahalya, incapable of returning to her earlier self, embodies disillusionment with established gender norms. When Rama brings her back to life, she realizes she can no longer confidently interact with men. She constantly questions the purity of her intentions and whether her words and actions convey what she desires them to express:

> The stone lodged in her heart had not budged. She wished to conduct herself in a way that wouldn't arouse suspicion in others or cause them to purposely stare. Consequently, she forgot how to be natural. Her whole demeanor changed. Everyone around her appeared to be Indras, and fear froze Ahalya's heart. The laughter and playfulness of her earlier days vanished. She rehearsed each word a thousand times, examining it from every angle to make sure it was right before she spoke. She agonized over Gautama's words, too, wondering whether they held some deeper meaning. Life itself became hellish torment.[113]

Crushed by the trauma of Indra's rape, Ahalya is now a ghost of herself.

Gautama is also plagued by guilt, and he loses his peaceful comportment. "In his mind, Ahalya moved about free of blemish. He was the unworthy one, he felt. The anger that had incited his fiery curse tainted him instead. . . . His faith dried up and vanished into nothingness."[114] Gautama begins to understand the place of emotion in life, but the couple becomes increasingly estranged. They journey together in search of reconciliation, crossing landscapes "identical to the oppressive dried-up hope [*nampikkai vaṟaṭci*] within them."[115] Despite their efforts, Gautama and Ahalya find that their heterosexual bond—built on the ideal masculine and feminine qualities they once possessed—no longer holds.

Ahalya seeks comfort in Rama's wife Sita, who models the happy marital life she hopes to regain. But when she learns that Sita stepped into fire to prove her chastity to Rama after king Ravana abducted her, Ahalya shudders:

> "Did he ask you to do it? Why did you do it?" she asked.
>
> "He asked me, I did it," Sita quietly replied.
>
> "He asked you?" Ahalya screamed. . . . One law for Ahalya, and another for Rama? Was it betrayal? A justice born from the bowels of Gautama's curse?

> Both were silent a while. Sita laughed softly, "Didn't he have to prove it to the world?"
>
> "Isn't it enough to know it within oneself? Can the truth really be proven to the whole world?" asked Ahalya. Words abandoned her. "Is it only true if you prove it? Even if it doesn't touch your heart? Let it be. What's this world anyway?"[116]

Ahalya gives up. If Rama—who once delivered her from her curse—still questioned his own wife's virtue, what change could the future possibly hold? Gautama approaches Ahalya in hopes of conceiving a child, but Ahalya petrifies into stone to ease her heart's burden. This ending confirms Pudumaippittan's literary philosophy of disillusionment (*nampikkai vaṟaṭci*) and its secret truth of isolation (*taṉimai*).

Together, the Ahalya stories suggest the inarticulability of feminine desire, the lack of a place for it anywhere in the world. The irreconcilable schism between Ahalya's mental "purity" and her physical "pollution" suggests that feminine desire is, perhaps, the most isolating desire. Utterly corporeal, it can never be accepted, fulfilled, or overcome. In Ahalya's case, however, to abandon feminine desire is to annihilate the self. Her dilemma symbolizes the lonely desperation of the modern individual, whose rich emotional life lies deep in the heart of the short story, but not yet free in the world beyond.

FORMAL LOCATIONS

Ahalya's loneliness was Pudumaippittan's response to the polarized Tamil landscape that troubled him throughout his writing career. Dutiful, devoted, and sacrificing, her character cited the spiritually elevated desires of the ideal feminine type. Withdrawn, doubting, and estranged, she also undermined these desires by disclosing their unsustainability in contemporary times. She was an affront to Tamil Brahmin sentiments, which valorized Hindu values of kinship and tradition in service of national unity, as well as to Tamil non-Brahmin sentiments, which violently opposed Hindu culture for oppressing Dravidian identity. Ahalya's repudiation of the heterosexual bond was a rejection of both prevalent frameworks of sociality.[117] The female character, in Pudumaippittan's short stories, was a symbol rather than a type—an emotionally charged metaphor for *nampikkai vaṟaṭci*, the utter loneliness of human desire. This truth was linked to the specific Tamil ethnolinguistic dynamics of Pudumaippittan's time and place.

Padma also displaces ideal feminine norms, but her affective force is different. Ahalya willingly hardens into a solitary state because it offers her the space to explore and fortify her identity. Even though Padma, like Ahalya, finds herself ultimately alone, her tears express psychological turbulence and existential precariousness instead. Padma does not reject the conventional heterosexual bond. Rather, she discovers her ineligibility for this relationship that she desires. This realization contains an uneasiness that the ties holding the Hindi-speaking, Hindu community together—ties built on the spiritualized desires of the ideal feminine type—may be loosening. Longing for sanctioned wifehood and motherhood, Miss Padma cites the kinship structures and social conventions associated with this community. *Ānand*—literary bliss, the specific emotional response that her tears attempt to evoke in readers—emerges out of a critique of both Western and Indo-Persian representations of female desire and sexuality. In the face of these nationalist anxieties, Padma is an omen of the Hindi-Hindu community's impending disintegration, a trope born of Premchand's time and place.

Padma and Ahalya demonstrate how social relations were deeply embedded into the form of Premchand's and Pudumaippittan's stories themselves. Fashioned by a dialogue between title and content, these female characters shaped the short story's citational structure, which referenced local discourses of the Indian woman and reworked them into geographically specific aesthetic insights. The issue was not one of "compromise between western formal influence . . . and local materials," as Franco Moretti has argued in his discussion of the novel's global circulation.[118] On the contrary, in Premchand's and Pudumaippittan's cases, the short story's brevity is better understood through this form's relationship to content, rather than as something modular and separate as Moretti might argue. These writers compel us to take seriously the pressures of content on a genre's formal manifestations, illustrating how privileging form over content (or content over form) obscures the multiple worlding acts that writers and texts perform, the diverse readerships that these acts address, and the multiscalar webs of meaning that they produce.

As the female characters in Hindi and Tamil short stories became increasingly unhinged from existing gender norms, the citational structure of the short story grew increasingly tropological. Characters dissociated from their metaliterary referents and became singularities in their own right. Accordingly, late colonial–era short story titles gradually transformed from descriptive statements of subject matter into metaliterary commentary on content. Premchand's and Pudumaippittan's prolific short story careers exemplify this shift, portending new forms of postcolonial modernist realism that were nascent, bubbling, ready to come.

CHAPTER 3

Modernist Realism

The Literary Historical Imperative of Postindependence Indian Literatures

REALISM, MODERNISM, LITERARY HISTORY

Neither realism—a disciplinary mode shaped by rationalism, empiricism, and colonial order—nor modernism—an aesthetic of experimentation and protest against imperial power and capitalism—corresponded with the aura of hopeful cooperation and solidarity that Indian independence heralded. Both modes foregrounded the regional, caste, and communal schisms fueled by colonialism, in terms that were too visceral to meet the unifying goals of the postcolonial state. Hindi and Tamil short stories of the 1950s and 1960s scarcely mentioned colonialism or confronted the upheaval of decolonization—including the atrocities of Partition, frenzied debates about national language, agitation surrounding land and other resources, and conflict over communal and regional identities. Prompted by a utopian impulse and an ideological imperative to imagine a landscape absent of the scars of imperial subjugation, postindependence Hindi and Tamil short story writers turned to literary history instead. Literary history offered an alternative epistemological foundation for building postcolonial understandings of community.

In contrast to realist and modernist modes, which were linked to ideologies of "truth" and "reality," literary history provided a noncontroversial discursive terrain for articulating dissatisfaction, discontent, and estrangement—experiences that were incongruent with the new state's promises of freedom and equality. Emerging as a consistent interchange between literary and metaliterary texts, literary history seeded a narrative of what Neil Lazarus calls "postcolonial disconsolation"—fashioned, in the case of Indian literatures, by bracketing the residues of colonial violence.[1] Instead of postulating unity based on nationalist and anticolonial feelings, literary history proposed an egalitarian relationship among readers and characters, a relationship constructed through shared aesthetic lineages. These lineages provided the ground for establishing Indian English, Hindi, and Tamil communities built around practices of producing and comprehending literary sentiment.[2]

Consequently, literary history was—and continues to be—integral to shaping the realism-modernism debate in postindependence India, although it has been largely overlooked in contemporary scholarship. In the early 1990s Geeta Kapur characterized Indian modernism as a dialectic between the national and the modern—the former concerned with indigenous landscapes and "folk" traditions and the latter informed by international style. In her view Indian modernism differs from Western modernism because "it is manifestly social and historical," rather than driven by a "hypostasis of the new."[3] Kapur's framework has led to a murky teleological periodization of Indian modernism in which trends seen as realist in the classical European sense acquire modernist import only once they engage with modernity using legibly European modes of critique.[4] A binary reading that pits nationalist realism against transnational modernist style sidelines the ways in which Indian writers have defined and changed the definitions of realism and modernism for themselves. As this chapter demonstrates, postindependence Hindi and Tamil writers synthesized the justice-seeking impetus of realism with modernism's stylistic explorations of interiority through literary historical mapping. In each case, literary history offered a resolution to debates about the social function of literature, superseding tensions between realist and modernist modes.

Literary history traced distinct genealogies in each literary sphere. As I showed earlier, Premchand and Pudumaippittan had already consolidated influential—yet divergent—understandings of Hindi and Tamil literariness during the late-colonial period. Locating their origins in the work of these predecessors, 1950s and 1960s Hindi and Tamil writers revised Premchand's and Pudumaippittan's key concepts, adapting them to their different postindependence settings. Hindi writers coalescing around the Nayī Kahānī (New Story) Movement took their cues from Premchand's idealistic realism (*ādarśommukhī yathārthvād*), which emphasized writerly compassion and responsibility. They regarded this literary philosophy as their inheritance, portraying individuals within a North Indian landscape both riven and silenced by communalism.

By contrast, Tamil writers promoted by the little magazine *Eḻuttu* (Writing) viewed their examination of the human condition as an extension of Pudumaippittan's worldview of disillusionment (*nampikkai vaṟaṭci*). To this notion, they added emphases on language, emotion, and writerly style, which they used to counter the provincializing tendencies of Tamil ethnolinguistic nationalism. For this reason, these writers incorporated everyday speech into their work, whereas their Hindi counterparts focused on relationships between their characters' interior states and external environments. These literary historical positionings were strikingly different not only from each other but also from the postcolonial state's narrative of "one literature, though written in many languages."[5] They shaped Hindi and Tamil writers' equally distinct responses to the realism-modernism dyad.

In this chapter I explore the production of divergent literary histories in the Hindi, Tamil, and Indian English literary spheres, especially in the two decades following independence. Across the three spheres, literary history became the cornerstone of a new modernist-realist mode constituted by an unstated mandate to suppress the legacy of colonial divisiveness. Modernist realism fulfilled the new state's aspiration to forge "unity in diversity." At the same time, it allowed differing—sometimes altogether contradictory—literary projects to emerge from immediate, intimate discussions about the nature and purpose of literature. Despite an overarching rootedness in literary history and a tendency to obscure colonial history, modernist realism contained a wide array of contextually specific literary practices that were both modernist and realist in scope. This mode therefore offered a means through which Hindi, Tamil, and Indian English writers could *world* their literary endeavors. Modernist-realist strategies and vocabularies enabled them to make the texts they produced intelligible as literature to different audiences across global, national, and regional scales.

I begin this chapter by discussing how contemporary thinkers understand modernist realism and suggest that persistent inattention to literary history has led to the privileging of a modernist aesthetic based on experimentation and innovation. The following sections revise this position by exploring how the Sahitya Akademi, Hindi *nayī kahānī* writers, and Tamil *Eḻuttu* writers all used literary history as a means for promoting new postcolonial literary projects. These projects produced forms of modernist realism that brought the requirements of realism and modernism together in different ways. Through a comparison of the Hindi, Tamil, and Indian English literary spheres, this chapter shows how modernist realism emerged as a postcolonial mode with diverse manifestations that reflected geographically located literary histories, rhetorical devices, and aesthetic techniques. I also argue, however, that this mode articulated a shared Indian middle-class ethos, fraught with anguish as well as hope, that was indexed to the realities of decolonization ongoing across the world.

MODERNIST REALISM, A MODE

The modernist realism that arose in the immediate postindependence Hindi, Tamil, and Indian literary spheres was concerned with literature's relationship to "truth"—some unnameable, universal, and humanist essence communicable through literature—as opposed to reality in and of itself. It proposed an intricate, reflexive, and indirect affiliation with external reality, rather than mimetic likeness. Modernist realism existed—like realisms and modernisms everywhere—along a discursive continuum concerned with the nature and representation of reality and individuals' relationships to it.[6]

Modernist realism functioned across the Hindi, Tamil, and Indian English spheres as a mode of enunciation that oriented readers toward texts. It therefore differed from—but also articulated with—the formal and thematic characteristics of genre. I understand genre to be a teleological formation comprised of community-based expectations and norms that both externally surround and internally structure texts. I view mode, by contrast, as the rhetorical techniques through which texts position both characters and authors in relation to readers—whether through the direct speech of the author, the represented speech of the characters, or some mixture of the two. In the wake of German Romantic thinkers' efforts to create a broader philosophy of genre, mode has come to designate a thematic quality equated with generic "natural form," "inner form," "style," "attitude," or "tone"—all of which suggest some primary quality inherent to a given genre that distinguishes it from all others.[7] Nonetheless, I find it useful to differentiate the effects of genres (such as the novel or short story) from those of modes (such as realism or modernism) to track the particular equalizing relationships between readers and characters that Sahitya Akademi, *nayī kahānī*, and *Eḻuttu* writers sought to establish. In all three instances, metaliterary discourses—particularly literary history and criticism—helped to construct a modernist-realist mode that could be transplanted across genres.

Modernist realism is not unique to the Indian context, but the literary historical injunction of Indian modernist realism suggests the insufficiency of existing models to explain its peculiar postcolonial aspiration. Take, for example, the Warwick Research Collective's (WReC) recent discussion of modernist realism, which seeks to revise the privileging of modernism over realism and its decidedly European orientation. Building on Fredric Jameson's perfunctory speculation that "a modernist realism would begin to emerge when the traditional methods of narrative representation (novelistic realism) are used and then undermined,"[8] the WReC argues that "one of the paradigmatic sites of emergence of a 'modernist realism' . . . is the world of the semi-periphery, in which 'local' and 'global' forces come together in conflictual and unsteady flux."[9] Modernist realism falls under the rubric of the WReC category of "peripheral realism"—a set of narrative strategies that registers the combined and uneven development of the world system. "Our assumption," the WReC writes, "is . . . that the effectivity of the world system will necessarily be discernable in any modern literary work" through formal features including "anti-linear plots, meta-narratorial devices, unrounded characters, unreliable narrators, contradictory points of view . . . discernable wherever literary works are composed that mediate the lived experience of capitalism's bewildering creative destruction (or destructive creation)."[10] Modernist realism, as the WReC conceives of it, appears to be nothing less than modernism, interpreted through the triangulated lens of capitalist transformation, imperial violence, and postcolonial discontent.

While postindependence modernist realism, like the WReC's peripheral realism, emerged in the "harsh glare of past and present imperial and colonial dispensations,"[11] I believe that this mode urges a reconsideration of a key WReC assumption—which is that peripheral realisms are rooted in definitive, previously prescribed narrative strategies that "undermine traditional methods of representation."[12] The WReC's starting point is a clearly delimited core-periphery world system within which peripheral realism proliferates—interrogating, transforming, and overturning the claims of traditional realism. For this reason, the WReC's peripheral realism only offers a picture of reality that is discordant or fantastical in comparison to realism's conventional forms.

But peripheral realisms can be considered in less monopolizing terms, such as those proposed by Jed Esty and Colleen Lye, which "approach the world-system as partially, potentially describable . . . [and] invite their publics to grasp the world-system via its local appearances or epiphenomenal effects, and not to imagine it as foreclosed or fully narrativized entity."[13] For Esty and Lye, peripheral realisms are shaped by the presence of unexpected forms, which have been incorporated into the realism-modernism continuum to address location-specific conundrums—for example, romance in colonial

African literature,[14] metonymy in postcolonial North Indian Dalit fiction,[15] or derangement in V. S. Naipaul's biographical reflections of Trinidad.[16] The case of Indian literatures offers an additional form—literary history—which has been integral to structuring the realism-modernism debate.

Literary history—a process of consolidating a canon through literary critical endeavors—combined with practices of fiction in the Hindi, Tamil, and Indian English literary spheres to develop unique, geographically specific aesthetic positions broadly classifiable under the rubric of a pan-Indian modernist-realist mode. Despite recent efforts to reach beyond Eurocentric models of center and periphery, new scholarship—including work on geomodernisms, peripheral realisms, and peripheral modernisms—has paid minimal attention to how canonization processes actively shape how realist and modernist formations construct notions of literariness.[17] I am not referring here to literary history "ordinarily conceived"—that is, studies of national literatures, histories of individual authors, or interpretations of texts over time.[18] Rather, in arguing for a literary historical approach, I am highlighting the need for understanding texts within not just their historical contexts—as, for example, Edward Said would have it—but also their literary historical contexts.[19] How writers conceive of literary history and position themselves within it affects how they define literature and try to express literary value in their texts.

Attending to the metaliterary alongside the literary need not reproduce the canonizing effects that texts and literary fields create. On the contrary, heeding the relationship between the literary and the metaliterary makes the exclusions that boundary-fixing processes create more obvious. The literary historical contests that took place in the immediate postindependence period, at the national as well as regional scale, were worlding enterprises that produced varied canonizing effects and engendered multiple core-periphery dynamics that did not always align. An equally generative and stabilizing force, the literary historical imperative of Indian literatures compels us to consider how peripheral realisms are always *relatively* peripheral and often centripetal, too.

NATIONAL LITERARY PURPOSE

The unity of Indian literature—at least in the Sahitya Akademi's view—served as a paradigm for broader Indian "unity in diversity," Prime Minister Nehru's catchphrase for promoting national integration. With Nehru at the Akademi's helm until his death in 1964 and Vice President of India Sarvepalli Radhakrishnan as second-in-command, the Akademi and its activities were intimately linked with the government's efforts to overcome regional linguistic divisiveness. "The most effective means of achieving national integration and international solidarity is by means of . . . literary productions," Radhakrishnan declared in his address at a 1962 symposium on "The Writer's Role in National Integration."[20] The institution's primary goal was to "promote mutual appreciation of the wealth and variety of literatures in all the languages of India," fashioning linguistic equality out of shared literary purpose.[21] Founded on the premise of the cohesiveness of Indian literature, the Sahitya Akademi took pains to justify the common roots of India's diverse literatures and to create opportunities for cross-regional literary dialogue.

The production of a singular Indian literary historical narrative was central to this effort. One of the first projects that the Akademi initiated was to publish book-length literary histories of all the major Indian languages. In 1954—the year of the Akademi's inception—its first secretary Krishna Kripalani appended a "Note on the Proposed Histories of Literature" to the institution's annual report in which he declared:

> [D]ifferences in language and script have tended to cloud the basic unity of Indian literature as a whole. . . . To illustrate the cultural unity of India, it may be desirable to stress the kinship of one language and literature with the others and discuss the interaction of mutual influence. . . . The debt to Sanskrit language and literature will no doubt be acknowledged by all."[22]

The literary history series was envisioned to disclose the Sanskritic past on which modern Indian unity was built. In his foreword to the *History of Bengali Literature*—the first of the series, published in 1960—Nehru argued for the essential Indianness of India's diverse languages, based on their historical participation in a shared aesthetic and intellectual environment:

> One of the principal functions of the Sahitya Akademi is to encourage all these great languages of India and to bring them closer to each other. Their roots and inspirations have been much the same and the mental climate in which they have grown up have been similar. . . . It may, therefore, be said that each of these languages is not merely a part of India, but essentially a language of India, representing the thought and culture and development of this country in its manifold forms.[23]

Through its literary historical endeavors, the Akademi traced a narrative of multilingual commonality from the precolonial past to the postcolonial present. It encouraged research in Sanskrit to substantiate how the language continued to interact with more modern Indian languages and literatures and inspire "fellowship, togetherness, [and the] reconciliation of peoples."[24] The rehabilitation of Sanskrit as a contemporary literature was just one of many projects that the Akademi introduced to develop a national literature. It commissioned translations of canonical regional texts into English and other Indian languages; funded writing workshops; ran regional, national, and international seminars and symposia; and instituted travel grants, scholarships, and other literary awards. Establishing its own publishing house, the Akademi compiled translated anthologies, conference papers, and national bibliographies of Indian literature, as well as "Who's Who" lists of Indian writers across regions. It also launched journals in English, Sanskrit, and, later, Hindi to foster national literary space. These activities were simultaneously literary historical and critical in function, and they allowed the Akademi to install a robust armature for constructing a present-day, pan-Indian canon rooted in the Sanskritic past.[25]

Repurposing Sanskritic concepts for its project of unification, the Akademi also developed a national vision of literary purpose, wherein the writer possessed extraordinary access to truth:

> We have a saying that all *kavya* [literary composition] is for *visva sreyas*, for the good of the world. The literary artist has not merely to reflect the world, he has to redeem the world. He has not merely to portray the experience he has, but he has to recreate that experience. He has to enter into solitude, glimpse the vision of truth, bring it down to earth, clothe it with emotions, carve it into words. That is the purpose of literature.[26]

Based on the writer's "intensity of experience" and ability to "express his or her ideas in clear and shining words, [and] in penetrating expressions," the Akademi's definition of literature joined a realist emphasis on authentic experience with modernist notions of writerly isolation and originality.[27] Sanskrit terminology lent this understanding a universalizing air of classical—if also Hindu—authority:

> Literature is a sacred instrument and through the proper use of it we can combat the forces of ignorance and prejudice and foster national unity and world community. Literature must voice

> the past, reflect the present and mould the future. Inspired language, *tejomayi vāk*, will help readers to develop a humane and liberal outlook on life, to understand the world in which they live, to understand themselves and plan sensibly for their future.[28]

The Sanskritic past charged Indian literature with ethical and aesthetic inspirations, fashioning a pan-Indian readership that cohered around an essentially Indian—yet also modern and liberal humanist—literary project. Within this framework, the ancient past folded directly into the postcolonial present, erasing all hints of colonial intervention.

Through its literary historical endeavors, the Sahitya Akademi fashioned a metaliterary worlding discourse—distinct from the literary techniques and devices of genre—that sought to dispose audiences to read texts through the lens of "unity in diversity." For this reason, I consider the Akademi's enterprises under the rubric of modernist realism, even if they did not endorse specific realist or modernist modes per se. These enterprises were motivated by a compulsion to produce a common literary lineage separate from Western influence. The ultimate aim of the Akademi's modernist realism was to create a national-scale community of readers joined by their mutual genealogical inheritance of a Sanskritic literary sentiment carved out of writerly exceptionality and civic responsibility. This sensibility helped the Akademi to orient readers toward a modern Indian future by translating diverse regional-scale literary trends into a national language of "unity," "truth," and "experience."

REPRESENTING HINDI AND TAMIL LITERATURE IN NATIONAL LITERARY SPACE

Despite the Akademi's efforts, however, numerous contentions arose over the ways in which the organization smoothed over literary differences—a problem with which the Akademi was miserably aware. As Radhakrishnan complained in the first issue of the Akademi's journal, *Indian Literature*:

> It is unfortunately true that we in India suffer from and are handicapped by our ignorance about ourselves. As things are, a Bengali poet or writer is likely to know a great deal about Ezra Pound or T. S. Eliot or Jean-Paul Sartre while knowing almost nothing or next to nothing about poets or writers in, say, Tamil

> or Malayalam or perhaps even in Hindi. The same is no doubt true of writers in every language. What is more regrettable is that ignorance breeds contempt and some of our writers are apt to imagine that nothing worth reading is being written in any Indian language save their own. There are fortunately some journals and literary organizations that are honestly and bravely trying to dispel the mists of this ignorance. . . . The present journal is one such humble effort.[29]

Nehru, too, worried that regional-language writers thought "much more of the literary coteries in which [they] move[d]" than of a wider pan-Indian audience.[30] Criticizing writers for expressing linguistic provincialism, the Akademi offered its English-language journal as a nonpartisan medium that could link regional understandings of literary value together within national literary space. Within this framework, English was a language of unification, rather than creation, serving as no more than a tool for asserting a more fundamental Sanskritic commonality.

Behind-the-scenes discussions of the regional literature overviews that appeared regularly in *Indian Literature* and other Akademi publications reveal that the Akademi's mission to generate literary camaraderie was often unsuccessful. For example, in two anthologies that bookended the first two decades of the Akademi's activities, major disputes arose over the writers selected to compose the Hindi reviews and what those authors chose to write. When the first of these anthologies was published in 1957, Hindi authors belonging to the Progressive Writers' Movement criticized their contemporary Sachchidananda Hirananda Vatsyayan "Agyeya" for the self-aggrandizing, biased overview of modern Hindi literature that he had composed. They felt that he had elevated modernist poetry—his own preferred genre and mode—and too harshly dismissed their more socially oriented, Marxist-leaning work. Hindi poet Ramdhari Sinha "Dinkar" wrote to Akademi secretary Kripalani, protesting Agyeya's partiality of view:

> In order to fully appreciate the feelings of the critics of Vatsyayan, you have to understand a significant position in Hindi. As the progressivists are branded Pro-Russian, even so the Vatsyayan group has begun to be described as Pro-American and there is hardly any doubt that due to their association with Shri Vatsyayan, some of the *prayogvadi* [experimentalist] writers are being looked upon as a literary wing of the cultural freedom congress. In between these two groups stand most of our writ-

> ers and poets who may be liked now by the progressivists and now by the *prayogvadis*. Most of these writers who do not belong to either group, have not liked Shri Vatsyayan's approach and their sympathies lie with the progressivists.[31]

Dinkar argued that Agyeya's controversial survey of Hindi literature could only be understood by those aware of the ongoing realism-modernism debate in the Hindi sphere. Hindi writers were divided into two camps, he explained: on one hand, progressivist (*pragativādī*) writers inspired by Soviet-style socialist realism and, on the other, writers funded by the American Congress for Cultural Freedom—an organization not so secretively linked with the CIA[32]—who espoused modernist experimentalism (*prayogvād*). Worried that Agyeya's *prayogvād* sympathies would diminish progressive realism in the eyes of non-Hindi readers—yet feeling that irrevocable damage had already been done—Dinker requested that the Akademi make Agyeya's biases evident in a postscript. He also asked that the Akademi oversee future overviews of Hindi literature by assembling a more impartial Hindi advisory board. In addition, Dinkar took offense with Agyeya's deletions of several incendiary passages in the Akademi's Hindi translation of the review. Dinkar's view, which was directly opposed to the Akademi's, was that Agyeya's literary politics should be exposed—rather than concealed—no matter how divisive and controversial they proved to be.

When the second anthology appeared in 1973, Namvar Singh's review of Hindi literature created another dispute in the Hindi world. By this time, Singh was an established literary critic who had written extensively in the 1950s and 1960s about the Nayī Kahānī Movement. His 1973 review reflected that his perspective on the movement had shifted, and he adopted a profound skepticism of Nehruvian-era humanism. Singh pinpointed what he viewed as the Hindu biases of postindependence writers, criticizing new poetry (*nayī kavitā*) and other "new writing" for elevating the "authenticity of feeling." According to Singh, this was an apolitical, middle-class stance that "in effect provided sustenance to the 'illusions' created by the Nehru Era."[33] Singh's survey undermined most of the modernist trends in postindependence Hindi literature. It mourned the dwindling of progressive politics, causing an uproar among his fellow writers and critics. As a result, the Akademi's Hindi advisory board requested that Singh include a "more balanced historical survey and a delineation of various trends and genres, which had been left out."[34] The anthology was temporarily taken out of circulation, and—as with the 1953 anthology—the Akademi appended an introductory caveat underscoring that the literary surveys did not reflect its own views. Despite the upheaval that both Agyeya's and Singh's essays caused, in these cases the Akademi papered over the contentious politics of the Hindi realism-modernism debate in its representation of Hindi literature in national literary space.

Similar disputes emerged over the way the Akademi portrayed the Tamil literary sphere. For example, in the first issue of C. S. Chellappa's magazine *Eḻuttu*, Ka. Naa. Subramanyam contested the first three Tamil recipients that the Akademi chose for its annual literary award:

> From the three prizes that it has conferred so far, it would seem that the Delhi Sahitya Akademi has not an iota of connection with the growth of Tamil literature. . . . Not one of three books receiving the prize has achieved good standing within the literary strain of Tamil literature. Aren't the Sahitya Akademi folks supposed to award prizes for literature? Instead, it seems that they have only taken into account the status of the writers themselves when giving out their awards. Since these books have now been translated into other Indian languages, it's possible that non-Tamilians will think there is no good literature in Tamil today.[35]

The three texts to which Subramanyam referred were *Tamiḻ Iṉpam* (The delight of Tamil), a collection of essays by R. P. Sethu Pillai that won the Sahitya Akademi award in 1955; *Alai Ōcai* (The sound of waves), a novel by R. Krishnamurthy "Kalki" that won in 1956; and *Cakkravartit Tirumakaṉ* (Chakravarti's divine son), a prose retelling of the *Rāmāyaṇa* by former Chief Minister of Madras C. Rajagopalachari that won the award in 1958. Writers associated with the modernist, "literary" strain of Tamil—such as Chellappa and Subramanyam—considered these works to be variedly didactic, entertainment oriented, or revivalist in perspective, rather than cosmopolitan and innovative. Instead of disclosing his own position within this camp, however, Subramanyam complained that the Sahitya Akademi's Tamil awardees were concerned with Tamil language, tradition, and the past. He claimed that these authors did not possess the same creativity of the other prize winners. He then listed several Tamil writers he felt were more deserving of recognition—for example, Na. Piccamurti and Laa. Sa. Ramamritham, both of whom belonged to Subramanyam's own coterie. Subramanyam concluded the op-ed by arguing that the Sahitya Akademi Tamil advisory committee had been hijacked by Tamil professors and editors of popular Tamil magazines. In Subramanyam's view, these individuals encouraged the "narrow," "parochial," and "jingoistic" elements of regional-language literatures, the very things that the Akademi had sought to overcome.[36]

For this reason, Subramanyam attempted to offset the Tamil advisory committee's biases by becoming a spokesperson for Tamil literature in the Akademi's publications. In multiple essays he wrote for the Akademi, he created a specific portrait of the Tamil literary field, lending visibility to his own literary camp. For example, in his 1959 overview of Tamil writing in *Indian Literature*—published just eight months after his *Eḻuttu* critique of the Akademi's Tamil awards—Subramanyam ignored the historical fiction that was popular among Tamil readers. Instead, he praised the incorporation of world literature into Mu. Varadarajan's work on Tamil poetry, described his own new writings as Tamil literary benchmarks, and hailed the debut of the journal *Eḻuttu* for its avant-garde and experimental content.[37] Similarly, in his 1964 overview for the journal, Subramanyam highlighted the work of R. Chudamani and D. Jayakanthan, championed as "literary" writers in *Eḻuttu* publications. He also applauded the launch of his own magazine *Ilakkiya Vaṭṭam* (The literary sphere), which featured modernist fiction and criticism.[38] As in the Hindi cases, Subramanyam's interventions evidence not just how "the very concept of a national literature was a highly crafted, manipulated, albeit discordant, entity," as Rosemary Marangoly George has compellingly argued.[39] They also show how literary history served as a key terrain on which local realist and modernist factions vied to shape the representation of regional literatures in national literary space.

THE *NAYĪ KAHĀNĪ* IN LITERARY HISTORY

Hindi and Tamil writers expressed deep skepticism about the Sahitya Akademi's intentions. For example, despite the Akademi's attempts to allay fears about government censorship of creative expression, Hindi writer Mohan Rakesh cautioned writers against accepting governmental support.[40] As his contemporary Mannu Bhandari recounts in her memoir, Hindi writers even protested the Akademi by boycotting its activities during a brief period in the 1960s.[41] Subramanyam's repeated complaints in Tamil little magazines about the Akademi's failures, together with Tamil writers' general avoidance of its activities, confirm that a comparable attitude prevailed in the Tamil literary sphere of the period.[42] It seems no coincidence, then, that Hindi and Tamil writers produced their own literary historical accounts about how the realism-modernism debate unfolded in their respective worlds, shaping readerships according to their localized interests and agendas. These accounts were addressed to these regional readerships but also responded to national and international perceptions of Hindi and Tamil literary endeavors.

In the Hindi sphere writers associated with the Nayī Kahānī Movement participated in the production of literary history most fervently. By the mid-1950s, they had created significant momentum around a new approach to short story writing through coffeehouse-style gatherings; larger-scale conferences taking place in Allahabad, Calcutta, and Delhi; and, most effectively, through short stories, critical essays, reviews, and letters to the editor published in contemporary literary magazines. From the mid-1950s through the 1960s, almost all major Hindi magazines featured articles and columns on the *nayī kahānī*.[43] This movement was comprised of a new generation of writers who were born in the late 1920s and early 1930s—too young to have meaningfully participated in the independence movement. Kamleshwar, Rakesh, and Yadav were considered the leaders of the movement, and Yadav's wife Mannu Bhandari was a central interlocutor in *nayī kahānī* discussions, many of which took place at Yadav's own publishing house, Akshar Prakaśan (Letter Publishing).[44]

Nayī kahānī writers generally belonged to upper-caste Hindu families, had university educations, lived in smaller cities across North India, and faced a new nation rife with possibility (despite being upended by the devastation of Partition). They were youthful, creative intellectuals who believed they were ready to break from past traditions and interrogate the postindependence condition with new energy. They felt that older-generation writers held omniscient control over characters, clinging to an old-fashioned understanding of reality, even though conditions had changed.[45] Postindependence short story writers maintained that no single morality could be fixed or superior during the transitional postindependence moment, particularly because, in their view, ideological rigidity and religious orthodoxy had led to Partition violence and communal divisiveness.[46]

Yet, however differently they viewed their work, *nayī kahānī* writers also recognized and rigorously documented their debt to the short story authors who had preceded them. They viewed this documentation as central to the movement itself. Yadav's *nayī kahānī* tracts, in particular, provided long lists, categorizing writers' contributions and specific pioneering stories.[47] In them, he reproduced the existing Hinduized historiography of the Hindi short story: its roots in the Vedas; its early development in the Puranas and epics; its stagnation in the medieval era; and, finally, its reinvigoration in colonial India. Affirming this historical mapping allowed Yadav to situate the *nayī kahānī* within a literary tradition already familiar to the middle-class, Hindi-speaking, Hindu community of readers that his predecessors had established, while also reconfiguring that tradition in the postindependence present.[48] In addition, Yadav clearly identified the modern Hindi forebears to the *nayī kahānī*, providing overviews of each writer's major stories and the ways in which each helped to develop the short-story form. In 1978, almost a decade after the movement had dissipated, Yadav observed that "the *nayī kahānī* was the first, and perhaps in any real sense, the last movement (*āndolan*) up till now in the entire journey of the Hindi story," affirming the overwhelming success of establishing the *nayī kahānī* as part of the Hindi canon.[49] Such moves elevated the short story above other genres in the postindependence Hindi literary field and made *nayī kahānī* writing intelligible as a movement.

Nayī kahānī writers also conscientiously situated their project in relation to *nayī kavitā* (new poetry) and *āñcalikatā* (regional writing), the two literary trends contemporaneous with the Nayī Kahānī Movement. This enabled them to distinguish the uniqueness of the short story as a means of examining the postindependence context. The term *nayī kavitā*, or new poetry, arose in the 1940s with Agyeya's theorization of *prayogvād*, or experimentalism.[50] Agyeya discussed *nayī kavitā* as a type of *prayogvādī* (experimentalist) writing that shifted Hindi literary concerns away from social relevance issues and toward the search for poetic essence, the integrity of the individual, and experimentation with language and form.[51] By defining the *nayī kahānī* in relation to *nayī kavitā*, Namvar Singh underscored the significance of the *nayī kahānī*. He brought the term into common parlance and marked a shift in focus, arguing that "from the perspective of literary forms, the short story alone is extremely modern."[52] According to *nayī kahānī* writers, not only was poetry—even "new poetry"—an older genre that lacked the same access to modernity as the short story, but its focus was also too individualistic, its theoretical framework too mired in tradition, and its perspective too detached from everyday readers. Conversely, the short story was linked to modern sociality, in which the writer took cognizance of the individual's responsibility towards others: "experience along with its circumstances, expression along with the reader—the art of the short story . . . is for understanding and consoling others, not the self."[53]

Nayī kahānī treatises took a slightly different approach in framing their relationship to *āñcalikatā*, the other major literary trend of the time. *Āñcal*, meaning "border," came to signify the margins—geographically, linguistically, and culturally—in Hindi literature. Writers who subscribed to *āñcalikatā* focused on the rural regions of the nation—rather than its urban centers—depicting the lives of peasants, fisher people, and tribals through their local dialects, customs, and traditions. *Nayī kahānī* writers viewed *āñcalikatā* as a trend that fell within the *nayī kahānī* project and argued that the distinction between urban and rural worlds was misguided.[54] According to Yadav and others, the forces affecting change in postindependence India were inherently urban, and this was what the *nayī kahānī* struggled to understand.[55] Although *nayī kahānī* writers often set their stories in remote mountain, seaside, or village landscapes, they focused almost exclusively on urban sensibilities—secular, nuclear, and middle-class domesticity; modern companionate romance; unrealizable individual desire; intellectual and emotional turmoil; and the transient lifestyles resulting from unstable white-collar working conditions. Uncertainty, disillusionment, self-doubt, skepticism, alienation, fragmentation, transitoriness—these were the compelling narrative tendencies that marked the quotidian lives of *nayī kahānī* characters.

THE MODERNIST-REALIST EQUATION

Situating themselves within this literary historical landscape, *nayī kahānī* writers theorized the aesthetics of form:

> [The *nayī kahānī* writer] had to grasp his truth through his own environment and feelings. This change in perspective [from the previous generation] began to alter the short story on several levels [*dharātal*]. Now the language of the story did not remain so singular. Such images [*bimb*], symbols [*pratīk*], and meanings [*arth*] began to arise in [the form] that portrayed credible individual experiences, but also sought to grasp larger social truths. These stories inadvertently began to operate on double and triple levels. . . . They attempted to capture the mutual relationship between the individual [*vyakti*] and the environment [*pariveś*] in its full complexity, or [in other words], this type of story became more profound, artistic, and impactful. Often two or three meanings resounded in them. They were superior stories of meaningful [*sārthak*] effort.[56]

Using plain, minimalist prose, *nayī kahānī* fiction worked through images, which "have become the essential medium of artistic expression in the modern age."[57] Writers valued the image for its impressionistic presentism, through which they could instantly convey a story's underlying meanings, without having to resort to authorial mediation. Aphoristically developing storylines through successions of descriptive imagery allowed *nayī kahānī* writers to express multiple levels of meaning without falling into didacticism or judgment. Writers created realistic depictions of ordinary events, within which readers could find symbols of intersecting social, historical, and existential conditions.[58] *Nayī kahānī* images wove fragmentary—yet detailed—descriptions of characters' external landscapes into monologic reflections about their emotional lives, establishing a specific *nayī kahānī* equation for modernist realism: *yathārth* (reality) equals *vyakti* (individual) plus *pariveś* (environment). Through the instantiation of *yathārth*, *nayī kahānī* writers tried to connect with readers, identifying with them on both personal and circumstantial levels.

I characterize *yathārth* as modernist realist because, in formulating this mode, *nayī kahānī* writers turned to literary history, innovating the experimental modernist tradition represented by Agyeya and the progressivist realist tradition embodied by Premchand—both of which crystalized at the height of the Independence Movement. They described Agyeya's short stories as focused on emotional experience, philosophical reflection, and linguistic and formal innovation and praised his literary efforts "to cast aside plot-centered narratives, [enabling] feeling, thought, and [internal] conflict to take their place."[59] *Nayī kahānī* writers argued that Agyeya's work established a more personal connection with the reader, a feature that soon became central to the *nayī kahānī* project.[60]

But they also critiqued Agyeya's work for being so individualistic and philosophical that it unmoored the short story from material reality altogether.[61] For this reason, *nayī kahānī* writers situated their movement in the lineage of Premchand. They characterized their commitment to *yathārth* as an innovation of Premchand's theorization of *ādarśommukhī yathārthvād*—or idealistic realism—a literary methodology for illustrating the material conditions of men's and women's everyday lives in ways that created space for social change. In chapter 2 I demonstrated how the Premchandian short story moved away from the didacticism and classism associated with novelistic idealism. This was also why *nayī kahānī* writers turned to Premchand as their short story forefather.

These writers characterized a shift in Premchand's writing from his earlier, less-refined literary examinations of social-realist character types—such as the widow or the peasant—toward more nuanced depictions of dehumanization. These later portrayals formed what *nayī kahānī* writers called Premchand's *saṃvedana dṛshṭi*—which might be translated as his "literary perspective" or "literary viewpoint" of sympathy, compassion, or sensitivity (*saṃvedana*). They understood his *saṃvedana dṛshṭi* as a mode—the manner through which the writer reaches out to establish a meaningful relationship with the reader, catalyzing a revelatory emotional or intellectual change in the reader's perspective. Motivated by the Premchandian writerly responsibility to society, *nayī kahānī* writers presented modernist-realist *yathārth* (reality)—that is, the perfectly poised illustration of personal and social experience—as striking the balance between realism and idealism that idealistic realism had failed to achieve.[62]

ELUTTU AND LITERARY TAMIL

Younger Hindi writers came together around *nayī kahānī* modernist realism because neither *pragativādī* (progressivist) nor *prayogvādī* (experimentalist) aesthetics seemed adequate to address the particular forms of modernization, urbanization, and the politics of language and nation that emerged in postindependence North India. Modernist-realist *yathārth* (reality), they believed, fashioned a worldview that was Hindi-based yet cosmopolitan in scope; secular yet informed by tradition; and commonplace yet rich in intertextuality. In the following chapters I show how this mode required *nayī kahānī* fiction to obscure embodied experiences of class, caste, religion, and gender, universalizing the upper-caste Hindu and middle-class perspectives that were presented to Hindi readers. Here, however, I want to identify how radically different the Tamil literary landscape was from this Hindi environment, which was more proximate—geographically, culturally, and politically—to the central government's efforts to create national unity and position India on the world stage. Whereas Hindi writers offered the *nayī kahānī* worldview as a counter to both English dominance and Hindi fanaticism, Tamil writers developed a modernist-realist mode that could contend with Tamil ethnolinguistic nationalism.[63]

In a manner similar to *nayī kahānī* writers, Tamil writers redoubled their efforts to develop Tamil literary history, criticism, and fiction beginning in the mid-1950s. Although they formed a diffuse group of individuals with diverse writing styles, literary outlooks, and political philosophies, they shared a desire to expand a "high literary" (*ilakkiya taramāṉa*) and "experimental" (*cōtaṉaiyāṉa*) strain of modern Tamil literature. Many of these writers traced their origins to the 1930s magazine *Maṇikkoṭi*, which was already renowned for inaugurating a high literary, modernist tradition in Tamil.[64] Some writers—such as Chellappa, S. Mani Iyer "Mauni," Piccamurti, Laa.

Sa. Ramamritham, N. Chidambara Subramanian, Subramanyam, and P. G. Sundararajan "Chitti"—had even begun their careers by writing in *Maṇikkoṭi.* Others—such as Jagadisa Thyagarajan "Ashokamitran," R. Chudamani, D. Jayakanthan, T. K. Doraiswamy "Nakulan," and Sundara Ramaswamy—were part of the younger generation that was ushered into the Tamil literary circle by 1950s' small magazines.[65] These, mostly Brahmin, writers had diverse educational and economic backgrounds and resided across the Tamil-speaking region. However, they eventually converged in Madras (now Chennai), which was the Tamil publishing center.[66]

In a 1956 essay "Ciṟukatai Ilakkiyam" (Short story literature), Chellappa argued that Tamil literature had stagnated after independence because Tamil criticism had not advanced enough to stimulate literary growth.[67] Known previously as a short story writer, Chellappa turned his focus to criticism. In the first issue of *Eḻuttu*—which Chellappa launched in 1959—he characterized the little magazine as a direct descendent of *Maṇikkoṭi,* noting that it aimed to develop literary experimentation and critical perspective: "*Eḻuttu* emerges from the belief that literary creation and taste can develop only through the exchange of ideas."[68]

Eḻuttu was the first Tamil literary magazine to claim this purpose, and by analyzing both past and present literature during its eleven-year run, Chellappa and other *Eḻuttu* contributors effectively constructed their own "Who's Who" list of authors and texts that should be included in the modern Tamil canon. This work neither constituted a cohesive movement—comparable to the *nayī kahānī*—nor reflected a singular critical perspective. Still, in this chapter, I use "*Eḻuttu* writers" as shorthand for authors who published in *Eḻuttu* and other contemporary little magazines, many of whom were promoted by Chellappa's publishing house Eḻuttu Piracuram (Writing Publications), which he established in Madras in 1962. These writers generated the literature and criticism that still represents a "high literary" strain of Tamil literature.[69]

A primary focus for *Eḻuttu* writers was the relationship between literature and language. Chellappa, for instance, highlighted the imbricated nature of these concepts while elucidating why he chose the name *Eḻuttu* for his magazine:

> Although the word "*eḻuttu*" can refer to a letter of the alphabet, grammar, scholarship, handwriting, a piece of evidence, or a painting, this magazine bears the meaning of "literary creation." But it's not that *Eḻuttu* puts aside all concerns of language. Language and literature function by falling in step with one another.[70]

Chellappa understood literary and linguistic evolution as co-constitutive processes. Thus, *Eḻuttu* contributed to the growth of language by facilitating literary creativity.[71] Subramanyam, who was probably next only to Chellappa in developing Tamil criticism, shared this view. In his many critical writings for *Eḻuttu* and other magazines, Subramanyam underscored the necessity of literary innovation for enhancing linguistic expression. This would then open Tamil culture to new intellectual horizons.[72]

The *Eḻuttu* stance was a response to several—sometimes overlapping—intellectual camps of this period, all of which were staking their own claims to Tamil language, literature, and culture. Both Chellappa and Subramanyam meticulously described this Tamil literary-linguistic terrain in their essays, sparing no disdain when critiquing existing trends. Chellappa's "Iṉṟu Tēvaiyāṉa Urainaṭai" (The prose style necessary for today), published in 1959, noted the multiplicity of contemporary linguistic positions—which included pure (*tūya*) Tamil, standard (*sṭāṇṭarṭ*) Tamil, spoken (*pēccuvaḻakku*) Tamil, written (*eḻuttu*) Tamil, vulgar (*koccai*) Tamil, English-inflected (*iṅkilīṣil niṉaittu tamiḻil eḻutuvatu*) Tamil, and traditional (*marapu vaḻi*) Tamil. Pure Tamil advocates, he explained, sought to cleanse Tamil of etymologically foreign words.[73] Standard Tamil advocates sought to erase the dialectical differences among the many Tamil regions. Supporters of spoken Tamil—among whom Chellappa placed himself—gave preeminence to the sounds and rhythms of speech, otherwise absent in written representations of this diglossic language. Advocates for written Tamil prioritized the grammatical conventions of refined Tamil (*centamiḻ*), many of which were steeped in ancient tradition. Describing these differences, Chellappa argued that each variety delimited Tamil language and literature within specific, politically motivated parameters. When taken together, however, these varieties confirmed the range and diversity of the language. This diversity, he further enjoined, was to be welcomed, not curbed.[74]

Chellappa, Subramanyam, and other *Eḻuttu* writers associated efforts to purify, standardize, and grammatically elevate Tamil with classicists such as R. P. Sethu Pillai and T. P. Meenakshisundaram, both of whom held university professorships, and Dravidianists like C. N. Annadurai and E. V. Ramasamy Naicker "Periyar," who were deeply involved in party politics.[75] *Eḻuttu* writers particularly condemned these Tamil activists' valorization of classical Tamil, which reached a peak after independence when Hindi threatened to replace English as the official language of the nation.

Following the ratification of the Indian Constitution in 1950, the central government implemented a fifteen-year transition period, during which time English functioned along with Hindi as an official language of India.

Nehru had hoped that this interim period would allow Hindi to establish sufficient presence in non-Hindi–speaking regions before replacing English altogether. Instead, South Indian resistance to Hindi only increased during this period, and the Dravidian anti-Hindi position reignited efforts to close Tamil off from outside influences.[76] This worried *Eḻuttu* writers, who considered such endeavors to be backward and provincial:

> [Dravidianists] take great pleasure in writing solely about Tamil *Caṅkam* literature, which is two thousand years old. . . . These pandits and professors are traditionalists. . . . They try to speak a de-Sanskritized Tamil, but never in history has a Tamil purified of Sanskrit existed. . . . They have no faith in the future of Tamil.[77]

Eḻuttu writers' trenchant critiques of the Dravidianist cooptation of language were part of their efforts to expand and cosmopolitanize the Tamil literary field. They employed these strategies, I believe, in the face of a profound threat that they must have felt to their predominantly Brahmin identity. At the same time, these strategies were a challenge to the revivalist project that scorned linguistic and literary innovation. Although they almost never discussed their caste position explicitly, *Eḻuttu* writers doubtless confronted opposition to their Brahminism in daily life.[78] Vehement, and sometimes violent, Dravidianist contempt for their English- and Sanskrit-inflected language, Vedic outlook, and Hindu ritualism hit hard at the very core of their existence. Surprisingly, the *Eḻuttu* writers' conservative impulse to uphold Brahmin caste identity aligned neatly with a progressive modernist impetus to reach beyond the strictures of culture and tradition through aesthetic experimentation. If postcolonial disconsolation emerged in the *nayī kahānī* because of the rupture of Partition, in *Eḻuttu* writings it came from the existential realization that not everyone could make the same claims to Tamil language, culture, and history.

Countering the Dravidianist resurrection of the classical Tamil past, *Eḻuttu* writers turned to modern Tamil literature to generate an alternative narrative of Tamil belonging, which was rooted in literary—rather than identity—politics. These writers saw this project as their *Maṇikkoṭi* inheritance, and they took up the late-colonial magazine's short story mantle as their own. In the first issue of *Eḻuttu*, for example, Subramanyam discussed the evolution of the Tamil short story, citing it as the first instance of high literary (*ilakkiya taramāṉa*) Tamil because of its deep connection with the development of world literature (*ulaka ilakkiyam*). He traced the rise of the

Tamil short story through North American, French, and Russian greats—such as Nathaniel Hawthorne, Guy de Maupassant, and Anton Chekhov—to the Bengali writer Rabindranath Tagore, and finally to V. V. S. Iyer, whom he, like *Maṇikkoṭi* writers before him, positioned as the father of the Tamil short story. In Subramanyam's view, Iyer sowed the seeds for the *Maṇikkoṭi* short story innovations that followed. His creative use of the short story paved a high literary path in contrast to the entertainment-oriented fiction of R. Krishnamurthy "Kalki," the *Maṇikkoṭi* writers' contemporary. Subramanyam listed the usual *Maṇikkoṭi* suspects—noting each's unique literary contributions—as well as the experiments of emerging postindependence writers such as D. Jayakanthan.[79] He remarked, "I discuss the nature and development of the short story to build the writer's consciousness of literary form [*ilakkiya uruvam*]."[80] For him, creating a literary historical and critical understanding of modern Tamil literature was necessary to craft a worldly literary sensibility among readers. This position stood in contrast to the narrow classicist one that they believed Dravidianists expounded.

Following Subramanyam's survey of the short story, Chellappa serialized what became a canonical collection, *Tamiḻ Ciṟukatai Piṟakkiṟatu* (The birth of the Tamil short story), in issues of *Eḻuttu* between 1964 and 1969. In these essays he supported Subramanyam's literary historical overview, which credited global, as well as local, literary influences. Like Subramanyam, Chellappa referenced the world story (*ulaka katai*) tradition and commended Iyer. According to Chellappa, one of Iyer's major accomplishments was that "he perceived the methods of a new manner of short story writing through reading Western literature and sought to bring these to Tamil."[81] Providing close readings of *Maṇikkoṭi* stories and authorial styles, Chellappa focused on innovation and experimentation. These qualities, in Chellappa's view, moved Tamil literature beyond the didacticism and conservatism that had hijacked the literary sphere at the time. Frustrated by questions of origin and prestige, Chellappa's tract endeavored to replace these questions with reflections on genre and mode:

> Was the American writer Edgar Allan Poe the father of the short story, or does the short story emerge from [ancient Tamil] *Caṅkam* literature, or did it originate in the [Sanskrit] *Pañcatantra* stories or in Boccaccio—we must put aside such useless debates about whether one side is right or the other. The short story is a literary genre [*tuṟai*] with unique characteristics and form. The task to which we must attend is a discussion that takes this [understanding] as its basis.[82]

Understanding the short story form entailed constructing a more recent and—at least compared to the Dravidianist perspective—rather divergent literary tradition, with roots that reached no deeper than the late nineteenth century, but which were spread across the globe.

A SEPARATE WORLD OF LANGUAGE, EMOTION, AND STYLE

The dynamics of Dravidianist politics made the coordinates of the realism-modernism debate in Tamil very different from those that emerged in the Hindi literary sphere. *Nayī kahānī* writers, who contended with the possibility of Hindi as the national language, embraced the Sanskritic past. As I discuss in later chapters, they even redeployed older literary tropes to convey a modernist-realist sensibility of alienation. In addition, *nayī kahānī* writers assimilated the seemingly opposed realist-progressivist and modernist-experimentalist Hindi trends that were circulating at the time, considering both as important influences on the *nayī kahānī* outlook. These strategies allowed *nayī kahānī* writers to posture their fiction as dynamic and innovative, while also remaining grounded in tradition. In the wake of Premchand's call to "maintain a distance" from European realist and idealist trends, the *nayī kahānī* constructed a modernist realism that could articulate a pan-Indian nationalist vision of inclusivity, even as it expressed a "Hindi" literary orientation.[83]

By contrast, Tamil literary debate, from the late-colonial era onward, revolved around Tamil language and tradition. For this reason, neither the Dravidian nor the Sanskritic past figured within the *Maṇikkoṭi*—and, later, *E̲luttu*—literary historical perspective. Encouraging readers to congregate around aesthetic rather than communal criteria, *Maṇikkoṭi* and *E̲luttu* writers drew freely from both realist and modernist positions. As I showed in the previous chapter, the line between realist and modernist techniques for *Maṇikkoṭi* writers was a blurry one. Both modes fell under a broader aesthetic of experimentation, which *Maṇikkoṭi* writers applied as much to their fictional accounts of personal events as to their fantastical stories. Following in *Maṇikkoṭi* writers' footsteps, *E̲luttu* writers developed a modernist-realist mode that maintained this ambiguity.[84] They constructed a three-fold understanding of literariness that gave equal emphasis to the incorporation of everyday speech, expression of unique writerly style, and evocation of an emotional response in readers. Although these criteria can be understood as all existing under the theoretical umbrella of classical European realism, *E̲luttu* writers formulated them as their literary historical response to Dravidianist linguistic and cultural rigidity.

Eḻuttu writers conceptualized modernist realism as a mode for building an aesthetic sphere independent of social or political interest; consequently, they viewed their endeavors as departures from conventional realism. Describing his own writerly stance, Chellappa described the *Eḻuttu* position on realism in an early-1960s series in the magazine that featured writers' reflections on literary purpose:

> Let me say this . . . as a writer—that is, as a writer who belongs to a literary faction whose practice is based on imagination [*kaṟpaṉai*], not issues [*vivakāram*]. . . . A completely realist practice [*yatārtta naṭaimuṟai*], the kind that demands thinking about the necessities for worldly survival in a knowledgeable and issues-focused way, is one literary method. Another literary method is that which wanders in a world of appearances, where the cloak of imagination spreads over everything. With regard to this difference, I have chosen the latter [method].[85]

Chellappa shifted the debate from a discussion about mimesis to an examination of writerly creativity. In other essays he further elaborated the process through which well-crafted fiction drew readers into a separate world:

> The words we find in a story establish lines, which evoke a sequence of events and give rise to an intensity of emotion [*uṇarcci tīviram*]. They create an expansive space for our conjectures [*yūkam*] and blend our feelings [*uṇarvu*] into it. We take part in the [story's] sorrowful drama and lose ourselves during that time as if we were characters. In short, we are taken to a separate world [*taṉi ulakam*]—a place of ecstasy—awakened by the lines of the story. The spell [*māyam*] brought into existence by that ecstasy is an accomplishment made possible by a great writer.[86]

For *Eḻuttu* writers the question was not whether the content of a story was realistic or fantastical, but whether its language and style successfully drew readers into an ulterior universe of aesthetic experience.

This universe was constructed out of pure, intense emotion (*uṇarcci*) and had its roots in the *Maṇikkoṭi* project, exemplified most famously by Pudumaippittan. In a 1957 lecture on Pudumaippittan's work, for example, Chellappa discussed the novelty of Pudumaippittan's aesthetic of disillusionment (*nampikkai vaṟaṭci*), which he characterized as a bold and singular "art for my sake" position.[87] Citing Pudumaippittan's own 1942 elaboration of *nampikkai vaṟaṭci*, Chellappa drew a correlation between the numbness and lack of faith that Pudumaippittan's worldview conveyed and the existential human predicament (*maṉita tollai nilai*) that Tamilians faced in the decades following independence.[88] In Chellappa's view, Pudumaippittan's portrayals of characters, such as Ahalya, created a powerful emotional response that was no less relevant to readers in the postindependence period.[89] The evocation of *uṇarcci* became a core aspiration of *Eḻuttu* modernist realism.

Equally important to *Eḻuttu* writers was the distinctive prose style (*taṉittaṉmaiyāṉa urainaṭai*) that a skillful writer employed to generate such intense feelings. Subramanyam posited a direct correspondence between writerly style (*naṭai* or *pāṇi*) and individual personality. Taking cue from Pudumaippittan's penname—which meant "crazy or mad for the new"—Subramanyam maintained that "without individuality (*taṉitvam*), writing cannot become literature. No literary writing takes shape when newness is not also combined with madness."[90] Through examinations of short stories by Pudumaippittan, Thi. Janakiraman, Jayakanthan, and Ramaswamy, Subramanyam observed that the nonconformist, eccentric personalities of *Maṇikkoṭi* and *Eḻuttu* writers were central to developing new short-story styles.[91]

Chellappa expanded on this argument, claiming these styles manifested as experimental language use, vocabulary choice, and sentence structure. For instance, in a 1957 essay on the Tamil short story, Chellappa performed meticulous close readings to document the unique word order, fragmented sentence structure, and emphasis on internal monologue that his contemporary Ramamritham used to produce experiential knowledge in readers. Chellappa ended by commenting on Ramamritham's admirable integration of spoken (*pēccu*) Tamil into his work—which, for Chellappa, was a trademark of Ramamritham's singular style. Quoting Ramamritham's own words, Chellappa argued that a literature lacking vulgar (*koccai*) language could not resonate with true experience. In the Dravidianist perspective, *koccai* Tamil referenced idiomatic spoken language in contrast to the *centamiḻ* (refined Tamil) used in classical literature and oratory. In Chellappa's framework, idiomatic language became a sign of the literary: "We could say that Ramamritham's vulgar-speech style breathes new life not only into stagnant matters but also into language itself. *Kaleer!* Its sounds echo in our ears."[92]

Chellappa offered a similar reading of an early short story by V. V. S. Iyer, which featured a peepul tree as its protagonist. The peepul tree character used dialectic rather than refined speech. For this reason, the story "put forth the view that one must write so that through the style of spoken Tamil, the beauty of sound resonates."[93] Repeatedly turning to the representation of spoken language in his analyses, Chellappa showed how each writer's use of spoken Tamil worked with other stylistic choices to fashion his unique writerly style.[94]

In the *Eḻuttu* worldview, only literary styles that emerged through spoken language could kindle aesthetic taste (*kalai racanai*) in readers, enabling the language to resound "like a song that resonates over and over in their ears."[95] Thus, spoken style (*pēccu naṭai*) was integral to how *Eḻuttu* writers conceived of literary purpose and sensibility.[96] If creating a self-contained aesthetic universe was the goal, and individual writerly style was the means, then spoken Tamil was *Eḻuttu* writers' most fundamental tool for generating shared emotional experiences in readers. *Eḻuttu* writers saw their use of spoken Tamil in literature as a form of mimesis, in opposition to the Dravidian exultation of a refined Tamil that *Eḻuttu* writers found to be a poor means for narrating everyday life. Yet, according to their own literary historical account, the *Eḻuttu* writers' representations of spoken language were innovative and experimental. Combining realist and modernist notions of language and style, the *Eḻuttu* project articulated a distinctly modernist-realist orientation.

A MIDDLE-CLASS IDEOLOGY

In her analysis of Indian popular culture, Patricia Uberoi writes that "Indian 'unity' may be the outcome of a modern process of 'class formation'—in particular, the formation . . . of a 'secular' middle class whose habits of mind and lifestyles are determined more by their *class* location than by their regional, caste, religious or linguistic affiliations."[97] This is one way of thinking about how the Sahitya Akademi's project overlapped with *nayī kahānī* and *Eḻuttu* endeavors. The Akademi's "unity in diversity" directive was, without question, a central component of Nehru's broader vision of expanding the postindependence middle class. Faced with the knotty problem of national integration, Nehru understood "unity in diversity" as a layered sense of Indian belonging, characterized by multiple affiliations to community, region, nation, and world. Rather than proffer economic parity, this political philosophy combined a shared cultural past with a modernized future, based on both aesthetic and technological advancement. This vision projected the middle class as a category to which all Indian citizens might eventually belong, sketching a postcolonial horizon wherein increasing numbers of citizens gradually shared in modernist progress.[98] The Sahitya Akademi's cultivation of national literary purpose was one means of instantiating this utopian class project.

Nayī kahānī writers also examined the struggles that seemed specific to the newly emerging postindependence middle class. In their fiction, individuals of this class came from *savarṇa* (caste Hindu) joint families that were now dispersing due to economic pressures, changing religious norms, and shifting kinship relations. *Nayī kahānī* protagonists were young Hindi-speaking men and women who, having distanced themselves from the ritualism and sectarianism of their parents' generation, came to larger cities to seek new forms of employment. This search for a white-collar, nuclear, urban way of life—alongside a decisive break from older forms of communal sociality—was aestheticized by *nayī kahānī* writers. "We can call this 'unity in diversity,'" Yadav wrote, riffing on Nehru's catchphrase, correlating it with the *nayī kahānī* worldview.[99] Hardly living the moneyed lifestyles of the Nehruvian bureaucratic elite, *nayī kahānī* writers offered an alternative view of the middle class, one rooted in Hindi literary history and aesthetics. "That middle class [*madhyavarg*] of which we were all a part . . . we [understood it as] avant-garde [*agragāmī*]. . . . We believed it would give us direction, and we assumed that all the world's philosophies and doctrines [*vicārdhārā*], everything, came from the middle class," Yadav recounted in a 2010 interview.[100]

The *E̱luttu* outlook was also interwoven with an aspirational middle-class politics. In the Nehruvian conception, "to be middle-class was to inhabit a particular orientation towards modernity."[101] This orientation was culturally Indian, while also being cosmopolitan, secular, and rational. The *E̱luttu* writers' explorations of aesthetic elevation, spoken language, and Tamil's worldly connections were linked to this sense of modernity. These literary criteria were deeply intertwined with *E̱luttu* writers' educational and employment advantages. As C. J. Fuller and Haripriya Narasimhan have argued, "Tamil Brahminhood and middle classness have become mutually constitutive of each other," particularly since the mid-twentieth century.[102] Their caste privilege notwithstanding, *E̱luttu* writers envisioned the middle class (*naṭuttara varkkam*) as an aesthetic—rather than an economic—category, a category fashioned from Tamil literary historical and literary critical knowledge. Artistic maturity, they argued, was tangential to, and more foundational than, financial gain. This maturity illuminated the human predicament and elevated the human spirit, providing an experiential basis for future communal cohesion.[103] In these ways, *Eḻuttu* writers advanced the ambitious pedagogic aims of Nehruvian "unity in diversity," while also promoting a localized literary historical worldview.

In contrast to Uberoi's position that Indian middle-class identity supersedes regional, caste, religious, and linguistic alliances, the case of postindependence Indian literatures suggests that the middle class—at least as it was envisioned by writers and thinkers in the two decades following independence—should be seen as a capacious signifier that obscured competing forms of difference. Metaliterary endeavors in the 1950s and 1960s across the Indian English, Hindi, and Tamil spheres abstracted and universalized this category by formulating a modernist-realist mode. Modernist realism channeled colonial histories of subjugation, violence, and division into geographically specific literary historical narratives of aesthetic affiliation. Within these narratives, experiences of difference became phenomenologically understandable as individual turbulence and loss, rather than social or political discord.

The middle class that postindependence modernist realism envisioned was not the more sure-footed one of today. On the contrary, it was a category constituted by its own unmooring from the certainties and traditions of the colonial past. To be sure, modernist realism reaffirmed the dominance of a historically entrenched, upper-caste Hindu logic across the Hindi, Tamil, and Indian English literary spheres. For this reason, it had deeply conservative consequences. Still, modernist realism aspired to create an aesthetic space where postcolonial disconsolation was common and collective. This mode provided an alternative to the isolating experiences of colonial violence—which could only be interpreted through the lens of class differentiation within existing realist and modernist frameworks.

Although I ground modernist realism in the Indian context, I consider it to be a distinctly postcolonial mode of literary experimentation. This mode took up the freedoms of form, language, and style typically associated with modernist writing. At the same time, it necessarily referenced the realities of decolonization. Responding to the forced relation of comparison with the West that colonialism imposed, modernist realism was characterized by an impulse to break away from colonial legacies, a sensibility of disconsolation, and an aspiration to transpose the positions of readers and characters.[104] It resisted rather than claimed a universalist platform. For this reason, I would argue that—even though I have described modernist realism as emerging out of geographically specific discussions and addressing geographically specific audiences—its attempts to synthesize existing realist and modernist practices resemble tensions between realism and modernism that were contemporaneously debated in other decolonizing contexts.[105] This mode served as a means for worlding Hindi, Tamil, and Indian English writers' literary historical projects, enabling them to become intelligible through the lenses of concurrent literary trends unfolding across the subcontinent and globe.

Rather than position the Sahitya Akademi's national-scale endeavors in opposition to the regional-scale *nayī kahānī* and *Eḻuttu* projects, I therefore consider them as complementary attempts to articulate a shared sense of injury. Postindependence writers conceived of the traumas of colonialism and decolonization as conditions of aesthetic possibility available to everyone—including those individuals whose experiences were too abominable to be articulated or sometimes even imagined. Modernist realism was a means for accommodating the breadth and unevenness of postcolonial experience in the Nehruvian era of hope.

CHAPTER 4

Empathetic Connections

Communalism, Caste, and Feminine Desire in Postindependence Hindi and Tamil Short Stories

THE ENIGMA OF FEMININE DESIRE

Female desire repeatedly undermined conventional notions of heterosexual propriety in Hindi and Tamil short stories from the 1950s and 1960s. Unlike late colonial-era fiction—in which depictions of feminine desire served to reinforce the Hindu conjugal family ideal—postindependence stories portrayed female desires as beyond patriarchal control.[1] The postindependence new woman worked outside the home, sought romantic companionships of her own choosing, postponed or rejected marriage, divorced, and even had affairs. She was a misfit, renegade, and seeker of pleasure. Her longings exceeded socially sanctioned behaviors and objectives, and, for this reason, the new woman's interiority became a promising cache, ripe for aesthetic exploration.

Rather than displaying wayward feminine desire as problematic, Hindi and Tamil short stories used this desire as a means to proffer the new woman as an archetypal sign of the times. They drew parallels between questions related to the new woman's position—What did she want? How would she fulfill her ambitions? Who would be her patriarchal guardian?—and anxieties about postindependence community. Just as these stories construed feminine desire as insatiable and unlocatable, so, too, did they assume the yearnings of readers to be without resolution. In this way, the new woman's inscrutable wants sought to give form to the uncertainties prompted by postindependence social and political transformations.

Discussing the portrayal of the feminine figure in 1950s and 1960s Indian literature and film, Geeta Kapur argues that "what is interrogated . . . is bad faith in inter-personal relationship[s]. . . . While in an earlier phase of nationalist consciousness there was an ebullience of self-discovery through mythic archetype, folk and popular forms . . . there is now the travail of the middle class worked out in psycho-social terms."[2] In Hindi and Tamil stories of the period, this middle-class psychosocial drama played out on the terrain of feminine desire. Bad faith—what Danielle Coriale defines as when a person "chooses to believe (falsely) in a story he has told himself so that he can avoid the truth of his own freely chosen actions"[3]—emerged from a tension between socially accepted models for heterosexual relations and the new woman, whose wants were consistently and hopelessly misaligned. Within this framework, the enigma of feminine desire conveyed a nebulous sense of agitation—the literary correlative of the precariousness comprising postindependence life.

Empathy was central to this process of signification. As I illustrated in chapter 2, Premchand's and Pudumaippittan's colonial-era short stories prompted a movement away from readerly sympathy by initiating a dissolution of the feminine type. Postindependence Hindi writers associated with the Nayī Kahānī (New Story) Movement and Tamil writers promoted by the publishing house Eḻuttu Piracuram (Writing Publications) sought to complete this project.[4] They did so by using narrative techniques designed to replace readers' sympathetic feelings for characters with empathetic identification. Inviting readers to step into the shoes of protagonists to experience these characters' discomfort and unbelonging firsthand, *nayī kahānī* and *Eḻuttu* writers attempted to place the positions of readers and protagonists on equal footing. The figure of the new woman facilitated this transposability by expressing the struggle to express and fulfill feminine desire as symbolic of the broader quest for human connection precipitated by postcolonial disconsolation.

This chapter explores how Hindi and Tamil short stories sought to build empathetic alliances between readers and protagonists through the universalization of feminine desire above religious and caste alliances. Within Hindi and Tamil frameworks of literary sentiment, apprehensions surrounding the new woman's hopes and ambitions served to bracket the problem of identitarian difference. This figure worked in tandem with literary history and criticism—which I described in the previous chapter—to inaugurate a postindependence modernist-realist mode that suppressed, rather than resolved, the legacy of colonial divisiveness. Through representations of the new woman, *nayī kahānī* and *E̱luttu* writers refracted bad-faith communal and caste relations through the lens of discordant heterosexual longing. Operating as a properly "literary" counterpart to the production of metaliterary discourses, *nayī kahānī* and *E̱luttu* interrogations of the new woman's desires aspired to unite readers through empathetic feelings aimed at superseding communal affiliations.

Narrative empathy manifested according to the parameters of the specific religious and caste dynamics characterizing the Hindi and Tamil contexts. In North India, Hindi writers were painfully aware of the weight of Partition on the cultural imaginary, and they could not ignore the emotional trauma that it triggered. At the same time, the overarching modernist-realist mandate to suture fractures of difference led them to avoid addressing the communal question head on. Partition entered into *nayī kahānī* stories obliquely; Muslim identity took on spectral manifestations; and secular critiques of the Indian bureaucracy replaced those confronting religious hypocrisy. Supplementing these moves, *nayī kahānī* representations of the new woman initiated the interiorizing of the profound experiences of loss, displacement, and brutal injury that Partition engendered. They mapped these mental and physical wounds onto the psychic anatomy of Hindi protagonists by portraying Partition's nightmarish events in the terms of unrequited love. Protagonists' inability to understand the new woman's desires—and the acute futility of their longings to establish companionate relations with her—stood in place of the communal question. These sentiments opened an admissible and intimate pathway for grappling with the inarticulable problem of religious difference.

In South India, Tamil writers faced a different historical conundrum, framed predominantly in the terms of caste. As I showed in chapter 3, the deep-seated anti-Brahminism of Dravidianist discourses spurred a paradoxical response among *E̱luttu* writers to cling to, rather than distance themselves from, Brahmin culture and identity. This inclination influenced the content of their short stories as much as the positions they expounded in their literary criticism. Using representations of the new woman, *E̱luttu* writers zoomed in on Brahmin geographies of domesticity: the layout of the Brahmin home and its immediate surroundings; the dialectical speech spoken within Brahmin spaces; and the hopes and dreams arising in opposition to antiquated Brahmin values, customs, and family structure. Confronted by anti-Brahmin sentiment in the political sphere, *E̱luttu* writers limited their settings to the interior realms that the new woman traversed, and they used her desires to translate their representations of Brahmin life into a rift between tradition and modernity. Within this framework, the new woman's reformist sensibilities provided an avenue for sidestepping the caste question by expressing it as an appeal for cultural modernization.

This chapter begins with a discussion of narrative empathy, illustrating how *nayī kahānī* and *Eḻuttu* writers attempted to draw readers into their distinct aesthetic worlds by posing the positions of readers and characters as interchangeable. The following sections explore *nayī kahānī* and *Eḻuttu* efforts to establish empathetic connection through the stories of Hindi writer Mohan Rakesh and Tamil writer D. Jayakanthan. Focusing predominantly on the enigma of feminine desire, Rakesh and Jayakanthan inscribed communal and caste anxieties onto the interior spaces of the home and the mind. Eliciting readerly empathy for the new woman's dilemmas through narrative techniques, such as monologic introspection and allegorical descriptions of landscape, these writers erased the lenses of religion and caste altogether. In their stories, the figure of the new woman became a horizon for imagining male-female relationships that had not yet found social expression, sublimating community and caste tensions along the axis of heterosexual relations. The new woman thus served as a key site through which the worlding of postindependence Hindi and Tamil short stories occurred—wherein this figure enabled these stories to accrue literary merit within differing regional, national, and global discussions about realism and modernism.

EMPATHETIC CONNECTIONS

A growing literature on narrative empathy has defined empathy as feeling *with* the emotions and experiences of a character. In contrast to sympathy, which generates feeling *for* a character's circumstances, empathy signals an intimate proximity between the dispositions of readers and characters. By forging empathetic connections, writers invite readers to step into the place of characters and see the world through their eyes. Yet, readers do not always engage with texts in the ways that authors anticipate or that texts encourage. Stories cultivate empathy unevenly, directing *some* readers to develop relationships with *some* characters while often blocking the formation of empathetic feelings toward other characters. Establishing empathetic connections depends on a range of factors, not fully predictable, which lie both within and outside the texts themselves.[5]

Scholarly discussions of narrative empathy have largely focused on how literature fosters this emotion, evaluating the merit of empathetic alliances between readers and characters through the altruistic actions that literature may or may not lead readers to perform in real life. I am interested, however, in how Hindi and Tamil writers sought to build new postindependence affiliations among readers through the use of narrative techniques commonly associated with evoking empathy. How did these writers understand the function of literature in society? What effects did they imagine literature to produce in readers? As I demonstrate below, Rakesh and Jayakanthan promoted readers' identification with their protagonists by attempting to draw readers into their characters' innermost desires and despairs. Such identification was crucial for understanding evolving postindependence demands. Rather than focusing on whether Rakesh's and Jayakanthan's efforts to generate empathy were felicitous, this chapter considers how these writers used criticism and fiction to conceptualize empathy as the foundation upon which to refashion postcolonial social relations. These theories moved Hindi and Tamil short story writing away from the colonial-era emphasis on readerly sympathy, generating new configurations of gender that were based on aesthetic—rather than social—relations and norms.

Suzanne Keen has observed that, despite its seeming rejection of both sympathy and empathy, European modernism "recast the representation of consciousness and feelings" through formal and linguistic experimentation.[6] The modernist turn did not dissolve empathetic connection. Instead, it interiorized and stylized the textual presentation of empathy, detaching it from its association with sympathy. Hindi *nayī kahānī* writers enacted a similar rupture, conceptualizing modernist-realist empathy as a literary historical response to their predecessor Premchand's idealistic realism (*ādarśommukhī yathārthvād*). As I showed in chapter 2, idealistic realism combined realist materialism with cultural idealism to summon readers' sympathy for characters' unjust living conditions. This mode was effective insofar as it motivated readers to work toward achieving a more utopian society.[7] *Nayī kahānī* empathy, by contrast, questioned the premise that sympathetic connection was possible in the postcolonial world.

Outlining the characteristics of the *nayī kahānī*, Rajendra Yadav clarified that it evoked "not *sahānubhūti* [sympathy], but *sah-anubhūti* [shared feeling]."[8] This formulation was a significant change from Premchand's understanding of sympathy, since it attempted to define empathy in a context where no concept for this feeling existed. As Yadav was well aware, *sahānubhūti* and its Hindi synonyms (*saṃvedanā, hamdardī*) denote both sympathy and empathy. He thus had to coin a word for empathy by separating *sahānubhūti* into its etymological components: *sah-*, a prefix meaning "shared," and *anubhūti*, a feminine noun meaning "perception" or "feeling."

Breaking the meanings of *sahānubhūti* apart, Yadav and other *nayī kahānī* writers severed the kinship between sympathy and empathy. They argued that, unlike sympathy, empathy enabled readers to breach the distance between self and other. By inviting readers to inhabit the worlds of characters, *nayī kahānī* empathy attempted to circumvent the competing moral and religious claims that they believed had torn post-Partition North India asunder. Empathy, they argued, entreated readers to recognize their own circumstances from the position of an "other," to relive the experiences of the other through the medium of literature.[9]

Sah-anubhūti—empathy—was therefore an integral component of *nayī kahānī* modernist realism, necessary for situating the circumstances of characters within a broader social topography. *Nayī kahānī* modernist realism—as I argued in Chapter 3—aspired to understand individuals (*vyakti*) within their external environments (*pariveś*). Narrative empathy provided an avenue through which readers could intuitively link the internal and external landscapes that *nayī kahānī* stories charted. Through empathy, the *nayī kahānī* sought to offer insights into the "totality of life," invoking a shared sense of the tenuous postcolonial condition within readers.[10] This was a condition of chaos (*halcal*), due to which individuals were "incapable of holding onto any one philosophical thread with certainty" because they had been cut off from their own sense of "worth and the life achievements associated with it."[11]

Nayī kahānī writers understood empathy to operate in the short story through an imagistic presentism, which produced the "harmony of image (*bimb*) and idea (*vicār*)—that is, the assembling of an image such that an idea explodes from within it, characters and events presented in the form of such tangible portrayals that the image itself illuminates the author's intention (*abhiprāy*) or symbol (*saṅket*)."[12] Symbolic imagery added metaphorical gravity to the metonymic details described in *nayī kahānī* stories, creating an emotional immediacy through which readers could bypass cognitive reflection. Through images, *nayī kahānī* writers solicited readers to feel with, rather than for, characters and to identify with the tense and complex nature of postindependence belonging. According to these writers, imagistic presentism produced an empathetic unsettling in readers, unveiling the universal truth of postcolonial alienation. Their approach shared resonances with the aesthetic strategies and philosophies developed in French New Wave and American New Criticism, but it was also tailored to address the specificities of the North Indian postcolonial condition.[13]

Tamil *Eḻuttu* writers further described the transformative effects of empathetic destabilization. Reflecting on his work in a 2006 interview,

Jayakanthan, for example, described narrative empathy as *kūṭu viṭṭu kūṭu pāytal*—literally, leaping into another's body. In this formulation, empathetic connection was a process through which identification with characters allowed readers to be "transported to unknown levels of intensity" to experience life anew.[14] In this way, literature fostered a type of heightened enlightenment in readers—what Jayakanthan characterized as maturity (*pakkuvam*)—that provided them with new insights for negotiating postindependence reality.[15] Narrative empathy was, in this sense, revelatory. It propelled readers through the problem of postcolonial alienation to spark the subjective conditions that *Eḻuttu* writers viewed as necessary to realign interpersonal relations.

Empathy was the distinguished outcome that *Eḻuttu* modernist realism pursued. As I showed in chapter 3, *Eḻuttu* writers constructed a modernist-realist mode through the aesthetic triangulation of spoken language (*pēccu Tamiḻ*), writerly style (*naṭai*), and intense emotional experience (*uṇarcci*). They furthermore specifically employed these rhetorical features to create an affective community of readers. Within this framework, *Eḻuttu* writers conceived of narrative empathy—similarly to *nayī kahānī* writers—as a means for circumventing rational deliberation. Language, style, and emotion came together to facilitate primal associations between readers and characters that were based on emotional sensation instead of intellectual rumination.

However, in contrast to the *nayī kahānī* emphasis on images and symbols, the writer's ability to wield language featured more centrally in *Eḻuttu* writings. This was because, as C. S. Chellappa pointed out, language itself enabled emotion and experience to converge within the reader:

> In true, pure art, emotions do not simply stimulate us. Through the power of the writer's words, an aesthetic relationship forms. . . . Emotions rise to the fore, entering [into literary creations] to help create a unity of experience. . . . The unity of emotion and experience is the foundation of literature. We could say that the quality of a literary creation depends on the writer's ability to achieve this unity.[16]

Employing distinctly aesthetic terms, Chellappa attempted to capture the elusive nature of narrative empathy. In his view, empathy was constituted through the artistry of a text. Yet, it also exceeded the text to generate profound lived experiences within readers. The empathetic connections forged through literature formed the touchstone of *all* experience—aesthetically generated or otherwise.[17] In this way empathy produced the affective foundation in readers that *Eḻuttu* writers deemed essential for coping in the postindependence world. Their conception of empathy drew from the sense of disillusionment (*nampikkai vaṟaṭci*) that their predecessor Pudumaippittan had conceptualized in his critiques of existing social norms.[18] At the same time, it shifted the experience of disillusionment from Pudumaippittan's grounding in both narrative content and generic form to one that emerged through the linguistic innovation. Giving preeminence to their formal experimentations with language, *Eḻuttu* writers transformed Pudumaippittan's disillusionment into an aesthetic of revelation. This aesthetic referenced the experience-based approach to art famously advanced by the American philosopher and education reformer John Dewey in *Art as Experience* (1934). At the same time, it spoke to specific postcolonial debates in the Tamil-speaking South about the relationship of literature to language.

In outlining the *nayī kahānī* and *Eḻuttu* positions, I am not arguing that these writers' theorizations of narrative empathy are prescriptions for how their fiction should be read. Rather, I offer their elaborations as inroads for exploring how writers across multiple Indian literary spheres engaged with empathy as a means for drawing readers into new interpersonal configurations. I believe that the distinctness of their views on empathy provides a useful starting point for understanding the unaligned literary sentiments that emerged in *nayī kahānī* and *Eḻuttu* fiction, despite a shared focus on empathy. The *nayī kahānī* emphasis on alienation aestheticized feelings of inertia, confusion, and incapacity. By contrast, the priority that *Eḻuttu* writers gave to revelation rooted literary purpose in a sense of moral outrage. As I elaborate in my readings of Rakesh's and Jayakanthan's stories below, these differing empathetic moods were fundamental to how *nayī kahānī* and *Eḻuttu* fiction erased religious and caste difference, respectively—the idealism of the *nayī kahānī* and *Eḻuttu* projects notwithstanding.

THE REFUGEE STATUS OF MAN

Illustrating the overlapping nature of communal and caste politics, Dilip Menon has outlined historical conjunctures during which "the problem of internal differences and hierarchy within Hinduism was temporarily resolved through the projection of united Hindu violence against Muslims."[19] The 1947 Partition of India and Pakistan was one such moment, during which Hindu-Muslim polarities elided contentions around caste inequality.

At the same time, the secular ethos of the Nehruvian era, encapsulated by a discourse of "unity in diversity," also placed limitations on the articulation of religious difference.[20] Censoring caste and communal questions simultaneously, Nehruvian secularism, as Vivek Dhareshwar writes, outlined "a trajectory of self-fashioning where the self gradually sheds its ethnic, caste, linguistic, and gender markers and attains the abstract identity of the citizen or becomes an individual."[21] *Nayī kahānī* stories participated in this self-fashioning by abstracting their protagonists from the material conditions of their existence. Collapsing caste, class, religion, and gender in the figure of the middle-class, *savarṇa* (caste Hindu) male, these stories portrayed this figure's inner turmoil as universal by cloaking it in the rhetoric of modernist-realist disconsolation.

Caste was deeply woven into the fabric of *nayī kahānī* stories, although it surfaced solely in the language of class. For example, Rakesh's "Mis Pāl" (Miss Pal) portrays its mountain-dwelling villager characters as ignorant, superstitious, and backward. They are contrasted to the urbanized male protagonist Ranjit and his friend Miss Pal, who intellectualize and psychologize the conditions of postindependence existence. Ranjit's and Miss Pal's economic status, level of education, and elevated Hindi diction immediately signal their *savarṇa* identity to any Hindi reader. Nonetheless, the story distinguishes these characters from the peripheral village dwellers through the class norms of propriety, civility, and hygiene—rather than through the terms of caste hierarchy. By extension, "Mis Pāl" poses any possible future redemption of the minor characters as a logical consequence of the class mobility promised by education. Consequently, caste is everywhere in the story, even though it is articulated nowhere.[22] In this way Rakesh's story—indicative of *nayī kahānī* fiction more generally—helped to consolidate a Hindu unity that was deeply structured by caste, despite its more utopian middle-class aspirations.

Nayī kahānī writing offered aspirational middle-class belonging to resolve the dilemma of caste hierarchy. But this conception was too rooted in *savarṇa* Hindu identity to also accommodate communal difference without further finessing. Menon's insight that fueling communal difference has been fundamental to establishing caste-based Hindu unity in North India helps me to think through some of the competing postcolonial mandates that *nayī kahānī* writers must have confronted—namely, on one hand, to reaffirm Hindu identity against Muslim outsiders and, on the other, to smooth over Hindu-Muslim religious differences for the sake of national unity. This paradoxical tension led *nayī kahānī* writers to focus more intently on the psychological dimensions of middle-class belonging, wherein Partition could be registered metaphorically as middle-class experiences of disillusionment and dislocation.

Nayī kahānī writers used Partition as a launching point for conceptualizing a more catholic sense of alienation in which physical brutality was located along a chain of lesser and greater injuries. In an essay describing the newness of the *nayī kahānī* in relation to Partition, Kamleshwar, for example, distinguished between external Partition violence and the internal upheaval to which it led:

> The terrible bloodshed and carnage that occurred with independence not only spurred caravans of refugees. But also man himself became a refugee [*śaraṇārthī*] within his own country, his home, and even his family. On an external level, disabled and terrified refugees came from across the border, but on an internal level, an entire community [*samudāy*] became a refugee. All those people who believed in secularism [*dharmnirpekshatā*] and—until the very moment of Partition [*vibhājan*]—believed it to be impractical and inconceivable—for whom the dream of Indian unity was ripe and who were born in an atmosphere in which religious forbearance and generosity were national values—they became refugees within themselves . . . . Those who understood themselves to belong to the nation's intellectual class were the most heartbroken of all because . . . that entire community found itself in a state of senselessness caused by the shattering of its values and beliefs. . . . For this reason, those whose humanist values [*mānvīya mūlya*] were murdered became refugees, more so than those who crossed national borders. . . . The individual as a refugee within himself, his condition of disillusionment [*mohabhaṅg kī sthiti*], and the fragmenting [*khaṇḍit honā*] of the middle- and lower middle-class family—these are truths that cannot be glossed over, even by dogmatism [*haṭhdharmitā*]. On the level of narrative [*kathya*], is this voice and its registration of terror not new? . . . The *nayī kahānī* has brought us face to face with human struggle, the interior world of man [*ādmī kī apnī duniyā*], and the existential condition [*astitva-bodh*].[23]

Kamleshwar moved fluidly from an image of refugees traveling in caravans to the inner splintering of intellectuals, transforming the refugee into a trope for the experiences he felt were common to middle-class citizens.

Alienation, in this context, was nothing less than man's refugee status, defined as the psychic separation of man from himself. This rationale placed stories explicitly dealing with Partition violence within the same category as stories examining individual isolation, just like Kamleshwar did in this essay.[24]

A handful of short stories and novels about Partition appeared in the two decades following the event. These were, as far as I know, written mostly by authors associated with the preindependence literary generation or with the Progressive Writers' Movement. As I argued in chapter 3, *nayī kahānī* writers sought to distance themselves from these groups. *Nayī kahānī* criticism engaged minimally, if at all, with the Partition fiction of Hindi and Urdu writers such as Agyeya, Upendranath Ashk, Rajinder Singh Bedi, Krishan Chander, Intizar Hussain, Qurratulain Hyder, Sa'adat Hasan Manto, and Yashpal. *Nayī kahānī* venues selectively published works by other writers—such as Ismat Chughtai, Amrita Pritam, Bhisham Sahni, and Krishna Sobti—giving preference to those short stories that resonated with *nayī kahānī* themes.

Partition fiction also grew more prolific after 1970. During the first two postindependence decades, the majority of *nayī kahānī* and Urdu *nayā afsānā* (new story) writers explored themes of alienation and disconnection through a secular humanist lens, while marginalizing the event of Partition itself.[25] As Aijaz Ahmad has observed, "for almost a whole generation [after Partition], the [literary] community tried to remain one while the nation-states became two."[26] This is one reason why modernist realism compelled so many writers within the Hindi and Urdu literary spheres, which were—by the 1950s—conceived of within institutional spaces (such as universities, publishing houses, and the Sahitya Akademi) as entirely separate fields.

PSYCHIC PARTITIONS

Of the writers centrally linked with the Nayī Kahānī Movement, only Kamleshwar and Rakesh depicted Partition in their fiction. Kamleshwar's most well-known works on Partition appeared in later decades. But one early story called "Aura Kitne Pākistān" (How many more Pakistans)—entirely different from his similarly titled 2000 novel *Kitne Pākistān* (How many Pakistans)—is dated to the late 1960s.[27] As Kamleshwar himself recounted, this story was initially lost and not published until 1994.[28] The story follows a love affair between the Hindu protagonist Mangal and his Muslim lover Bano. Confronted by social interdictions against interreligious marriage, the two are further torn apart by Partition. Rioting, brutality, and death all appear within the story's narrative frame.

Mangal metaphorizes this violence through a persistent questioning of the location and meanings of Pakistan. "Pakistan comes between us time and time again. It's not a country. . . . It's the name of an anguished truth," he laments.[29] "What would have happened if the Pakistan blazing within me had burst?" he later cries.[30] "Pakistan is the conception of man as smooth-tongued fragment, rather than complete being."[31] Finally, Mangal concludes the story in despair, acknowledging that he and Bano will never be together: "Is there nowhere to run that is not a Pakistan? Where I can become whole, taking all my longings and desires with me? Bano! Pakistan is everywhere. It beats us, wounds us, incessantly thrashes and humiliates us."[32]

Interspersing scenes of horror with loss and longing for his departed lover, Mangal's internal dialogue exemplifies what Kumkum Sangari has described as "the repositioning of *viraha* as an affective complex that could negotiate Partition."[33] By the story's conclusion, *viraha*—the poetic trope of anguish caused by separation from one's lover—eclipses Mangal's descriptions of violence, suggesting that Pakistan is the result of illicit love, rather than political contention. Mangal and Bano are doomed to eternal separation because of the parting that true love already requires of them. The circular logic of *viraha* enshrouds the story's depictions of Partition within layers of romantic torment and irresolvable desire.

Rakesh's three best-known Partition stories—"Malbe kā Mālik" (The owner of rubble, 1957), "Klem" (The claim, 1958), and "Paramātmā kā Kuttā" (God's dog, 1958)—examine Partition from a less-personal perspective than "Aura Kitne Pākistān."[34] All three are unusual within Rakesh's oeuvre, which centers almost exclusively on interpersonal relationships. "Klem" and "Paramātmā kā Kuttā" are vignette-like exposés that accuse the Indian bureaucracy of neglecting the poor while attempting to right the wrongs of Partition. Both stories touch on Partition violence but do not linger, directing readers to focus instead on the characters' present struggles for employment and survival.

"Malbe kā Mālik," by contrast, examines a single post-Partition day, during which a petty Hindu overlord named Rakkha meets his former Muslim neighbor Gani Miyan, who is visiting Amritsar (India) from his new residence in Lahore (Pakistan). Gani Miyan's sudden appearance forces Rakkha to remember how he brutally murdered Gani Miyan's son, daughter-in-law, and grandchildren during Partition so that he could acquire their property. Gani Miyan is heartbroken to find his home in ruins and his family gone, but he departs without learning what happened to them. In the final scene, an angry dog accosts Rakkha while he sits atop the ruins that he now owns. The dog's incessant growling channels the spirits of Gani Miyan's dead family members, haunting and paralyzing Rakkha, leaving him without any means for retribution.[35] Like in Kamleshwar's "Aura Kitne Pākistān," Partition emerges as a troubling and oppressive memory smoldering deep within postindependence individuals.

In comparison to these critical commentaries on Partition, Rakesh's 1960 story "Ādmī aura Dīvār" (The man and the wall) presents a more symbolic exposition. I view this story as part of a shift in Rakesh's writing toward abstraction, which began in the late 1950s and prevails in his most iconic *nayī kahānī* fiction.[36] This remarkable story reveals how the Nayī Kahānī Movement tried to absorb the injuries of Partition into a broader aesthetic of alienation. "Ādmī aura Dīvār" unfurls two narratives simultaneously. The first follows the protagonist Satte's fraught relationships with his sister Rajo, friend Harish, and neighbor Saroj. The second contemplates communal loss and longing. By the end of the story, the two storylines merge, mapping Satte's romantic desires onto the ruthless divisions caused by Partition.

"Ādmī aura Dīvār" is undeniably about Partition, although it functions tangentially within the plot. The opening scene, in which Satte stares at the unsightly graffiti on his bedroom wall, brings this immediately into focus:

> That wooden wall had a personality of its own. Different types of scripts, carved by nails and knives, were all over it. The shapes of the words made it seem as if the wall were smiling or sometimes grimacing. . . . In one corner was carved in deep Farsi letters: "Shirin Mumtaz alias [*urf*] Mumtaz Mahal." In the opposite corner—as if to balance out the communal account—someone much later had engraved her name in Devanagari letters: "Dammo alias [*athārt*] Damayanti." In the middle of the wall, spread out over something like one-and-a-half feet, someone had added his name: "Billu." Beneath it in crooked letters, someone had later appended: "Alias blue-black." In nearly the same place in Farsi letters was written: "Here I leave my soul [*rūh*]—Shirin Mumtaz, 8-13-47." A month-and-a-half later on 9-30-47 someone inscribed his acceptance: "I'm much obliged [*meharbānī*], thank you [*śukriyā*]." Where the wall abutted the doorframe, someone had written hurriedly, as if at the very moment of departure: "I love [*muhabbat*] you." Beneath this was a comment: "My love, are you male [*nar*] or female [*mādā*]?" . . . There was the eye of an otter, which put an ominous shadow

> over the whole wall, a deep wound created by a futile attempt to scratch out the wall in that spot.[37]

To a Hindi reader, the communalized identities of the various inscriptions are stark. Shirin—whose name and appearance in the Farsi script mark her as Muslim—compares herself to Mumtaz Mahal, for whom the Mughal emperor Shah Jahan built the Taj Mahal. Dammo counters with a Hindu rejoinder in Sanskritic Devanagari script, renaming herself Damayanti—the virtuous wife of King Nala in the ancient epic *Mahābhārata*. The unmistakable communal associations of these legendary characters seem to heighten the hostility between Shirin and Dammo. Billu, a nickname used for males of both communities, appears trivial by comparison. This name and its epithet "blue-black," both written in English in the Roman script, together suggest an emasculated identity. August 13, 1947, the eve of Indian and Pakistani Independence, is conspicuous among the inscriptions. The date intimates that Shirin's departure may have been compelled, or that she may have been killed or died by suicide. Her interlocutors use distinctly Perso-Arabic vocabulary to respond to her with love, longing, curiosity, and even mockery. Last, and most enigmatic of all, is the otter's eye, which has no script, vocabulary, or time stamp to signal its identity. In contrast to the scribblings, the eye appears as sheer violence, ready to swallow the voices calling out from the wall.

Throughout the story, the graffiti confronts Satte, unsettling and unnerving him. Satte is a writer unable to overcome his writer's block. Yet stories are all around him. Shirin, Dammo, Billu, the otter's eye—all of them develop intriguing personalities. They intrude into Satte's thoughts despite his repeated efforts to push them away. Each time Satte returns to his room or surfaces from a reverie, an inscription demands his acknowledgement. The messages are remnants of those whose desires have been blotted out by Partition:

> "Dammo alias Damayanti . . . !" Who was this Dammo? Why had she written her name on the wall? When did she live in that house? How did she look? How old was she? Where could she be now? Would she be happy if she were to come see her name written on the wall today? Or would a long sigh of sadness escape her? . . . And this Billu, when did he live in the house? Why did he feel it necessary to take up a foot-and-a-half to write his name? Did he wish to make his tall, broad stature evident, or to hide his shortness? And the person who changed the meaning

of his name to blue-black, why was he angry with Billu? . . . and Shirin Mumtaz? The only thing certain was that she was here before Partition—just two days before Partition. Did she leave the house exactly on 8-13-47? What was her intention in "leaving"? To leave the house, to leave the city . . . ? "Shirin Mumtaz alias Mumtaz Mahal!" Why did she think of herself as Mumtaz Mahal? Was there someone in her life, too, who wished to build her a Taj Mahal when she was gone? Or was the wall itself her Taj Mahal?[38]

The multiple ellipses in the passage suggest Satte's inability to explore the violent conditions in which the messages were possibly written. Instead he reflects on the longings they express. The romantic stories that Satte constructs around the names are tinged with *viraha*—suffering, anguish, and yearning. Dammo's and Shirin's links to the fabled love stories of Nala and Damayanti and Shah Jahan and Mumtaz, respectively, strengthen these sentiments. *Viraha* is Satte's persistent fascination. Through this affective complex, the story positions readers in a frame of empathetic identification with readily recognizable characters and tropes.

The narrative apposition of Satte's musings about the wall with his ruminations about his own experiences is not accidental. It serves to intertwine Satte's desires with the wall's multiple articulations, placing them together on a shared plane. The inscriptions prompt Satte to consider his own desires by revisiting his argument with Rajo, his jealousy of Harish, and his yearning for Saroj. For example, attempting to escape the glare of the otter's eye, Satte remembers how he beat Rajo that morning, having found her letters from Harish. Rajo's refusal to explain the letters, her audacity to defend her relationship with Harish, and the inscrutable spark in her eyes infuriate Satte. Most of Harish's letters are to Satte, but "there was one letter—and it was addressed solely to Rajo—at the end of which was an 'and' followed by three dots—many unwritten things were expressed in those three dots."[39] Similar to the wall inscriptions, Harish's ellipsis suggests forbidden love.

Satte juxtaposes his anger at both Rajo and Harish with the longing he feels for Saroj, a beautiful stranger with large black eyes, whom he used to watch from his bedroom window as she stood on the roof of a nearby apartment building. He obsesses about Saroj, unable to forget her: "How he wished he might sometime see Saroj up close and laugh with her, . . . but his desire remained only a desire."[40] Saroj, like the figures on the wall, is now gone. The roof has been built up, covering over her traces. Satte's memory of Saroj returns him to his preoccupation with Shirin, and his musings could

tensions it engendered did not encumber the Tamil cultural imaginary as much as in North India. Instead, as Dilip Menon notes, "unlike the north, the untouchables were party to the expansion of the sphere of public debate," making caste hierarchy central to South Indian discussion from the nineteenth century onward.[44] By the 1950s, Dravidianist, Pure Tamil, and Self-Respect discourses had cemented powerful critiques of Brahminism, which strongly influenced the trajectory of social and political reform in the Tamil-speaking region.

Within this highly politicized, anti-Brahmin atmosphere, how did *E<u>l</u>uttu* writers' depictions of Brahmin life, and of the Brahmin new woman in particular, accrue such considerable literary merit? One answer can be found in the *E<u>l</u>uttu* construction of modernist realism, which I examined in chapter 3. Undertaking what M. S. S. Pandian has described as "the subtle act of transcoding caste and caste relations into something else," this mode transformed representations of Brahmin dialectical speech into an aesthetic of linguistic experimentation.[45] Driven out of a political arena dominated by questions of caste, *E<u>l</u>uttu* writers took refuge in literature. Literature provided a space where they could freely wield Tamil—a language to which they arguably could stake no claim—to explore tensions specific to Brahmin identity.

Thus, I view the *E<u>l</u>uttu* turn to language as a reaction to colonial processes of vernacularization. Observing how the prevalence of English in Indian public life puts caste at a linguistic remove, Vivek Dhareshwar argues that "caste, then, becomes represented by being driven into the private domain—a domain, significantly enough, where very often the vernacular is deployed."[46] At one level, Dhareshwar's argument offers a rationale for why Brahmin life emerged so centrally in *E<u>l</u>uttu* fiction. Constituted through an opposition to the secularizing forces of English, the "vernacular" is a realm in which caste necessarily imbues language. As I have argued throughout this book, however, "literary" Tamil writers viewed their endeavors in both conversation and conflict with English and other literatures.

These writers developed their "worldly" position by explicitly disavowing Dravidianist rationalities of the vernacular, which had, by their very logic, expelled Brahmin writers from the vernacular domain. Here, as Geeta Patel has argued in the case of Miraji's Urdu poetry, the vernacular lost its purchase. For this reason, I read the Tamil case through Patel's insight that "it is in the absence of speaking on the vernacular, perhaps, in the absence of laying claim to it as a site where one can return, as though guilelessly, to truth value that those who have to live the legacy of vernacularization can find hopes that might bear something more than the brutal."[47] Perhaps the search for something more than the brutal—for a Tamil future that could accommodate Brahmin ways of being—propelled *Eḻuttu* writers to pose their depictions of caste as universal.[48]

Among *Eḻuttu* writers, Jayakanthan spoke most candidly about the relationship between caste, language, and literature. Iconoclastic, argumentative, and outspoken—an "enfant terrible," as he once called himself—Jayakanthan was simultaneously singular and exemplary of the *Eḻuttu* position.[49] He was, and continues to be, popular and literary, acclaimed and controversial, widely translated and broadly critiqued. Unlike the majority of his *Eḻuttu* contemporaries, Jayakanthan wrote about the lowest echelons of society as well as the highest, even if he favored depictions of Brahmin life. The literary community both praised and denounced him for his sexualized descriptions of male and female bodies, unapologetic documentations of perverted desire, and trenchant critiques of class hypocrisy. But it also unequivocally celebrated him for his representations of Brahmin dialectical speech, which his contemporaries claimed no one had so realistically portrayed before.[50] A non-Brahmin himself, Jayakanthan's thinking on Brahminism legitimized and strengthened the *Eḻuttu* position.

In a memoir about postindependence-era Tamil politics, Jayakanthan railed against Dravidianist party leaders, deeming their contention that Brahmins were not Tamilians backwards. "It seemed unjust and irrational to me to deny that those whose only language was Tamil were not Tamilians, to kick them out for being foreigners and 'Aryans,'" he reflected.[51] Critiques of Brahminism, he argued, mistakenly construed Brahmin domination as a caste issue, rather than the outcome of the "feudal cruelties" sedimented by class hierarchy.[52] These views went hand in hand with Jayakanthan's understanding of literary purpose, which undermined Dravidianist classicism and linguistic purification:

> Literature emerges through the speaking of a language. It cannot take shape if it boycotts life. For contemporary Tamil literature to find a place within university departments around the world, its prose style [*urai naṭai*] must be developed. Prose style must not be constructed like that of verse. Prose evolves to the extent that it is in harmony with our lifestyles and practices—to the extent that prose is connected with [life's] beauties and progresses. Furthermore, contemporary literature must bring the people we daily meet into its characters. Perceiving the uniqueness of a character—its time, its milieu, its geographical location, its economic class—occurs through [the character's]

> thoughts and conversations and the author's descriptions. It is impossible for Pure Tamil—which is a futile effort—to achieve this. Because Pure Tamil is an illusion, not a life truth. In other words, it is the desire of a small coterie.[53]

Critiquing the Pure Tamil interest in literature as functionalist, Jayakanthan emphasized that language and literature shared an intimate, complementary relationship. Tamil language, he argued, developed through the exploration of literary characters using the dialects in which they realistically thought and spoke. Jayakanthan's examinations of Brahmin speech and life fit neatly into this aesthetic framework.

In many of his stories Jayakanthan theorized Brahminism as a means of modernization. For example, *Pirammōpatēcam* (The initiation of the Brahmin)—one of his controversial novellas, first serialized in *Āṉanta Vikaṭaṉ* and then published as a book in 1963—depicts a Brahmin protagonist, Sankara Sarma, who confronts his atheist friend Seshadari's radical anti-Brahminism. When Seshadari elopes with Sankara's daughter, rescuing her from her father's conservative trappings, Sankara angrily disowns her. But Sankara also performs the Brahmin initiation ceremony for a pious young non-Brahmin man whom he decides to adopt in her place. Responding to criticisms that the story touted a conservative Brahminism rather than the progressive socialism he claimed to support, Jayakanthan prefaced the novella with a rejoinder:

> A man who wears a [Brahmin] tuft is a conservative. An atheist is a progressive [*muṟpōkku*]. . . . In truth, classifying conservatives and progressives according to such qualities is not becoming of enlightened men. He who rejects selfishness, who refrains from enmity against one or more sections of humanity, who strives for progress and to make life excellent for all humankind . . . is a progressive deserving the respect of all who have a heart. Seen in this light . . . Sankara Sarma is a great revolutionary! . . . Yes, he attempts to make the Vedas new. . . . He is a theist, a spiritualist. [But] Seshadari is a true atheist, materialist, and communist because he understands that [Sankara's] true social objectives must not be doubted.[54]

Through such expositions, Jayakanthan conceived of Brahminism as a politics of humanism that could overcome caste and class oppression. True Brahminism, he argued, encouraged *manita apimāṉam*—deep pride and respect for humankind—which he held as the fundamental aim of progressivism.[55] In this way Jayakanthan justified his literary depictions of Brahmin life, deflating the accusations of casteism that Dravidianist and Pure Tamil activists made against him.

BRAHMIN GEOGRAPHIES OF INTERIORITY

Jayakanthan's thinking on language, literature, and caste exemplifies how *Eḻuttu* modernist realism bracketed questions of caste by translating Brahminism into a call for progress. *Eḻuttu* fiction assisted in this reformulation by focusing on the Brahmin home, where changing caste-based norms could be rearticulated in a universal discourse of tradition and modernity. The vast majority of *Eḻuttu* stories were set in Brahmin domestic spaces, exploring tensions within the Brahmin family. They mapped Brahmin geographies onto the Brahmin woman's body, using the structures of the Brahmin home to outline the contours of the new woman's oppressions, strengths, and irresolvable desires.

Sundara Ramaswamy's 1959 story "Kiṭāri" (Heifer), for example, details a Brahmin compound—the large two-story house, the cow shed, the backyard, the firewood room, and the storage sheds—around which the old patriarch of the family moves. His daughter is quarantined in an upstairs bedroom, sick with tuberculosis, and his granddaughter lies confined in a room downstairs, having just delivered her fifth child, another girl. Ironically, everyone in the compound rejoices in the recent birth of a young heifer while regretting the arrival of the baby girl. Meanwhile, the granddaughter weeps silently, cursing the fate that refuses to grant her a son. In this story, the gender-differentiated spaces of the Brahmin compound accentuate female oppression, marking the limits of the female characters' abilities to realize their desires.

Another example is Chellappa's "Māmiyiṉ Vīṭu" (Aunt's house, 1967). In this story the Brahmin protagonist Raghu returns to his childhood home, which had formerly been his aunt's prize possession. The home was razed to make room for a municipal sewage drain. Walking around the planned layout of the neighborhood, Raghu nostalgically remembers the home's Brahmin features: the upper and lower porches (*tiṇṇai*), front foyer (*rēḻi*), central hall (*kūṭam*), passageways (*naṭai*), courtyard (*muṟṟam*), well (*kiṇaṟu*), and cattle shed (*koṭṭam*). Upon the gridlike geography of the modernized city, Raghu reconstructs his aunt's house: "the sixty by forty plot, ten feet in front, five in the back, five feet on each side, the main hall beginning right at the street—as if exposing all of the home's internal affairs to the street—here was the kitchen, the bedroom. . . . [T]he story of that lane's birth was also the story of my own."[56] Raghu recalls how his aunt Bhagirathi had courageously fought to retain possession of the place after she was widowed, so that she could provide for her children and nephew. He describes the meticulous chores she performed to care for the home, pouring herself into its architecture. He then recounts how Bhagirathi's body deteriorated when the municipal corporation demolished her house. The lane on which it once stood was now named after her. "My aunt will not be forgotten, even after I . . . [am] gone," Raghu concludes.[57] This story, like Ramaswamy's, uses the inner spaces of the Brahmin home to showcase the interiority of the Brahmin woman. Combining a sense of loss for an older way of life with a recognition of the need for reform, the story configures the Brahmin woman's struggles as the primary ground on which modernization unfolds.

Eḻuttu stories inscribed caste into the Brahmin woman's interiority, linking Brahmin identity to the pathways of modernity. Jayakanthan's "Nāṉ Jaṉṉalarukē Uṭkārntirukkiṟēṉ" (I sit by the window) chronicles this process beautifully. Published in 1969 the story is presented as the stream of consciousness of an unnamed elderly Brahmin woman. Entirely in dialectical speech, the narrator recounts her life story as she sits on the windowsill, watching the street from her home. Her tone is irreverent and angry, a challenge to patriarchy. In the opening lines, she asks: "Yes, I sit right on the windowsill . . . so what? Why shouldn't I? . . . That's how I've always sat. . . . *Adee amma!* I've been sitting here for ages. And I'll go on sitting here. What's wrong with that?"[58] She describes how her father and stepmother, whom she calls Chitti, relegated her to the status of a servant after her mother died and how she was forced to care for her siblings instead of attending school. Denied the right to marry, she began looking out from the window in search of respite. Refusing to budge from the sill for years, she mourns her life's stasis while the world has changed around her. At the story's conclusion, however, she realizes that she has also grown and that her conditions have improved. She is now seen as a grandmother to her brother's grandchildren, cared for and loved.

The story's basic plot is quite ordinary—a recognizable tale of patriarchal oppression in which the Brahmin woman's suffering sheds light on the need for social reform. Dispossessed and unmarried, the narrator's circumstances recall that of the Brahmin widow, a feminine type bringing dilemmas of female guardianship and regulation to readers' attention. The story's representation of the narrator draws on the canonical authority of this type, which, as Susie Tharu has noted, "lies in its ability to survive and resurface, and in its power to effect reiteration across generations."[59] For this reason, the oppression that the narrator experiences requires little narratorial justification.

But I also view Jayakanthan's depiction of the narrator's life as extraordinary for the way it circumscribes feminine desire. The edifice of the home, particularly the window, illuminates her longings. The window functions as the narrator's eyes. It also offers her life-giving breath. As she remarks: "What's a window for? For air. To see the street. For those inside to breathe. . . . Why should a person breathe? Are you also going to ask why a house needs air? What kind of questions are these? Can you even call it a house if there aren't any windows? That would be a tomb."[60] Necessary for the narrator's survival, the window forms a physical threshold between inside and outside, a threshold at which she may live out the experiences she was never allowed. She views the window as an extension of her own corporeality: "If I sit with my back against one wall of the window frame and press my feet against the other, *vinnu*, it fits me perfectly. . . . I am the window and the window, me."[61]

When the narrator's father catches her watching a marriage procession from the window one day, she wonders:

> "Appa, when will you get me married?" I asked. What was wrong with that? I still don't feel it was wrong. I had hardly asked the question when suddenly my father's countenance changed. He scowled at me as if I were disgusting. . . . Did the man even answer my question? As if anger were some kind of response. As if he was the only one to feel anger! Wouldn't I, too, be angry? . . . Everyone started gossiping—I shouldn't have asked such a question, I was a disgrace, crazy for marriage, wild for men. They said all sorts of crude things. . . . Was this man even my father? He was Chitti's husband. . . . *Adee amma!* I've had enough in this lifetime simply because I've been born a woman.[62]

The narrator's father reads her question as an expression of excessive sexual desire that must be contained. In retrospect the narrator scathingly attacks the hypocritical patriarchal norms that have construed her own desires as prurient, while sanctioning her father's overindulgent sexual attraction to his new wife. Through her angry ramblings, she exposes society's deep anxiety to control feminine desire with which the story contends.

This event serves as a turning point, after which the narrator feels more scrutinized than ever:

> Chitti would sneak up behind me as I sat by the window like a cat putting one paw in front of the other. If a man walked past in the street, she would think I was waiting there just for him. If some vagrant sat under the peepul tree smoking a beedi, she would think I'd completely fallen for him. Whoever was out there, supposedly I was ogling him. And if no one was there, then supposedly I was waiting for him![63]

The narrator finds herself reduced to sexual desire. At the same time, she questions whether such desire could be wrong, even if it is also futile: "Slowly I too began to wonder, was I looking for someone? Who could it be? Was I wrong to search? . . . If whoever I was searching for were to actually come, as if I could jump out the window and run away with him."[64] Stifled, isolated, and confused, the narrator seems incapable of pinpointing the exact nature of her own desires. Through intimate glimpses into the narrator's tenuous position, the story invites readers to enter into an empathetic web with the narrator. Within it, the narrator's afflictions summon readers' shared sense of indignation toward the strictures of outdated tradition.

With nowhere else to go, the narrator moves inward, into surreal spaces. She describes a dreamlike sequence of events, which she has come to view as ordinary:

> Suddenly one day I was surrounded by only window [. . .] a huge window [. . .] all the walls were window [. . . .]
>
> . . . The peepul tree was gone, the pond behind it was gone, the neighbor Sivanandan's house was gone, there were no marriage or funeral processions going by. Only window. Not like the beautiful, small window of my house. There was no sill. Nowhere to lean back against or prop my feet. Nothing [. . . .] It was like a cage, a cave, a prison. Could it have been a lie? A dream? I'm not sure how to explain it. Just forget it. I'm now back at the windowsill again!
>
> Another time, an elephant came in through the window. It was the same elephant that I'd seen in religious processions going through town. *Adee amma*, what a big elephant! How furtively it stretched out its trunk as if it were calling to me. It slipped its waving trunk between the bars of the window and touched my cheek. I shivered but it also felt good [*nalla*]. I climbed off the windowsill where I'd been sitting and went to the center of the room. The elephant stuck its long trunk completely into the

> room and groped around to catch hold of me. . . . Little by little that elephant flattened his body into a piece of black cloth—as if transforming into a large curtain that had been cut out in the shape of an elephant—and slid itself entirely through the window bars. Now it stood in its original shape in the middle of the room, its back smashed against the ceiling. *Adee amma!* How pleasurable [*cukam*] it was! How joyful [*cantōṣam*]! No fear. Not even a little. . . . It wrapped its trunk around my neck, holding me, tugging me to come with it. . . . Carrying me in its trunk, the elephant retreated the way it had come—undulating like cloth it slipped back through the window bars. When I got to the window, I leaned my back firmly against one side of the frame and pushed my feet up against the other as if latching a bolt across a door. How could I have slipped out like the elephant?[65]

The narrator then watches the elephant retrace its path to the peepul tree and morph into the Ganesh (elephant god) idol that always stands beneath. Remarking that the elephant visits her in this manner now and then, she notes, "[T]he elephant comes in, but I don't go out. Would that even be possible?"[66] The narrator then moves into the present moment, concluding the story by recounting a playful conversation with her great granddaughter. Surprised to be surrounded by so many generations, she remarks: "*Adee amma!* There was so much to observe on this side of the window, and I had never paid attention!"[67] Despite her circumstances, the narrator discovers that she has matured.

Sandwiched within this mundane narrative arc, the double dream sequence is enigmatic and highly sexualized. The windowed space without frame or sill, outside of which no landscape appears, unsettles the narrator. She views the all-encompassing window as both bounded and boundaryless—almost unimaginable and possibly unreal. By contrast, her physical contact with the elephant is descriptively concrete. It incites pleasure and excitement. The elephant's association with the Hindu god Ganesh spiritualizes their intimate, corporeal encounter. The experience seems to satiate the narrator's otherwise irresolvable desire, leading her to accept, and even to affirm, the impossibility of crossing the perimeter of the Brahmin home.

Fusing the Brahmin woman's body to the structural skeleton of the Brahmin home, the story critiques outdated Brahmin traditions while also resurrecting the Brahmin woman as a central figure of modernity. She must stay confined within the home because this is the only sanctioned place for her to grow. While her family members view the narrator's body—and, by extension, the Brahmin home—as requiring protection, the dream sequence illustrates how this edifice is nonetheless vulnerable to penetration. As if to lessen the threat, the narrator casts vulgar feminine desire into a private, fantastical realm. The incident both confirms and transgresses conservative Brahmin norms. Against this impulse to reinvent Brahminism, the narrator's dream of the unbounded window emerges as an aporia. It suggests the narrator's inability to imagine a world unbounded by caste—going even beyond gender—a place where all desire may have limitless expression. Closing off this possibility, the narrator replaces a potential interrogation of caste with a tentative resolution to the question of feminine desire, which she adeptly interiorizes to pass on to new generations.

REALIGNING HETEROSEXUAL RELATIONS

Both "Ādmī aura Dīvār" and "Nāṉ Jaṉṉalarukē Uṭkārntirukkiṟēṉ" worry about the unknowable nature of feminine desire. They offer their protagonists' internal ruminations as an invitation for readers to participate in the postcolonial discontent spurred by the incomprehensibility of feminine desire. Rakesh's Satte ruminates on the longings that he imagines Dammo, Shirin, Rajo, and Saroj must have felt. His suspicions about their lovers madden him, possess him, and drive him to destructive ends. Similarly, Jayakanthan's narrator confronts the limits of expressing feminine desire. She wonders what kinds of longings are permissible, whether she can freely explore them, and who is responsible for their existence. Her inability to find satisfying answers leaves her trapped in her home. Through such concerns, Rakesh's and Jayakanthan's stories obscured communal and caste questions by guiding readers through an emotionally agitated interrogation of what the new woman wants.

In the following two stories I explore this interrogation to consider how Rakesh and Jayakanthan used the problem of feminine desire to position male and female characters in new heterosexual paradigms. Rakesh's "Ek Aura Zindagī" (Another life) and Jayakanthan's "Akkiṉip Piravēcam" (Trial by fire) replace the respective communal and caste anxieties of the postindependence Hindi and Tamil contexts with a male unease over trying to understand feminine desire. These stories thus extend the questions about feminine desire that "Ādmī aura Dīvār" and "Nāṉ Jaṉṉalarukē Uṭkārntirukkiṟēṉ" initiate. They elaborate how a generalized sense of postcolonial turmoil could be broached through the disconnects emerging from misaligned heterosexual relations.

No Longer a Feminine Type

Rakesh's "Ek Aura Zindagī" was first published as part of his eponymous collection, in 1961, and then again, in 1963, in the magazine *Naī Kahāniyāṁ*. Written in the third person, the narrative of this short story is focalized through the perspective of Prakash, the protagonist, who has been staying a few days in Khilanmarg, a valley in Kashmir. The plotline is fairly simple: Prakash has divorced his first wife, Bina, and desperately misses their young son, Palash. He is also estranged from his second wife, Nirmala, and has arrived in Khilanmarg after walking out on her. Fortuitously, Prakash meets Bina and Palash, who are vacationing in the mountains. Nothing momentous happens in "Ek Aura Zindagī": Prakash spends a couple of afternoons in Khilanmarg with Palash, contemplates his relationships with Bina and Nirmala, and experiences an ambiguous connection with Bina. At the story's conclusion, Prakash is as alone as he was in the beginning, seemingly unmoved by his interactions with Bina and Palash or the dreary Kashmiri rain and fog.

The changing weather—torrential rain, shifting clouds, dense fog—is almost character-like in the story. Descriptions of its unpredictable, unreadable moods feature prominently, more prominently than any descriptions of Prakash's actions or mental states. The narrative offers these descriptions in lieu of insights into Prakash's desires to give readers a sense of how much Prakash lacks mental clarity and how lonely, fumbling, and depressed he feels.

> The fog slowly grew so dense that no form or color was visible from [Prakash's] balcony. . . . Sitting in his chair, he sometimes felt as if the balcony . . . were some kind of secret province in the skies—sky upon sky above and below, a bottomlessness over which the balcony held authority as a complete and independent world of its own.[68]

The fog hampers Prakash's ability to distinguish between internal and external realities. It maps Prakash's inner state, drawing readers into his ulterior reality. Within this hazy realm, Prakash is enveloped by uncertainty. Does he truly see Bina and Palash, or are they a figment of his inner desire?

> His mind, roaming among clouds of fog, suddenly returned again to the balcony. Many people wandering the streets of Khilanmarg were riding horses—like the extinguishing figures of a faint painting. . . . The tip of the snow-covered mountain on his left emerged from a small [layer of] fog, illuminated by the rays of a hidden sun. A bird drifting in the fog soared before the summit, its wings suddenly golden—but the very next moment it was lost in the mist.
>
> Prakash stood up from his chair, leaned over [the balcony railing] and peered toward the street. Wasn't that voice Palash's?[69]

Prakash's relationships with Bina and Palash are as wavering as his visions of the landscape among the clouds and fog—sometimes present and luminescent, sometimes hidden and lost. Prakash adores his son, yet he has forsaken his paternal responsibilities. By missing Palash's birthdays and maintaining inconsistent contact with Palash, Prakash has become a peripheral figure in his son's life. Bina questions Prakash's right to be in contact with Palash and presses him to forget his past.

Narratively, Palash serves to constantly remind readers of Prakash's failures as a father, husband, and man. His presence discloses Prakash's deep desire for human connection, a desire that is heterosexual at heart. Prakash's deep dissatisfaction and unease with both his wives—Bina, whom he divorced several years before, and Nirmala, from whom he has now run away—prevent him from establishing "another life." His major dilemma is that he doesn't know what kind of woman he wants.

In a flashback that lies at the core of the story, Prakash pits Bina against Nirmala:

> The question arose in his mind afresh: why couldn't he free himself completely from the past? . . . But when he began to imagine starting a new life, he kept coming up against a doubt. . . . How could he say that his second attempt would be successful when his first attempt was not? . . . Whenever he imagined a woman as a future wife, the shadow of his earlier life appeared in her face. Although he hadn't given it clear thought, it seemed to him that he wanted to spend his life with the kind of woman who was completely the opposite of Bina. Bina was extremely arrogant, educated equally to him, earned more than him. She took great pride in her independence and believed that she could confront

> any situation on her own. Physically, too, Bina was quite tall. She was stronger than him. And she spoke openly, as would a man [*mardānā ḍhaṅg*]. Now, Prakash wanted a woman who was dependent on him in every way, whose weaknesses [*kamzorī*] required her to take refuge in a man.
>
> And Nirmala was just such a woman. . . . She was a simple [*sīdhī-sādī*], naive [*māsūm-sī*] girl, who lowered her eyes when she spoke. She was of average education and lived an ordinary life. Prakash unwittingly felt sympathy [*sahānubhūti*] toward her when he saw her. She was twenty-five or twenty-six but looked no more than eighteen or nineteen.[70]

Bina emerges as a type: a new modern woman, whose independence and intellectual and physical superiority threaten Prakash. Nirmala is Bina's foil: a traditional good wife (*satī*) who stirs Prakash's sympathy and hope for a normal, settled life.

Yet the story also undermines the validity of these types, questioning their relevance in the postindependence moment. For example, after their marriage, Prakash soon discovers that Nirmala is crazed, possibly insane:

> She would loosen her hair like a "goddess" and say, "You want to divorce me like you did Bina? Bring a third one into your house? But I'm not Bina. She wasn't a good wife [*satī nārī*]. . . . I am a good wife, I will unsettle this house brick by brick. Come, come, come!
>
> If Prakash tried to placate her, she would say, "Look, stay away from me. Don't touch me. I am a wife. I am a goddess. Do you wish to destroy my wifehood [*satītva*]? Do you wish to defile me? When did I marry you? I'm still a virgin [*kaṃvārī*]. I'm a small child. No man in this world can touch me. I live a divine life. . . . But I won't leave here. You must let me sleep beside you. Am I a widow [*vidhavā*] who should sleep alone? I am an auspicious married woman [*suhāgin*]. Does any married woman sleep alone? I took the sacred vows of wifehood when I circled the fire with you and came to your house.[71]

Nirmala's perverted mobilization of traditional understandings of wifehood is striking. Even as she intentionally embodies prescribed womanhood, she exceeds its boundaries, exposing its horrifying impracticality to meet Prakash's needs as a modern man. Her madness renders the *satī* type literarily excessive and logically impossible, driving Prakash into an alienated mental state: "his mind felt as if free-falling in a dark well. . . . Nothingness surrounded him on all sides. . . . He felt as if dead, suffocated inside."[72]

Bina, too, moves beyond the type of the new woman, contributing to Prakash's sense of isolation. Her desires are illegible. Upon meeting in Khilanmarg, Prakash and Bina share a few momentary glimpses, but, like the impenetrable fog, Bina's inner state remains opaque: "Apart from the reflected sky, it was unclear what emotion lay in Bina's glance."[73] Prakash discovers that Bina and Palash are traveling with another woman, whose relationship to Bina is ambiguous yet also seemingly sordid. When Prakash has a brief interchange with the woman before taking his son for the afternoon, Bina calls after him:

> "Look, I wanted to tell you something . . ." [said Bina].
>
> "Tell me," [Prakash replied].
>
> Bina remained quiet a moment, thinking. Then she said, "Don't tell [Palash] anything that might . . ."
>
> Prakash felt as if something were lacerating his nerves. He lowered his eyes and slowly replied, "No, I won't mention anything like that."[74]

Unspoken, though implied in the ellipses in this passage, is the possibility of Bina's love affair with the strange woman and with other men. Bina sits uncomfortably with the new-woman type. Her masculine physicality and mannerisms, inscrutable gazes and actions, and romantic relationships with other men and possibly women make her unknowable—rather than the predictably Westernized, lecherous, and materialistic new woman of the late-colonial era.

Bina and Prakash's final meeting in Khilanmarg, which brings Bina to inexplicable tears, propels Prakash into deep depression. As the story ends, Prakash drunkenly walks out into the torrential night rain, having gambled away his money:

> Suddenly a new shudder ran through his body. He felt that he was no longer alone on the road. . . . He turned to look. Beside him trotted a wet dog—ears flapping, silent and introspective![75]

Prakash, like the dog, is an outcast who wanders in the pouring rain—aimless, lonely, buried in thought. He is alienated because he desires something different than the socially accepted norms that the good-wife and new-woman types represent. In the fog and rain he searches for a new form of interpersonal relations that remains unrealized, hidden deep within Prakash's subconscious desires. The bad faith that sets Prakash adrift is the result of the wrongs that Prakash feels Bina and Nirmala have committed against him. Both women fail to fulfill the requirements of the types they reference, propelling Prakash into an unknowable abyss.

Questioning the relevance of the good wife and the new woman, Bina and Nirmala represent a departure from the use of feminine types in preindependence Hindi fiction. Earlier, the good wife (*satī*) was a character that evoked sympathy in both protagonists and readers. For example, the eponymous female protagonists in Premchand's *Nirmalā* (1928) and Jainendra Kumar's *Sunītā* (1935) are traditional good wives who return to the socially sanctioned domestic fold, even if they initially deviate from it. Even Premchand's incorrigible Miss Padma and Miss Malti—characters I examined in chapter 2—ultimately evoke readers' understanding. The desires of these new women align with the social types that they portray, suggesting that they are worthy of readerly sympathy and compassion. Rakesh's Bina and Nirmala, by contrast, are almost unrecognizable as types. Their motivations and desires are difficult to identify. For this reason, these characters push readers to move beyond the subjectivities associated with the new-woman and good-wife types. Focalized through Prakash's perspective, the story aligns readers with male confusion about and estrangement from postindependence feminine desire, gesturing toward a new, as yet unsolidified, configuration of heterosexual relations.

Female Maturation

Although Jayakanthan's "Akkiṉip Piravēcam" (Trial by fire) is a very different story, it employs landscape descriptions to develop its characters and explore feminine types in a manner similar to Rakesh's "Ek Aura Zindagī." Published in 1966, the story immediately aroused controversy for depicting the rape of an adolescent Brahmin girl.[76] Responding to his readers' criticisms that he should not have let the female protagonist go unpunished, Jayakanthan extended the story into two novels—*Cila Nēraṅkaḷil Cila Maṉitarkaḷ* (Some times, some people, 1970) and *Kaṅkai Eṅkē Pōkiṟāḷ?* (Where is Ganga going?, 1978). The novels give the young girl a name (Ganga), describe her Brahmin family background, and follow her lifelong journey for retribution. Despite these novelistic attempts to tame the short story's provocative claims, however, "Akkiṉip Piravēcam" remains an unusual portrayal of the postindependence new woman's relationship to sexual desire.

Written in the third person, the story follows the unnamed female protagonist during an evening in which she is raped and then ceremoniously purified by her mother. The narrative is highly cinematic. From a vivid description of a rainbow-colored flock of college women huddled under umbrellas in the pouring rain, it turns to the protagonist—standing alone, younger than the rest, exceptional because of her tattered clothes. Lower-middle-class, naive, and unprotected, she waits to catch the bus home. The narrator portrays her as both virginal and extraordinary: "Standing there, now drenched by rain, her shapely ivory legs turned blue and trembling, her worn blouse and half sari glued to her body, her tiny figure shrunken in the cold—she is poised like a goddess, and one feels like simply carrying her away."[77] As darkness descends and the downpour increases, the narrator describes her innocence and beauty as risks.

A handsome young man stops to offer her a ride, and the girl is drawn to his car: "She stares at the beautiful car, sweeping her eyes over it from the rear all the way to the driver's seat, in astonishment."[78] The young man ushers her inside his vehicle under the pretense of rescuing her from the rain. As he drives her through the city, the girl observes glowing streetlamps, wide streets, tall buildings, and beautiful bungalows. The glamour of these urban surroundings envelopes the young girl, conveying to readers her sense of unbelonging.

Fearfully, the girl soon realizes that the young man has taken her somewhere out of the city. Still, she continues to feel exhilarated by the new things around her—the car's motorized gadgets, plush seats, and blaring radio. She also begins to observe the man:

> He is pretty good looking. Tall, brown clothes tightly clinging to his body. His skin glows in the dim light; she is reminded of the beauty of a magnificent, deadly serpent. Looking at him from behind, she can only see his left eye. It draws light and sparkles. Hair worn cropped, so short that no wind could dishevel it, and longish sideburns that glimmer in the diminishing light. When he looks back through the rearview mirror, she thinks for a moment that it would be nice if that bright face had a thin mustache.[79]

Told from the girl's perspective, this passage charts her sexual attraction to the stranger. Bracketed by the ominous landscape—enveloping darkness, roaring thunder, flashing lightening, torrential rain, and the desolate field in which the car now stands—her attraction for the man is unhindered. The narrative continually moves between portentous descriptions of the environment and the girl's curiosity and desire, countering her physical sensations of arousal with more socially permissible feelings of terror linked to her current vulnerability. Through filmic cutting between the menacing landscape and the girl's observations, the story encourages readers to identify with the girl's artless exhilaration, while simultaneously foreshadowing impending danger.

When the young man climbs into the backseat beside her, tempting her with chocolate and gum, the girl's arousal remains firm: "Refusing to place [the gum] in her hand, he holds it up to her face, places it upon her lips, and lightly brushes it across them. Her head feels on fire and a pleasant burning sensation runs through her body."[80] Even when he assaults her, a trace of this sensation lingers:

> "May I kiss you?" [he asks in English]. She has no idea what to say. Her tongue is lolling. In the cold her face is sweating and her body, trembling. Suddenly, as if the tips of her ears, her cheeks, and her lips were being scorched by fire, she shudders in his arms. "Please, please," she screams as he embraces her with violent passion. Her shrieks grow fainter and fainter and finally cease. Then, as if arbitrating his final verdict, her hands fasten tightly around his neck. Outside . . . The sky is torn apart! Lightning scatters! Sounds of thunder rumble and crackle! Oh! Where has the thunder struck![81]

The alarming weather mirrors the terrible event taking place in the car. The young man overpowers the girl and violates her. Attempting to retain control of her body, the girl clasps her hands around his neck—an action astonishingly close to a reciprocating embrace. This is not to argue that the girl's response is one of roused passion or even resigned acceptance. The brief passage is not detailed enough to suggest either of these readings. Yet the narrator's ambivalent choice of words to describe this fateful moment leaves a space for the girl to retain possession of her sexual desire, the judgment of the stormy skies notwithstanding.

Throughout the story, the young man is portrayed as manipulative, callous, and self-serving. Even when he tries to apologize, he only attests to his degenerate nature:

> He feels regret as he looks at her standing beside him—short, dimly lit by a distant streetlamp, brimming with tears. It occurs

> to him that he has become a lowly slave to his own sense of freedom. "Yes, a slave—a slave to feeling!" he feels in his heart. He says to her [in English], as if in secret, "I'm sorry!" She looks up at his face . . . Oh, that attractive face![82]

As in many of Jayakanthan's stories, the young man's sexual desire is depicted as intrinsic to his masculinity. Masculine desire is the ugly underbelly of urbanized modern urban freedom. This is why the girl must return home to find safety and redemption.

When the girl tells her mother what has happened, her mother beats her with disgust. Suddenly realizing the uselessness of punishing her daughter, the mother pulls her into the bathroom, strips her, and bathes her with buckets of water. She advices her daughter to never tell a soul about the incident, exclaiming: "You're clean now, child. Clean. The water I've poured on you isn't water. Think of it as fire. There are no blemishes upon you now." Then she continues:

> Don't you know the story of Ahalya? They say that she was purified when the dust from Lord Rama's foot touched her. But her mind was never impure. That is why the dust of Rama's foot fell upon her. . . . Take care that your own mind doesn't become impure. . . . Forget what happened as if it were a bad dream.[83]

The mother forces her daughter to undergo the proverbial trial by fire—named after the *agni parīkshā* (test of fire) episode in the ancient epic *Rāmāyaṇa* in which Sita steps into flames to prove her loyalty to her husband Lord Rama. She also compares her daughter to Ahalya, whose ascetic husband turned her to stone after the god Indra disguised himself as her husband to sleep with her. Emphasizing Ahalya's purity of mind, the mother reinforces her daughter's moral fortitude and renews her virginal purity. The girl now moves with savvy through the modern city, careful not to cross paths with luring cars or strange men. She walks with confidence, her eyes shining with the "light of maturity [*vaḷarcci*] and womanhood [*peṇmai*]."[84]

The light in the girl's eyes represents her new knowledge about how to negotiate masculine desire. Yet the light also suggests that the spark of her own sexual desire remains steady within her, although it is now regulated by her newfound wisdom. This horrifying coming-of-age story refashions the goddess type. It marks a significant shift from Pudumaippittan's late colonial-era representations of Ahalya, who becomes paralyzed after her rape. In Pudumaippittan's stories, Ahalya's trauma causes her to retreat into herself and to question her ability ever to be physically intimate with her husband again. She breaks apart heterosexual relations, offering no formula for their reconciliation.[85] Jayakanthan's protagonist, by contrast, transforms the trauma of rape into a revelatory insight about the maturity required to channel feminine desire and navigate patriarchal violence.[86] The girl re-emerges as a woman in the modern world, challenging the debauched new man to become her worthy partner. As in Rakesh's "Ek Aura Zindagī," this story portrays a bad-faith alliance between male and female characters that spurs a provisional realignment of heterosexual relations.

THE UNIVERSALIZATION OF FEMININE DESIRE

In Rakesh's and Jayakanthan's stories, a careful charting of landscape aspired to produce empathetic alliances between readers and protagonists. Descriptions of the intimate spaces surrounding Rakesh's and Jayakanthan's main characters invited readers into their inner lives. Satte's wall, bedroom, and view of the neighboring apartment building; the elderly woman's home, window, and the street; Prakash's contemplation of the clouds and fog from his balcony; and the adolescent girl's observations of the car, weather, and urban cityscape—these environments prompted, and sometimes even replaced, the protagonists' introspections. Rakesh's and Jayakanthan's stories used landscape to plot the misanthropic dimensions of postindependence middle-class interiority. Efforts to forge readers' empathetic connections with protagonists paradoxically generated disconnection with the stories' other characters.

In both cases, this disconnection was fashioned by anxiety about managing feminine desire. Questions surrounding what the postindependence new woman wanted, whether her longings were defensible, and who would be responsible for overseeing her ambitions propelled the actions of *nayī kahānī* and *Eḻuttu* protagonists. Unable to pinpoint the longings of the women around him, Satte violently effaces the wall. Deprived of romantic connection by her family members, the elderly woman escapes into dreamy realities. Unnerved by Bina's and Nirmala's excessive personalities, Prakash drunkenly roams. And pushed to the unspeakable ends of sexual attraction, the girl emerges matured. These stories document how *nayī kahānī* and *Eḻuttu* fiction universalized feminine desire as the preeminent concern of postindependence existence. In place of communal and caste affiliations, this fiction constructed feminine desire as the constitutive intuition for creating empathetic connections with protagonists.

The problematic of feminine desire replaced the varied social and political traumas of decolonization with a shared sense of turmoil around heterosexual relations. It served as a means for worlding the *nayī kahānī* and *Eḻuttu* literary projects, making them intelligible through the lens of general postcolonial discord. In *nayī kahānī* stories, the inscrutability of feminine desire masked the inarticulability of communal division. These stories reformulated an interdiction against crossing communal lines into an incapacity to attain heterosexual companionship. The new woman and the new man were both morally bankrupt, and neither could achieve interpersonal connection. This incapacity shaped literary sentiments of stasis, isolation, and estrangement. In *Eḻuttu* stories the sexualized nature of feminine desire concealed the distinctly Brahminical topography within which it arose. *Eḻuttu* stories refashioned discourses of caste hierarchy into a critique of patriarchal subjugation. Here the new woman was constructed as visionary and the new man as depraved, even corrupt. This gendered imbalance gave expression to a literary sentiment of indignation.

A common interest in feminine desire nonetheless brought these divergent aesthetic frameworks together. Modernist-realist empathies were built on it, joining *nayī kahānī* alienation and *Eḻuttu* indignation within the web of postcolonial disconsolation. Across these two Indian literatures, bad-faith relationships between male and female characters realigned bad-faith communal and caste alliances around precarious new paradigms of heterosexual relations.

be about either of them: "How he wished he had known the girl. . . . Where was she today? What was she thinking?"[41]

Saroj, the new floor of the building, the inscriptions, Harish's letter—these characters, spaces, and objects come together to extend the metaphor of Partition. Among them, the bedroom wall is the most blatant symbol of all:

> Some tenant had put up the wooden partition to divide the large room into two parts. . . . The other side now stored useless things. . . . empty bottles, old gas cylinders, torn burlap sacks, broken chairs, different kinds of baskets, sickles, wooden platters, and a tin tub that had not been used to heat water for years. That room was like a small graveyard where countless things had been buried for who knows how long, their ancient histories gathered up within them.[42]

The inventory in this passage forms a metonymic chain that leads straight to Partition, suggesting that Partition itself must be partitioned off from reality, like the useless items tucked behind the wall. Satte's longings are etched over their concealed histories. At the end, Satte takes a knife to the wall. Exhausted, he then sits back to observe his creation: "Now no indication of Shirin Mumtaz remained, but that deformed eye, more deformed than before, stared back at him through the gaping hole that he had made."[43] Satte's first act of postindependence writing is an unconsciously driven, vexed effacement of Partition that submerges its histories within the cavernous recesses of his mind.

A NEW BRAHMINISM

Rakesh's story illustrates how *nayī kahānī* stories carved Partition onto the interiorities of their protagonists, burying the event beneath a psychic schism. Evocations of love and longing, expressed through male protagonists' preoccupation with feminine desire, now stood in Partition's place. In its very erasure, Partition constructed the *nayī kahānī's* aesthetic scaffolding. It shaped the questions that *nayī kahānī* writers posed in their explorations of the new woman.

In the *Eḻuttu* case, though, representations of the new woman emerged from a different historical dialectic, which took shape in the terms of caste. Due to geographical distance, the trauma of Partition and the communal

CHAPTER 5

The Right to Write

Authorizing Feminine Desire in the Hindi and Tamil Canons

A LANGUAGE OF ENTITLEMENT

By the 1950s the Hindi and Tamil literary spheres had assimilated notions of equality and platonic companionship between men and women, notions that now circulated widely alongside discourses of individual and women's rights. *Nayī kahānī* and *Eḻuttu* writers not only portrayed male and female characters who questioned traditional gender roles but also began to integrate the voices of women writers into their circles in an effort to create a more broadly appealing and comprehensive humanist aesthetic. Few women writers had gained prominence in the Hindi and Tamil literary spheres thus far, but following independence, conditions were more favorable for women who wanted to enter the traditionally male literary scene.

In this transitional context, during which women writers were considered as potential but not yet properly "literary" writers, Mannu Bhandari and R. Chudamani rose to prominence within the *nayī kahānī* and *Eḻuttu* writers' circles, respectively. Remarkably, Bhandari's and Chudamani's short stories from the 1950s and 1960s candidly portray female characters who have as much desire for sexual expression, economic independence, and human equality as their male partners do. Yet, despite introducing characters who challenged the social and sexual mores of their time, Bhandari and Chudamani escaped prevalent criticisms that women writers were too didactic, social reformist, or sentimental, or that they were primarily interested in producing "shock value" or entertainment for popular consumption.[1] Bhandari and Chudamani published in the same elite venues as *nayī kahānī* and *Eḻuttu* male writers did, and they have since been translated and anthologized internationally in volumes of Indian literature and women's writing.[2]

How did Mannu Bhandari and R. Chudamani gain recognition within the largely male-dominated Hindi and Tamil canons, while also depicting feminine desires that had previously been considered "unliterary"? They did so, I argue in this chapter, by using an idiomatically inflected language of entitlement—characterized by terms such as *nyāy*, *adhikār*, and *apanatva* in Hindi and *niyāyam*, *atikāram*, *urimai*, and *kaṭamai* in Tamil—to legitimize their status as writers and to articulate feminine desire using the lenses of Hindi and Tamil literary humanism that were gaining currency at the time. Since the late nineteenth and early twentieth centuries, these common words have designated liberal understandings of individual freedom, rights, and entitlements, and by the 1950s, had become mainstays of international and national political discourse. But these terms of entitlement also describe longer-standing power relations within Hindi and Tamil frameworks of kinship, patronage, and religious community. While these ideas are legally associated with rights and entitlements, they are also embedded in several affective and moral frameworks, ones that can sometimes sustain conflicting conceptualizations of the self. In their fiction Bhandari and Chudamani employed a language of entitlement to express their mastery of literary humanist methods, thereby authorizing themselves to portray female desires, duties, and commitments as fundamentally human in nature. In doing so, Bhandari and Chudamani introduced new understandings of rights and freedoms for women into the Hindi and Tamil canons.

Bhandari and Chudamani developed their individual, idiomatically inflected uses of a language of entitlement during a period of heightened constitutional and public debate over the rights of women and minorities. The pressing question was whether women's rights should be adjudicated on the liberal basis of women's identity as individuals who bear self-interest, or on the nonliberal basis of women's affiliations to the specific religious communities toward which they bear obligation.[3] In this context Bhandari's and Chudamani's uses of a language of entitlement were unique because they combined a liberal narrative of women's self-ownership with a nonliberal narrative of women's self-surrender to communities of kinship. The incorporation of these narratives allowed Bhandari and Chudamani to consider women's rights from within, rather than outside, the sphere of the family and community. In other words, Bhandari's and Chudamani's uses of a language of entitlement enabled them to reconcile an individual-rights perspective with one based on community rights. At a time when feminist politics were dismissed as antagonistic to national integration and women's writings were considered substandard to so-called literary writing, Bhandari and Chudamani brought a discourse of women's freedoms and entitlements to bear on the Hindi and Tamil canons, expanding the scope of literary humanism to allow room for feminine desire.

This chapter begins with an overview of women's writing in colonial India, contending that Bhandari's and Chudamani's works enabled new perspectives on women's rights to emerge within the postindependence literary sphere. I turn next to their short stories, through which I describe how Bhandari and Chudamani wield a language of entitlement to express feminine desire in literature. Ultimately, I suggest that Bhandari's and Chudamani's writings move us beyond criticisms of postindependence women's writing that claim authors turned away from feminist struggles to focus more apolitically on domestic concerns and internal conflicts of the self.[4] By engaging with women's rights and freedoms in literary terms, Bhandari and Chudamani enabled these topics to enter the realm of high literature for the first time, inaugurating a new literary humanist tradition of women's writing across the Hindi and Tamil literary spheres. At the same time, the distinct literary norms to which these writers responded disclose how women's writing was regionally variable and could never be reduced to a singular category, such as "Third World" or "postcolonial" women's writing.[5] Through their uses of a language of entitlement, Bhandari and Chudamani worlded Hindi and Tamil women's writing, making it intelligible as both literary and feminist.

WOMEN'S WRITING IN INDIA

The first phase of women's writing in India, between the 1850s and the 1910s, arose during social-reform debates surrounding the women's question. Issues such as widow immolation, widow remarriage, child marriage, women's health, and women's education became key cultural battlegrounds on which Indian nationalists rallied against colonial rule.[6] The rise of women's writing fueled this nationalist activism by constructing images of Indian women and expectations for their behavior. This writing mainly consisted of literature that was *strī upyogī* (useful for women)—namely, advice columns and didactic fiction written by men for women's self-improvement—and a handful of autobiographical accounts by women.[7]

The second phase, what Francesca Orsini calls the "radical-critical phase" of women's writing, occurred when women writers and editors entered into the public sphere from the 1920s through the 1940s.[8] For the first time, women publicly voiced their views on social and family norms and nationalist politics in newspapers and popular magazines, articulating their "right to feel"—that is, women's right to express their emotions and needs.[9] As a result, women's writing played a crucial role in what Mrinalini Sinha has shown to be the "rhetorical invention of new subject positions for women," which later facilitated the emergence of the Indian's women's movement and its liberal demand for women's rights.[10] The dovetailing of women's articulations of their "right to feel" with women's activism was most clearly exemplified by key leaders of the Indian women's movement, such as Rameshwari Nehru and Sarojini Naidu, who developed widely recognized careers as editors and writers.[11]

While this period saw an immense increase in the number of women writers, as well as the growth of a vibrant publishing market for women's magazines, few women were considered to be "literary"—as opposed to social-reformist, feminist, political, entertainment-oriented, or simply "women" writers. In the Hindi and Tamil literary spheres, for example, only two notable writers come to mind: Hindi writer Mahadevi Varma and Tamil writer Vai. Mu. Kothanayaki Ammal. Early in her career, Varma's poetry was critiqued for being too sexualized and romantic. It was only in the late 1930s, when she took on editorship of the influential Hindi magazine *Cāṅd*, that she began to establish a place among Hindi literary greats.[12] The literary reception of Kothanayaki Ammal, however, has been lukewarm, and her social-reformist activism is more highly regarded than her prolific fiction writing and editorship of the Tamil women's magazine *Jagaṉmōhiṉi*.[13]

Orsini argues that the rise of literary women's writing resulted from the taming of its radical-critical edge, a development marked explicitly by Mahadevi Varma's editorship of *Cāṅd* from 1935 to 1938.[14] In her efforts to appeal to a more literary readership, Varma censored overtly political or social-reformist texts. She emphasized fiction and poetry and replaced challenges to social norms with an ideology of womanly *maryādā*—which, in Varma's case, signaled *savarṇa* (caste Hindu), middle-class notions of women's correct behavior, decorum, and honor within the family and community. For Varma, literature was not meant to convey society's problems and possible solutions but rather to capture the experiences, insights, and transformations of the individual.[15]

But this conservative shift in women's writing must be viewed as part of a broader schism between "literary" and "political" camps that occurred in the 1930s Hindi and Tamil spheres. In both cases—as I described in previous chapters—younger generations of "high modernist" writers, deeply embedded in international discussions on the function of literature, began to critique the social-reformist tones and overtly political messages of dominant literary trends. Although these Hindi and Tamil writers were responding to very different cultural and sociopolitical contexts, their views on the purpose of literature coincided with Varma's position on women's literature: they all elevated "literary" messages that focused on linguistic innovation and psychological introspection above "political" ones that focused on social change and nationalist progress.[16] By defining themes of womanly *maryādā* and individual experience as "literary," the home and the family became the central subjects of high literature after the late 1930s.[17] Thus, Orsini's observation that women's journals turned to domestic concerns after Independence pertains not only to women's writing but also to postindependence high literature in general.[18]

Not until the postindependence period, in the wake of this turn to the literary, did women writers like Bhandari and Chudamani begin to be placed on a literary par with men.[19] Only two other Hindi women writers, Krishna Sobti and Usha Priyamvada, achieved this status during the 1950s and 1960s.[20] Although all three writers have been described as part of the canonical Nayī Kahānī Movement, only Bhandari participated in the otherwise all-male discussions that defined the movement's characteristic literary techniques and philosophical outlook. Similarly, Chudamani's only "literary" female contemporary in the early postindependence moment was Rajam Krishnan. Literary critics have been less laudatory of Krishnan's writing, arguing that it lacks sophistication and is overtly polemical.[21] Conversely, Chudamani has consistently been viewed as part of the Tamil literary canon. She was, for instance, the only woman writer to have her work published or reviewed in the journal *Eḻuttu*, which, as I showed in chapter 3, served as a key venue for cultivating an aesthetic sensibility that still shapes Tamil understandings of literariness.

Considering the argument that literariness became limited to domestic and personal concerns in postindependence India, I contend that Bhandari and Chudamani's articulations of feminine desire within the sphere of the literary need to be recognized as considerable achievements.[22] These women writers enabled a discourse of women's rights and entitlements to be not just compatible, but also coterminous, with the norms and conventions of high literature of the time. Bhandari and Chudamani authorized the representation of feminine desires that had previously been considered too polemically charged to be literary, bringing a tradition of female writing concerned with women's freedom and the right to feel into the male-centric Hindi and Tamil canons. In doing so, they also staked a claim to the sphere of the literary, whereby women writers' writing could be viewed on equal terms with other literary writing.

THE CLAIM TO AUTHORSHIP

Nayī kahānī and *Eḻuttu* writers successfully controlled how literary value was defined—as I demonstrated in chapter 3—because they wrote prolifically about what did and did not make short stories literary. Although Bhandari and Chudamani did not talk or write about the process of writing or produce literary criticism like their male contemporaries, they were nonetheless able to claim an authorial position within the Hindi and Tamil canons through their fiction.[23] In the exemplary stories to which I turn here, Bhandari's and Chudamani's protagonists explore contemporary understandings of literariness and demonstrate their mastery of the short story using a language of entitlement that emerges from a focus on justice and injustice (*nyāy* and *anyāy* in Hindi; *niyāyam* and *aniyāyam* in Tamil). These stories explore the meaning of "just" representation—that is, representation that is true to life, as well as artful, at least according to the norms and conventions of Hindi and Tamil high literature. In doing this, the protagonists—and, by extension, Bhandari and Chudamani themselves—assert the right to write, to exist as respected authors within their fields. These otherwise ordinary stories are remarkable because they illustrate how Bhandari and Chudamani laid the necessary groundwork that allowed them to entitle their female characters to express feminine desire in their other stories. As I show in the following section, the right to write also implies the right to portray feminine desire in a just, truthful, and artful manner.

Life Is the Story, the Story Life

Mannu Bhandari's "Paṇḍit Gajādhar Śāstrī" (1957), written in the first person, narrates the story of a young man, a writer, who is vacationing alone at a hotel near the beach in Puri (a city outside the Hindi-speaking region). As the story opens, the unnamed narrator meets his neighbor, Pandit Gajadhar Sastri, who is a *paṇḍit*, or scholar, of Hindi literature and short story writer like himself. But each time the two men meet, the pandit dismisses the narrator's writerly talent and talks incessantly. Through short, repeated phrases such as "defeated in the end (*ākhir hār kar*) . . . ," the narrator articulates that he can hardly get in a word edgewise.[24] The pandit constantly cuts off the narrator's attempts to converse by recounting his own successes as a Hindi short story writer and his theories about literature.

Despite the pandit's one-sided speech, the narrator manages to discredit the pandit's expertise through a private dialogue with the reader. He often inserts his own thoughts parenthetically within the pandit's words. For example, as the pandit is lecturing to the narrator about what makes a good writer, the narrator interjects the pandit's speech in an aside to the reader. The pandit says (and the narrator intervenes), "Undoubtedly, my ideas, my emotions, my literature (by which he means a single story), and my life are synonyms."[25] Such asides make readers privy to the skepticism the narrator feels each time the pandit asks him a question without letting him answer or holds forth about his own accomplishments.

Several times in the story, the pandit expounds on his main writing philosophy to the narrator—namely, that writing and life are inseparable: "Simply understand that for me life itself is for the story, the story itself is for life; life itself is the story, the story itself is life [*jīvan hī kahānī hai, kahānī hī jīvan hai*]."[26] As the narrator observes the pandit further, he underscores the enigma of this chiastic aphorism: neither does life fit within the bounds of the story nor does the story exactly match up with life. This is because, even as the pandit insists that he writes according to this philosophy, the narrator reveals the pandit's failure either to represent himself truthfully or to write successfully. In one scene the narrator finds the pandit standing on the beach, observing a young woman splashing in the water. The pandit claims to watch her so that he may find new material for a story, but in the eyes of the narrator, the pandit is ogling her: "[The pandit] was savoring the sight of her with large desirous eyes."[27] In another scene the pandit lectures to the narrator that a true writer must have compassion for thieves because of their dire straits. But, the very next day, the pandit ruthlessly beats the servant boy clearing away dishes in his room, whom he mistakes for a thief.[28]

The narrator thus shows the impossibility of any easy identification between writing and life. Nevertheless, the narrator himself writes his experience truthfully in the form of the story of his interaction with the pandit—to which we, as readers, have now been given access. The narrator ends the story by saying, "Unwittingly indeed, he [the pandit] has become the primary character of my story. He was a great soul—it simply wouldn't have been just [*pūrā nyāy bhī nahīṃ hotā*] not to give him the position of main character!"[29] If there is any correlation between writing and life—if indeed life is the story and the story is the life—it exists in the narrator's clever rehabilitation of the pandit's skewed philosophical expositions by showing the pandit's true character. This rehabilitation is meaningful insofar as it serves as the creative impetus of the story, providing the means through which the narrator brings the writerly project to fruition, thereby entitling himself to write fiction.

Although Bhandari's language of entitlement takes most forceful shape in this conclusion, it also operates subtly throughout the story, whenever the narrator engages with the pandit's writerly vision. For example, while discussing the elements of language, style, and plot, the pandit describes a new short story he is writing, and the narrator takes his comments to heart:

> I said with a start, "But isn't the appearance of a sermon in a story an obstacle to its essential quality?" [The pandit] began cackling with laughter, as if I'd asked a hugely foolish thing. When his laughter subsided somewhat, he said, "From your questions, it appears that you have a lack of practice. . . . You know the power of literalness, irony, and symbolism in language, don't you? . . . Now look, you yourself have become a plot in my short story. . . . You see, I'm in the habit of always speaking the truth. Without it, we haven't even come close to being literary. . . . I can't give you the position of main character in my story, but yes, I can portray you well as a secondary character. You could successfully be presented in the form of a short story writer who hardly knows the basics of language and who is dying to be a writer. When he doesn't receive praise for his works, he turns away from his readers and finds them at fault, but he doesn't see his own fault. This is the fundamental matter." Then he gave a snicker and burst out laughing. I, too, laughed ashamedly, concurring.[30]

In moments like this, the narrator considers the pandit's expositions on writing seriously, going so far as to doubt his knowledge of short story writing in the process of entertaining the pandit's ideas (the exact ideas he will bring to fruition in the conclusion). In this scenario writerly entitlement is posed as a question that needs exploring. The narrator's humility in the face of the pandit's arrogance, self-doubt in comparison to the pandit's self-assurance, and thoughtful responses in contrast to the pandit's blathering garrulousness undermine the pandit's authority. These wavering, self-reflexive reactions are how Bhandari's language of entitlement presents readers with a "truer" picture of what constitutes literary merit, earning the narrator the right to write.

This idiom of self-doubt—an idiom of *hār*, or defeat, as it might be called—permeates many of Bhandari's stories.[31] It appears in Bhandari's very first short story "Maiṃ Hār Gaī" (I lost), published in the journal *Kahānī* in 1955, and persists throughout her fiction. The protagonist of "Maiṃ Hār Gaī," a woman writer herself, attempts to control the wayward natures of her characters and is ultimately defeated by their willful personalities. In a similar gesture to the narrator's interactions with the pandit, she chooses to relinquish the narrative to her characters. At the same time, Bhandari herself establishes her skillful hand as a storyteller by truthfully recounting the writing process. In other stories, such as "Yahī Sac Hai" (This is the truth), which I examine below, Bhandari uses the idiom of *hār* to characterize her protagonists' incapacity to act in the world. In each case Bhandari's protagonists cannot realize their will and give in to their circumstances, while Bhandari herself successfully attains authorship and often portrays feminine desires that are customarily unsanctioned to appear within the sphere of high literature.

Bhandari's idiom of *hār* made her language of entitlement comprehensible within the philosophy of the Nayī Kahānī Movement. This idiom is perfectly legible in the terms of the ambivalence, loss, disconnection, and moral disintegration that *nayī kahānī* writers sought to convey from the new nation's capital as they made sense of what modern India would look like. Bhandari's idiom of *hār* resonates with the movement's use of the short story to portray individuals' "unnamed restlessness of the mind," their "search for new relationships," and their "internal struggles and conflicts of the mind" that arose during postindependence transition and turmoil.[32] The self-deprecation through which the narrator of "Paṇḍit Gajādhar Śāstrī" assumes authorship fits within the *nayī kahānī* worldview that characterized the search for the individual's sense of self as a fundamentally aesthetic enterprise. By articulating writerly entitlement in the idiom of *hār*, Bhandari earned a place in the male-dominated Nayī Kahānī Movement, which produced authoritative standards for high literature in the 1950s and 1960s Hindi literary sphere.

The Proper Subject of Fiction

Chudamani's short story "Katai Poruḷ" (The content of fiction, 1965) shares concerns with Bhandari's "Paṇḍit Gajādhar Śāstrī"—namely, what it means to be a good writer and what comprises the proper subject of fiction. Yet, although Chudamani's story, like Bhandari's, uses a language of entitlement to underscore the literary value of truthful representation, it does so in a different idiom—an idiom of *cīṟṟam*, meaning wrath or rage. Written in the third person, the narrative of "Katai Poruḷ" focuses on emotional life of the protagonist Thyagarajan. Thyagarajan is not a writer, but he learns what writing means through his friend Patanjali. The story begins as Thyagarajan grumbles to himself, "Does being a writer mean one can write whatever he feels like?"[33] He has just opened the latest issue of a literary magazine to find that Patanjali has written a story about his beloved brother's death. Thyagarajan seethes with anger that Patanjali, who had consoled him when he lost his brother, should now so publicly display Thyagarajan's profound sadness and loss:

> Thyagarajan's body shook with anger [*kōpam*]. . . . Yes, the story was about him. The Vaisnava Brahmin lines on his forehead marked in the center by vermillion, his tendency to screw up his forehead, each description from top to bottom was of him. . . . With what unsympathetic selfishness [Patanjali] had detailed as fiction the truth of his brother's death! Who could be so unjust [*aniyāyam*]?[34]

He thinks further: "What else was this but treachery? What kind of morality [*muṟai*] uses an intimate friend's profound sadness, his sacred inner feelings, as content for a story [*katai poruḷ*]?"[35] For Thyagarajan, Patanjali's realistic descriptions of his appearance and emotions are unjust and immoral. Thyagarajan immediately sets off, boiling with rage (*cīṟṟam*), to confront his callous friend about this exploitation.[36]

En route, Thyagarajan is stopped by a neighbor, who excitedly tells him the newest neighborhood gossip: Patanjali's wife has left him for a younger man! Thyagarajan ignores the neighbor—he cannot contain his anger—and marches off to see his writer friend anyway. He finds Patanjali distraught, lying on the floor in the dark, and looking similarly to how he himself had felt during his own brother's death. But even as he recognizes, and can even sympathize with, Patanjali's loss, Thyagarajan's rage keeps him from embracing and consoling his friend. He walks away without a word, wondering whether the writer, who had assumed that it was his right (*taṉ urimai poruḷāka eṭuttu*) to use others' feelings to create fiction, finally understands the deeply private sadness of loss.[37]

A month passes. The two men do not meet. One day, Thyagarajan opens a new issue of the literary magazine to find that Patanjali has published his own experience—a writer's loss of his young wife—in all its veracity! Thyagarajan wonders: "Are his own sadness and insult—are even these simply materials for stories for Patanjali?"[38] At first, Thyagarajan feels Patanjali will do anything to write a compelling story. Yet he then concludes in a complete reversal of thought:

> Was he [Patanjali] stone hearted? Or . . . ?
>
> Or was he a true writer, for whom writing was the sole means by which he could wholeheartedly and without guile express sympathy, sadness, and other emotions and receive consolation [from others]?[39]

The wrath that has driven Thyagarajan throughout the story culminates in an epiphanic understanding of what makes a true writer and how the necessity to write connects a writer to others. A true writer is one for whom writing is the only means by which he can fully and truthfully express emotional experience to others, thereby finding consolation and establishing human connection. His realization validates the short story Patanjali has written about him and enables him to understand the writer's craft. Thyagarajan can now see the justness and morality that has compelled Patanjali to chronicle their private emotional lives. The result is the short story "Katai Poruḷ," a window through which readers can learn what comprises the proper content of fiction. Thyagarajan's recognition of Patanjali's writerly obligation arises out of his overcoming of deep anger (*cīṟṟam*)—an anger that shakes his body, screws up his forehead, and brings tears to his eyes. He now views Patanjali as a writer, not just a friend, and accords him a position of authorship.

The anger through which Thyagarajan questions Patanjali's right to write belongs to a more general idiomatic style in Chudamani's writing. Particularly in her earlier stories, her characters their express moral outrage through intense bodily reactions. These outbursts escalate towards a catharsis that is both emotionally and ethically charged. For example, in "Cītaiyait Teriyumā?" (Don't you know Sita?), Chudamani's protagonist Nalayini rages against her philandering husband, even threatening suicide.[40] Nalayini's anger leads her to a moment of self-reckoning, in which she realizes that she is enabling her husband by staying with him, that her moral duty is to leave him. *Cīṟṟam* helps to express the injustice of Nalayini's situation and to rationalize the bold course of action she resolves to take. Similarly, in "Katai Poruḷ," Thyagarajan's *cīṟṟam* facilitates a moral inquiry into the proper subject of fiction writing, ultimately legitimizing life experience as the true writer's raw material. Chudamani seemingly published no fiction other than "Katai Poruḷ"—and she authored only one brief response to readers—in which she explored the question of authorship. For this reason,

I view "Katai Poruḷ" as significant not only because it provides insight into how Chudamani viewed the task of the writer but also because it interrogates the writerly project using the same language of entitlement inflected in the same idiom of *cīṟṟam* as her other stories that explore women's rights, freedoms, and entitlements. I examine one such story, "Maṉitaṉāy Māṟi" (Becoming human), below.

Not surprisingly, Chudamani's idiom of *cīṟṟam* speaks to the high literary humanism of the *Eḻuttu* writers that I have discussed in earlier chapters. As part of their literary endeavor to emphasize the existential human predicament (*maṉita tollai nilai*) above Tamil linguistic and ethnolinguistic nationalism, these writers insisted that good literature should evoke *uṇarcci*—feeling, emotion, or sentiment—in readers. As C. S. Chellappa, editor of the magazine *Eḻuttu*, notes: "The emotion that human life evokes . . . is appropriate to and one with experience [*aṉpavam*]. This unity of emotion and experience is . . . the very means through which an artistic creation impacts a reader, and the way that it should impact a reader, too."[41] Chudamani's idiom of *cīṟṟam* and the Brahminical settings in which it unfolds should be viewed as part of this broader literary humanist aesthetic, which valorized the ability of literature to incite an emotional response and human connection within readers. This is how Chudamani was able to assume a respected position of authorship within the postindependence high Tamil literary sphere.

FEMININE DESIRE IS HUMAN DESIRE

Through the language of entitlement, the male characters in "Paṇḍit Gajādhar Śāstrī" and "Katai Poruḷ" earn the right to write by demonstrating their mastery of "true" writing. These characters actualize their desire for authorship through an understanding of human nature. For this reason, although these stories do not address women's authorship directly, I view them as part of the more general claim that Bhandari and Chudamani make, which is that feminine desire—writerly or otherwise—is human desire. In the following two stories, Bhandari and Chudamani articulate this claim explicitly by using the language of entitlement to demand womanly rights and freedoms for their female characters.

The Truth about Feminine Desire

Mannu Bhandari's short story "Yahī Sac Hai" (This is the truth) is a series of diary entries in the first-person voice of Deepa, a young woman living alone in the provincial North Indian city of Kanpur while she completes her postgraduate degree.[42] As the story opens, Deepa is waiting for a visit from Sanjay, her lover. She is irritated because he is late, being insensitive to the time she needs to write her thesis. Deepa is also anxious to tell Sanjay about an upcoming job interview in Calcutta. When Sanjay finally arrives, and the fragrance of the *rajnīgandhā* flowers he customarily brings takes hold of her, Deepa's anger melts away into caresses. As the story progresses, however, we learn that Deepa's love and longing for Sanjay are not as permanent as they seem. Indeed, the "truth" that Deepa comes to understand is one of vacillation, of her feelings' ability to suddenly shift between Sanjay and her former boyfriend, Nishith, whom she meets again during her Calcutta interview.

Deepa's narrative explicates truth through a language of entitlement. Specifically, it develops the meaning of truth through the authority and rights Deepa possesses over Sanjay and Nishith—and they, over her. Truth and entitlement are interlocking terms that constitute Deepa's selfhood. For example, when Deepa tells Sanjay about her upcoming trip to Calcutta, she is delighted he feels happy for her and is willing to transfer to Calcutta if she gets the job. At the same time, she worries that he suspects she still has feelings for Nishith, who lives there now. So, she quietly appeals to Sanjay in her heart, telling him that he is her only love and the center of all her future plans:

> Sanjay thinks that I still have a soft spot in my heart for [Nishith]. Chi! I hate [Nishith]. . . . Sanjay, think about this: if such a thing were the case, would I have surrendered myself [*ātmasamarpaṇ karna*] like this to you, to your every proper, and improper, gesture? Would I have let myself dissolve in your kisses and embraces? You know that no woman gives someone all these entitlements [*adhikār*] before marriage. But I've given them. Isn't it only because I love you, I love you very, very much? Have faith, Sanjay, that our love is the truth [*sac*]. My love for Nishith was simply a fraud, a confusion, a lie.[43]

In a time and place where women are prohibited from meeting with men outside their families, Deepa entitles Sanjay to treat her as only a husband should. She does this by surrendering herself to him (literally, handing her soul/self over to him) in a physically intimate way. Her willingness to go against the social norms of womanly propriety convinces her that Sanjay is the man she desires. Nishith was no more than a foolish and painful mistake.

Once in Calcutta, however, Deepa finds herself drawn toward Nishith, whom she runs into at a coffee house on the evening of her arrival. Nishith assists Deepa in securing her new job, although he never mentions their past or why he abandoned her. Deepa accepts Nishith's offer to contact some influential people in her field, even if hesitantly, realizing: "I had become quite hopeful [about getting the job] after [Nishith's] daylong efforts. How necessary it was for me to get this job, if I did, how pleased Sanjay would be, how happily we would spend the beginning of our married life!"[44] Deepa first justifies her interactions with Nishith as time spent toward achieving her own goals.

Things quickly change after Deepa has a successful interview. She and Nishith make plans to go out to celebrate and, again, the question of entitlement begins to trouble Deepa:

> I remembered, Nishith really likes the color blue, and I put on a blue sari, of course. I got dressed eagerly and meticulously. And repeatedly I stopped myself—all of this was happening to please whom? Wasn't this absolute madness?
>
> On the stairs Nishith said with a smile: "You look beautiful in that sari." My face became flushed; my temples reddened. Truly, I wasn't prepared for this statement. . . . I wasn't at all in the habit of hearing such things. Sanjay never noticed my clothes, nor did he talk this way, even though he had every right [*adhikār*] to. And [Nishith] said such things without any right? . . .
>
> But I don't know why, I couldn't get angry with him; rather I felt a delightful thrill [*pulakamaya siharan*]. . . . My heart, thirsting to hear such a comment, felt washed over by pleasure [*ras se nahā jānā*]. But why did Nishith say such a thing? What right did he have?
>
> Did he really have no right? . . . None?[45]

The same shivers Deepa felt at Sanjay's touch now arise with Nishith's words, and she begins to wonder whether Nishith has the right to notice and say things that she wishes Sanjay would say. In Kanpur Deepa had entitled Sanjay to be intimate with her based on the pleasure she felt from his caresses and flowers, as well as her excitement about their future plans together. Now, in Calcutta, she slowly gives Nishith these same entitlements to intimacy, as he becomes increasingly involved in her career plans, and she, in turn, grows more passionate about him. Soon, her feelings toward Nishith become true—true as Deepa's love for Sanjay was earlier. By the end of her Calcutta trip, Deepa revokes Sanjay's rights to intimacy and places them in Nishith's hands. She surrenders herself fully to Nishith, wanting nothing less than the commitment of marriage: "I glanced at him full of deep submission, compassion, and imploring, as if saying, why don't you tell me, Nishith, that you still love me, that you want me by your side always, that you want to . . . marry me. Despite all that happened, maybe I still love you—not maybe, I truly love you."[46] As Thomas de Bruijn notes, scenes like this from "Yahī Sac Hai" evoke the medieval poetic trope of the *virahiṇī*, "the woman waiting for her husband or lover who is far from home," which is used to "symbolize the longing for reunion with the divine" and which has a "strong connotation of unfulfilled love and sexual desire."[47] This reference to long-standing canonical literary representations of sexual desire situates Deepa's longing within an already familiar idiom of surrender, or *hār*, while also expressing entitlement. Deepa's pining for Nishith evokes a submissive desire for a reunion with the divine, as well as a liberal sense of self-ownership and mutual reciprocity between lovers.

On her last day in Calcutta, Deepa finally receives the reciprocation she yearns for. Nishith turns up at the station, momentarily clasping her hand as her Kanpur-bound train departs. Surprised and elated, Deepa silently screams:

> I understand everything, Nishith, I understand everything! This momentary touch has conveyed everything you couldn't during these past four days. Believe me, if you are mine, then I, too, am yours, yours alone. . . . I feel that it is this touch, this happiness, this moment that is the truth, all the rest was a lie; an unsuccessful attempt to forget myself, deceive myself, trick myself.[48]

This feeling of possessing Nishith and being possessed by him is integral to the way Bhandari's language of entitlement emerges. As soon as Deepa returns to Kanpur, she writes Nishith, recounting that she had been angry and hurt when he abandoned her several years ago, but the way he treated her as his own during her recent visit drew her to him again. She tells her readers: "As soon as I saw him, it was as if all my anger melted away. Being possessed this way, how could my anger possibly remain?"[49] The word Bhandari uses, which I have here translated as "being possessed," is *apanatva*—a word that signifies ownership, of being "one's own"—and through it Deepa expresses the intimate, even family-like, manner in which Nishith behaved with her in Calcutta. Deepa sees this treatment as the possessiveness that exists between partners, and she accepts it in a gesture of complete surrender. *Apanatva,* the feeling of possessing and being possessed by one's lover, goes hand in hand with the *adhikār*—or entitlement to intimacy—that she gives him and seeks in return.

This sense of *apanatva* that Deepa reads into Nishith's treatment of her is more than a symptom of her desire for Nishith: Nishith's ownership of Deepa is tantamount to her ownership of her own self. Day after day, Deepa awaits Nishith's response, pining for the postman's delivery. Unable to bear the waiting, she wanders the streets, thinking to herself: "Where should I go? I seemed to have lost my way, lost my destination. I myself didn't know where I should end up. Nevertheless, I wandered aimlessly. But how long could I roam this way? Defeated [*hār kar*], I turned back."[50] Without Nishith's recognition of their shared entitlements and possession of each other, Deepa is confused and loses her self-assurance. She finds herself directionless and thwarted, uncertain of her desires and life goals.

In his long-awaited reply, Nishith does not acknowledge his feeling of possession over or right to be intimate with Deepa. But Deepa has no time to react. Just as she finishes reading Nishith's letter, she sees Sanjay at her door with a fresh bouquet of flowers. Overcome by joy, Deepa suddenly realizes another truth: along with physical intimacy, she also needs emotional stability and support, something only Sanjay provides. She thus comes back to the "truth" of Sanjay:

> I couldn't speak. I simply clasped my arms around him tightly, more tightly. The scent of the *rajnīgandhā* flowers slowly washed over me. Just then I felt Sanjay's lower lip brush my forehead, and it seemed to me that this touch, this happiness, this moment, this is the truth [*satya*], all of that was a lie, it was false, it was a confusion.[51]

In this final moment of the story, Deepa professes her loyalty to Sanjay—despite everything, it is he who fulfills her after all. Even though Deepa has had passionate feelings for and premarital physical relationships with more than one man, through these experiences she learns to love, respect, and feel commitment toward the one man she will marry. In such a reading, "truth" is the truth of the conjugal bond, which Deepa affirms wholeheartedly. Deepa surrenders her unpredictable and continually changing feminine desires for a community-approved, stable, and mature married life. From the perspective of women's freedom and equality, Deepa's return to Sanjay seems like the defeat of feminine desire because, at every turn in the story, Deepa's desire for physical intimacy is matched by an equally intense desire for conjugal allegiance and the broader structure of the extended family of which it is necessarily a part. Deepa repeatedly intimates that Sanjay provides her with the support her brother, sister-in-law, and father would have given her if they had been present, alluding to the extended family in relation to which she understands her relationship with Sanjay.[52] In light of the contemporary debates on marriage, family, and community in the political and cultural spheres, I read Bhandari's meditation on Deepa's vacillation as an exploration of the extent to which feminine desire can be accommodated within a communitarian family model.[53]

Directing our attention to Bhandari's use of a language of entitlement, however, allows us to read otherwise. By considering her desires in the terms of *adhikār* (rights and entitlements) and *apanatva* (ownership and possession), Deepa pushes the boundaries of what constitutes a normative heterosexual relationship. Her language of entitlement allows her to articulate and claim her womanly right to experience multiple loves, which are situationally specific and profoundly constitutive of Deepa's selfhood. In those moments when Deepa feels paralyzed by her desire, she claims possession of her self-interests by entitling Sanjay or Nishith to them. Even as the outcome of Deepa's actions conforms with a worldview that valorizes women's self-sacrifice and "romanticiz[es] the sentiments of the extended family," and in which it is men who exercise rights over female bodies, it does not negate Deepa's ownership of her feminine desire.[54]

Bhandari herself commented on the radicalness of her portrayal of Deepa, even in 2007: "Now, a woman being torn between two men is an extremely taboo [*gopanīya*] topic in our society. Taboo and also prohibited in a way, so in order to illuminate [Deepa's] internal conflict, it was necessary to take recourse to the diary form."[55] Popular and critical reception of "Yahī Sac Hai" confirms that this literary strategy was overwhelmingly successful. In a 1978 essay, for instance, Rajendra Yadav—whose work I have discussed at length in earlier chapters—interpreted Deepa's expression of feminine desire in the terms of the Nayī Kahānī Movement's project to portray the individual's inner turmoil in the postindependence moment:

> When I expressed another type of interpretation of Mannu's story "Yahī Sac Hai"—that it wasn't a story about love and emotional contradiction or a girl who accepts two lovers; that it was a story of the fragmented mentality of the 1950s–1960s, when the Indian mind perceived itself as divided in two mental states at the same time, on one side was her past (the story's first lover) who still today remained true to her, and on the

> other side was her present; both were true to her and she had to choose one—at that time Mannu said this interpretation was "a long shot" and made fun of me. But to me my interpretation seems true even today.[56]

Here, Yadav reframes Deepa's novel understandings of feminine choice and desire in the more universal terms of individuals' conflicted affiliations to the past and the present. His comments offer just one example of how Bhandari's work has been understood through a canonical Hindi lens, while also expanding what could be expressed within it. "Yahī Sac Hai" broadens expression by, at every instance, dually inflecting the meanings of *adhikār* and *apanatva* with, on one hand, the affective ties of community relations of kinship and, on the other, liberal self-ownership. The two meanings cannot be parsed. Precisely when Sanjay and Nishith express kinship-like affection toward Deepa, offering emotional, financial, or career support, her other truth—self-affirming, sexual desire—is most intensely aroused.

The novelty of Deepa's expressions of feminine desire is not that they challenge the sexual mores of their time, but rather that they do so on literary terms. In other words, the idiom of *hār* enables Bhandari's portrayal to operate on the level of realism—wherein Deepa's expressions of sexual desire appear contentious, transgressive, and liberal, at least in the context of existing social norms—as well as the level of metaphor—in which these expressions craft a *nayī kahānī* literary aesthetic defined by the post-independence struggle to make sense of the tensions between past and present, tradition and modernity. Accomplishing this rhetorical simultaneity is what allows Deepa's expressions of feminine desire to substantiate a narrative of women's self-interest (the story read as realism) and a narrative of women's self-sacrifice (the story read as metaphor), folding these narratives into each other in inseparable ways.

Feminine Desire Becomes Human

While the premise of R. Chudamani's story "Ma<u>n</u>ita<u>n</u>āy Mā<u>r</u>i" (Becoming human), published in 1964, diverges from Bhandari's "Yahī Sac Hai," the two stories share a literary concern with the entitlements men and women possess over one another.[57] Putting the two stories in conversation enables us to track the broader formation of a language of entitlement that these women writers employ. "Ma<u>n</u>ita<u>n</u>āy Mā<u>r</u>i" problematizes the entitlements that a husband has over his wife, suggesting that some other type of husband-wife relationship might be possible: "Vanita worked outside the home to help her parents; she also did the housework for her husband's sake. But his sense of entitlement [*urimai*] and selfhood [*taṉmai*] stood in the way." "And so . . . ?" asks the opening teaser, leaving us to wonder what will happen next—that is, what Vanita will do to remedy her situation.[58] The plot centers on Vanita's struggles to satisfy her husband and to maintain her household while also working to support her sick parents. Vanita's husband Shekar is angry and resentful of her financial independence and responsibilities to others, and Vanita is torn because she cannot find a balance between her commitments to her natal family and her domestic requirements as a good wife. Ultimately, the story critiques Shekar's sense of entitlement, emphasizing the necessity of "becoming human," or developing sensitivity, compassion, and respect for others.

Because Chudamani's story portrays a married couple, its stakes are different than Bhandari's. Deepa's flirtations with premarital relationships create unsettling ripples in the institution of marriage by raising the possibility that women possess preexisting romantic desires other than those they promise to their husbands. And Vanita destabilizes conventional understandings of marriage by suggesting that women maintain strong loyalties to their natal families, even after marriage. Considering the existing disputes over dowry and inheritance—the Hindu inheritance laws that were passed just ten years before "Maṉitaṉay Māṟi" was published remain contentious even today[59]—Chudamani's suggestion that modern Indian daughters are obligated to care for their elderly parents (just as sons do) was certainly bold for its time. Vanita's most pressing desire is for Shekar to understand her love for her parents and to recognize her freedom to fulfill her responsibility to them.

Yet sexual desire invades the terrain of parental love. Vanita and Shekar are just as modern a couple as Deepa and Sanjay in the sense that they, too, come together on their own terms, rather than through a family arrangement: "The factory where she worked was on the way to his office, and the two took the same bus daily. Their mutual feelings of connection and their [eventual] marriage developed out of those meetings."[60] At various moments in the story such as this, the narrator shows us that Vanita and Shekar share an attraction for each other and desire each other equally. Phrases like "ācai mayakkam" (the intoxication of desire) and "tāmpattiyam iṉimai" (the sweetness of conjugal life) characterize Shekar's feelings for Vanita,[61] and passionate physical responses evidence Vanita's attraction toward Shekar. For example, when Vanita and Shekar are talking after dinner, they begin to flirt, reminiscing about how they used to go to evening films when they were first courting. Shekar whimsically asks:

> "Shall we go to a movie tonight?"
>
> He gently joined his hand with hers. There was a feeling of entitlement [*urimaiyuṇarcci*] in his desire [*aṉpu*], a pride steeped in his right [*atikāram*] to think, "she's mine."
>
> "Sure, let's go!"
>
> "Vanita!"
>
> "Hmm? Tell me, what is it? What's the meaning of your staring at me like this without saying anything?"
>
> "Meaning? What am I saying that's meaningless, Vanita? You look so beautiful today." A pressing pleasure [*itam*] from the invigorating depth of his grasp. Her heart was also moved, and her cheeks reddened and shone.
>
> "Shall we go to the cinema? What do you say?"
>
> "Anything you say."
>
> "Yes! That's precisely the proper quality [*laṭcaṇam*] of a good wife [*nalla maṉaivi*]."
>
> He took pride in the thought that she, from the depth of love [*aṉpu*], had surrendered herself to him.
>
> For a while, time stood still. He felt as though he were wandering in a kind of heaven. She was sitting in the chair beside him, her head resting on his shoulder. A few soft whisperings. And finally, silence between them. Even in silence his heart was absorbed, intoxicated by pleasure [*iṉpu mayakkmāy*].[62]

Here, the word *urimai* (an etymologically Dravidian word, which means rights or entitlements) and its synonym, *atikāram* (an etymologically Sanskritic word, cognate of the Hindi word *adhikār*), underscore the intimate way in which Shekar's physical desire for Vanita is heightened by the sense of entitlement he feels over her. Vanita, in turn, happily participates in the romantic exchange, demurely bewildered by Shekar's ogling, blushing at his touch, assenting to his every word, and murmuring softly while leaning on his shoulder.

Vanita responds to Shekar's advances through an idiom of surrender that, at first glance, seems to possess a lesser sense of ownership and entitlement than Deepa expresses in her relationships with Sanjay and Nishith. Shekar views Vanita's self-surrender as essential to being a good wife, and she willingly, lovingly accedes. Nonetheless, Vanita's pleasure stands out in those brief fragmentary moments when the narration blurs Shekar's perspective with Vanita's, rather than taking Shekar's perspective or the form of direct dialogue.[63] Notice how the passage progresses from Shekar's direct speech

("You look so beautiful today") to a sentence fragment that has no verb or object ("A pressing pleasure from the invigorating depth of his grasp") to Vanita's physical response ("Her heart was also moved, and her cheeks reddened and shone"). This discursive movement allows the narrative voice to express Vanita's physical desire, marking an equal narrative terrain on which the two relate to each other, even if it is Shekar who wields the language of entitlement and Vanita who reacts to it.

Chudamani's movement between direct dialogue, the omniscient voice, and Shekar's point of view gives shape to her language of entitlement through the idiom of *cīṟṟam*. The story's shifting third-person voice enables the narration to contrast the terms of reciprocity defining Vanita and Shekar's conjugal relationship with Shekar's contradictory sense of entitlement over Vanita. It leads the reader to rhetorically and negatively insert Vanita's desires and the injustice of her position into the forefront of the story, even though the anger and the entitlements are Shekar's. Take, for example, the following scene, in which the story turns seamlessly from a dialogue between Shekar and his father to Shekar's internal rumination, punctuated by third-person omniscience. Together, these subtle shifts in narrative voice highlight Shekar's unbending, patriarchal illogic. When Shekar suggests Vanita cares more for her parents' well-being than his, Vanita doesn't respond. But Shekar's father does:

> "I earn a pension. But if I didn't, wouldn't you take care of me?"
>
> "How could I not? It's my duty [*kaṭamai*] to take care of you. That's what is right [*nyāyam*]," [Shekar said].
>
> "Because you're my child, right?"
>
> "Right."
>
> "Vanita is her parents' child. Don't forget that." The old man quickly walked out.
>
> Shekar stood without moving, inwardly seething [*porumal*] and confused. Vanita was her parents' child—was he the only one who didn't get this? Still, he felt despair in his heart. Gangrene and suffocation [*puraiyōṭum pukaiccal*]. Was it a disgrace to his manhood? It wasn't even that. What Vanita earned never entered the house. Even the smallest things she needed, she bought with his salary. She had always given her husband that respect. So why did he feel so enraged [*ericcal*] inside?[64]

In the opening lines of this passage, the narrative articulates a notion of gender equality through Shekar's father—not Vanita. He authoritatively, yet compassionately, expresses humanist reason on Vanita's behalf, emphasizing that Vanita and Shekar have the same responsibilities when it comes to taking care of their parents. Still, Shekar is paralyzed, overcome with confusion and irrational anger. "Gangrene and suffocation," interjects an omniscient narrative voice, characterizing Shekar's human compassion gone awry. The fragment operates as an interpolation that further accentuates the odious way in which Shekar's entitlement over Vanita conflicts with what his father tries to convince Shekar to see as Vanita's duty. The very mention of Vanita's separate salary suggests her ability to be independent from Shekar and his inability to be the true man of the house. In this way, the narrative exposes the threat Shekar feels, even though he himself does not understand why he is so angry. In contrast to the despair eating away at his heart, the words Shekar uses in response to his father—*kaṭamai* (duty, responsibility) and *nyāyam* (justice, what is just, what is right)—belong to Chudamani's language of entitlement. They gesture toward rights and responsibilities that both he and Vanita possess, but that are not dictated by their conjugal bond. These rights and responsibilities are simultaneously liberal and nonliberal: Vanita's and Shekar's right to work and to earn their own money is also their duty toward their families and their well-being.

As the story progresses, Shekar becomes more incapable of bearing the idea that Vanita's energies are directed toward her job as much as him. The narration, too, becomes more polemical—charged with *cīṟṟam*—even as it centers on Shekar's perspective:

> His anger [*āttiram*] continued to grow. [Vanita] was his possession [*uṭaimai*], and she was straining herself. Why? Laboring for someone else.
>
> She belonged to him [*avaḷ avaṉuṭaiya conta poruḷ*]. Yet, she was so tired that she couldn't share in his pleasure [*ullācam*]. He raged [*cīṟṟam*]; it was as if a thing that he had paid for was now damaged and useless to him.[65]

Shekar views Vanita as someone he possesses—as his *uṭaimai* (property) and his *conta poruḷ*, or his "own," a phrase with similar connotations to Deepa's sense of *apanatva*. Here, however, the phrase is reduced to its basest meaning: Shekar sees Vanita as an object, a purchased good that no longer serves its purpose. Although Shekar feels that Vanita manages their household well despite her job, he has no sympathy for Vanita's working-woman lifestyle. The sense of ownership he expresses stands in stark contrast to the moments of pleasure that the couple experience, as well as the love with which Vanita treats Shekar.

In the end, no amount of love and longing is enough to reconcile their opposing views. When Shekar finally puts his foot down, declaring that Vanita must quit work, she calmly decides to leave him—and she does. In a stunning instance of first-person voice, Vanita explains her actions in a letter to Shekar, chastising him for disregarding her filial and financial duties to care for her parents:

> When you heartlessly said, so what if my abandoned parents are ruined and destroyed, I couldn't bear the shock, despite my love and desire [*aṉpu*] for you. It's my duty [*kaṭamai*] to take care of my parents. I'm going there. You've got a lot of the qualities of a husband, but I don't see the qualities of a human being [*maṉitaṉ*] in you.[66]

Here, in a moment of clarity and self-realization, Vanita exercises her right to commit to her natal *kaṭamai* (duties or responsibilities), which for her are just as definitive of who she is as are her love for her husband and her duties as a good wife. In making this decision, she elucidates what it means to be human. Being human means heartfulness, as opposed to Shekar's heartlessness, a compassion for others, and a commitment to one's own responsibilities. This humanity is something Vanita feels she deserves from her husband if he is going to be her equal partner. Vanita's letter considers her duty toward her parents as interchangeable with her right to be treated as a human being. It makes an argument for gender equality through the language of self-sacrifice. When Vanita's parents ask her if she has had a quarrel with Shekar, Chudamani ends the story with Vanita's indictment of Shekar's lack of humanity: "'What fight? No, it's nothing like that,' Vanita said calmly. 'One day for sure he'll become human [*maṉitaṉāy māṟi*] and come here to take me home.'"[67] Love and desire are not enough to sustain a marriage; mutual respect and universal standards of humanity are also required.

On one hand, Vanita's final words rattle the stronghold of marriage no less than Deepa's expressions of desire for more than one man. The terms of human relations (here: shared compassion and respect) trump the terms of conjugal loyalty and devotion, and Shekar's failure to recognize this causes him to lose his husbandly entitlements over Vanita. Consequently, we might interpret Chudamani's ending as a liberal argument for the acknowledgement of women's self-interests over women's self-sacrifice. Despite the story's focus on Shekar's entitlements and desires, the narration gives the final word to Vanita and underscores her right to work and to maintain her natal family connection. The shifting third-person voice undermines Shekar's authority, dehumanizes his perspective, and ultimately writes it out of the story altogether. Conversely, it gives Vanita the respect and equality she deserves as a human being, paying utmost attention to her desires.

On the other hand, Vanita's dedicated, family-oriented feminine character facilitates Chudamani's language of entitlement. Throughout the story, Vanita adheres to the ideals of a conventional good wife. She skillfully performs her domestic duties, respects her husband's authority, and even manages to look beautiful despite being exhausted from work. She furthermore expresses a commitment toward her natal family in terms that elevate her moral character and deem her admirable. When Vanita says, "One day for sure he'll become human," she indicates that Shekar will realize that Vanita is equally human, and that she has a right to maintain her role as a daughter alongside her role as a wife. In expressing this sentiment, Vanita endorses a narrative of women's self-sacrifice in the interests of family and community, no less than Deepa. As with Bhandari's "Yahī Sac Hai," Chudamani's "Maṉitaṉāy Māṟi" complicates the binary between women's self-interest and women's self-sacrifice. The story's shifting third-person voice corrects Shekar's skewed understandings of *urimai* and *atikāram* (synonyms, both referring to rights or entitlements) and *taṉmai* (selfhood) by juxtaposing these with Vanita's self-assurance, compassion, and filial duty. Chudamani's language of rights and entitlements articulates Vanita's affective ties to her community in tandem with and inseparable from her liberal conceptions of self-ownership.

The circumscription of Vanita's feminine desire within this framework of universalizing humanism—a characteristic move in Chudamani's stories—has enabled her work to be read as "literary," placing her alongside other well-established writers of her time. For instance, in his review in *Eḻuttu* of one of Chudamani's early short story collections, the influential critic P. G. Sundararajan describes the resistance to tradition that her female characters display not as expressions of feminine choice or desire, but rather as Chudamani's method of evoking a feeling of human connection within her readers. Sundararajan finds this method exemplary of Chudamani's humanistic prose style. Commenting on her portrayals of disconnected husbands and wives, he writes: "[Her stories] reflect the effects of a shared internal human emotion [*uṇarcci*] existing between two people separated by differences of mere opinion."[68] Here, Sundararajan tames the expressions of individuality that Chudamani's female characters voice by calling them expressions of the shared emotions that all individuals—that is to say, husbands and wives alike—feel. Rather than reading Chudamani's writing as part of a discourse of gender justice, Sundararajan situates them within the project of canonical postindependence Tamil short story writers. In doing so, his interpretation aligns Chudamani's fiction with the contemporary aesthetic aims of Tamil high literature.

On the level of plot, Chudamani's "Maṉitaṉāy Māṟi" facilitates a literary humanist interpretation like Sundararajan's. Centered on Shekar's point of view, the story expresses his deep perplexity regarding Vanita's desire to work and the marital strife caused by the couple's irreconcilable difference of opinion. But on the level of rhetoric, Chudamani's language of entitlement—inflected in the idiom of *cīṟṟam*—simultaneously offers a different reading: her shifting third-person narrative voice powerfully authorizes Vanita to take full ownership of her desires and entitlements. Chudamani's language of entitlement thus shows how readings such as Sundararajan's only get us so far. They preclude us from recognizing the innovative literary ways in which writers like Bhandari and Chudamani imagined the scope of women's entitlements and feminine desire at a moment when these issues were contentious and their definitions were in flux.

LABELING WOMAN WRITERS

Despite their bold examinations of women's desires and entitlements, both Bhandari and Chudamani managed their authorly personas with finesse, expressing deep ambivalence about speaking in feminist terms, or being labeled as "women writers." Bhandari, for example, describes feeling pleased that her photo was not printed alongside some of the first short stories that launched her writing career. She recalls that, when the stories came out: "My name wasn't clearly gender specific, so most [readers'] letters arrived addressed to 'Dear Brother.' . . . I laughed a lot, but I also felt a sense of satisfaction that this praise was absolutely not out of kindness because I was a woman."[69] In another instance, an interviewer asked Bhandari about her protagonist Darshana's extramarital affair in the story "Tīn Nigāhoṃ kī Ek Tasvīr" [A picture of three perspectives], published in 1958:

> Researcher: In your opinion is Darshana's extramarital love acceptable? If it is acceptable, then what becomes of the institution of wifely allegiance and duty [*pātivratya dharma*]?

> Mannu Bhandari: There's a difference between attraction [*ākarshaṇ*] and love [*prem*]. Because if attraction gives rise to expression then it would be love, but Darshana doesn't express it.[70]

In this exchange, from the early 2000s, Bhandari evaded the researcher's question about the acceptability of extramarital love. She refused to put Darshana's actions in transgressive terms, almost as if she were depoliticizing Darshana's affair by disallowing its articulation in a moral framework. Similarly, in a 2002 interview, Chudamani was asked about the psychology of one of her female characters, who, when her husband leaves her and later returns, discovers that she no longer wants him. Chudamani replied: "It isn't necessary to completely describe everyone in a story. Just as we can't understand a person fully in real life, so it is in literature."[71] Like Bhandari, Chudamani interpreted her character's actions by appealing to human emotion and experience, rather than by challenging gender or other social norms.

Bhandari and Chudamani are not alone in their apparent disavowal of feminist politics. Among their postindependence literary contemporaries, Anita Desai (English), Ismat Chughtai (Urdu), Krishna Sobti (Hindi), Saroj Pathak (Gujarati), and Anusuya Shankar "Triveni" (Kannada)—to name a few—have all expressed a tension between "literary writing" and "women's writing." For these writers, literary writing signals an aesthetic universal humanism that conflicts with the feminist-political particularities of women's writing.[72] In their groundbreaking two-volume anthology *Women Writing in India*, Susie Tharu and K. Lalita write of the work of this new postindependence generation of women writers: "In many senses their well-crafted writing does not seem to be disputing the ground laid out for it any more than the mainstream writing [of canonical male writers of the time]. But it is also possible to read the women's writing of this period as engaged in a bitter and difficult debate about women and the kind of hospitality gender received within the universalist claims of the postindependence years."[73] Newly arising "literary" women writers—who were, for the most part, well educated, middle class, upper caste, and Hindu—began to search for ways to resolve the question of how women (and women writers) did, could, and should be situated within the category of the human in postcolonial India. Bhandari's and Chudamani's languages of entitlement illustrate one avenue through which some women writers worked out a solution by rearticulating feminine desire and freedom in the aesthetic terms of literary humanism.

Bhandari's and Chudamani's approach to sexual difference and authorship—indeed, their attempt to erase sexual difference in the realm of the literary—might be interpreted as their resistance to one of the dilemmas of the category of women's writing: that it assumes an unbroken continuity between writer and text (female writer equals feminine text), in which the value of the text is determined by the author's signature. Early theorists of women's writing did just this in the 1970s. In an attempt to reclaim the lost tradition of women's literature, American feminists, on one hand, used women's writing to offer alternative images about women, by women, and for women.[74] French feminists, on the other hand, searched for ways to theorize the unrepresentable of phallocentric discourse marked by the "feminine," which they considered as "elusive, phantasmal, [and] . . . that can't be observed at the level of the sentence but only glimpsed as an alternative libidinal economy."[75] Both these branches of feminist thought, however, invariably defined women's writing as writing by women, the "woman author as origin, and her life as the primary locus of meaning."[76]

By contrast, theories arising in the 1980s and 1990s—that underlined the "death of the author," the primacy of the text, and the performativity of gender—undermined the category of women's writing by deconstructing the very notions of authorship and gender that defined it.[77] These philosophical challenges to essentialism conflicted with the feminist project of promoting women writers, bringing theoretical discussions of women's writing to a standstill. As a result, Toril Moi argues, "the question of what the sex or gender of the author has to do with literature" remains unresolved. What we are left with are theories about gender construction—or "how gender is created or comes into being." But, as Moi goes on to say, "*Theories of origins simply do not tell us what we ought to do once gender has come into being.*"[78] In other words, how should a writer respond when she has already been categorized as a "woman writer"? What *does* the sex or gender of the author have to do with literature?

"Nothing!" At least this is what Bhandari and Chudamani seem to say in interviews such as those I cited above, at those critical junctures when they have been called on to speak not as "writers" but as "women writers." When they have been compelled to reconcile their writerly identities with a gender already come into being, Bhandari and Chudamani have responded by emphasizing the "human" rather than "feminine" emotions and actions of their characters, locating their work in the realm of the literary rather than the feminist political. Still, I do not interpret their responses as a championing of the death of the author or an argument for the constructedness of gender, both readings that see Bhandari and Chudamani as repudiating feminist politics. As I hope to have highlighted in my readings of their short stories, emphasizing the humanist rather than the feminist dimensions of

Bhandari and Chudamani's writing does not diminish the latter aspects of their work. This becomes clearer, I believe, if we shift the stress we hear in the claim, "I am a writer, not a woman writer!" from the latter half ("not a woman writer"), to the beginning half ("I am a writer"). What if we understand Bhandari and Chudamani as struggling against the provocation not that they are women writers and therefore not "true" writers but rather that, as women writers, they cannot be "true" writers?[79] I am suggesting, in other words, that Bhandari and Chudamani are trying not to erase sexual difference or eschew feminist politics, but rather to demonstrate how feminine desire and experience are just as universal as the desire and experience of their masculine counterparts. It is precisely this move, I believe, that enabled Bhandari and Chudamani to broaden the field of women's writing and the scope of literary humanism in the two decades following independence.

A LITERARY HUMANIST TRADITION OF WOMEN'S WRITING

The depiction of feminine desire was not solely the province of women writers. In the previous chapter, I showed that a fascination with human desire—its wayward passions and impossible inclinations—compelled many *nayī kahānī* and *Eḻuttu* writers to focus on man-woman relationships, and in their stories feminine desire seems knottiest of all. For this reason, Bhandari's and Chudamani's focus on feminine desire, and their inflection of it through vocabularies of entitlement, should be understood as worlding strategies that made their short stories intelligible within the literary humanist frameworks of their male contemporaries. These strategies furthermore indexed their stories to pan-Indian and global conversations about gender and interpersonal relations, which were transforming through ongoing processes of decolonization.

At the same time, Bhandari's and Chudamani's languages of entitlement made their engagement with feminine desire unique. Unlike their male contemporaries, for whom feminine desire was enigmatic and unfulfillable, Bhandari's and Chudamani's female characters evince clarity and rightful ownership of their desires. Deepa and Vanita view the affection, love, and companionship they share with their partners as something they possess. Such ownership stands in stark contrast to *nayī kahānī* and *Eḻuttu* male writers' depictions of the postindependence new woman. For example, Yadav and Bhandari each published a story in 1957 called "Ek Kamzor Laṛki kī Kahānī" (The story of a weak girl)—which were likely written in conversation.[80] Both stories explore the possibilities for a woman to express her love for a man other than her husband in the face of social injunction, family circumstance, and personal feelings of incapacity and powerlessness. But a key difference is that Bhandari's protagonist Rup uses the language of *adhikār* (entitlement) to consider to which man she will give possession of her body and soul. Rup explores how the new woman might negotiate contradictory social pressures and personal desires. By contrast, Yadav's protagonist Savita loses consciousness, leaving her fate in the hands of the two men vying for her devotion. No language of entitlement provides the leeway for Savita to escape becoming—or even to complicate—the trope of the weak girl.

In Chudamani's case, "Cītaiyait Teriyumā?"—which I briefly mentioned above—provides a good comparison. The protofeminist undertones of this story are clear, especially when placed in conversation with D. Jayakanthan's controversial story "Akkiṉip Piravēcam" (Trial by fire). As I discussed in the previous chapter, Jayakanthan's story, like Chudamani's, references the trial by fire that Sita, the heroine of the Sanskrit epic *Rāmāyaṇa*, faces to prove her chastity and loyalty to her husband. But it does so in a very different way than "Cītaiyait Teriyumā?" When a stranger rapes Jayakanthan's young Brahmin female protagonist, her mother cleanses her daughter to wash away the girl's innocence and mark the maturity she has acquired for facing modern life. Jayakanthan's language in "Akkiṉip Piravēcam" is highly descriptive and the girl sexualized. In contrast to the story's focus on the girl's physical condition—rather than her mental turmoil or emotional transformation—Chudamani charts the evolution of the interiority of her protagonist Nalayini. Nalayini's ultimate realization that she must maintain her self-integrity is juxtaposed with an outcaste sweeper woman's blind devotion to her husband and her unnecessary physical suffering. The world opens up for Nalayini because of the claims to justice she makes. Chudamani authorizes Nalayini to leave her husband, portraying an ending just as defiant of social norms as Jayakanthan's resurrection of a raped woman, but more interested in female subjectivity. In doing so, Chudamani offers a glimpse of the philosophical strains of thought and the caste and class materialities shaping the trope of the educated, middle-class, upper-caste Tamil new woman in postindependence India.

In Bhandari's and Chudamani's stories, the language of entitlement negotiates feminine desire and human desire. It features female interiority, translating the "right to feel" that earlier women writers had voiced into a postcolonial aesthetic. Entirely novel in the immediate postindependence moment, this language opened an avenue for ensuing generations of women writers to use literary humanism as a lens for exploring feminine desire. Many women have now become recognized authors. For example, in the Hindi context, Bhandari's influence is evident in the work of Raji Seth, who began writing in the 1970s. In one of Seth's first short stories, "Apne Viruddh" (Against myself), published in 1979, the protagonist Ruchi's desire to write comes to a head with her subordinate position to her partner Shyam, also a writer. Unable to overcome Shyam's possessiveness over her daily life as well as her writing, Ruchi finds herself at a loss and ultimately gives up her writing.[81] "Apne Viruddh" takes up the question of women's writing where Bhandari's early postindependence stories leave off by depicting a woman's right to write as part of her fulfillment as a human being. In more contemporary times, notable Hindi women writers such as Geetanjali Shree, who resists the label "woman writer," and Archana Varma, who explicitly claims a feminist-political stance, both portray themes of feminine desire in their work, often evoking the existential sensibilities of loss, alienation, and disillusionment as a way to connect their work to discourses of humanism within the Hindi literary tradition.[82]

In the Tamil context an even more evident link exists between Chudamani's early expressions of literary feminism and contemporary women's writing. Chudamani served as an early mentor and lifelong confidante to the well-known woman writer Ambai (the pen name of C. S. Lakshmi, whose literary humanist portrayals of feminine desire have become definitive of contemporary middle-class Tamil literary feminism.[83] Ambai's stories, many of which were first published in the elite journal *Kaṇaiyāḻi*, push back against Tamil literary norms prescribing the depiction of feminine desires and entitlements. In stories like "Ciṟakukaḷ Muṟiyum" (Wings), published in 1967, her female characters rage inwardly at a patriarchal system that requires women to suppress their sexual desire and sacrifice their dreams, just so they can please their parents and husbands. Other stories, such as "Aṇil" (Squirrel), published in 1986, explore the tradition of Tamil women's writing, women's desire to write, and the possibility of women finding a knowledgeable readership.[84]

Since the early 2000s Ambai's humanist portrayals of feminine desire, including the desire to write, have taken more pronounced shape in the poetry of the women writers Rajathi Salma, Malathi Maithri, Sukirtharani, and Kutti Revathi, whose work has been the subject of recent literary controversy for its unabashed emphasis on women's right to express sexual desire in literature. Ambai supported these poets' struggle to claim their right to literary expression, comparing their situation to one she faced early in her career and linking their literary efforts to her own: "Many years ago a male Tamil writer wrote to a senior male writer that reading the stories of Ambai gave him the feeling that she was not physically fully satisfied. . . . The recent controversy about language some Tamil women poets use has made it clear that . . . such men never cease to exist."[85] Seth's and Ambai's fiction and that of the following generation of women writers have found a place within the realms of Hindi and Tamil high literature. Picking up in the wake of Bhandari's and Chudamani's uses of a language of entitlement, these writers continue to forge a tradition of women's writing that views literature as a humanist endeavor and feminine desire as a human one.

CONCLUSION

Ten Theses on the Idea of Indian Literature

This book's comparison of Hindi and Tamil literature has explored the feasibility and durability of the idea of Indian literature and its capacity to collect diverse literary and linguistic strategies and aims beneath the auspices of a single rubric. Hindi, representing the universalizing aspirations of the nation, and Tamil, epitomizing the particularizing ambitions of the region, are conventionally viewed as the extreme poles of the multilingual continuum comprising Indian literature. This book has shown, however, that during the twentieth century, these spheres were co-constitutive of each other and of the idea of Indian literature itself. Through mutually imbricated theories and practices of translation, citation, genre, literary history, rhetoric, and style, writers worlded Hindi, Tamil, and Indian literature—producing innovative, influential theorizations of literariness that claimed the literary as the terrain on which to define and contest the postcolonial condition. Powerful acts of worlding, these theorizations created new forms of aesthetic affiliation between readers, writers, and texts by framing how texts should be positioned and received. The affiliations they forged were tied to the fissures of language and region yet also exceeded these fissures through the promise of readerly communion in multilingualism and translation. The unrealizability of this promise breathes life into the idea of Indian literature and its ambition to circumvent the politics of language, while linking literature to nation.

The view of Indian literature that this book has offered may be framed in the following ways:

1. Indian literature is an abstract idea—rather than a concrete fact, a specific corpus of texts, or the literary correlative to a predetermined language or body of languages. This idea is real and enduring and possesses animating force because of—not despite—its indeterminacy, multiplicity, and continual evolution alongside the shifting dynamics of multilingualism in India.
2. The animating power of the idea of Indian literature hinges on the thesis of translatability. This thesis necessitates translation between Indian languages and postulates perfect translatability between them. The impossibility of translating that which must be translated constitutes the paradoxical ground on which the idea of Indian literature finds aesthetic expression.
3. Indian literature is a modern idea that emerged in the twentieth century. This idea was born from colonial processes of vernacularization and represents a rejection of the condition of vernacularity that these processes imposed on Indian languages. The idea of Indian literature is a critique of vernacularity that generates passions for conversation, collaboration, and aesthetic congregation without presupposing unification.
4. The idea of Indian literature crystalizes around representations of gender and uses of genre. Gender and genre function as citational and iterative components of content and form that move across literary spheres, becoming intelligible to multiple readerships simultaneously. This intelligibility is built upon collective understandings as well as misunderstandings, differences, and disarticulations of meaning—all of which allow gender and genre to draw on and respond to disconnected literary conversations occurring concurrently at regional, national, and global scales. Gender and genre are intersectional and multiscalar, not modular, and function as aesthetic nodes through which the idea of Indian literature coheres.
5. The idea of Indian literature compels regional literary histories to convene readerships around aesthetic, rather than communal, affiliations. These narratives accomplish aesthetic congregation through the evocation of shared literary sentiments that can never be truly shared because they emerge from disparate social, historical, and aesthetic concerns. Together, regional Indian literary histories give shape to an ambiguous idea of Indian literature that is fashioned by

the universalizing yet nebulous feelings of discontent, anguish, and hope.

6. The idea of Indian literature recruits readers into relations of sympathy and empathy through the creative use of rhetorical modes that make the positions of characters and readers recognizable (realism) and transpositional (modernist realism). Through these modes, the idea of Indian literature functions as a capacious signifier for diverse experiences of colonial and postcolonial indignation and disconsolation.
7. The idea of Indian literature is continually (re)constituted by vocabularies, such as those of gender or caste justice, which seek to span multiple Indian languages. Through such vocabularies, the idea of Indian literature offers the potential for writers and readers to assemble around ideological and aesthetic perspectives and strategies that are utopian and activist, rather than cultural or linguistic, at their core. Transregional and multilingual vocabularies may reinforce the structural pillars of caste, class, and religion that buttress the idea of Indian literature, but they may also challenge and undermine these pillars, thereby throwing the idea into crisis and even disrepair.
8. The idea of Indian literature exists at a tangent to the nation. As an idea of multilingual dialogism, it is not contingent on comprehension or communication and therefore embodies possibilities of imagining and reinforcing, as well as subverting and dismantling the cultural cohesion proposed by the nation.
9. The idea of Indian literature proffers a multilingual dialogic horizon for fiction and theory, as well as scholarship and criticism. Scholarship and criticism can produce, perpetuate, destabilize or undo the idea of Indian literature—as much as readerly or writerly claims and challenges to Indian literature as a literary field.
10. The idea of Indian literature is an idea of comparative literature—the idea of a literary field threatened dissolution by the very components it longs to bring together.

Notes

INTRODUCTION

1. Sujit Mukherjee, preface to *The Idea of an Indian Literature*, vi.

2. For more on this, see Casanova, *World Republic of Letters*, 75–78; Mufti, *Forget English!*, 59–66; and Yildiz, *Beyond the Mother Tongue*, 6–7. For discussion of the philological revolution's influence on Orientalist scholars working in the subcontinent, see Dalmia, *Nationalization of Hindu Traditions*, 161–62, and Mufti, *Forget English!*, 104–6. The philological revolution in Europe—prompted by the German philologist Johann Gottfried von Herder's views—produced what Yasemin Yildiz calls the "monolingual paradigm" in which the notion of the mother tongue figures languages as separate and distinct and connects each language with identifiable characteristics rooted in geography, history, culture, and biology. See also Young, "That Which Is Casually Called a Language." In the subcontinent, processes of monolingualization have always existed both in tandem and in tension with multilingual forms of sociality and textuality. For further discussion, see also chapter 1.

3. Weber, "The Name 'Indian Literature,'" 1–2. This excerpt first appeared in Weber's book *The History of Indian Literature*, originally published in German, in 1852, and translated into English, in 1878, as part of the London-based Trübner's Oriental Series. For more on this series and its role in producing ideas of "literature," see Orsini, "Present Absence."

4. Sujit Mukherjee, *Towards a Literary History of India*, 232.

5. For more on Hindi language politics, see Dalmia, *Nationalization of Hindu Traditions*; Christopher King, *One Language, Two Scripts*; Mody, *Making of Modern Hindi*; Mufti, *Enlightenment in the Colony* and *Forget English!*; Orsini, *Hindi Public Sphere*; and A. Rai, *Hindi Nationalism*. Hindi and Urdu share a common syntax and vocabulary, but beginning in the late nineteenth century, Hindi began to be identified as the language of the Hindus, written in the Devanagari (or Nagari) script,

and Urdu as the language of the Muslims, written in the Nastaliq (or Perso-Arabic) script.

6. For more on Tamil language politics, see Nambi Arooran, *Tamil Renaissance*; Pandian, *Brahmin and Non-Brahmin*; and Sumathi Ramaswamy, *Passions of the Tongue*.

7. This is in direct contrast to the slogan of the Sahitya Akademi (India's National Academy of Letters), which insists that "Indian literature is one though written in many languages." For more discussion on this, see Raveendran, "Genealogies of Indian Literature."

8. Ahmad, *In Theory*, 288.

9. For example, see Chatterji, *Languages and Literatures*; K. M. George, *Comparative Indian Literature, Vol. 1* and *Comparative Indian Literature, Vol. 2*; and Gonda, *History of Indian Literature*.

10. See, for example, Chaudhuri, "Modernisms in India"; Das, *A History of Indian Literature, 1800–1910* and *A History of Indian Literature, 1911–1956*; Dev, "Comparative Literature in India"; V. Dharwadker, "Modernist Novel"; Pollock, *Literary Cultures in History*; and A. K. Singh, "Interliterariness." See also Subrahmanyam et al., "A Review Symposium."

11. Orsini, "Multilingual Local," 346. See also Ciocca and Srivastava, introduction; Kothari, *Multilingual Nation*; Nerlekar, *Bombay Modern*; Orsini, "Multilingual Literary History"; Sadana, *English Heart, Hindi Heartland*; Sangari, "Aesthetics of Circulation"; and Shankar, *Flesh and Fish Blood*.

12. Pollock, "Cosmopolitan Vernacular" and *Language of the Gods*.

13. Novetzke, *Quotidian Revolution*.

14. Beecroft, *Ecology of World Literature*.

15. Orsini, "Multilingual Local."

16. Shankar, "Comparatism" and *Flesh and Fish Blood*.

17. Chatterjee, introduction; Gajarawala, "Mother Russia."

18. Ghosh, "In Difference," 200.

19. Shankar, "The Vernacular: An Introduction," 191.

20. Gupta et al., "Literary Sentiments," 813. For more skeptical positions on the term "vernacular," see A. Dharwadker, "Mohan Rakesh"; Orsini, "Vernacular: Flawed but Necessary?"; and Selvamony, "Vernacular as Homoarchic Mode of Existence."

21. Needless to say, an examination of premodern South Asian literary cultures is outside the scope of this book. For a discussion of how Pollock's understanding of vernacularization might not account for the case of premodern Tamil, see Shulman, *Tamil: A Biography*. The point I want to make here is that even the revolutionary potential some scholars and writers attribute to modern uses of the vernacular is conceptualized as a resistance and corrective to colonial-era vernacularization. For example, Dalit writers working in different Indian languages have turned to vernacular linguistic realism since the 1970s to counter processes of linguistic purification, standardization, and Sanskritization that began in the nineteenth century. For more on this, see Brueck, "Mother Tongues"; Geetha, "History and the Caste Imagination"; Nerlekar, *Bombay Modern*; and Shankar, *Flesh and Fish Blood*.

22. For Pollock, Beecroft, and others, the primary difference between premodern and colonial-era processes of vernacularization is that the latter explicitly tie language to cultural identity and territory. See, for example, Dalmia, *Nationalization of*

Hindu Traditions; Kaviraj, *Imaginary Institution of India*; Mitchell, *Language, Emotion, and Politics*; and B. Raman, *Document Raj*. I am interested here in exploring this linkage more deeply using vernacularization as a lens through which to consider how Indian multilingualism—particularly in the realm of literature—was reconfigured and continued to evolve during the nineteenth and twentieth centuries.

23. Novetzke, *Quotidian Revolution*.

24. Annamalai, "Challenge of Spoken Language"; Dhareshwar, "Caste and the Secular Self"; and Pandian, "One Step Outside Modernity."

25. For example, neither Yildiz's monolingual paradigm, which created a "homology between language and ethno-cultural identity" (*Beyond the Mother Tongue*, 26) nor Beecroft's national literature ecology, which sealed literature's role in maintaining this homology (*Ecology of World Literature*, 199), accounts for the vernacularizing role of English and other imperial languages on the varied histories of multilingualism outside Europe. Unlike in Europe, the nationalization and monolingualization of languages in colonial India configured them as parallel and distinct, yet also incommensurate, to English.

26. Mitchell, *Language, Emotion, and Politics*, 159.

27. Mitchell, *Language, Emotion, and Politics*, 163.

28. Importantly, this was also the period when the term "vernacular" began gaining more currency in Europe. For example, the *Oxford English Dictionary* online database shows that, although the term appears in English in the seventeenth century, its usage increases significantly during the nineteenth century. This increase suggests that ideas of what constitutes the vernacular and vernacularization may have evolved in Europe as much as in the colonies during this time—very possibly through the increasing interactions taking place between them.

29. Dalmia, *Nationalization of Hindu Traditions*, 168; Patel, "Vernacular Missing," 134.

30. Dalmia, *Nationalization of Hindu Traditions*, 154; Pollock, *Language of the Gods*, 20–22.

31. Patel, "Vernacular Missing," 134. For more on the impact of Herder's views in the subcontinent, see Dalmia, *Nationalization of Hindu Traditions*, 161–62; and Mufti, *Forget English!*, 101. This new understanding of the vernacular constituted Sanskrit as a "classical" instead of "cosmopolitan" language—which consequently became understood as exemplary of ancient Indian civilization, while also being out of touch with the everyday lives of the Indian people. For more on this, see Sawhney, *Modernity of Sanskrit*.

32. See, for example, Dalmia, *Nationalization of Hindu Traditions*; Mitchell, *Language, Emotion, and Politics*; B. Raman, *Document Raj*; Trautmann, *Languages and Nations*; and Venkatachalapathy, "From *Pulavar* to Professor." The production of grammars and manifestos that launched the European vernacular revolution in the fourteenth century did not occur for South Asian languages until the colonial era—with the exceptions of Kannada, Tamil, and Telugu (Pollock, *Language of the Gods*, 471). Pollock attributes premodern vernacularization in South Asia to the literarization—rather than standardization—of regional languages. He uses the terms "cosmopolitan" and "vernacular" as glosses for the Sanskrit theory of *mārga* (way) and *deśī* (place), which became established around the seventh century and came to describe processes of vernacularization occurring during the second millen-

nium in South Asia (204–22, 397–410). These glosses permit Pollock's comparison with processes of vernacularization happening contemporaneously in Europe. As I argued above, Pollock's understandings of the vernacular and vernacularization do not map onto the appearance and usages of these terms in colonial India. For a discussion of vernacularization in medieval Europe, beginning with Dante's 1305 Italian manifesto *De Vulgari Eloquentia*, see Beecroft, *Ecology of World Literature*, 145–93.

33. B. Raman, *Document Raj*, 77.

34. Das, *Sahibs and Munshis*; Annamalai, *Social Dimensions of Modern Tamil.*

35. B. Raman, *Document Raj.*

36. Mitchell, *Language, Emotion, and Politics.*

37. Dalmia, *Nationalization of Hindu Traditions*; Alok Rai, *Hindi Nationalism.*

38. Kaviraj, "Two Histories of Literary Culture."

39. Yashaschandra, "From Hemacandra to *Hind Swarāj*."

40. Punjabi was the exception, however. As Farina Mir has shown, the colonial state accorded vernacular status to Urdu—rather than Punjabi—in the Punjabi-speaking region, thereby depriving it of the institutional and financial resources that fueled vernacularization in other Indian languages. Compared to other Indian languages, Mir argues that "Punjabi literary culture enjoyed a relative independence from the colonial state . . . [which] allowed greater scope for continuity with precolonial practices. Punjabi literary culture offers, therefore, a particular instance of stability through a period usually marked for its ruptures" (*Social Space of Language*, 4).

41. Let me also underscore, however, that the interactions between English and Indian languages were under no circumstances unidirectional. As Vinay Dharwadker has argued, Indian languages and English share a historical "intertexture" developed through zones of interracial contact and acculturation so that "the highly crafted 'English' of Indian English literature is full of the long shadows of the Indian languages" ("Historical Formation," 261).

42. Many scholars observe efforts to bring written language forms closer to their spoken counterparts across regions in nineteenth-century India. See, for example, Dalmia, *Nationalization of Hindu Traditions*; Mitchell, *Language, Emotion, and Politics*; and B. Raman, *Document Raj*. My point here is that these efforts were fundamental to nineteenth-century vernacularization processes and configured colonial-era language dynamics differently from Pollock's cosmopolitan-vernacular paradigm, which is rooted in the concretization and unification of written forms through their aesthetic proximity to Sanskrit (*Language of the Gods*, 23–26). See Cohn, "Command of Language," for more on how colonial ambitions for knowledge and power required the acquisition of Indian languages.

43. Ebeling here quotes from the *4th Annual Report from the Governors of Madras University*, published in 1845, and the Advocate General of Madras George Norton's pamphlet *Native Education in India; Comprising a Review of its State and Progress within the Presidency of Madras*, published in 1848. The 1845 report states: "It is to be observed that the vernacular languages of this Presidency namely Teloogoo, Tamil, Canarese, Malyalum, and Tuluva are almost totally barren of what Europeans deem useful or substantial knowledge. All their ancient, original, valued literary compositions are in *Poetry*. The existing Prose works, very few of which can, we believe, be recommended as exhibiting a correct or sensible style, are but translations. . . . As regards the Poetic compositions, their merit by the Native Standard is very different

from that of any European compositions. Difficult verbal feats by complex reduplications of the same words with various, and even contrary, meanings—by various alliterations—and by perversely ingenious artifice in the structure of sentences and verses—form the staple of what are considered fine writings" (as quoted in Ebeling, *Colonizing the Realm*, 166).

44. See, for example, Coppola, *Urdu Poetry*; and Shulman, *Tamil: A Biography*.

45. M. Mukherjee, introduction to *Early Novels in India*, xi–xii. See also Chaudhuri, "Bengali Novel."

46. M. Mukherjee, *Realism and Reality*, 18.

47. Premodern vernacularization, by contrast, instituted a new diglossia by generating vernacular literary conventions, modeled on Sanskrit, which were distinct from existing spoken forms of regional languages. See Pollock, *Language of the Gods*.

48. Macaulay, "Minute on Indian Education," 237.

49. See, for example, Anjaria, "Introduction: Literary Pasts, Presents, and Futures"; and Sadana, "Writing in English."

50. See, for example, Dalmia, *Nationalization of Hindu Traditions*; and B. Raman, *Document Raj*.

51. Anjaria, "Introduction: Literary Pasts, Presents, and Futures," 6. Emphasis in original.

52. Early colonial-era claims to the vernacular were therefore dominated by upper-caste social and political concerns, in contrast to contemporary arguments that view vernacular arenas as promising sites for the recovery of marginalized identities and histories.

53. Rethinking methodologies of comparison between East and West, Kumkum Sangari proposes a "critical aesthetic of circulation that understands co-constitution and can step out of usual questions of influence, comparability, commensurability, and set aside hierarchies based on centers/peripheries or the metropolitan/global market presence of art and literature. Co-constitution may be economic, social, patriarchal, ideological, cultural, linguistic, political (as in anti-colonial and anti-imperialist struggles), and anchored in subtle and complex histories of translation, circulation and extraction that span these fields. An analysis of co-constitution discloses visible or subcutaneous connections between seemingly discrete, disparate, or binarized entities" ("Aesthetics of Circulation," 9).

54. See, for example, Chaudhuri, "Bengali Novel"; Dalmia, "Merchant Tales"; Ebeling, *Colonizing the Realm*; M. Mukherjee, *Early Novels in India*; and Padikkal, "Inventing Modernity."

55. See C. King, *One Language, Two Scripts*; and A. Rai, *Hindi Nationalism*.

56. Dalmia, "Locations of Hindi." For discussion of the fluidity between Hindi and Urdu in nineteenth-century literary production, see Dubrow, *Cosmopolitan Dreams*; and Orsini, *Print and Pleasure*.

57. For more on Dwivedi's role in standardizing modern Hindi, see Mody, *Making of Modern Hindi*; and Orsini, *Hindi Public Sphere*, 127–31.

58. For more on Adigal and the Pure Tamil Movement, see Sumathi Ramaswamy, *Passions of the Tongue*, 144–54; and Vaithees, *Religion, Caste, and Nation*, 126–29.

59. For more on these events in South India, see Sumathi Ramaswamy, *Passions of the Tongue*, 197–99. For more on contemporaneous language debates in the North, see Orsini, *Hindi Public Sphere*, 126–41.

60. As quoted in N. Menon, "When the National Poet Spoke up for Tamil."

61. For more on Premchand, see chaps. 1 and 2.

62. Premchand, "Rāshṭrabhāshā Hindī," 150.

63. Premchand, "Rāshṭrabhāshā Hindī," 153.

64. See, for example, Premchand, "Antarprāntīya Sāhityak Ādān-Pradān ke Liye." The original publication date of this work is unavailable.

65. See, for example, Premchand, "Dakshiṇ meṃ Hindī Pracār."

66. See Premchand, "Dakshiṇ meṃ Hindī Pracār."

67. Premchand, "Rāshṭrabhāshā Hindī," 163.

68. In his speech Premchand positioned premodern Hindi poetry within the aesthetic framework of eroticism (*śṛṅgāra*), which he identified as the dominant poetics of the Islamicate era and the result of the preferences and patronage politics of courtly culture. He marked a shift in nineteenth-century Hindi poetry toward realism, while arguing that Urdu poetry remained connected to the aesthetics of the Islamicate past ("Rāshṭrabhāshā Hindī," 163–64). Premchand was not alone in viewing Urdu's association with Persian poetic traditions as indicative of the language's inability to express Indian modernity in the same way as Hindi—which, as he and others were well aware, was constructed as a distinct language and literature only in the nineteenth century. As Vasudha Dalmia, Sujata Mody, and Valerie Ritter have illustrated, late nineteenth- and early twentieth-century Hindi writers sought to Sanskritize yet also modernize Hindi poetry by ridding it of the erotic themes associated with the Islamicate era. See Dalmia, *Nationalization of Hindu Traditions*; Mody, *Making of Modern Hindi*; and Ritter, *Kama's Flowers*.

69. Premchand also briefly addressed the relationship between Hindi, Urdu, and Hindustani: "Call it Hindi, call it Hindustani, call it Urdu—it's all the same thing" ("Rāshṭrabhāshā Hindī," 154). But in the rest of the speech he used the terms Hindi (linked explicitly to Devanagari texts written by Hindu authors) and Urdu (represented by Nastaliq texts written mainly by Muslim authors) to designate distinct languages and literatures. His Hindi list included writers such as Mahadevi Varma, Jaishankar Prasad, Sumitranandan Pant, Makhanlal Chaturvedi, and Suryakant Tripathi "Nirala." His Urdu list, by contrast, included writers such as Abdul Halim Sharar, Mirza Hadi Ruswa, Sajjad Hussain, Nazir Ahmed Dehlvi, and Khwaja Hasan Nizami.

70. While nineteenth-century writers who had been educated in English—such as Bengali writer Bankimchandra Chattopadhyay, Tamil writer Samuel Vedanayakam Pillai, and Hindi writer Bharatendu Harischandra made a conscious choice to work in Indian languages, they also maintained a foothold in English-language publishing and viewed their endeavors as part of a process of introducing European linguistic and literary conventions into Indian languages. They furthermore viewed English readers as audiences for their vernacular writings. For more discussion on this, see Chaudhuri, "Bengali Novel"; Dalmia, *Nationalization of Hindu Traditions*; Ebeling, *Colonizing the Realm*; and M. Mukherjee, *Realism and Reality*. My argument is that this foothold became increasingly politicized during the early twentieth century so that by the 1930s many Indian writers felt compelled to reject English in favor of Indian languages despite their ability to work in both.

71. I am not arguing that Indian writers entirely stopped working in English, but rather that they began to hold English in a subordinate position to Indian languages

in their aesthetic and political stances. Apart from Premchand's position against English, consider, for instance, the case of Tamil writers associated with the 1930s literary magazine *Maṇikkoṭi*. Several of these writers deliberately switched from writing in both English and Tamil to writing exclusively in Tamil as an overt expression of their nationalism. At the same time, they took a firm stance against Tamil linguistic purism and embraced the diversification of Tamil through the integration of English vocabulary, syntax, and translation. Writers belonging to the Progressive Writers' Association offer another example. Although they wrote their 1935 manifesto for Indian literature in English and advocated the use of Roman script for Indian languages, they also recognized the impossibility of supporting English as a primary all-India language. See chapter 1 for more discussion of these writers. Indian writers did, of course, produce important Indian English fiction during the late colonial period. But, as Snehal Shingavi has argued, even Mulk Raj Anand, Raja Rao, and R. K Narayan—now credited with establishing the Indian English canon—did not receive literary recognition in India until the postindependence period (*Mahatma Misunderstood*).

72. The INC declared its demand for full independence in 1929.

73. Urdu authors and texts were not the only ones excluded from Premchand's canon. Elsewhere, he also discouraged translations into Hindi of texts from other languages. For more on Premchand's understanding of the Hindi canon, see chapter 1.

74. A more extreme misalignment between language and literature arose in the Tamil-speaking South. Nineteenth-century colonial and missionary efforts to reduce diglossia in Tamil led to an early twentieth-century backlash by Tamil pandits and Dravidian activists, who sought to reaffirm classical Tamil literary language and even employ it for political oratory and journalism. For more on this, see Bate, *Tamil Oratory*; B. Raman, *Document Raj*; and Venkatachalapathy, "From *Pulavar* to Professor." In chapter 1, I demonstrate how Tamil writers associated with the magazine *Maṇikkoṭi* sought to intervene in this ethnonationalist agenda for Tamil language in the 1930s by reclaiming literature as a cosmopolitan space of cultural intermixing and worldly aspiration.

75. It is remarkable, though, that Premchand did not explicitly mention the presence of anti-Hindi sentiment in Madras in this piece. As A. R. Venkatachalapathy and Sumathi Ramaswamy have shown, Tamil language devotion conferences and political rallies were at a new height during the period when Premchand visited the South (see Sumathi Ramaswamy, *Passions of the Tongue*; Venkatachalapathy, "From *Pulavar* to Professor" and *In Those Days*). I can only speculate that Premchand may have wanted to focus his Hindi readers' attention on the commitment necessary for developing Hindi in the South, rather than the obstacles that Hindi faced in the region.

76. Premchand, "Dakshiṇ meṃ Hindī Pracār," 268–69.

77. Sakai, *Translation and Subjectivity*, 4.

78. Sakai, *Translation and Subjectivity*, 4.

79. See, for example, Premchand, "Bhāratīya Sāhitya Parishad," "Rāshṭrabhāshā Kaise Samṙddh Ho," and "Sāhityik Kluboṃ kī Āvaśyakatā."

80. Premchand, "Antarprāntīya Sāhityak Ādān-Pradān ke Liye," 232. I discuss this new investment in the idea of Indian literature across the Indian English, Hindi, and

Tamil literary fields in chapter 1 and show how writers were motivated by divergent and sometimes contradictory interests in it. For instance, in his 1934 speech to Tamil students of Hindi in Madras, Premchand argued that a pan-Indian literature would come to fruition when more writers from non-Hindi–speaking regions contributed to the Hindi corpus. But I also show in chapter 1 that Premchand sought to narrow the boundaries of Hindi by discouraging translation and other outside influences.

81. For more on dialogism, see Bakhtin, *Dialogic Imagination* and *Speech Genres*. Bakhtin, writing contemporaneously with Premchand, but focused on the Russian context, noted that dialogism exists at several levels: (1) between utterances within a single language, (2) amid social languages within a national language, and (3) among national languages within a single culture. He restricted his own explorations of dialogism to the first and second levels and was interested in exposing the centrifugal forces of heteroglossia existent within monolinguistic national culture. The multilingual makeup of late-colonial India, I would argue, requires deeper examination along the lines of Bakhtin's third level of dialogism—that is, among national languages within a single culture. I would also suggest, however, that the emergence of dialogism among regional Indian languages—once they became fully associated with distinct cultural and territorial identities in the late-colonial era—was in part responsible for the consolidation of the notion of a single national Indian culture.

82. Nambi Arooran, *Tamil Renaissance*, 109. See also Sumathi Ramaswamy, *Passions of the Tongue*, 261n12.

83. For more on language politics, leading up to and following Indian independence, and the formation of linguistic states, see J. Das Gupta, *Language Conflict*; Forrester, "Madras Anti-Hindi Agitation"; and R. King, *Nehru*. The reorganization of state boundaries along linguistic lines was set in motion by the States Reorganization Act in 1956 and the creation of Andhra Pradesh as a Telugu state. This reorganization was a highly contentious process that unfolded over several decades and continues to impact linguistic movements in contemporary India. Disputes across the subcontinent over whether English or Hindi should become the national language following Independence were related to the creation of linguistic states. These disputes prompted Jawaharlal Nehru, the first prime minister of India, to implement a fifteen-year grace period—until 1965—during which time Hindi could be further integrated at the regional level before assuming its mantle as the national language. But these efforts were unsuccessful, and anti-Hindi protests persisted throughout the grace period, especially in the South. In the North, by contrast, Hindi advocacy remained strong. To quell the situation, Nehru brought the Official Languages Bill before the Lok Sabha (lower house of Parliament) early and ushered its passing in 1963. This extended the deadline for phasing out English beyond 1965, effectively stalling the national language question. Yet the bill's promise that English would be retained indefinitely for official purposes alongside Hindi fell into question with Nehru's death in 1964. Despite the addition of an amendment to the Official Languages Act in 1967 to slow down the Hindi-ization process, language riots continued into the late 1960s in the South. This led national leaders to effectively shelve the national language question. Still today, India has two official languages of the Union (English and Hindi), twenty-two scheduled languages of the regions, and no national language.

84. I discuss this new vision for Hindi literature in detail in chaps. 3–5.

85. Yadav, "Ek Duniyā Samānāntar," 17–18.

86. For more on the notion of autonomy in modernist fiction, see Goldstone, *Fictions of Autonomy*; and Kalliney, "Modernism." The very name—*nayī kahānī* (new story)—that Yadav and his contemporaries used for advancing their postindependence Hindi agenda references the "making it new" of modernism expounded by Ezra Pound in late 1920s. For examples of national-scale discussions about modernism and artistic autonomy in Indian literature, see essays published in the Sahitya Akademi's journal *Indian Literature,* such as Joshi, "Modernism and Indian Literature"; and Tagore, "Modernism in Literature." Based in Delhi and active in its literary culture, Yadav was invested in debates happening at the Sahitya Akademi, although he sometimes viewed himself at odds with the Akademi's literary agenda. See, for example, his wife's autobiographical reflections in Bhandari, *Ek Kahānī Yah Bhī*. Yadav also referenced globally iconic modernist writers, such as Joyce and Eliot, and drew on existentialist understandings of autonomy, particularly those of Jean-Paul Sartre. See, for example, the essays included in Yadav, *Kahānī*.

87. In chapters 3 and 4 I also show that specters of Partition trauma and communal conflict can be read into the erasures that Yadav's literary worldview enacted.

88. Chellappa, *Tamil̲ Cir̲ukatai Pir̲akkir̲atu*, 30. For the full quote, and more discussion on Chellappa's views and *El̲uttu*, see chapter 3.

89. S. Radhakrishnan, "Editorial Note," 1. For the full quote and further discussion, see chapter 3.

90. Kaviraj, *Imaginary Institution of India*, 151–52.

91. For arguments against the persistence of English, see, for example, M. Mukherjee, *Perishable Empire*. I hasten to add that recent scholarship has productively complicated this binary understanding of English as a realm entirely separate from Indian languages. See, for example, Anjaria, " Introduction: Literary Pasts, Presents, and Futures"; Nerlekar, *Bombay Modern*; Sadana, *English Heart, Hindi Heartland*; and Shingavi, *Mahatma Misunderstood*.

92. A different multilingual configuration would emerge by the 1970s and 1980s, exemplified by the work of Hindi writer Geetanjali Shree (1957–) and Tamil writer C. S. Lakshmi (1944–). Both instituted a linguistic division between their academic nonfiction written in English and their fiction written in Hindi and Tamil, respectively. As Shree pointed out in a 2018 lecture, the bilingualism of her generation differed from that of the previous literary generation. She argued that, having been educated in English in post-Partition India—by which time the separation between Hindi and Urdu (and other regional languages) had become institutionally entrenched—she could possess, unlike her predecessors, no sense of a mother tongue and had to return to Hindi via English (Shree, "My Language"). See also Sadana, *English Heart, Hindi Heartland*, 116–35; and Shree, "Writing Is Translating." Similarly, C. S. Lakshmi—who uses the penname Ambai for her fiction—has noted that she uses a Tamil that is outside of Tamil, even though it is the language to which she intuitively turns for writing fiction (Doctor, "Her Own Language"). Both Shree and Lakshmi express, according to Sadana, a "multilingual consciousness of regionally located literary practitioners [that] incorporates English-language discourse . . . [so that] the expression of one's regionality relies on English" (Sadana, *English Heart, Hindi Heartland*, 105). I would argue that this consciousness was made possible by

the position given to English following the fizzling out of the national language question after 1965.

93. Anderson, *Imagined Communities*, 22. Anderson later observes that the newly arising field of philology—pioneered by Orientalists like William Jones—brought European languages into comparison with languages existing elsewhere. This prompted the printing, in Europe, of new vernacular-language grammars and dictionaries, which could provide a clear demarcation of what constituted European languages and literatures vis-à-vis philology's sudden pluralization of "extra-European antiquity" (Anderson, *Imagined Communities*, 70). The central role of comparative philology in the consolidation of European vernaculars into national languages suggests a fundamental interrelation between linguistic processes in Europe and contemporaneous ones unfolding in the colonial world—an interrelation that Anderson himself overlooks. The process of colonial-era vernacularization that I have outlined in this chapter—which constituted English as a model vernacular for Indian languages because it epitomized a one-to-one relation between language, people, and territory—urges us to consider how the elevation of vernaculars to the standing of national languages in Europe was contingent on the assignation of a vernacular status to languages in colonial contexts like India.

94. This and the preceding quotation are from Anderson, *Imagined Communities*, 30.

95. This and the preceding quotation are from Anderson, *Imagined Communities*, 34–35.

96. Jameson, *Political Unconscious*, 138. For more on the revolutionary challenges that the novel was seen to raise against traditional class hierarchies, centrality of religion, and aristocratic norms of propriety and civility, see Bakhtin, *Dialogic Imagination*; Lukács, *Historical Novel* and *Theory of the Novel*; Moretti, *Way of the World*; and Watt, *Rise of the Novel*.

97. See, for example, Chaudhuri, "Bengali Novel"; V. Dharwadker, "Modernist Novel in India"; Ebeling, *Colonizing the Realm*; Kailasapathy, *Tamil̲ Nāval Ilakkiyam*; M. Mukherjee, *Early Novels in India*; Padikkal, "Inventing Modernity"; and G. Rai, *Hindī Upanyās kā Itihās*.

98. Jameson, *Political Unconscious*, 138.

99. For more on understanding realisms and modernisms as modes, see chapter 3.

100. Anderson, *Imagined Communities*, 27–28.

101. Anderson, *Imagined Communities*, 32. Emphasis in original.

102. Chaudhuri, "Bengali Novel," 102.

103. Dalmia, *Nationalization of Hindu Traditions*, 222–37; Ebeling, *Colonizing the Realm*, 205–46.

104. Chaudhuri, "Bengali Novel," 108.

105. Genette, *Paratexts*, n.p.

106. Pratt, "Short Story," 100. Pratt's essay is one of a very few that explores the formal features of the short story. Apart from hers, Charles May's examinations of the short story ("*I Am Your Brother*"; "Reality in the Short Story"; and *Short Story Theories*) and his edited volumes of writers exploring their own short story practices (*New Short Story Theories* and *Short Story Theories*) offer insights into the nature, development, and ambitions of the genre. Other studies and anthologies provide

general overviews of the short story in different regions of the world, rather than explications of the genre's inner workings. See, for example, Head, *Modernist Short Story*; Hunter, *Cambridge Introduction to the Short Story in English*; March-Russell, *Short Story*; Parts, *Russian Twentieth-Century Short Story*; and Scofield, *Cambridge Introduction to the American Short Story*. Numerous literary histories of Indian short story writing exist for each of the regional languages. In the cases of Hindi and Tamil, see, for example, Ashk, *Hindi Kahānī*; Kennedy, "Two Tamil Literary Renaissances"; Kennedy, "Public Voices, Private Voices"; Madhuresh, *Hindī Kahānī kā Vikās*; G. Rai, *Hindi Kahānī kā Itihās*; Roadarmel, "Theme of Alienation"; D. Singh, *Hindī Kahānī*; and Sundararajan and Sivapathasundaram, *Tamiḻil Ciṟukatai*. But in contrast to these histories, only the Hindi and Tamil writers I examine in this book have sought to theorize the form.

107. For example, Tagore published his first short stories in the 1870s—the same period that Edgar Allan Poe's short story writing and theories gained circulation in the US and Europe (several decades after his death). For more on Poe's work and reception, see March-Russell, *Short Story*, 32–42. Poe's stories—along with Tagore's—were translated widely into Hindi and Tamil and inspired much short story experimentation in these languages by the 1910s (see Kennedy, "Public Voices, Private Voices," 80; and Mody, *Making of Modern Hindi*, 178–213). This was the same moment that O. Henry's "well-made story" became popular in North America and Europe (March-Russell, *Short Story*, 39). Poe's major contribution was to validate the periodical market as a "source for artistic innovation" (March-Russell, *Short Story*, 33), but this idea did not gain currency until Brander Matthews called attention to it in *The Philosophy of the Short-Story* in 1901. Matthews's interpretation of Poe, Paul March-Russell writes, "effectively distance[d] the short story form from its popular and folk roots in order to present it as an object of aesthetic value equivalent to the novel . . . aid[ing] magazine editors as much as . . . individual writers" (*Short Story*, 35). Nonetheless, Pratt shows that the short story has maintained a subordinate position compared to the novel in Western literary criticism ("Short Story"). By comparison, I show in chapter 2 that Hindi and Tamil writers viewed the novel as an inferior form that lacked the aesthetic value of the short story. This perspective was based on their association of the novel with didacticism and popular fiction.

108. See, for example, Auerbach, *Mimesis*; Bakhtin, *Dialogic Imagination*; and Lukács, *Historical Novel* and *Theory of the Novel*.

109. I thank Jonathan Alba Cutler for prompting me to explore Pratt's arguments in light of the colonial conditions particular to India.

110. In the case of Tamil, A. R. Venkatachalapathy has shown that, beginning in the 1920s, writers began to critique the novel for its social-reformist didacticism, pulpiness, and derivativeness of English romance and detective fiction. See Venkatachalapathy, *Province of the Book*, 76–98. The rise of the Tamil short story, by contrast, was linked to the establishment, in the 1930s, of the first Tamil magazine devoted to high literature and to conversations among writers about the differences between "popular" and "literary" Tamil literature. See Mani, "Literary and Popular Fiction." See also chapter 2. In the case of Hindi, I discuss in chapter 2 how an anxiety about the derivativeness of the Hindi novel led writers like Premchand to emphasize the literary merit of the Hindi short story instead.

111. Considering the case of Tamil, K. Kailasapathy and Richard Kennedy have also connected the rise of the short story to the maturing of the middle class in the 1930s, which was highlighted by short story's narrow focus on individual experiences of urban modernization. See Kailasapathy, *Tamil̲ Nāval Ilakkiyam*, 194–206; and Kennedy, "Two Tamil Literary Renaissances."

112. Dalmia, *Nationalization of Hindu Traditions*, 282–91; Mody, *Making of Modern Hindi*, 135–77.

113. Rosenstein, "Introduction," 4.

114. For more on this, see Sumathi Ramaswamy, *Passions of the Tongue*, 34–36.

115. I also want to note, however, that some Tamil writers—such as Na. Piccamurti, Ku. Pa. Rajagopalan, and Ka. Naa. Subramanyam—continued to write poetry throughout the late-colonial era, even if their poetry did not feature centrally in literary discussions until the postindependence period. I thank Sascha Ebeling for bringing this point to my attention.

116. Harsha Ram offers an alternative multiscalar approach to questions of world literature by calling for researcher-scholars to perform a kind of analytical scale jumping that brings to light the intersecting local, national, and transregional modernist conversations occurring contemporaneously in any given location. See Ram, "Scale of Global Modernisms." I am making the slightly different argument that we must understand the dialogism that shapes literary texts as multiscalar in nature—that is, as engaging multiple, dissociated, and sometimes hypothetical readerships across global, national, regional, and local scales—even when these readerships are not immediately evident to us from the words on the page.

117. This and the preceding quotation are from Mufti, *Enlightenment in the Colony*, 180.

118. Mufti, *Enlightenment in the Colony*, 182.

119. Mufti, *Enlightenment in the Colony*, 197.

120. For another examination of Manto's innovative explorations of gender, see Gopal, *Literary Radicalism in India*, 89–122.

121. Charu Gupta has argued that in late-colonial India: "For Hindu bourgeois ethics an attack on prostitutes and the courtesan culture of the pre-colonial period became another way of condemning the supposed decadence and lewdness of Muslim kings, especially of the late medieval period" (*Sexuality, Obscenity, Community*, 112). At the same time, changing middle-class norms around marriage and monogamy led to a Hindu condemnation of the prostitute as the embodiment of the "other" of middle-class Hindu society. For more on how these critiques have impacted courtesan culture, see Oldenburg, "Lifestyle as Resistance."

122. Mufti reveals the influence of Western criticism's bias toward the novel on his argument when he compares the Urdu tradition to it, writing that, in Urdu, "the development of the novel form has not constituted anything like the sort of coherent and canonical tradition that we associate with the major languages of Western Europe, with Arabic and Japanese, or even with other Indian languages like Bengali" (*Enlightenment in the Colony*, 182–83).

123. For more on Bharati's representations of *Tamil̲ tāy*, see Sumathi Ramaswamy, *Passions of the Tongue*, 51–52. For more on Gupt's and other poets' representations of *Bhārat mātā*, see Gupta, *Sexuality, Obscenity, Community*, 202–13.

124. See, for example, M. Mukherjee, *Realism and Reality*, 68–100.

125. Premchand wrote *Bāzār-e-Ḥusn* in 1917, but he did not find a publisher until 1924. *Sevāsadan* was published in 1918.

126. Anantharam, "Change in Aesthetics." For more discussion of the two novels together, see also Shingavi, "Premchand and Language."

CHAPTER 1

1. This idea of Indian literature departed from the colonial construction of eighteenth- and nineteenth-century literature—what Aamir Mufti has called the formation of "the institution of Indian literature" through Indological preoccupations with Sanskrit and efforts to standardize Indian languages. According to Mufti, the eighteenth-century Oriental encounter invented Indian literature, a national corpus that could join world literary space. European Indologists and the indigenous colonial intelligentsia conceptualized Indian literature through a mutual sense of elation, apprehension, awe, and reverence for the literature of the other—"a sort of philological sublime" (*Forget English!*, 105). Together, they elevated the classical Sanskritic canon and set modern Indian vernaculars on the path of literary development (see also Ahmad, *In Theory*). As "counter-Orientialist," social-reformist, and regional-identitarian movements arose in the twentieth century, and the nationalist movement expanded, this cohesive notion of Indian literature became increasingly untenable. For more discussion on this, see the introduction.

2. But at the 1936 meeting of the *Akhil Bhāratīya Sāhitya Parishad* (All-India Society for Literature) in Nagpur, Gandhi "laid down the ruling that the language of the *Parishad*, and by implication the language of the country, was not going to be 'Hindustani' in which the now much reduced Urdu could still have claimed a half-share, but 'Hindi or Hindustani' in the Nagari script" (Trivedi, "Urdu Premchand," 107).

3. See the introduction for more on this. For discussion of Gandhi's, Nehru's, and the INC's views on language politics, see J. Das Gupta, *Language Conflict*; and R.King, *Nehru*.

4. The Sahitya Akademi constitution was established to "work actively for the development of Indian letters and to set high literary standards, to foster and coordinate literary activities in all the Indian languages and to promote through them all the cultural unity of the country" (as reproduced in Rao, *Five Decades*, 258). The second goal of the constitution was "to encourage or to arrange translations of literary works from one Indian language into others and also from non-Indian into Indian languages and *vice-versa*" (as reproduced in Rao, 258). Two excellent recent studies—Rosemary Marangoly George's *Indian Literature and the Fiction of National Language* and Rashmi Sadana's *English Heart, Hindi Heartland*—have documented how the Sahitya Akademi has privileged English despite its supposed goal of creating linguistic equality among all Indian languages.

5. S. Radhakrishnan, "Writer's Role," 25.

6. See, for example, Banerji, "Current Publishing Trends"; A. Das Gupta, "Translating Antigone"; R. K. Das Gupta, "Indian Response," and "Western Response"; Machwe, "Problem of Translation"; Nehru, "Creative Writing"; and Tagore, "Modernism in Literature."

7. Banerji, "Current Publishing Trends," 55.

8. Banerji, "Current Publishing Trends," 58.

9. Nehru, "Creative Writing," 67.

10. Thus, numerous *Indian Literature* articles also considered whether modern "Indian Literature" actually existed and how to most effectively develop this field. See, for example, Bhattacharya, "Modern Indian Literature: Myth or Reality?"; R. K. Das Gupta, "Problems of Research"; Isenburg, "Modern Indian Literature"; and Joshi, "Modernism and Indian Literature."

11. Ahmad, *In Theory*, 243. Emphasis in original.

12. Ahmad, *In Theory*, 249.

13. Ahmad, *In Theory*, 281.

14. M. Mukherjee, *Perishable Empire*, 188.

15. Merrill, "Translations from South Asia," 168. See also Devy, *In Another Tongue*; and Merrill, *Riddles of Belonging*.

16. Discussing the recent boom in the publication of writing translated from Indian languages, Arunava Sinha writes: "while there is no stemming the flow of original works in English, India's biggest English language publishers—the majority of whom are global corporations—are warming up to the idea of commissioning and publishing more works in translation from regional languages. . . . Translations are now being presented as examples of best in class writing" ("Big Story").

17. Ahmad, *In Theory*, 243–44.

18. Yildiz's focus is on Europe. But Aamir Mufti has shown that the philological revolution—which gave rise to the monolingual paradigm—was made possible by the Orientalist encounter with the "East." Through this encounter, Mufti writes, "a concept of world as an assemblage of 'nations'" was articulated for the first time (*Forget English!*, 35).

19. Yildiz, *Beyond the Mother Tongue*, 2.

20. I discuss this premise in greater detail in the introduction and chapter 3.

21. Yildiz, *Beyond the Mother Tongue*, 3–4. Speaking about translation more generally, Robert Young has recently asked: "What if translation required the invention of the monolingual (and then the multilingual) for it to come into existence? . . . Wedded to the written form, translation is sustained by the ideology of discrete unitary languages, assuming and requiring monolingualism, for without that separated distinction the conversion of one language into another would never take place—and would never be needed" ("Called a Language," 1217–18). Although linguistic pluralism remains prevalent in speech forms across the subcontinent, the standardizing and translational impulses of the modern Indian literary sphere lean toward the type of monolingualism that both Young and Yildiz identify. See the introduction for more on this.

22. Khilnani, "Gandhi and Nehru," 154–56.

23. Damrosch, *What Is World Literature?*, 4.

24. Damrosch, *What Is World Literature?*, 287.

25. Variations of this model appear in Franco Moretti's notion of "distant reading," which views world literature as a system for evaluating the evolution and variation (in short, the translation) of form on a global scale, and in Pascale Casanova's "world republic of letters," which provides peripheral literatures entry into world literary space through recognition from more established literatures, primarily through translation (Casanova, *World Republic of Letters*; Moretti, "Conjectures on World Literature" and "More Conjectures"). Casanova, Damrosch, and Moretti

advance concepts such as *littérisation*, consecration, translatability, and literary evolution, which define the literary qualities of texts that become part of the world literary canon. Preserved by "autonomous critics" (most of whom are located at elite European institutions), the global publishing market, and international literary prizes, these concepts are curiously solipsistic in nature. What travels is translatable; what is translatable receives consecration; and what is consecrated achieves *littérisation* "by means of which a text comes to be regarded as literary by the legitimate authorities" (Casanova, *World Republic of Letters*, 136). Who are these "legitimate authorities," and what does it mean to be considered "literary"? Is a text translatable because it is literary, or is it literary because it is translatable? For two critiques of this prevailing world-literature position, see Orsini, "Multilingual Local"; and Shankar, "Literatures of the World."

26. Damrosch, *What Is World Literature?, 288.*

27. Ahmad, *In Theory*, 244, 255.

28. Damrosch, *What is World Literature?*, 288. For Damrosch, "a work enters into world literature by a double process: first, by being read *as* literature; second, by circulating out into a broader world beyond its linguistic and cultural point of origin" (6; emphasis in original). Attending to worlding processes, I argue, allows us to see how writers use a variety of nonaligning strategies, techniques, and conventions to not only make texts "literary" but also define what counts as "literary" in the first place.

29. See, for example, Hayot, *On Literary Worlds*; Johnson, "Archive of Errors"; Shankar, "Literatures of the World." These studies offer alternatives to the prevailing world-system approach to world literature taken by, for example, Beecroft, *Ecology of World Literature*; Casanova, *World Republic of Letters*; Moretti, "Evolution, World-Systems, *Weltliteratur*"; Mufti, *Forget English!*; and Warwick Research Collective, *Combined and Uneven Development.*

30. Kadir, "To World, to Globalize," 6–7.

31. Worlding processes need not therefore necessarily invoke "world literature"—as the examples in this chapter do—to make texts intelligible as literature.

32. Cheah, *What Is a World?*, 26.

33. Cheah, *What Is a World?*, 37.

34. Cheah, *What Is a World?*, 9–10.

35. Cheah, *What Is a World?*, 129.

36. According to Cheah, a text must meet four specific criteria to belong to this category: (1) it must take globalization as one of its themes and express how a given society is situated in the world system; (2) it must show how a nation is part of a world through an activist stance that is oppositional to globalization; (3) it must view the world as a "limitless field of conflicting forces that are brought into relation and that overlap and flow into each other without return"; and (4) it must register the process of worlding—that is, "receiving a world or letting it come . . . showing the possibility of opening onto another world . . . [that is] immanent to the present world" (*What Is a World?*, 210–12).

37. Heidegger, "Origin."

38. Spivak, "Rani of Sirmur," 253n218. See also Spivak, *Critique of Postcolonial Reason*, 211–13, and "Three Women's Texts," 253–54. Cheah argues that Spivak's use of worlding to describe imperialist discursive cartography "obscures what is truly

valuable about Heidegger's concept for understanding the relation between world literature and globalization. . . . Worlding is not a cartographical process that epistemologically constructs the world by means of discursive representations but a process of temporalization. Cartography reduces the world to a spatial object. In contradistinction, worlding is a force that subtends and exceeds all human calculations that reduce the world as a temporal structure to the sum of objects in space" (*What Is a World?*, 8). In other words, Cheah contends that by using the concept of worlding to describe a problem of epistemology, Spivak overlooks the fundamentally ontological nature of worlding, thereby using the term in a "derived sense." I would argue, however, that in emphasizing the all-pervasive ontological nature of worlding, Cheah disregards the context-specific nature of the world that each instance of worlding discloses. Literary processes of worlding have both ontological and epistemological force.

39. For an account of the London PWA meetings and the drafting of the manifesto, see Anand, "Progressive Writers' Movement"; and Zaheer, "Reminiscences." For an account of the first All-India PWA conference in Lucknow, see Zaheer, *Light*. Shabana Mahmud has demonstrated that Mahmuduzzafar, a key PWA member, first articulated the idea of a "League of Progressive Authors" in 1933, in response to widespread denunciation of *Angāre* ("Angāre," 451). This Urdu collection was published in Lucknow in 1932, and it included short stories by Mahmuduzzafar, Sajjad Zaheer, Rashid Jahan, and Ahmed Ali. But the London PWA writers' manifesto was the first *concerted* articulation of a new pan-Indian literature, since it was the first to define the aims and objectives of progressive writing and to coordinate PWA efforts across the subcontinent.

40. Apart from Anand (who was responsible for the first draft) and Zaheer (who prepared the final draft), several other London-based Indian writers were also involved in creating the manifesto. See Anand et al., "Manifesto"; and Zaheer, "Reminiscences."

41. Every PWA study that I have consulted incorrectly cites the original publication date of Premchand's translation of the London PWA manifesto in *Haṃs* as October 1935, rather than the correct date of January 1936. See, for example, Ahmed, *Literature and Politics*; Coppola, "All-India Progressive Writers' Association" and *Urdu Poetry*; Jalil, *Liking Progress, Loving Change*; and Merrill, *Riddles of Belonging*. Coppola cites the *Haṃs* translation's publication date based on Khalilur Rahman Azmi's Urdu reproduction of the manifesto in his study of Urdu progressive literature. See Azmi, *Urdū meṃ Taraqqī Pasand*, 35–37. Other studies draw from Coppola's English translation from Urdu, rather than examining the *Haṃs* version.

42. The PWA manifesto that was published in the *Left Review* underwent some revisions before it was approved at the first All-India PWA Conference, held in Lucknow. In his recollections of the first conference, Zaheer writes: "The manifesto of the Progressive Movement was also presented at the conference and was accepted unanimously. Only a few words were changed in the original document which had been prepared in London, at the behest of the Maharashtra representatives, and the revision was approved by everybody" (*Light*, 71). Yet there are no records of the exact changes made to the manifesto at the first All-India PWA conference. Another amended manifesto was adopted at the second All-India PWA Conference in Cal-

cutta in December 1938. This manifesto is reproduced in Pradhan, *Marxist Cultural Movement*, 20–22.

43. Anand et al., "Manifesto," 240.

44. See Anand, "Progressive Writers' Movement"; and Zaheer, "Reminiscences." Singling out phrases such as "spirit of progress" and "spirit of reaction" as typical of "leftist-liberal criticism of the period" (Coppola, "All-India Progressive Writers' Association," 9), Coppola and others have vaguely noted the manifesto's connection to communist and socialist thought. See, for example, Ahmed, *Literature and Politics*, 21–28; Coppola, "All-India Progressive Writers' Association," 3–5, and *Urdu Poetry*, 62–114; and Jalil, *Liking Progress, Loving Change*, 191–211. But these scholars have not examined near-verbatim similarities in language appearing in the PWA manifesto and speeches from the Soviet Writers' Congress and Paris Congress.

45. Jalil argues that, although there is no direct evidence that Zaheer attended the Soviet Writers' Congress, "money came from Britain for the dispatch of Indian students for training and to pay for the Indian delegates to attend the [Seventh World Congress of the Comintern held in Moscow in 1934]." She further contends that Zaheer drew inspiration from Moscow, possibly had a "clandestine discussion somewhere in Europe" about what happened at the Congress, and likely received money from Moscow to start a communist magazine in India (*Liking Progress, Loving Change*, 216–17).

46. Zaheer, "Reminiscences," 40.

47. Gorky, "Soviet Literature," 27–32.

48. Zhdanov, "Soviet Literature," 19.

49. Radek, "Contemporary World Literature," 150.

50. Radek, "Contemporary World Literature," 170–74.

51. Radek, "Contemporary World Literature," 157.

52. Gide, "Individual," 448.

53. This and the preceding quotation are from Gide, "Individual," 450–52.

54. Ali, "Progressive View of Art," 80–81.

55. Anand, *Conversations in Bloomsbury*, 94–102, 129–32, 144–51.

56. Anand, "Progressive Writers' Movement," 10.

57. Anand, "Progressive Writers' Movement," 8.

58. Anand, "Progressive Writers' Movement," 10.

59. For example, Anand writes: "Indian culture had during the last hundred years, suffered from the bias of European scholars in favour of British Imperialism, while the significance of many aspects of our art and literature has never been brought out in an objective manner. . . . [But] for the first time there is a scheme through which we can have a voice in international discussion" ("Progressive Writers' Movement," 15–16).

60. Zaheer, "Reminiscences," 40.

61. Anand, "Progressive Writers' Movement," 20.

62. The PWA's progressivism still maintains prominence in contemporary discussions of world literature. For example, in her comparison of the PWA writer Mulk Raj Anand and James Joyce, Jessica Berman has used Anand's work to argue for international modernism's progressive agenda ("Comparative Colonialisms").

63. Talat Ahmed suggests that the London PWA writers' location outside of India also contributed to their vision of a progressive, pan-Indian literature in a common

language and script: "In London, linguistic or religious differences amongst the small Indian community would have seemed immaterial compared to their status as Indians and the cohesion this would have engendered" (*Literature and Politics*, 21).

64. Nehru, "Creative Writing," 67.

65. See, for example, Denning, *Age of Three Worlds*; and Gopal, *Literary Radicalism in India*.

66. Coppola, "All-India Progressive Writers' Association," 10–11. See also Coppola, *Urdu Poetry*, 85.

67. Azmi's Urdu reproduction of Premchand's manifesto, on which Coppola relies, does not include Premchand's opening and closing remarks. Azmi's version was published in 1977. In it, some of the clauses present in the *Haṃs* version appear reordered; descriptive phrases are sometimes added and sometimes missing; and, in some instances, "Urdu" (Arabic- and Persian-derived) vocabulary replaces "Hindi" (Sanskrit-derived) words.

68. Premchand, "Landan meṃ," 117.

69. Premchand, "Landan meṃ," 117; compare sentences 4–9 from the London PWA manifesto above.

70. Orsini, *Hindi Public Sphere*, 108–9. *Rāso* is an early Hindi genre of martial ballad (circa the sixteenth century), sung to an accompaniment of music and acting. *Bhakti* devotional currents arose in South India in the seventh century, moved northward by the tenth century, and maintained a strong presence across the subcontinent throughout the nineteenth century. "The dark age of Muslim occupation" references Shukla's characterization of the periods of rule by the Delhi Sultanate (twelfth to fifteenth century) and the Mughals (fifteenth to nineteenth century). The *rīti* period is named for the *rīti* (high style) poetry that flourished due to Mughal court patronage during the sixteenth through nineteenth centuries. For a chronology of subcontinental history, see Dalmia and Sadana, *Cambridge Companion*, xi–xxii. For a definition and overview of *bhakti*, see Hawley, *Storm of Songs*, 1–11. For a discussion of the *rāso* and *rīti* poetic traditions, see Busch, *Poetry of Kings*.

71. Milind Wakankar elaborates: "from Shukla's perspective in the 1930s, Kabir's idiom . . . seemed suspiciously 'mystical' and 'foreign' to the generally accessible, more Hindu (and therefore more Indian) values enshrined in the work of Surdas and Tulsidas" ("Moment of Criticism," 997).

72. See Wakankar, "Moment of Criticism," 1001–7.

73. See Premchand, "Sāhityā kā Uddeśya," 6. This turn was exemplified by texts like *Baitāl Paccīsī* (The twenty-five tales of Baital), *Bāgh-o-bahār* (Garden and spring), *Sahastra-rajani-caritra* (The story of the thousand nights), and *Candrakāntā Santati* (Chandrakanta's sons). *Baitāl Paccīsī* is an eleventh-century compilation of Sanskrit stories about King Vikramaditya and his pursuit of a vampire spirit who animated dead bodies. *Bāgh-o-bahār* is the Urdu title of poet Amir Khusrau's thirteenth-century collection of allegorical stories in Persian (also called *The Tale of the Four Dervishes*). *Sahastra-rajani-caritra* is the nineteenth-century Hindi translation of the Persian *Arabian Nights*. *Candrakāntā Santati* is a multivolume sequel by Devkinandan Khatri and his son Durgaprasad Khatri. It draws on the Persian *dāstān* tradition of tales of wonder and adventure. See Premchand, "Kahānī Kalā 1," 27, and "Sāhityā kā Uddeśya," 7.

74. Premchand, "Kahānī Kalā 1," 30.

75. In chapter 2, I discuss how Premchand's investment in classical Indian idealism shaped his literary philosophy of idealistic realism (*ādarśommukhī yathārthvād*).

76. These critiques are also evident in Premchand's address to the South India Society for the Propagation of Hindi (Dakshiṇa Bhārat Hindī Pracār Sabhā) in December 1934, discussed in the introduction in this book. Viewed in conjunction with the speech, Premchand's stance on medieval-era Indian literature in his translation of the London PWA manifesto can be understood through the lens of nineteenth-century vernacularization processes, which had construed prose as modern in contrast to the traditional conventions of poetry.

77. Premchand, "Landan meṃ," 117–18; compare sentences 10–11 of the London PWA manifesto.

78. Coppola, "All-India Progressive Writers' Association," 11. See also Coppola, *Urdu Poetry*, 85–86.

79. See A. K. Singh, "Premchand On/In Translation"; and Trivedi, "Urdu Premchand." Harish Trivedi contends that Premchand wrote increasingly in Hindi not just because the Hindi publishing market was more profitable—although this was the explanation that Premchand himself offered in some of his letters. He argues that Premchand switched because, as a Hindu, he saw himself as an outsider to Urdu, which became more associated with Islamic culture and tradition during the late colonial period. Premchand's most compelling portrayals of Hindu village life—epitomized in his final novel *Godān* (The gift of a cow, 1936)—emerged when he wrote in Hindi about "the life of the villages and villagers which he knew best through upbringing and observation" (Trivedi, "Urdu Premchand," 114). Trivedi's assessment confirms how, over the course of his career, Premchand came to view some of settings, themes, and character types as more suitable for a Hindu audience and others as more appropriate for a Muslim one. Yet I would also argue that understanding the ways in which Premchand moved between languages requires more research than is possible here. For example, to what extent did translators, editors, and publishers alter Premchand's texts before publication in Hindi and Urdu venues, rather than Premchand himself? For more discussion on Premchand's movements between Hindi and Urdu, see chapter 2.

80. See, for example, Premchand, "Kahānī Kalā 3," and "Sāhitya kī Pragati."

81. Premchand, "Upanyās," 37.

82. Premchand, "Premcanda kī Prem-Līlā," 70.

83. Avadhesh Kumar Singh has pointed to the same two passages to argue: "Premchand was pragmatic in his attitude towards translation. . . . He acknowledged the significance of translation but did not overestimate it" ("Premchand On/In Translation," 130–31). I believe, however, that Premchand was driven by more than just pragmatism. As I show further in this chapter, his views on translation were intimately linked with his efforts to elevate the status of Hindi on the national stage.

84. Premchand, "Bhāratīya Sāhitya aura Paṇḍit Javāharlāl Nehrū," 106.

85. Premchand, "Bhāratīya Sāhitya aura Paṇḍit Javāharlāl Nehrū," 107.

86. For more discussion of the two novels, see the introduction in this book.

87. Shingavi, "Premchand and Language," 163.

88. Premchand, "Landan meṃ," 118.

89. For more on Premchand's paradoxical stances on Hindi language and literature, see the introduction.

90. Premchand, "Landan meṃ," 18.

91. Premchand, "Landan meṃ," 18.

92. The absence of any PWA influence in Tamil Nadu during this period is likely due to the failure of the Communist Party of India (CPI) to influence politics in the region more generally. V. K. Padmanabhan has argued that, because the CPI's actions and policies were determined by leaders outside of Tamil Nadu (as well as South India), the party was largely disconnected from Tamil politics of caste, gender, and identity in the preindependence period. He further notes, "Marxism in Tamil Nadu spread as a political programme rather than a new world view or a cultural movement. The communists of Tamil Nadu served both as promoters of Marxist thought and builders of a political movement. But their role as activists overshadowed their role as ideologues. Consequently, the Marxian concept of politics as both the fruit and the seed of deeper critical consciousness did not develop in Tamil Nadu" ("Communist Parties," 228). The Tamil leader P. Jeevanandam more successfully linked Tamil literature and culture using a Marxist lens in his writings and public speeches after independence. Jeevanandam founded the *Tamiḻnāṭu Kalai Ilakkiyap Perumaṉṟam* (Tamil Nadu Arts and Literature Forum) in 1961—which replaced the unsuccessful Tamil Nadu branch of the Progressive Writers' Association, founded in 1948—as a "conscious attempt to unite and give direction along Left ideological lines to the varied cultural art-literary associations operating independently in Tamil Nadu at the time" (Vaitheespara and Venkatasubramanian, "Beyond the Politics of Identity," 556). Later, a more successful Tamil Nadu branch of the Progressive Writers' Association, associated with the Communist Party of India (Marxist) party, was established in 1975. For more on this, see Cody, *Light of Knowledge*, 140-48.

93. The founding editors of *Maṇikkoṭi* were T. S. Chokalingam, K. Srinivasan, and V. Ramaswamy Iyengar. The three quickly recruited B. S. Ramaiah to join them and eventually turned editorship over to him in 1935. For an account of the *Maṇikkoṭi* era and the writers involved with the magazine, see Kennedy, "Public Voices, Private Voices"; Ramaiah, *Maṇikkoṭi Kālam*; and Vallikkannan, *Tamiḻil Ciṟu Pattirikkaikaḷ*, 19–22. Although many writers published in *Maṇikkoṭi*, key figures associated with the group include Ramaiah, Pudumaippittan, C. S. Chellappa, N. Chidambara Subramaniam, Ka. Naa. Subramanyam, Ku. Pa. Rajagopalan, Na. Piccamurti, S. Mani Iyer "Mauni," La. Sa. Ramamritham, and P. G. Sundararajan "Chitti." Almost all these writers were Brahmins. None of them intentionally or explicitly articulated a connection between the *Maṇikkoṭi* literary worldview and caste identity. Still, I read their use of modern Tamil literature to circumvent identitarian politics and to inspire national unity as a reflection of the threat that these writers must have felt to their social position and senses of selfhood and community. M. S. S. Pandian has argued that "claiming the Brahminic as the national was an important move made by Tamil Brahmins. It was a move which implicitly reduced non-Brahmins and religious minorities as being inadequately Indian" (*Brahmin and Non-Brahmin*, 35). *Maṇikkoṭi* writers' efforts to expose Tamil to other languages, both Indian and European, inadvertently supported this claim.

94. Ramaiah, *Maṇikkoṭi Kālam*, n.p.

95. Ramaiah, *Maṇikkoṭi Kālam*, 59–60.

96. Sumathi Ramaswamy, *Passions of the Tongue*, 147.

97. For more on S. Vedachalam Pillai "Maraimalai Adigal," see Sumathi Ramaswamy, *Passions of the Tongue*; and Vaithees, *Religion, Caste, and Nation*. Adigal was a Saivite (devotee of Shiva) and viewed Saivism as the original religion of the Tamil people (Pandian, "Notes on the Transformation of 'Dravidian' Ideology"). However, he also sought to reform Saivism, calling for "vegetarianism and teetotalism, and . . . the excision of 'irrational' customs and rituals . . . which were the very stuff of village and popular religion" (Sumathi Ramaswamy, *Passions of the Tongue*, 25). For a discussion of the relationship between the Pure Tamil and Self-Respect Movements, along with the different ideologies comprising the Dravidian movement, see Pandian, *Brahmin and Non-Brahmin* and "Notes on the Transformation of 'Dravidian' Ideology"; and Venkatachalapathy, *In Those Days*. For discussion of Periyar, see Geetha and Rajadurai, *Non-Brahmin Millennium*; and Nambi Arooran, *Tamil Renaissance*.

98. *Maṇikkoṭi* writers' efforts to distinguish modern Tamil literature from Dravidianist and Pure Tamil politics effectively bifurcated the Tamil literary field into two streams—an aesthetic stream built "on the model of the spoken word" (Bate, *Tamil Oratory*, 65) and political stream that sought to create a public version of *centamiḻ* or "'high,' 'pure,' grammaticalized Tamil" (Shulman, *Tamil: A Biography*, 319). This bifurcation remains to this day and has further entrenched diglossia within the contemporary Tamil sphere. David Shulman theorizes the focus on spoken Tamil within the literary sphere as a modern form of vernacularization, wherein "modern communications [have] create[d] better conditions for . . . the full autonomization and cultural privileging of colloquial dialects—than existed in medieval times" (*Tamil: A Biography*, 320). In the introduction in this book, I argue that the emphasis on colloquial dialects in literary Tamil—in contrast to the privileging of a classical Tamil style in political discourses and journalism—has its roots in nineteenth-century shifts in the subcontinent's multilingual landscape. I also want to note that the aesthetic stream of Tamil literature that *Maṇikkoṭi* writers developed in the 1930s was itself shaped by internal contentions. Apart from the Self-Respect and Pure Tamil movements, *Maṇikkoṭi* writers also positioned their work against the entertainment-oriented endeavors of *Āṉanta Vikaṭaṉ*, the fastest growing Tamil magazine at the time. They criticized the *Āṉanta Vikaṭaṉ* editorship for focusing on circulation numbers instead of literary quality and viewed its fiction as trivial and didactic. For more on these debates, see Mani, "Literary and Popular Fiction."

99. See especially Ramaiah, *Maṇikkoṭi Kālam*, 56–68.

100. Kennedy, "Public Voices, Private Voices," 128.

101. Pudumaippittan, "Tamiḻaip paṟṟi," 84–87.

102. Dravidianists used the term *tamiḻpaṟṟu*—meaning adherence, attachment, affection, support, love, and devotion to Tamil—to reference the growing devotion that many Tamil speakers expressed toward their language and culture. In the *Maṇikkoṭi* writers' view, such devotion was excessive, even fanatical. For more on *tamiḻpaṟṟu*, see Sumathi Ramaswamy, *Passions of the Tongue*.

103. Piccamurti, "Taṟkālat Tamiḻk Kavikaḷ," 46.

104. See, for example, Ramaiah, *Maṇikkoṭi Kālam*, 33, 59–61. According to Sumathi Ramaswamy, in the Indianist's view: "British colonialism and English . . . had to be replaced by the Indian nation with its family of 'national' languages, of which

Tamil would be the language of the region while Hindi would be the 'official' language of communication with other Indians. . . . In contrast to Dravidianists, who imagined (away) India in very Tamil terms, [Indianists] framed their concern with Tamil in terms of India. . . . Indianism reminded Tamil speakers that the liberation of Tamil would have to proceed in tandem with the liberation of India. . . . In general, Indianism's strategy was to gloss over all internal sources of contention and difference in favor of closing ranks against the real enemy, the English-speaking colonial" (*Passions of the Tongue*, 46–49). Taking cue from Bharati, the *Maṇikkoṭi* writers articulated an Indianist approach to Tamil literature and national politics. For more on Dravidianist critiques of Bharati's work, see Sumathi Ramaswamy, *Passions of the Tongue*, 200–201.

105. The year 1937 was also when the Government of Madras implemented Hindi education in schools, leading to violent protests in the region from 1937 to 1940. For more on this, see Nambi Arooran, *Tamil Renaissance*, 186–218.

106. Several writers wrote under pseudonyms for some of the work they published in *Maṇikkoṭi*. One reason could have been to give readers the impression that more writers contributed to the magazine than actually did. It is also possible that some writers wished to dissociate some of their political and literary viewpoints from their more established writerly personas.

107. Lokasundari Raman was married to the Tamil physicist C. V. Raman. For more details on her life, see Parameswaran, *Lady Lokasundari Raman*.

108. Batasari, "Yātrā Mārkkam: Nākari Eḻuttu," 30.

109. Pudumaippittan, "Yātrā Mārkkam," 75.

110. Pudumaippittan, "Yātrā Mārkkam: Cantēkat Teḷivu," 56.

111. Ramaiah, *Maṇikkoṭi Kālam*, 69.

112. Batasari, "Yātrā Mārkkam," 56.

113. Vyasan, "Yātrā Mārkkam," 57.

114. Batasari, "Yātrā Mārkkam," 56–57.

115. Pudumaippittan, "Yātrā Mārkkam: Taḻuvalum Moḻi Peyarppum," 69–70.

116. Only two writers who published in the series—N. Chidambara Subramanian and Ka. Naa. Subramanyam—favored adaptation over translation. Both argued that literature should convey shared qualities of human qualities across cultures and that adapting foreign texts to accommodate the Tamil language was inevitable. For this reason, Ka. Naa. Subramanyam insisted that all translations are actually adaptations. See Subramanian, "Yātrā Mārkkam"; and Subramanyam, "Yātrā Mārkkam." Subramanian's and Subramanyam's views of adaptation did align, however, with the general *Maṇikkoṭi* approach, which sought to replace ethnolinguistic particularism with humanist universalism.

117. Vyasan, "Yātrā Mārkkam: Taḻuvalum Moḻi Peyarppum." Ramaiah's example of adaptation was therefore also part of his effort to expand the Tamilian worldview beyond a Dravidianist focus on caste.

118. This and the previous quotation are from Apter, *Against World Literature*, 2–3.

119. Apter, *Against World Literature*, 320–34.

120. Apter, *Against World Literature*, 34.

121. Mufti, *Forget English!*, 10–11. Emphasis in original.

122. Mufti, *Forget English!*, 9. Emphasis in original.

123. Mufti, *Forget English!*, 35.
124. Mufti, *Forget English!*, 112. Emphasis in original.

CHAPTER 2

1. For overviews of these writers' lives and works, see Holmstrom, "Making It New,"; Orsini, introduction; and Venkatachalapathy, *In Those Days*, 73–85.
2. Premchand, "Galpāṅk kā Prastāv," 39.
3. See, for example, Premchand, "Kahānī Kalā 1"; and Pudumaippittan, "Kataikaḷ."
4. For further discussion, see, for example, Das, *Struggle for Freedom*; and Sogani, *Hindu Widow*.
5. M. Mukherjee, *Realism and Reality*, 7. See also M. Mukherjee, "Introduction to *Early Novels in India*."
6. See, for example, Anjaria, *Realism in the Twentieth Century*; Denning, *Age of Three Worlds*; Gopal, *Literary Radicalism in India*; Holmstrom, "Making It New"; and Venkatachalapathy, In Those Days, 73–85.
7. Gopal, *Literary Radicalism in India*, 27.
8. For more on the PWA and Premchand's relationship to the organization, see chapter 1.
9. Rather than endorsing the PWA's aims, Premchand distanced himself from the organization's literary progressivism in his address: "The Progressive Writers' Association: in my opinion this name seems wrong. A writer or artist is by nature progressive. . . . He perceives a deficiency, both within himself and outside. To correct this deficiency, his soul is restless. . . . [But] not every writer or author holds the same understanding of advancement or progress. The stages that one community considers to be progress, another may undoubtedly view as decadent, and so a writer must never subject his art to any objective" ("Sāhitya kā Uddeśya," 13–14). Hindi writers would later define progressivism in much narrower terms, but Premchand sought to embrace a range of literary perspectives and approaches.
10. Premchand, "Sāhitya kā Uddeśya," 6.
11. Premchand, "Sāhitya kā Uddeśya," 13.
12. Premchand, "Sāhitya kā Uddeśya," 10–11.
13. Premchand, "Sāhitya kā Uddeśya," 9.
14. For recent examples, see Anjaria, *Realism in the Twentieth Century*, 41; and Gajarawala, *Untouchable Fictions*, 48.
15. Premchand, "Sāhitya kā Uddeśya," 8.
16. Premchand discussed his literary project in a letter to fellow Hindi writer Jainendra Kumar when describing his work in comparison to that of the Hindi poet Jaishankar Prasad. This letter is reproduced in Jainendra Kumar, *Premacanda*, 94.
17. Premchand, "Kahānī Kalā 1," 30. See chapter 1 for the full quote and further discussion of Premchand's understanding of idealism.
18. Premchand, "Jīvan meṃ," 98–99. The original publication date of this essay is unavailable.
19. Anand et al., "Manifesto," 240. For more on the PWA's literary politics, see chapter 1.
20. Premchand, "Kahānī Kalā 3," 43.
21. Premchand, "Sāhitya kā Uddeśya," 9.

22. Premchand, "Kahānī Kalā 2," 31–33.

23. Premchand's paradoxical stance on the construction of character—his insistence on true-to-life character portrayals, on one hand, and the exaggeration of character traits, on the other—has led to contrasting interpretations of his work. For example, while Anjaria views Premchand's Hori—the protagonist of his novel *Godān* (1936)—as psychologically nuanced and round (*Realism in the Twentieth Century*, 33–59), Gajarawala describes Hori as a flattened type (*Untouchable Fictions*, 32–67). This seeming contradiction is explained, I would argue, by Premchand's broader focus on inspiring readers. He insisted that "literature arose for the very sake of begetting love in man toward what is good or beautiful—and therefore conducive to his welfare—and hatred in man toward what is bad or ugly and therefore false" ("Jīvan aura Sāhitya meṃ," 57). Premchand's characters emerged sometimes as round, sometimes as flat, depending on the contours of the particular moments through which he sought to evoke readers' emotions. I discuss Premchand's uses of round and flat characters in more detail later in the chapter. His short story characters were neither flat nor round, but rather citations of existing character types.

24. Premchand, "Upanyās," 35.

25. Premchand, "Jīvan meṃ," 90.

26. Premchand, "Sāhitya kā Ādhār."

27. Premchand, "Upanyās," 35.

28. For an overview of *rasa* theory, see Schweig and Buchta, "*Rasa* theory." For an overview of changing meanings of the term *rasa*, see Pollock, "An Intellectual History."

29. Gupta, *Sexuality, Obscenity, Community*, 40.

30. For example, see Dwivedi's essay on *nāyak-nāyikā bhed*—the classical literary convention describing different types of heroes and heroines to express the erotic sentiment. He linked the use of this convention in *rīti* poetry to a wrongful elevation of luxury and pleasure in Muslim court culture ("Nāyikā Bhed"). Dwivedi published the early works of many canonical Hindi writers, including Premchand, in his journal *Saraswatī*. For more on Dwivedi, see the introduction in this book.

31. This view is expounded, for instance, in Shukla's seminal essay "Kavitā Kyā Hai?" (What is poetry?), first published in 1903. Shukla viewed *rasa* as a common thread that could be traced through Hindi literature, and he wrote extensively about *bhāv* and its relationship to literature and art. See, for example, the essays collected in *Cintāmaṇi: Pahalā Bhāg*. In his monumental *Hindī Sāhitya kā Itihās* (History of Hindi literature), Shukla viewed Premchand's work as pathbreaking and definitive of a new trend in Hindi prose that focused on social issues (539–40). For more discussion of Shukla's views, see chapter 1.

32. For more on the movement and its poets, see Schomer, *Mahadevi Varma*.

33. Premchand, "Sāhitya kā Uddeśya," 13.

34. Premchand, "Sāhitya kā Uddeśya," 7–8.

35. Premchand, "Sāhitya kā Uddeśya," 7.

36. Premchand, "Abhilāshā," 67.

37. See Dalmia, *Nationalization of Hindu Traditions*, 273.

38. See Ritter, "Proper Female Subject," 122–23.

39. Sawhney, *Modernity of Sanskrit*, 165.

40. For example, the Urdu version of Premchand's "Sāhitya kā Uddeśya"—first published in 1941 in the Urdu magazine *Nayā Adab*—uses a completely different terminology than that of *rasa* to discuss the role of emotion in literature. See Premchand, "Adab kī Gharaz-o-Ghāyat." His uses of words such as *jazbā* (emotion) and *ishq* (passion)—rather than *bhāv* (emotion) and *śṛṅgāra* (erotic sentiment)—index debates around social reform that were prevalent in nineteenth- and early twentieth-century Urdu literature. Margrit Pernau has shown that new understandings of emotion arose among North Indian Urdu speakers in the late nineteenth century. Ideas of compassion, friendship, and passion—which were rooted in Urdu poetic imagery—became central to community building in this period. See Pernau, *Emotion and Modernity*, and "Love and Compassion." Premchand was aware of these debates, and they likely informed his writings. It is unclear whether Premchand wrote his PWA speech in Hindi or Urdu and whether he himself translated the speech and his other writings from one language to the other in their various iterations. Nonetheless, the use of different terminology in his criticism—and different plot lines and characterizations in his fiction—discloses how the Hindu and Urdu versions of Premchand's texts were directed toward separate and distinct audiences.

41. Premchand, "Kahānī Kalā 2," 37–38.

42. Pudumaippittan, "Ilakkiyattiṉ Uṭpirivukaḷ," 122–24.

43. Pudumaippittan, "Ilakkiyattiṉ Irakaciyam," 118–19.

44. This and the previous quotation are from Pudumaippittan, "Uṅkaḷ Katai," 223–24.

45. Pudumaippittan, "Ciṉṉa Viṣayam," 109.

46. Pudumaippittan, "Kataikaḷ," 114.

47. Pudumaippittan, "Uṇarcci Vēkamum Naṭai Nayamum," 129.

48. For discussion on medieval Tamil poetics, see Shulman, *Tamil: A Biography*, 167–72. For more on interiority, see Lukács, *Theory of the Novel*.

49. Pudumaippittan, "Taṉimai," 61.

50. Holmstrom, "Making It New," 246.

51. Venkatachalapathy, *In Those Days*, 76.

52. Pudumaippittan, "Eṉ Kataikaḷum Nāṉum," 177–78.

53. For more on Pudumaippittan's positions on literary and popular writing, Tamil scholarship, and language politics, see Mani, "Literary and Popular Fiction."

54. Pudumaippittan, "Eccarikkai!," 779.

55. Pudumaippittan, "Eṉ Kataikaḷum Nāṉum," 173–75.

56. Pudumaippittan, "Uṇarcci Vēkamum Naṭai Nayamum," 128.

57. For example, Pudumaippittan and Ramaiah—who both wrote for the journal *Maṇikkoṭi*—decided to each create a short story about a young woman they encountered on a street corner in a remote Madras neighborhood. The short stories they each produced represented two different—yet "true"—depictions of everyday reality. See Sundararajan and Sivapathasundaram, *Tamiḻil Ciṟukatai*, 184–86.

58. For more on this separation in European modernism, see, for example, Lewis, *Cambridge Introduction to Modernism*.

59. Pudumaippittan's short story "Ciṟpiyiṉ Narakam" (The sculptor's hell), first published in *Maṇikkoṭi* in 1935, offers one example of this argument. For discussion of this story, see Mani, "Literary and Popular Fiction."

60. For more on these debates, see Sreenivas, *Wives, Widows, Concubines*.

61. I am grateful to George Hart for our discussions of the representation of *tanimai* in premodern Tamil literature. He offered helpful insight into how jolting Pudumaippittan's theorizations of loneliness and isolation must have been to contemporary readers with a strong sense of Tamil community.

62. Pudumaippittan, "Cirukatai," 142. Pudumaippittan's was the first in a series of essays on the short story, by various writers, that were published in the influential magazine *Maṇikkoṭi*. Beginning in 1935 the magazine defined itself as exclusively focused on short story writing. Pudumaippittan published essays and stories regularly in *Maṇikkoṭi*, and he played a key role in developing its repute as a harbinger of short story writing and modernism in Tamil. It could be argued that strains of modernist individualism may be found in the earlier work of V. V. S. Iyer, who is considered the father of the Tamil short story. For example, Iyer's first short story collection *Maṅkaiyarkkaraciyin Kātal Mutaliya Kataikaḷ* (Mankaiyarkkaraci's love and other stories), first published in 1917, focuses on unrequited or tragic love between men and women, featuring the inner workings and process of self-discovery of the antihero. For more on Iyer, see Kennedy, "Public Voices, Private Voices," 65–94. Yet I would also add that the social-realist novel remained the preeminent form in modern Tamil literature until the concerted efforts of Pudumaippittan and his *Maṇikkoṭi* contemporaries to develop the short story in the 1930s. For discussion of the early Tamil novel, see Ebeling, *Colonizing the Realm*, 205–46; and Kennedy, "Two Tamil Literary Renaissances." For discussion of the rise of popular novels in Tamil, see Venkatachalapathy, *Province of the Book*, 76–98.

63. The previous quotations are from Premchand, "Kahānī Kalā 1," 28 and 36, respectively.

64. For Bakhtin, heteroglossia—the representation of diverse speech genres and social and historical forces—is the preeminent feature of the novel. Rather than defining the generic boundaries of the novel, however, Bakhtin was interested in documenting the "novelization" of literary forms, which renewed language and made it dialogic. Within his framework, the short story and other modern genres also participated in the novelization process. Necessarily circumscribed, the short story does not have the capacity for the extensive representation of heteroglossia that the novel does. Nonetheless, as I demonstrate later in this chapter, the short story epitomizes the parody and irony so central to novelistic discourses. Premchand's and Pudumaippittan's short stories are full of the parodic stylization Bakhtin associated with the novel. Parody, I argue, is an integral element of the short story's citational structure. See Bakhtin, *Dialogic Imagination*.

65. Many of Premchand's and Pudumaippittan's Anglo-European and Russian predecessors and contemporaries shared a similar understanding of the short story. See, for example, the selections by well-known short story writers anthologized in May, *New Short Story Theories* and *Short Story Theories*.

66. For more on the relationship between the novel, the short story, and poetry, see the introduction.

67. Premchand wrote no poetry, and—as far as I am aware—he did not discuss why he never experimented with the genre. I would argue that he was not drawn to poetry because he associated it with the decadence and individualism of the medieval era, which—as I show in this chapter—he critiqued in several of his essays.

68. See, for example, Premchand, "Hindī Galp-Kalā."

69. See, for example, Premchand, "Upanyās."

70. Premchand, "Kahānī Kalā 1," 29.

71. Pudumaippittan, "Kataikaḷ," 112.

72. Pudumaippittan, "Ciṟukatai," 142–43.

73. Pudumaippittan, "Ciṟukatai: Maṟumalarccik Kālam," 235.

74. This and the previous quotation are from Pudumaippittan, "Ciṟukatai: Maṟumalarccik Kālam," 237–38.

75. Premchand, "Kahānī Kalā 2," 32–34.

76. May, "*I Am Your Brother*," 53.

77. May, "Reality in the Short Story."

78. Genette, *Paratexts*, 55–103.

79. It might be argued that short story titles function similarly to chapter titles or section headings, which Genette considered to be kinds of paratexts. But he was primarily interested in the book form and argued that paratexts work together with the main text to construct the impression of a comprehensive whole. I would suggest that short stories—as well as other genres—published in journals and magazines operate differently because they can also be (and often are) read separately, rather than as components of a larger whole.

80. All these stories are available in Premchand, *Mānasarovar*.

81. These stories are collected in Pudumaippittan, *Putumaippittaṉ Kataikaḷ*.

82. The dating of the *Cilappatikāram* is contested. While some scholars believe it is was written around the first century CE, others date it from the third to seventh century CE. For more discussion on this, see Shulman, *Tamily: A Biography*, 101–2; and Zvelebil, *Smile of Murugan*, 174–76.

83. Pudumaippittan, "Poṉṉakaram," 68.

84. Forster, *Aspects of the Novel*, 103–4.

85. Forster, *Aspects of the Novel*, 118.

86. See Lukács, *Historical Novel* and *Theory of the Novel*.

87. Chakrabarty, *Provincializing Europe*, 133.

88. Gajarawala, *Untouchable Fictions*, 45.

89. Ramamurthy, "Modern Girl." See also Weinbaum et al., "Modern Girl as Heuristic Device."

90. Premchand, "Mis Padmā," 58.

91. "Unmād" is included in Premchand's *Mānasarovar*, vol. 2. In this story, Jenny, Manhar's second wife, is European, fickle, selfish, and always in search of pleasure. "Do Sakhiyāṁ" is included in *Mānasarovar*, vol. 4. The story compares the divergent paths of Padma—who believes in women's rights and marries out of choice—and her friend Chanda, who happily marries into a joint-family situation. Ultimately, Padma discovers that wifely love, dedication, and sacrifice are necessary to make a marriage successful.

92. The original publication date of the Hindi and Urdu versions of "Mis Padmā" are unknown. Based on its themes and tone, however, scholars generally agree that "Mis Padmā" appeared toward the end of Premchand's career. The Hindi story was later published in *Mānasarovar*, vol. 2, in 1936. The Urdu story appeared in his 1936 collection *Zād-e-Rāh*. Premchand's novel *Godān* was also published in 1936.

93. See, for example, Gupta, "Portrayal of Women"; and Pandey, "How Equal?"

94. Premchand, "Mis Padmā," 62.

95. Roye, "Politics of Sculpting," 238.

96. The recent translations of Premchand's Hindi and Urdu short stories orchestrated by M. Asaddudin have brought to light the extent to which Premchand worked in both languages throughout his life, moving back and forth between them as a writer working through drafts. In-depth study of the relationship between Premchand's Hindi and Urdu fiction is, however, yet to be done. See Premchand, *Premchand: The Complete Stories.*

97. Premchand, "Miss Padma," 599.

98. Premchand, *Godān,* 53.

99. Premchand, *Godān,* 310–11.

100. Hutcheon, *Theory of Parody,* 11.

101. Ramanujan, "Three Hundred Ramayanas," 135. Ramanujan's translation of this passage is from Sanskrit poet Valmiki's text.

102. For an overview of some of the Ahalya retellings, see Das, *Struggle for Freedom,* 134; and Sundararajan and Sivapathasundaram, *Tamiḻil Ciṟukatai,* 185–86.

103. Sundararajan and Sivapathasundaram, *Tamiḻil Ciṟukatai,* 184–86.

104. Pudumaippittan, "Akalyai," 133.

105. For a summary of the evolution of the Ahalya myth from its earliest appearance in the *Rāmāyaṇa,* see Söhnen-Thieme, "Ahalyā Story."

106. Pudumaippittan, "Akalyai," 132.

107. Pudumaippittan, "Akalyai," 133.

108. Pudumaippittan, "Akalyai," 134.

109. Pudumaippittan, "Akalyai," 135.

110. Pudumaippittan, "Kāñcaṉai."

111. Pudumaippittan, "Cellammāḷ."

112. Pudumaippittan, "Cāpa Vimōcaṉam," 535.

113. Pudumaippittan, "Cāpa Vimōcaṉam," 538–39.

114. Pudumaippittan, "Cāpa Vimōcaṉam," 539–40.

115. Pudumaippittan, "Cāpa Vimōcaṉam," 544.

116. Pudumaippittan, "Cāpa Vimōcaṉam," 547.

117. A. R. Venkatachalapathy recounts that "C. Rajagopalachari, the self-appointed custodian of Indian (Hindu) culture . . . wrote a veiled rejoinder in the form of a re-telling of the Agaligai story from the Ur-text of Valmiki" (*In Those Days,* 81) immediately following Pudumaippittan's publication of "Cāpa Vimōcaṉam." Rajagopalachari's position on the Ahalya myth represented the Hindu viewpoint of the Indian National Congress—the leading political party across the subcontinent. Pudumaippittan's Ahalya also offered a different position on heterosexual relations than the reformed marriage practices that the Self-Respect Movement advanced, which emphasized equality and free will as opposed to kinship and tradition.

118. Moretti, "Conjectures on World Literature," 58.

CHAPTER 3

1. Lazarus, *Postcolonial Unconscious,* 31-32.

2. For this reason, I understand these communities to be what Jacques Rancière defines as a "community of sense," which is "not a collectivity shaped by some common feeling . . . [but rather] a frame of intelligibility that puts things or practices

together under the same meaning. . . . A community of sense is a certain cutting out of space and time that binds together practices, forms of visibility, and patterns of intelligibility" ("Politics of Aessthetics," 31).

3. Kapur, *When Was Modernism*, 298.

4. See, for example, Berman, "Comparative Colonialisms."

5. Sahitya Akademi, *Progress Report*, 3.

6. South Asian thinkers were not alone in theorizing the path from literature to reality as tortuous or even duplicitous. For more on realism in South Asia, see, for example, Anjaria, *Realism in the Twentieth Century*; Kapur, *When Was Modernism*; M. Mukherjee, *Realism and Reality*; and Sangari, "Politics of the Possible." For discussion of classical Western realism, see, for example, Adorno et al., *Aesthetics and Politics*; Auerbach, "Figura"; Auerbach, *Mimesis*; Barthes, "Reality Effect"; Jakobson, "Realism in Art"; Jameson, *Antinomies of Realism*; Lukács, *Meaning of Contemporary Realism*; and Lukács, "Narrate or Describe?"

7. See Bakhtin, *Dialogic Imagination*, 3–83; Bakhtin, *Speech Genres*, 60–102; Frye, *Anatomy of Criticism*, 33–51; Genette, *Architext* and *Narrative Discourse*; Jameson, *Political Unconscious*, 89–136; Lukács, *Theory of the Novel*, 11–69; Todorov, *Genres in Discourse*, 13–26; and Wellek and Warren, *Theory of Literature*, 235–44.

8. Jameson, "Realism-Modernism Debate," 475.

9. Warwick Research Collective, *Combined and Uneven Development*, 67.

10. Warwick Research Collective, 20, 51. The WReC acknowledges that these features could also be addressed under the name of modernism—and indeed a large part of their chapter on "irrealism" overlaps with WReC member Benita Parry's earlier work on peripheral modernism (Parry, "Aspects of Peripheral Modernism"; Warwick Research Collective, 81–95). However, they also insist that "to read modernist literature in the light of combined and uneven development is to read it with one eye towards its realism" (Warwick Research Collective, 67). This vaguely realist dimension of the WReC's irrealism references the "real" of globally dispersed systemic crises of modernity, rather than any particular realist strategies or techniques per se.

11. Warwick Research Collective, *Combined and Uneven Development*, 52

12. Warwick Research Collective, 52.

13. Esty and Lye, "Peripheral Realisms Now," 285.

14. Gikandi, "Realism."

15. Gajarawala "Casteized Consciousness."

16. Krishnan, "V. S. Naipaul."

17. In addition to the scholarship cited above, I am thinking of recent work such as Doyle and Winkiel, *Geomodernisms*; Friedman, "Definitional Excursions"; Friedman, "Periodizing Modernism"; and Friedman, "Planetarity."

18. Casanova, *World Republic of Letters*, 142.

19. Said, *Culture and Imperialism*.

20. S. Radhakrishnan, "Key-Note," 3.

21. Rao, *Five Decades*, 2.

22. Sahitya Akademi, *Annual Report*, appendix 6, 20–21.

23. Nehru, foreword, v.

24. S. Radhakrishnan, "Key-Note," 1. For more examples, see R. K. Das Gupta, *Western Impact*; Raghavan, "Sanskrit."

25. These activities continue in the present, sustaining the Akademi's mission to produce and maintain a national canon, even though—as I show further in this chapter—they are also often disputed and disregarded.

26. S. Radhakrishnan, "Speech at Inaugural Ceremony," 4.

27. S. Radhakrishnan, "Key-Note," 2–3.

28. S. Radhakrishnan, foreword, v.

29. S. Radhakrishnan, "Editorial Note," 1–2.

30. Nehru, "Question of Language," 251.

31. Dinkar as reproduced in Rao, *Five Decades*, 311.

32. Pullin, "Congress for Cultural Freedom."

33. This quotation and the preceding one are from Namvar Singh, "Hindi," 83–85.

34. Rao, *Five Decades*, 113.

35. Subramanyam, "Cāhitya Akāṭami Tamil̲ Paricu," 4.

36. Sahitya Akademi, *Annual Report*, appendix 6, 20.

37. Subramanyam, "Tamil Literature."

38. Subramanyam, "Tamil Literature" (1964).

39. George, *Indian English*, 171.

40. For example, in the first issue of *Indian Literature*, Radhakrishnan wrote: "There seems to be a misconception in the minds of some writers regarding the role of the Sahitya Akademi. They seem to think that the Akademi having been founded by the State is necessarily under the control of the Government and is nothing but a camouflaged organ of propaganda and patronage. These writers who are earnest advocates of freedom of individual creative expression—as all writers and indeed all intelligent human beings should be—are therefore suspicious of the Akademi's expanding programme of activities and have a genuine fear that it may strangle rather than help true literary expression. This fear is, however, groundless" ("Editorial Note," 2). For his exhortation that writers must defend their freedom of expression, see Rakesh, *Sāṁskṛtik*, 21–25.

41. Bhandari, *Ek Kahānī Yah Bhī*, 97–98.

42. See Subramanyam, "Ilakkiyat Taram Uyara," "Tamil̲il Cir̲ukatai," and "Ulaka Ilakkiyam."

43. The primary magazines that published *nayī kahānī* fiction and essays were *Dharmayuga*, *Jñānodaya*, *Kahānī*, *Kalpanā*, *Naī Kahāniyāṁ*, and *Sārikā*. Other journals also played a role in the circulation of *nayī kahānī* stories and debates, such as *Haṃs*, *Lahar*, *Māyā*, *Nikash*, *Pratīk*, and *Saṅket*. Apart from regular articles and reviews on contemporary short stories and the short story form in these magazines, columns definitive of *nayī kahānī* debates and philosophies include the following: "Āj kī Hindī Kahānī" (The Hindi short story today), published in *Kahānī* and authored by a different writer each month; Mohan Rakesh's "Bakalam Khud" (Alone with a pen) and Namvar Singh's "Hāśiye Par" (From the margins), both published in *Naī Kahāniyāṁ*; and the 1964 yearlong series of autobiographical reflections by *Nayī Kahānī* writers titled "Ek Kathā Daśak" (A decade of the story), published in *Dharmayuga*.

44. See Bhandari, *Ek Kahānī Yah Bhī*; Rakesh, *Mohan Rākeś kī Ḍāyarī*; and Yadav, *Muṛ-Muṛke Dekhtā Huṁ*. Tyagi, in "Nayī Kahānī ke Trikoṇ par Ek Ṭeḍī Nazar," discusses the contemporary perception of Kamleshwar, Rakesh, and Yadav as front-runners of the movement. For a list of writers and critics generally asso-

ciated with the movement, see Madhuresh, *Hindī Kahānī kā Vikās*; Roadarmel, "Theme of Alienation"; and D. Singh, *Hindī Kahānī*. Those now identified with the movement were, in practice, sometimes at odds with its philosophies or only marginally involved. For example, Nirmal Verma's stories have been hailed as paragons of the *nayī kahānī* (see, e.g., N. Singh, *Kahānī*, 52–65), although Kamleshwar, Rakesh, and Yadav, as well as Verma himself, considered him an outsider to the movement. See, for example, de Bruijn, "Nirmal Varma"; and Rakesh, "Bakalam Khud: Udās-Dhaṛkanem̐"; compare Verma, *Hara Bāriś Mem̐* and "Nayī Kahānī." Namvar Singh saw his role in the movement as that of an antagonist (*Kahānī*, n.p.). *Nayī Kahānī: Sandarbh aura Prakr̥ti*, edited by Hindi critic Devishankar Awasthi, provides a compendium of differing perspectives on the movement, which were written during the period that it took shape.

45. The older generation to which *nayī kahānī* writers referred—exemplified by the psychological (*manovaijñānik*) tradition of Jainendra Kumar, the progressivist (*pragativādī*) tradition of Yashpal, and the experimentalist (*prayogvādī*) tradition of Agyeya—was still active in the 1950s and 1960s. *Nayī kahānī* writers characterized the writers of this generation as "against the times" (*samay ke prati*) because of the overt and rigid, albeit varied, ideological stances they put forth in their writing. Kamleshwar, *Nayī Kahānī kī Bhūmikā*, 95–102. See also Rakesh, *Sām̐skr̥tik*, 30–45; and Yadav, "Ek Duniyā Samānāntar."

46. See, for example, Kamleshwar, *Nayī Kahānī kī Bhūmikā*, 96.

47. See Yadav, "Ek Duniyā Samānāntar," "Kahānī," and *Kahānī*.

48. Compare Premchand, *Kuch Vicār*. See also chapter 2.

49. Yadav, *Premacanda*, 93.

50. See Agyeya, "Dūsra Saptak," and "Tār Saptak."

51. See Lotz, "Rāhoṃ ke Anveṣī"; Rosenstein, "Introduction"; and N. Singh, *Kavitā ke Naye Pratimān*.

52. N. Singh, *Kahānī*, 13.

53. Yadav, "Ek Duniyā Samānāntar," 48.

54. See, for example, Rakesh, "Bakalam Khud: Udās-Dhaṛkanem̐," 77.

55. Yadav, "Ek Duniyā Samānāntar," 40–41. See also Rakesh, *Sām̐skr̥tik*, 34–35; and N. Singh, *Kahānī*, 29. For more on the centrality of representations of urban life in Hindi literature, see Dalmia, *Fiction as History*.

56. Yadav, *Premacanda*, 98–99.

57. N. Singh, *Kahānī*, 33.

58. See Rakesh, *Sām̐skr̥tik*, 38–39; N. Singh, *Kahānī*, 32–33; and Yadav, "Ek Duniyā Samānāntar," 67–69.

59. Yadav, "Kahānī," 26.

60. See Kamleshwar, *Nayī Kahānī kī Bhūmikā*, 12; Rakesh, *Sām̐skr̥tik*, 46; Yadav, "Kahānī," 26–27, and *Kahānī*, 25, 46–47. For more on Agyeya's short story writing, see Orsini, "Ajñeya's Stories."

61. For *nayī kahānī* critiques of Agyeya's short story writing, see, for example, Yadav, "Ek Duniyā Samānāntar."

62. See Kamleshwar, *Nayī Kahānī kī Bhūmikā*, 9–20; Rakesh, *Sām̐skr̥tik*, 31–32; Yadav, "Kahānī," 14–15; and Yadav, *Premacanda*, 85–92.

63. For more on Hindi and Tamil linguistic nationalism, see the introduction and chapter 1.

64. For more on *Maṇikkoṭi*, see chaps. 1 and 2.

65. Apart from *Eḻuttu*—which I discuss in more detail in the rest of this chapter—little magazines of the 1950s include *Cānti*, *Tīpam*, and the Marxist-leaning *Carasvati*. The more popular magazine *Kalaimakaḷ* and the Communist Party of India's Tamil magazine *Tāmarai* also sometimes published "literary" fiction during this period. In the 1960s a handful of new little magazines—including *Ilakkiya Vaṭṭam, Kaṇaiyaḻi*, and *Naṭai*—helped to expand the field. These magazines competed for readerships with the more widely circulating magazines *Āṉanta Vikaṭaṉ*, *Kalki*, and *Kumutam*. For more on postindependence-period small magazines, see Rajamarttandan, "Kaṉavukalum Yatārttamum"; Sundararajan and Sivapathasundaram, *Tamiḻil Ciṟukatai*; and Vallikkannan, *Tamiḻiḷ Ciṟu Pattirikkaikaḷ*.

66. Other writers considered to belong within the 1950s and 1960s Tamil high-literary circle include: Thi. Janakiraman, Tharamu Sivaram "Piramil," Ki. Rajanarayanan, Tho. Mu. Ci. Raghunathan, and Ra. Cu. Krishnasamy "Vallikkanan." Yet this list is by no means exhaustive, and several writers published their work in both widely circulating popular magazines as well as more exclusive, high-literary small magazines. B. S. Ramaiah—who took *Maṇikkoṭi* to literary heights in the 1930s and revived the magazine for a brief, unsuccessful five-issue run in 1950—even criticized Chellappa and Subramanyam for holding writers to rigid standards, instead of considering how literary styles and tastes had changed in the postindependence era. After independence, Ramaiah published most of his work in popular magazines, such as *Āṉanta Vikaṭaṉ*, rather than in venues like Chellappa's *Eḻuttu*. For more on the postindependence Tamil literary sphere, see Sundararajan and Sivapathasundaram, *Tamiḻil Ciṟukatai*; and Vallikkannan, *Carasvati Kālam*.

67. Sundararajan and Sivapathasundaram, *Tamiḻil Ciṟukatai*, 203.

68. Chellappa, "Eḻuttu Vaḷara," 2.

69. For example, Chellappa and Subramanyam—the two most active Tamil literary critics of the immediate postindependence period—had a falling out and went separate ways. But they continued to engage with each other in literary forums, such as the little magazines, and to share a drive to develop "high" Tamil literature and criticism.

70. Chellappa, "Eḻuttu Vaḷara," 2. Vallikkannan recounts that in choosing the name *Eḻuttu* for his magazine, Chellappa was also inspired by the English-language little magazines *Writing* and *New Writing* (*Tamiḻiḷ Ciṟu Pattirikkaikaḷ*, 64).

71. For more on the contentious relationship between language and literature that arose with Indian independence, see the introduction.

72. See, for example, Subramanyam, "Ilakkiyattil Karuttum Urupamum" and "Ulaka Ilakkiyam."

73. For more on the rise of the Pure Tamil Movement in the colonial period, see chapter 1.

74. Chellappa, "Iṉṟu Tēvaiyāṉa Urainaṭai," 147–51.

75. See, for example, Subramanyam, "Iṉṟaiyat Tamiḻ Ilakkiyam."

76. For more on India's language policy following independence, see the introduction in this book. For discussion of the colonial-era Dravidian Movement and its relationship to the Pure Tamil Movement, see chapter 1. Although the two movements held differing positions on multiple issues, I use the term "Dravidianist" in this chapter to characterize attempts made by both Dravidian and Pure Tamil activ-

ists to resurrect classical Tamil language and the ancient Tamil past for the purposes of defining postindependence Tamil community and identity.

77. Subramanyam, "Iṉṟaiyat Tamiḻ Ilakkiyam," 68. See also Jayakanthan, "Tamiḻum Taṉittamiḻum."

78. See Fuller and Narasimhan, *Tamil Brahmins*. One exception is D. Jayakanthan. Although not a Brahmin himself, Jayakanthan took Dravidianist critiques of Brahminism head on, arguing that a true Brahmin derives his identity from his efforts to encourage the progress of humanity—rather than from family, tradition, or belief. See, for example, the preface to his 1963 novelette *Pirammōpatēcam* (The initiation of the Brahmin) in which he defended his portrayal of Brahminism as an ethical way of life, rather than as an insidious system of oppression rooted in birthright (Jayakanthan, "Muṟpōkku"). In his fiction, Jayakanthan often portrayed the struggle of lower-class Brahmin characters overcoming the backwardness and close-mindedness associated with Brahmin tradition. For more on Jayakanthan, see chapter 4.

79. For more on writers belonging to the *Maṇikkoṭi* group, see chapter 1.

80. Subramanyam, "Ciṟanta Tamiḻc Ciṟukataikaḷ," 8.

81. Chellappa, *Tamiḻ Ciṟukatai Piṟakkiṟatu*, 23.

82. Chellappa, *Tamiḻ Ciṟukatai Piṟakkiṟatu*, 1.

83. For more on Premchand's stance on European realism and idealism, see chapter 1.

84. For example, Subramanyam characterized late colonial-era Tamil poet Subramania Bharati as the initiator of poetic innovation and Tamil literary renaissance, as well as a representative of a realism committed to truth. See Subramanyam, "Kavi Pāratiyār."

85. Chellappa, "Etaṟkāk Eḻutukiṟēṉ," 45.

86. Chellappa, *Tamiḻ Ciṟukatai Piṟakkiṟatu*, 29–30.

87. Chellappa, "Putumaippittaṉ Kataikkaru," 352.

88. For discussion of Pudumappittan's literary approach of *nampikkai vaṟaṭci* (disillusionment), including the 1942 essay "Eṉ Kataikaḷum Nāṉum" (My stories and I) that Chellappa cites, see chapter 2.

89. Chellappa, "Putumaippittaṉ Kataikkaru," 354–59. Chellappa also turned to the work of *Maṇikkoṭi* writer B. S. Ramaiah to elaborate his understanding of *uṇarcci* (emotion). See, for example, Chellappa, *Tamiḻ Ciṟukatai Piṟakkiṟatu*, 12–13. See chapter 2 for discussion of Pudumaippittan's portrayals of the character Ahalya.

90. Subramanyam, "Tamiḻc Ciṟukataiyil Veṟṟi Kaṇṭavarkaḷ," 74.

91. See, for example, Subramanyam, "Mūṉṟu Ciṟukatāciriyarkaḷ."

92. Chellappa, "Nalla Ciṟukatai Eppaṭi Irukkum?" 445.

93. Chellappa, *Tamiḻ Ciṟukatai Piṟakkiṟatu*, 31.

94. While some of Chellappa's contemporaries, such as P. G. Sundararajan "Chitti," wrote reviews and criticism about fiction written by women, Chellappa—as far as I am aware—never did. For discussion of Sundararajan's analysis of women's writing, see chapter 5.

95. Chellappa, *Tamiḻ Ciṟukatai Piṟakkiṟatu*, 5.

96. Tamil literary critics and scholars recognize *Eḻuttu* writers—and the magazine—for developing Tamil new poetry (*putukkavitai*) as much as for advancing literary criticism and short fiction. I want to suggest that the understanding of

spoken Tamil style that *Eḻuttu* writers developed through their literary historical and critical analyses of short story writing provided an avenue for theorizing the spoken style that became characteristic of new poetry. For discussion of the centrality of speech and sound to new poetry, see Chellappa, "Putukkavitai paṟṟi"; and Subramanyam, "Tamiḻil Puṭuk Kavitai." For an example of the scholarly reception of new poetry in *Eḻuttu*, see Rajamarttandan, "Ci. Cu. Cellappāvum."

97. Uberoi, *Freedom and Destiny*, 22. Emphasis in original.

98. Nehru's policies favored the existing middle-class minority that had risen to power through colonial educational and bureaucratic channels—an affluent, rationally inclined, upper-caste Hindu, English-speaking minority that comprised no more than five to ten percent of the population. The administration actively imagined this class as a proxy representing the interests of the nation and as a pedagogic body responsible for ushering the larger populace into the middle-class fold. For more on the Indian middle class, see Deshpande, *Contemporary India*, 142–8; "Mapping"; Fernandes, *India's New Middle Class*, 1–28; and Kaviraj, "State, Society and Discourse." For more on Nehru's understanding of Indian identity, see Khilnani, *Idea of India*.

99. Yadav, *Kahānī*, 92.

100. Yadav, "Sunie."

101. Baviskar and Ray, introduction to *Elite and Everyman*, 5.

102. Fuller and Narasimhan, *Tamil Brahmins*, 27.

103. See the essays by various *Eḻuttu* writers collected in Subramanyam, "Etaṟkāk Eḻutukiṟēṉ?"

104. Robert Young similarly observes that "postcolonial authors have always written comparative literature. . . . For postcolonial writers had no choice: that work was done by the violent, historical imposition of colonialism, which forced postcolonial society and its literature into comparison in the first place" ("Postcolonial Comparative," 688).

105. For an example of how some of these tensions played out in the African context, see Kalliney, "Modernism." Examining the role of the CIA-funded Congress for Cultural Freedom in supporting modernist projects in Africa, Kalliney illustrates how Anglophone African writers reworked modernist notions of aesthetic autonomy—which had been prevalent in interwar Europe—to distance themselves from the political commitments of realism, while simultaneously articulating an anti-imperialist stance.

CHAPTER 4

1. I borrow the phrase "conjugal family ideal" from the work of Mytheli Sreenivas. Examining changing notions of the family in colonial India (particularly, Tamil Nadu), Sreenivas writes: "we find a growing emphasis on the conjugal relationship that challenged, but did not fully replace, a 'joint family' composed of several generations of patrilineal kin. This emphasis developed into what I term the 'conjugal family ideal,' where the relationship between husband and wife was figured as a central axis of affect and property ownership within families. . . . Advocates of a conjugal family ideal looked to the husband-wife relationship as foundational to the quality of all other family relations" (*Wives, Widows, Concubines*, 6). The conjugal family ideal

included a number of emerging understandings of the family, including a gendered division of domestic space, labor, and behavior—wherein women were conceived as loving mothers and faithful, companionate wives.

2. Kapur, "Mythic Material," 80–81.

3. Coriale, "Existential Eliot." Coriale offers this definition in her analysis of Fredric Jameson's *Antinomies of Realism*. Focusing on Jameson's reading of George Eliot, she explains that Jameson views Eliot's realism as anticipating the existentialist concept of mauvaise fois, or bad faith.

4. For more on the Nayī Kahānī Movement and Eḻuttu Piracuram, see chapter 3.

5. On narrative empathy, see Hammond and Kim, *Rethinking Empathy*; Keen, *Empathy and the Novel*, "Narrative Empathy," and "Theory of Narrative Empathy"; and Lindhé, "Paradox of Narrative Empathy."

6. Keen, *Empathy and the Novel*, 58.

7. For more on sympathy in Premchand's work, see also Gajarawala, *Untouchable Fictions*, 45–48; and Rai, "Kind of Crisis."

8. Yadav, "Kahānī," 27.

9. See, for example, Kamleshwar, *Nayī Kahānī kī Bhūmikā*, 17; and Yadav, *Muṛ-Muṛke Dekhtā Huṁ*, 31–37.

10. Rakesh, "Interview with Mohan Rakesh," 17.

11. Rakesh, *Sāṁskṙtik*, 45.

12. Rakesh, *Sāṁskṙtik*, 38.

13. For more on the cosmopolitan sensibility of postindependence Hindi writing and how it intersected with forms of Euromodernism—especially with regard to Rakesh's playwrighting—see Aparna Dharwadker, "Mohan Rakesh."

14. Jayakanthan, "D. Jayakanthan in Conversation," 160–61.

15. See, for example, Jayakanthan, "Etaṟkāka Eḻutukiṟēṉ?" and "Katāpāttirattiṉ Āḷumaiyaik Kākkum Tāymaikkural."

16. Chellappa, "Uṇarcci Veḷiyīḍu," 109.

17. Chellappa, "Uṇarcci Veḷiyīḍu," 111.

18. For more on Pudumaippittan's understanding of literary disillusionment, see chapter 2.

19. Menon, *Blindness of Insight*, 14.

20. For more on this Nehruvian ethos, see chapter 3.

21. Dhareshwar, "Caste and the Secular Self," 116.

22. Rakesh, "Mis Pāl." For more discussion of this story and other examples of how *nayī kahānī* stories elided caste through the language of class, see Mani, "What Was So New."

23. Kamleshwar, *Nayī Kahānī kī Bhūmikā*, 69–72. These reflections are from Kamleshwar's essay "Śaraṇārtī Ādmī aura Mohbhaṅg: 'Naye' kā Ek aura Koṇ" (Refugee, man, and disillusionment: "Newness" from another angle, 1966), included in the volume.

24. Kamleshwar, *Nayī Kahānī kī Bhūmikā*, 71–72.

25. I thank Mehr Farooqi for sharing her insights on Urdu *nayā afsānā* fiction with me.

26. Ahmad, "In the Mirror," 111–12.

27. In the preface to his collection *Koharā* (Fog)—in which "Aura Kitne Pākistān" first appeared—Kamleshwar notes that he wrote the story around 1966 or 1967

("Bhūmikā se Pahale," 6). Kamleshwar's volume of collected stories, however, records the story as "Mumbai 1969" ("Aura Kitne Pākistān," 615).

28. I am not sure what to make of this tidbit. Could it suggest a conscious or unconscious attempt on Kamleshwar's part to keep the story out of circulation because of the social and political restrictions he may have felt around depicting Partition? Or, conversely, does the story's exploration of Partition violence suggest that the social and historical conditions for representing Partition were changing by the late 1960s?

29. Kamleshwar, "Aura Kitne Pākistān," 604.

30. Kamleshwar, "Aura Kitne Pākistān," 608.

31. Kamleshwar, "Aura Kitne Pākistān," 612.

32. Kamleshwar, "Aura Kitne Pākistān," 615.

33. Sangari, "*Viraha*," 261.

34. See Rakesh, "Klem," "Malbe kā Mālik," and "Paramātmā kā Kuttā."

35. Stray dogs appear often in Rakesh's stories, including "Ek aura Zindagī" (Another life), which I examine later in this chapter. Could the dog function as a specter of Partition violence that travels through postindependence life?

36. Theo Damsteegt confirms this shift in his analysis of Rakesh's deletions of explanatory narrative content from his 1950s stories when he republished them in the 1960s and 1970s. These deletions evidence a general tendency in Rakesh's work toward minimalism and symbolism. See Damsteegt, "Early Short Stories."

37. Rakesh, "Ādmī aura Dīvār," 163.

38. Rakesh, "Ādmī aura Dīvār," 165. Ellipses in original.

39. Rakesh, "Ādmī aura Dīvār," 168.

40. Rakesh, "Ādmī aura Dīvār," 170–71.

41. Rakesh, "Ādmī aura Dīvār," 171.

42. Rakesh, "Ādmī aura Dīvār," 165.

43. Rakesh, "Ādmī aura Dīvār," 172.

44. Menon, *Blindness of Insight*, 12.

45. Pandian, "One Step Outside Modernity," 1735.

46. Dhareshwar, "Caste and the Secular Self," 118.

47. Patel, "Vernacular Missing," 143.

48. For more on how vernacularization processes impacted Tamil writers from the 1930s onward, see the introduction.

49. Jayakanthan, "Enfant Terrible."

50. See, for example, Sundararajan and Sivapathasundaram, *Tamiḻil Ciṟukatai*, 247. Jayakanthan's literary path was also exceptional because he began his career as a member of the Communist Party of India (CPI) and published his first works in Tamil CPI magazines. Like many writers across Tamil Nadu and India more broadly, he became disillusioned with the CPI's positions after the Hungarian Revolution of 1956. He therefore left the CPI and, by the late 1950s, began to develop trenchant critiques of the progressivism he associated with leftist politics. Jayakanthan's discussion of progressivism in the preface to his novella *Pirammōpatēcam* that I discuss later in this chapter expresses this stance. In the late 1950s and early 1960s, his work became increasingly recognized and published by more established *Eḻuttu* writers such as Subramanyam and Chellappa. Jayakanthan would later question the high-literary stance that *Eḻuttu* represented. Nonetheless, his writing was and continues

to be legible through the general conventions for literariness that *Eḻuttu* writers developed.

51. Jayakanthan, *Ōr Ilakkiyavātiyiṉ Araciyal Aṉupavaṅkaḷ*, 71.

52. Jayakanthan, *Ōr Ilakkiyavātiyiṉ Araciyal Aṉupavaṅkaḷ*, 71–72. Later in the memoir Jayakanthan explains that, while Brahmins may have formally inhabited the top of the class hierarchy, in the postindependence era their position was so eroded that they could hardly be considered middle class, since they constituted a small minority of the Tamil population (161).

53. Jayakanthan, "Tamiḻum Taṉittamiḻum," 158–59.

54. Jayakanthan, "Muṟpōkku," 183–84.

55. See Jayakanthan, "Muṟpōkku," 184, and *Ōr Ilakkiyavātiyiṉ Araciyal Aṉupavaṅkaḷ*, 225.

56. Chellappa, "Māmiyiṉ Vīṭu," 19–20.

57. Chellappa, "Māmiyiṉ Vīṭu," 23.

58. Jayakanthan, "Nāṉ Jaṉṉalarukē Uṭkārntirukkiṟēṉ," 474. Ellipses in original.

59. Tharu, "Impossible Subject," 1312.

60. Jayakanthan, "Nāṉ Jaṉṉalarukē Uṭkārntirukkiṟēṉ," 474–75.

61. Jayakanthan, "Nāṉ Jaṉṉalarukē Uṭkārntirukkiṟēṉ," 475.

62. Jayakanthan, "Nāṉ Jaṉṉalarukē Uṭkārntirukkiṟēṉ," 480–81.

63. Jayakanthan, "Nāṉ Jaṉṉalarukē Uṭkārntirukkiṟēṉ," 481.

64. Jayakanthan, "Nāṉ Jaṉṉalarukē Uṭkārntirukkiṟēṉ," 482.

65. Jayakanthan, "Nāṉ Jaṉṉalarukē Uṭkārntirukkiṟēṉ," 483–85. Bracketed ellipses in original.

66. Jayakanthan, "Nāṉ Jaṉṉalarukē Uṭkārntirukkiṟēṉ," 485.

67. Jayakanthan, "Nāṉ Jaṉṉalarukē Uṭkārntirukkiṟēṉ," 487.

68. Rakesh, "Ek Aura Zindagī," 161–62.

69. Rakesh, "Ek Aura Zindagī," 175–76.

70. Rakesh, "Ek Aura Zindagī," 168–70.

71. Rakesh, "Ek Aura Zindagī," 172–75.

72. Rakesh, "Ek Aura Zindagī," 171.

73. Rakesh, "Ek Aura Zindagī," 192.

74. Rakesh, "Ek Aura Zindagī," 188. Ellipses in original.

75. Rakesh, "Ek Aura Zindagī," 200.

76. Although her caste is never mentioned, her dialectical speech implies a Brahmin identity.

77. Jayakanthan, "Akkiṉip Piravēcam," 98.

78. Jayakanthan, "Akkiṉip Piravēcam," 99.

79. Jayakanthan, "Akkiṉip Piravēcam," 102.

80. Jayakanthan, "Akkiṉip Piravēcam," 103.

81. Jayakanthan, "Akkiṉip Piravēcam," 103–4. Ellipsis in original. Throughout the story, the young man speaks in English, obscuring his caste identity while making his class identity clear. Had the story portrayed the young man as a non-Brahmin, I imagine that the rampant controversy surrounding the story would have been even greater.

82. Jayakanthan, "Akkiṉip Piravēcam," 105. Ellipsis in original.

83. This and the above quotation are from Jayakanthan, "Akkiṉip Piravēcam," 108. Ellipses in original.

84. Jayakanthan, "Akkiṉip Piravēcam," 109.

85. For discussion of Pudumaippittan's stories about Ahalya, see chapter 2.

86. Jayakanthan viewed his representation of the girl as part of a literary lineage of representations of Sita and Ahalya, emphasizing that his story was an attempt to reconceptualize Ahalya's *cāpa vimōcaṉam*—her deliverance from her husband's curse. In doing so, he directly referenced Pudumaippittan's Ahalya retellings. See Jayakanthan, "Katāpāttirattiṉ Āḷumaiyaik Kākkum Tāymaikkural."

CHAPTER 5

1. Prior to independence, criticisms of obscenity and writing for "shock value" were leveled against both men and women writers who depicted aberrant sexuality and desire—for example, members of the Progressive Writers' Association such as Ismat Chughtai and Sa'adat Hasan Manto. For more on these writers, see, for example, Chughtai, *Life in Words*; Gopal, *Literary Radicalism in India*; and Kumar and Sadique, *Ismat*. Anxieties about the depiction of sexuality and desire also undergirded characterizations of women's writing as resisting conventional understandings of propriety and decorum. For discussion of the prevalent themes in and the reception of women's writing during the colonial period, see Bannerji, "Fashioning a Self"; Lakshmi, *Face Behind the Mask*; Nijhawan, *Women and Girls*; Orsini, *Hindi Public Sphere*, 243–89; Sreenivas, *Wives, Widows, Concubines*, 94–119; and Tharu and Lalita, *Women Writing, Vol. II*, 1–116.

2. For discussions of Bhandari's and Chudamani's work and their continued reception as "literary" writers, see Bhandari, "Mannu Bhandari," and "Śodhanārthinī"; Chudamani, "Kavarccikkāka Iṉṟi"; D. Kumar, "Tokuppurai"; Lakshmi, *Face Behind the Mask* and "Crest Jewel"; Narayanan and Seetharam, "Narratives That Linger"; and Roadarmel, "Theme of Alienation." Their stories are included in well-known anthologies of women's writing in India, such as Mohanty and Mohanty, *Slate of Life*; and Tharu and Lalita, *Women Writing, Vol. II*.

3. I borrow this language from Rochona Majumdar's work on the debates concerning women's rights following independence. During post-1947 constitutional debates, some feminist activists embraced state legal intervention to protect women's freedoms, while others promoted a narrative of communal belonging. For the latter group, Indian religious traditions—which held women's roles as mothers, daughters, sisters, and wives as the bedrocks of social order and cultural posterity—took precedence over their identities as women and individuals. "At issue," writes Majumdar, "was a tussle between a modern liberal idea of the individual as a bearer of interest and an equally modern romanticization of the sentiments of the extended family" ("Self-Sacrifice," 20). As fiction and film of the time demonstrates, these debates about women's place in society were also prevalent in the broader cultural sphere.

4. Apart from the overview provided by Tharu and Lalita in their survey of twentieth-century women's writing in India, postindependence women's writing is little examined. Tharu and Lalita describe women's writing during this period as part of a "new curriculum" that was "charged with the ethical responsibility of shaping the new citizen" (*Women Writing, Vol. II*, 93). They write: "The [women] writers represented in this volume inherited a culture in which many of the authorities that

had administered the lives of women like themselves in the nineteenth and early twentieth centuries had been questioned and reconstituted. Yet surprisingly, neither the women's texts that emerged around the middle of the twentieth century, nor those of their male contemporaries, bear marks of those political encounters. Significations won, in the thick of battle as it were, are drained of the drama that attended their birth and of the history that shaped them. The new world is cleared of detail, not only of the Imperial conquest begun in the eighteenth century but in many ways continuing into the postindependence period, but also of all resistance to domination, as it becomes the setting for universal rituals of self-realization" (*Women Writing, Vol. II*, 91). Their critique of women's writing during this period echoes critiques of Indian feminism prevalent during the 1950s and 1960s, which argued that activists had laid aside their struggles for women's freedom to support the state's goal of national integration. See Desai, "From Accomodation to Articulation"; Forbes, *Women in Modern India*; John, "Women's Movement"; and R. Kumar, *History of Doing.*

5. See, for example, Boehmer, *Stories of Women*; Spivak, "Literary Representation"; and Trinh, *Woman, Native, Other.*

6. See Forbes, *Women in Modern India*, 10–31; and Sangari and Vaid, *Recasting Women.*

7. See Dalmia, "Generic Questions"; Orsini, "Domesticity and Beyond" and *Hindi Public Sphere*; Sarkar, *Hindu Wife, Hindu Nation*, 95–134; Tharu and Lalita, *Women Writing, Vol. I*, 43–116, and *Women Writing, Vol. II*, 145–86.

8. Orsini, "Domesticity and Beyond."

9. Orsini, *Hindi Public Sphere*, 274–89. See also Orsini, "Domesticity and Beyond." Orsini discusses women's writing in Hindi, while others have described similar developments in languages such as Bengali, Marathi, Tamil, and Urdu. See Bannerji, "Fashioning a Self"; Kosambi, *Women Writing Gender*; Minault, "Urdu Women's Magazines"; Sreenivas, "Female Subject," and Sreenivas, *Wives, Widows, Concubines*, 94–119.

10. M. Sinha, *Specters of Mother India*, 210. For discussion of the intersections between the rise of women's writing and the women's movement, see Nijhawan, *Women and Girls*; Orsini, *Hindi Public Sphere*, 243–308; and M. Sinha, *Specters of Mother India*, 49–50). For an overview of the rise of the Indian women's movement, see Forbes, *Women in Modern India*; and R. Kumar, *History of Doing.*

11. See Alexander, "Sarojini Naidu"; Nijhawan, *Women and Girls*; and Orsini, "Domesticity and Beyond," and *Hindi Public Sphere*, 243–308.

12. See Orsini, *Hindi Public Sphere*; and Schomer, *Mahadevi Varma.*

13. For example, most canonical histories of Tamil literature fail to mention her work. Furthermore, as far as I know, Kothanayaki Ammal's work has not been translated into English, nor has it been anthologized, both being important markers of a writer's canonical status within the Tamil literary sphere. See Guy, "Icon in Her Time"; and Lakshmi, *Face Behind the Mask*, 67.

14. See Orsini, *Hindi Public Sphere*, 243–308.

15. See Anantharam, "Mahadevi Varma"; Orsini, "Domesticity and Beyond," 158–60, and *Hindi Public Sphere*, 273, 304–8; and Schomer, *Mahadevi Varma.*

16. As previous chapters elaborate, these writers—such as Agyeya and Jainendra Kumar in Hindi, and Ramaiah and Pudumaippittan in Tamil—viewed their literary

turn to domestic concerns as a highly political response to the distinct linguistic nationalisms and identity politics prevalent in Hindi and Tamil contexts at the time. Through their emphases on linguistic innovation, psychological innovation, and the examination of the home and the family, these writers offered a politics of the literary.

17. While no figure like Varma—who sought to make women's writing more "literary"—emerged in the Tamil literary sphere during the 1930s and 1940s, a similar shift in women's writing did take place, so by the postindependence period, domestic concerns overshadowed the radical-critical politics of Tamil women's writing. See Lakshmi, *Face Behind the Mask*; and S. Raman, "Face Behind the Mask."

18. For instance, I show in chapter 4 that *nayī kahānī* stories and the stories of the *E̱luttu* writers focused almost exclusively on man-woman relationships within families.

19. Tharu and Lalita call the few "literary" women writers emerging at this time the "eleventh among ten" (*Women Writing, Vol. II*, 93–94).

20. See Jain, *Kathā-Samay*; and Roadarmel, "Theme of Alienation."

21. See, for example, Lakshmi, *Face Behind the Mask*, 133; Sundararajan and Sivapathasundaram, *Tami̱lil Ci̱rukatai*, 227–28; and Tharu and Lalita, *Women Writing, Vol. II*, 20–7.

22. For discussions of a comparable anxiety surrounding women's desires in film during this period, see Prasad, "State In/Of Cinema"; Srivastava, "Idea of Lata Mangheshkar"; and Uberoi, *Freedom and Destiny*.

23. Bhandari and Chudamani have not discussed why they did not write "metaliterary" texts, such as criticism. But both authors have indicated in interviews and autobiographical reflections that, early in their careers, they aimed to write truthfully and straightforwardly and resisted delving into the intricacies of language and symbolism, which distract readers from forming an emotional connection with characters. See Bhandari, *Ek Kahānī Yah Bhī*, and "Mannūjī ke Tamām Raṅg"; and Chudamani, "E̱luttararaṅkam," and "Kavarccikkāka Iṉri̱."

24. Bhandari, "Paṇḍit Gajādhar Śāstrī," 54. Ellipsis in original.

25. Bhandari, "Paṇḍit Gajādhar Śāstrī," 58.

26. Bhandari, "Paṇḍit Gajādhar Śāstrī," 57.

27. Bhandari, "Paṇḍit Gajādhar Śāstrī," 57.

28. Bhandari, "Paṇḍit Gajādhar Śāstrī," 59–60.

29. Bhandari, "Paṇḍit Gajādhar Śāstrī," 60.

30. Bhandari, "Paṇḍit Gajādhar Śāstrī," 58–59.

31. I use "idiom" similarly to how Bakhtin uses the notion of speech genre. For Bakhtin, a speech genre is a linguistic model of representation that reflects and shapes the world and stratifies, as well as unifies language. It mediates between singular utterances and social reality. See Bakhtin, *Speech Genres*. Bhandari's idiom of *hār* reflects her individual style, while simultaneously demonstrating the larger concerns and conventions operating within the Hindi cultural context. This is also respectively the case with Chudamani's idiom of *ci̱ṟram*, which I discuss later in this chapter.

32. Yadav, "Kahānī," 52.

33. Chudamani, "Katai Poruḷ," 100.

34. Chudamani, "Katai Poruḷ," 100.

35. Chudamani, "Katai Poruḷ," 103.
36. Chudamani, "Katai Poruḷ," 104.
37. Chudamani, "Katai Poruḷ," 108.
38. Chudamani, "Katai Poruḷ," 111.
39. Chudamani, "Katai Poruḷ," 112. Ellipsis in original.
40. This story was published in Chudamani's 1969 collection *Anta Nēram*. In the acknowledgments Chudamani notes that all the stories in this collection were previously published in a range of Tamil magazines. Yet I have not been able to locate the publication details of this story.
41. Chellappa, "Uṇarcci Veḷiyīḍu," 109, 118. See also Chellappa, "Etaṟkāk Eḻutukiṟēṉ?," 46–48.
42. This story was first published in the June 1960 issue of the popular Hindi magazine *Naī Kahāniyāṁ*. It was also the title story of Bhandari's influential 1966 collection. Following its publication, "Yahī Sac Hai" was praised in popular Hindi magazines and interviews, as well as adapted into the award-winning 1974 film *Rajnīgandhā* directed by Basu Chatterjee. See Bhandari, *Ek Kahānī Yah Bhī*, "Mannu Bhandari," and "Śodhanārthinī"; and Rakesh, "Bakalam Khud: Prem-Tikon."
43. Bhandari, "Yahī Sac Hai," 264–65.
44. Bhandari, "Yahī Sac Hai," 268.
45. Bhandari, "Yahī Sac Hai," 268–69. Ellipses in original except following, "I felt a delightful thrill [*pulakamaya siharan*]."
46. Bhandari, "Yahī Sac Hai," 272.
47. de Bruijn, "Under Indian Eyes," 207.
48. Bhandari, "Yahī Sac Hai," 273.
49. Bhandari, "Yahī Sac Hai," 275.
50. Bhandari, "Yahī Sac Hai," 276.
51. Bhandari, "Yahī Sac Hai," 277.
52. See, for example, Bhandari, "Yahī Sac Hai," 274. Bhandari chose to give Deepa's extended family a more prominent role in the 1974 film adaptation of the story, for which she wrote the script. In the opening scene of the film, viewers learn that Deepa lives with her brother and sister-in-law. Her sister-in-law approves of Deepa's relationship with Sanjay and encourages her to pursue it further. Moreover, in several of Bhandari's other stories examining feminine desire, the extended (Hindu) family figures prominently in how female characters define marriage and conjugality. See, for example, Bhandari, "Ek Kamzor Laṛki" and "Tīn Nigāhoṃ."
53. The postindependence dilemma of defining women's freedoms and desires in terms of either individual choice or community values took shape during discussions about whether marriage should be viewed as an expression of personal right (i.e., individual choice) or community right (i.e., ordained by divine sacrament and arranged according to community norms). By retaining the personal law category, the new postcolonial state endorsed a communitarian model of marriage, while also offering citizens the option of selecting a secular model through the Special Marriage Act (1954). For discussion of family, community, and conjugality in modern India, see, for example, Sarkar, *Hindu Wife, Hindu Nation*; Sreenivas, *Wives, Widows, Concubines*; and Uberoi, *Freedom and Destiny*. For discussion of postindependence juridical debates on marriage, see, for example, Majumdar, *Marriage and Modernity*, 206–37; Parashar, *Family Law Reform*; and Uberoi, "Hindu Marriage."

54. Majumdar, "Self-Sacrifice," 20.

55. Bhandari, *Ek Kahānī Yah Bhī*, 47.

56. Yadav, *Premacanda*, 107.

57. Chudamani's story was published in *Kalaimakaḷ*, one of the most well-known Tamil magazines of the postindependence period.

58. Chudamani, "Ma̱nitaṉāy Māṟi," 77. Ellipsis in original.

59. See Basu, *To Take Her Rights*.

60. Chudamani, "Maṉitaṉāy Māṟi," 79.

61. See, for example, Chudamani, "Maṉitaṉāy Māṟi," 80.

62. Chudamani, "Maṉitaṉāy Māṟi," 81.

63. For more on direct dialogue, see Genette, *Narrative Discourse*, 162–94. Genette uses "external focalization" to describe the omniscient third-person narrative voice and "internal focalization" to describe a third-person narrative voice focused only on a given character's point of view.

64. Chudamani, "Maṉitaṉāy Māṟi," 77–79.

65. Chudamani, "Maṉitaṉāy Māṟi," 81–82.

66. Chudamani, "Maṉitaṉāy Māṟi," 82.

67. Chudamani, "Maṉitaṉāy Māṟi," 82.

68. Sundararajan, "Cūṭāmaṇi Kataikal," 53.

69. Bhandari, *Ek Kahānī Yah Bhī*, 39.

70. Bhandari, "Śodhanārthinī," 284.

71. Chudamani, "Kavarccikkāka Iṉṟi," 46.

72. See Chughtai, *Life in Words*; Jussawalla and Dasenbrock, "Anita Desai"; Kuchedkar, introduction to *Whom Can I Tell?*; Sobti, "Author's Integrity Is Supreme"; and Tharu and Lalita, *Women Writing, Vol. II*, 285–86, 312–13.

73. Tharu and Lalita, *Women Writing, Vol. II*, 94.

74. See, for example, Gilbert and Gubar, *Madwoman in the Attic*; Moers, *Literary Women*; and Showalter, *Literature of Their Own*.

75. Jacobus, "Is There a Woman?" 109. See Cixous, "Laugh of the Medusa"; Irigaray, *Not One*; and Kristeva, *Kristeva Reader*.

76. Jacobus, "Is There a Woman?" 108. See also Moi, *Sexual/Textual Politics*; and Tharu and Lalita *Women Writing, Vol. II*, 15–37.

77. See Barthes, "Death of the Author"; Butler, *Bodies That Matter* and *Gender Trouble*; Derrida, "Signature Event Context"; and Foucault, "What Is an Author?"

78. This and the previous quotation are from Moi, "Not a Women Writer," n.p. Emphasis in original.

79. Moi is interested in how a women writer might maneuver within a discourse that has hailed her, or called her into being, as a women writer. I am differently interested in how our own commitments to feminist politics of varying kinds might lead us to misread the terms on which writers like Bhandari and Chudamani see themselves being hailed in the first place.

80. See Bhandari, "Ek Kamzor Laṛki"; and Yadav, "Ek Kamzor Laṛki." In her memoir Bhandari mentions that, after Yadav and Bhandari met in the mid-1950s, they often discussed their writing. By 1957, when both of their collections that included "Ek Kamzor Laṛki kī Kahānī" came out, they knew each other quite well. Consequently, the use of the same title and choice of similar subject matter for both stories is in all likelihood not coincidental. Bhandari, *Ek Kahānī Yah Bhī*, 34–40.

81. See Seth, "Apne Viruddh."

82. For example, Shree's novel *Māī* (Mother) explores a woman's capacity to break free from the social expectations that her mother's generation has placed on her. The protagonist Sunaina uses a language of humanism—of "being," "being human," and "nonbeing"—to consider her place as a modern woman in the world (see, for example, *Māī*, 116–19). In her struggles to realize her desires and aspirations, Sunaina experiences profound loneliness and defeat, just as Bhandari's female characters do. In Varma's case, the short story "Behada" (Without boundaries)—which was published in her 1981 collection *Sthagita* (Delayed)—provides a good example. Ritu, the female protagonist of this story, uses a language of existential uncertainty and angst to point out the limitations of gender on her freedom of choice. For Shree's and Varma's positions on feminism and women's writing, see Shree, "I'm Waiting" and "Past Is Ever Present"; and Varma, "Grand Celebration."

83. Ambai has discussed her relationship with Chudamani in several places, including Lakshmi, "Crest Jewel"; Lakshmi, "Maṉattukkiṉiya Oru Tōḻi"; Lakshmi, "Maṉattukkiṉiyavaḷum Maraṇamum." She also dedicated *The Face Behind the Mask*, her study of Tamil women writers, to Chudamani.

84. These stories are available in Ambai, *Ampai Kataikaḷ*.

85. Lakshmi, "Landscapes of the Body."

Bibliography

Adorno, Theodor, Walter Benjamin, Ernst Bloch, Bertolt Brecht, Frederic Jameson, and Georg Lukács. *Aesthetics and Politics*. London: Verso, 2007. First published 1977.

Agyeya. "Dūsra Saptak" [The second heptad]. New Delhi: Bharatiya Jnanpith Prakashan, 1996. First published 1952.

———. "Tār Saptak" [A heptad of strings]. New Delhi: Bharatiya Jnanpith Prakashan, 1995. First published 1943.

Ahmad, Aijaz. "In the Mirror of Urdu: Recompositions of Nation and Community, 1947–65." In *Lineages of the Present: Ideology and Politics in Contemporary South Asia*, 103–25. London: Verso, 2000.

———. *In Theory: Classes, Nations, Literatures*. London: Verso, 1992.

Ahmed, Talat. *Literature and Politics in the Age of Nationalism: The Progressive Writers' Movement in South Asia, 1932–1956*. London: Routledge, 2009.

Alexander, Meena. "Sarojini Naidu: Romanticism and Resistance." *Economic and Political Weekly* 20, no. 43 (1985): WS68–71.

Ali, Ahmed. "Progressive View of Art." In Pradhan, *Marxist Cultural Movement in India*, 67–83.

Ambai. *Ampai Kataikaḷ, 1972–2014: 42 Āṇṭuk Kataikaḷ* [Short stories of Ambai, 1972–2014: 42 years of stories]. Chennai: Kalachuvadu, 2016.

Anand, Mulk Raj. *Conversations in Bloomsbury*. London: Wildwood House, 1981.

———. "On the Progressive Writers' Movement." In Pradhan, *Marxist Cultural Movement in India*, 1–22.

Anand, Mulk Raj, K. S. Bhatt, J. C. Josh, S. Sinha, and S. S. Zaheer. "Manifesto of the Indian Progressive Writers' Association, London." *Left Review* 2, no. 5 (1936): 240.

Anantharam, Anita. "A Change in Aesthetics and the Aesthetics of Change: A Comparative Study of Premchand's *Bazaar-E-Husn* and *Sevasadan*." *South Asian Review* 33, no. 2 (2012): 177–202.

———. "Mahadevi Varma (1907–1987): Between Tradition and Feminist Emancipation." In *Mahadevi Varma: Political Essays on Women, Culture, and Nation*, edited by Anita Anantharam, 1–26. Amherst, NY: Cambria Press, 2010.

Anderson, Benedict. *Imagined Communities: Reflections on the Origin and Spread of Nationalism*. London: Verso, 2006. First published 1983.

Anjaria, Ulka. "Introduction: Literary Pasts, Presents, and Futures." In *The History of the Indian Novel in English*, edited by Ulka Anjaria, 1–30. New York: Cambridge University Press, 2015.

———. *Realism in the Twentieth Century Indian Novel: Colonial Difference and Literary Form*. New York: Cambridge University Press, 2012.

Annamalai, E. "The Challenge of Spoken Language to Creative Writers." In *History and Imagination: Tamil Culture in the Global Context*, edited by R. Cheran, D. Ambalavanar, and C. Kanaganayakam, 63–75. Toronto: TSAR Publications, 2007.

———. *Social Dimensions of Modern Tamil*. Chennai: Cre-A, 2011.

Apter, Emily. *Against World Literature: On the Politics of Translatability*. London: Verso, 2013.

Ashk, Upendranath. *Hindi Kahānī: Ek Antaraṅg Paricay* [The Hindi short story: An intimate survey]. Allahabad: Nilabh Prakashan, 1969.

Auerbach, Erich. "Figura." In *Scenes from the Drama of European Literature*, 11–76. Translated by Ralph Maheim. Minneapolis: University of Minnesota Press, 1984. Originally published 1944 in German.

———. *Mimesis: The Representation of Reality in Western Literature*. Translated by Willard R. Trask. Princeton, NJ: Princeton University Press, 2003. Originally published 1946 in German.

Awasthi, Devishankar, ed. *Nayī Kahānī: Sandarbh aura Prakṙti* [The new story: Context and nature]. New Delhi: Akshar Prakashan, 1966.

Azmi, Khalilur Rahman. *Urdū meṃ Taraqqī Pasand Adabī Tahrīk* [The progressive literary movement in Urdu]. Aligarh: Anjuman-i-Taraqqi Urdu, 1972.

Bakhtin, Mikhail. *The Dialogic Imagination: Four Essays*. Translated by Caryl Emerson and Michael Holquist. Austin: University of Texas Press, 1981.

———. *Speech Genres and Other Late Essays*. Edited by Caryl Emerson and Michael Holquist. Translated by Vern W. McGee. Austin: University of Texas Press, 1986.

Banerji, C. R. "Current Publishing Trends in India." *Indian Literature* 5, no. 2 (1962): 49–58.

Bannerji, Himani. "Fashioning a Self: Educational Proposals for and by Women in Popular Magazines in Colonial Bengal." *Economic and Political Weekly* 26, no. 43 (1991): WS50–62.

Barthes, Roland. "Death of the Author." In *Image, Music, Text*, 142–48. Translated by Stephen Heath. New York: Hill and Wang, 1977. Originally published 1967 in French.

———. "The Reality Effect." In *The Rustle of Language*, 141–48. Translated by Richard Howard. Berkeley: University of California Press, 1989. Originally published 1968 in French.

Basu, Srimati. *She Comes to Take Her Rights: Indian Women, Property and Propriety*. Albany: State University of New York, 1999.

Batasari. "Yātrā Mārkkam" [The journey's path]. *Maṇikkoṭi* 5, no. 5 (1937): 55–56.

———. "Yātrā Mārkkam: Nākari Eḻuttu, Tamiḻ Ilakkiya Caṅkam, Puttakappiracuram" [The journey's path: The Nagari script, the Tamil Literary Association, new publications]. *Maṇikkoṭi* 5, no. 1 (1937): 30–31.

Bate, Bernard. *Tamil Oratory and the Dravidian Aesthetic: Democratic Practice in South India*. New York: Columbia University Press, 2010.

Baviskar, Amita, and Raka Ray. Introduction to *Elite and Everyman: The Cultural Politics of the Indian Middle Classes*, edited by Aita Baviskar and Raka Ray, 1–23. New Delhi: Routledge, 2011.

Beecroft, Alexander. *An Ecology of World Literature: From Antiquity to the Present Day*. London: Verso, 2015.

Berman, Jessica. "Comparative Colonialisms: Joyce, Anand, and the Question of Engagement." *Modernism/Modernity* 13, no. 3 (2006): 465–85.

Bhandari, Mannu. *Ek Kahānī Yah Bhī* [This too is a story]. New Delhi: Radhakrishna Prakashan, 2007.

———. "Ek Kamzor Laṛki kī Kahānī" [The story of a weak girl]. In *Maiṃ Hār Gaī* [I lost], 42–64. New Delhi: Radhakrishna Paperbacks, 2001. First published 1957.

———. "Maiṃ Hār Gaī" [I lost]. In *Sampūrn Kahāniyāṁ: Mannū Bhanḍārī*, 21–26. First published 1957.

———. "Mannu Bhandari: Inner Recesses of Creativity." Interview by Ranavira Rangra. In *Women Writers: Literary Interviews*, 109–24. New Delhi: B. R. Publishing, 1998.

———. "Mannūjī ke Tamām Raṅg" [The many colors of Mannu-Ji]. Interview by Ajit Singh. In *Triśaṅku aur Anya Kahāniyāṁ* [Trishanku and other stories], 6–37. New Delhi: Akshar Prakashan, 1978.

———. "Paṇḍit Gajādhar Śāstrī" [Pandit Gajadhar Sastri]. In *Sampūrn Kahāniyāṁ: Mannū Bhanḍārī*, 54–60. First published 1957.

———. *Sampūrn Kahāniyāṁ: Mannū Bhanḍārī* [Complete short stories: Mannu Bhandari]. New Delhi: Radhakrishna Prakashan, 2008.

———. "Śodhanārthinī kā Mannū Bhanḍārī Jī se Kiyā Gayā Sākshatkār" [Researcher's interview with Mannu Bhandari]. Interview by Bina Rani Gupta. In *Mannū Bhanḍārī kā Kathā Sāhitya: Pārivārik Jīvan kī Samasyāeṁ* [The short fiction of Mannu Bhandari: Problems of family life], 280–89. Hapur: Sambhavna Prakashan, 2006.

———. "Tīn Nigāhoṃ kī Ek Tasvīr" [A picture of three perspectives]. In *Sampūrn Kahāniyāṁ: Mannū Bhanḍārī*, 124–33. First published 1958.

———. "Yahī Sac Hai" [This is the truth]. In *Sampūrn Kahāniyāṁ: Mannū Bhanḍārī*, 261–77. First published 1966.

Bhattacharya, Lokenath. "Modern Indian Literature: Myth or Reality?" *Indian Literature* 9, no. 1 (1966): 78–86.

Boehmer, Elleke. *Stories of Women: Gender and Narrative in the Postcolonial Nation*. Manchester: Manchester University Press, 2005.

Brueck, Laura. "Mother Tongues: The Disruptive Possibilities of Feminist Vernaculars." *South Asia: Journal of South Asian Studies* 43, no. 5 (2020): 988–1008.

Busch, Allison. *Poetry of Kings: The Classical Literature of Mughal India*. Oxford: Oxford University Press, 2011.

Butler, Judith. *Bodies That Matter: On the Discursive Limits of "Sex."* London: Routledge, 1993.

———. *Gender Trouble: Feminism and the Subversion of Identity*. New York: Routledge, 1990.

Casanova, Pascale. *The World Republic of Letters*. Translated by M. B. DeBevoise. Cambridge, MA: Harvard University Press, 2004.

Chakrabarty, Dipesh. *Provincializing Europe: Postcolonial Thought and Historical Difference*. Princeton, NJ: Princeton University Press, 2000.

Chatterjee, Partha. "Introduction: History in the Vernacular." In *History in the Vernacular*, edited by Partha Chatterjee and Raziuddin Aquil, 1–24. Ranikhet, India: Permanent Black, 2008.

Chatterji, Suniti Kumar. *Languages and Literatures of Modern India*. Calcutta: Bengal Publishers, 1963.

Chaudhuri, Supriya. "The Bengali Novel." In *The Cambridge Companion to Modern Indian Culture*, edited by Vasudha Dalmia and Rashmi Sadana, 101–23. Cambridge: Cambridge University Press, 2012.

———. "Modernisms in India." In *The Oxford Handbook of Modernisms*, edited by Peter Brooker, Andrzej Gąsiorek, Deborah Longworth, and Andrew Thacker, 942–60. Oxford: Oxford University Press, 2010.

Cheah, Pheng. *What Is a World? On Postcolonial Literature as World Literature*. Durham, NC: Duke University Press, 2016.

Chellappa, C. S. "*Eḻuttu* Vaḷara" [The rise of *Eḻuttu*]. *Eḻuttu*, no. 1 (1959): 1–4.

———. "Etaṟkāk Eḻutukiṟēṉ?" [Why do I write?]. In Subramanyam, *Etaṟkāk Eḻutukiṟēṉ?* [Why do I write?], 43–49.

———. "Iṉṟu Tēvaiyāṉa Urainaṭai" [The prose style necessary for today]. In *Tamiḻil Ilakkiya Vimarcaṉam*, 143–54. First published 1959.

———. "Māmiyiṉ Vīṭu" [Aunt's house]. *Eḻuttu*, no. 97 (1960): 19–22.

———. "Nalla Ciṟukatai Eppaṭi Irukkum?" [What makes a good short story?]. In *Tamiḻil Ilakkiya Vimarcaṉam*, 379–446. First published 1957.

———. "Putukkavitai paṟṟi" [On new poetry]. *Eḻuttu*, no. 15 (1960): 62–63.

———. "Putumaippittaṉ Kataikkaru" [Pudumaippitan's short story themes]. In *Tamiḻil Ilakkiya Vimarcaṉam*, 352–78. First published 1957.

———. *Tamiḻ Ciṟukatai Piṟakkiṟatu* [The birth of the Tamil short story]. Chennai: Eluttu Prachuram, 1974. First published 1964–69.

———. *Tamiḻil Ilakkiya Vimarcaṉam* [Literary criticism in Tamil]. Chennai: Eluttu Prachuram, 1974

———. "Uṇarcci Veḷiyīḍu" [The expression of emotion]. In *Tamiḻil Ilakkiya Vimarcaṉam*, 109–18. First published 1961.

Chudamani, R. "Cītaiyait Teriyumā?" [Don't you know Sita?]. In *Anta Nēram* [That time], 174–89. Chennai: Malikai Veliyeedu, 1969.

———. "Eḻuttaraṅkam (Periyavaṉ Katai)" [The *Eḻuttu* stage (a big man)]. *Eḻuttu*, no. 7 (1959): 222.

———. "Katai Poruḷ" [The meaning of fiction]. In *Avaṉ Vaṭivam* [His face], 100–112. Chennai: Annai Nilayam, 1965.

———. "Kavarccikkāka Iṉṟi Tarattukkāka Eḻuta Vēṇṭum" [Writing for the sake of quality, not appeal]. Interview by Ma. Mangaiyartilakam. *Kaṇaiyāḻi*, 2011, 44–48. First published 2002.

———. "Maṉitaṉāy Māṟi" [Becoming human]. *Kalaimakaḷ* 7 (1964): 77–82.

Chughtai, Ismat. *A Life in Words: Memoirs*. Translated by M. Asaduddin. New Delhi: Penguin Books, 2012. Originally published 1979–80 in Urdu.

Ciocca, Rossella, and Neelam Srivastava. "Introduction: Indian Literature and the World." In *Indian Literature and the World*, edited by Rossella Ciocca and Neelam Srivastava, 1–32. London: Palgrave Macmillan, 2017.

Cixous, Hélène. "The Laugh of the Medusa." *Signs* 1, no. 4 (1976): 875–93.

Cody, Francis. *The Light of Knowledge: Literacy Activism and the Politics of Writing in South India*. Ithaca, NY: Cornell University Press, 2013.

Cohn, Bernard. "The Command of Language and the Language of Command." In *Colonialism and Its Forms of Knowledge*, 16–56. Princeton, NJ: Princeton University Press, 1996.

Coppola, Carlo. "The All-India Progressive Writers' Association: The European Phase." In *Marxist Influences and South Asian Literature*, edited by Carlo Coppola, 1–34. South Asia Series Occasional Paper no. 23, vol. 1. East Lansing: Asian Studies Center, Michigan State University, 1974.

———. *Urdu Poetry, 1935–1970: The Progressive Episode*. Karachi: Oxford University Press, 2017.

Coriale, Danielle. "Jameson's *The Antinomies of Realism*: Existential Eliot." nonsite .org, no. 11 (2014). https://nonsite.org/jamesons-the-antinomies-of-realism/.

Dalmia, Vasudha. *Fiction as History: The Novel and the City in Modern North India*. Ranikhet, India: Permanent Black, 2017.

———. "Generic Questions: Bharatendu Harischandra and Women's Issues." In *India's Literary History: Essays on the Nineteenth Century*, edited by Vasudha Dalmia and Stuart Blackburn, 402–34. Delhi: Permanent Black, 2004.

———. "The Locations of Hindi." *Economic and Political Weekly* 38, no. 14 (2003): 1377–84.

———. "Merchant Tales and the Emergence of the Novel in Hindi." *Economic and Political Weekly* 43, no. 34 (2008): 43, 45–47, 49–60.

———. *The Nationalization of Hindu Traditions: Bharatendu Harischandra and Nineteenth-Century Banaras*. Delhi: Oxford University Press, 1997.

Dalmia, Vasudha, and Rashmi Sadana, eds. *The Cambridge Companion to Modern Indian Culture*. Cambridge: Cambridge University Press, 2012.

Damrosch, David. *What Is World Literature?* Princeton, NJ: Princeton University Press, 2003.

Damsteegt, Theo. "The Early Short Stories of Mohan Rakesh." *Journal of South Asian Literature* 19, no. 1 (1984): 141–55.

Das, Sisir Kumar. *A History of Indian Literature, 1800–1910: Western Impact: Indian Response*. New Delhi: Sahitya Akademi, 1991.

———. *A History of Indian Literature, 1911–1956: Struggle for Freedom: Triumph and Tragedy*. New Delhi: Sahitya Akademi, 1995.

———. "The Idea of an Indian Literature." In *The Idea of an Indian Literature: A Book of Readings*, edited by Sujit Mukherjee, 202–7. Mysore, India: Central Institute of Indian Languages, 1981. First published 1973.

———. *Sahibs and Munshis: An Account of the College of Fort William*. New Delhi: Orion Publications, 1978.

Das Gupta, Alokeranjan. "Translating Antigone." *Indian Literature* 3, no. 2 (1960): 45–50.

Das Gupta, Jyotindra. *Language Conflict and National Development: Group Politics and Language Policy in India*. Berkeley: University of California Press, 1970.

Das Gupta, R. K. "Indian Response to Western Literature." *Indian Literature* 12, no. 2 (1969): 57–67.

———. "Problems of Research in Modern Indian Languages." *Indian Literature* 9, no. 1 (1966): 17–32.

———. "Western Response to Indian Literature." *Indian Literature* 10, no. 1 (1967): 5–15.

Dasiketan. "Yātrā Mārkkam" [The journey's path]. *Maṇikkoṭi* 5, no. 3 (1937): 41–43.

de Bruijn, Thomas. "Nirmal Varma: A Hindi Author on the Shores of Modernity." *IIAS Newsletter* 26 (2001): 24–25.

———. "Under Indian Eyes: Characterization and Dialogism in Modern Hindi Fiction." In *Chewing over the West: Occidental Narratives in Non-Western Readings*, edited by Doris Jedamski, 183–212. Amsterdam: Rodopi, 2009.

Denning, Michael. *Culture in the Age of Three Worlds*. London: Verso, 2004.

Derrida, Jacques. "Signature Event Context." In *Margins of Philosophy*, 308–28. Translated by Alan Blass. Chicago: University of Chicago Press, 1985. Originally published 1972 in French.

Desai, Neera. "From Accomodation to Articulation: Women's Movement in India." In *Women's Studies in India: A Reader*, edited by Mary John, 23–27. New Delhi: Penguin Books, 2008. First published 1986.

Deshpande, Satish. *Contemporary India: A Sociological Perspective*. New Delhi: Penguin Books, 2003.

———. "Mapping the 'Middle': Issues in the Analysis of the 'Non-Poor' in India." In *Contested Transformations: Changing Economies and Identities in Contemporary India*, edited by Mary E. John, Praveen Kumar Jha, and Surinder S. Jodhka, 215–36. New Delhi: Tulika Books, 2006.

Dev, Amiya. "Comparative Literature in India." *CLCWeb: Comparative Literature and Culture* 2, no. 4 (2000). http://dx.doi.org/10.7771/1481-4374.1093.

Devy, G. N. *In Another Tongue: Essays on Indian English Literature*. New York: Peter Lang, 1993.

Dhareshwar, Vivek. "Caste and the Secular Self." *Journal of Arts and Ideas*, no. 25/26 (1993): 115–26.

Dharwadker, Aparna. "Mohan Rakesh, Modernism, and the Postcolonial Present." *South Central Review* 25, no. 1 (2008): 136–52.

Dharwadker, Vinay. "The Historical Formation of Indian-English Literature." In Pollock, *Literary Cultures in History*, 199–267.

———. "The Modernist Novel in India: Paradigms and Practices." In *A History of the Indian Novel in English*, edited by Ulka Anjaria, 103–18. Cambridge: Cambridge University Press, 2015.

Doctor, Vikram. "Her Own Language." *Economic Times*, March 10, 2007. https://economictimes.indiatimes.com/her-own-language/articleshow/1744275.cms?from=mdr.

Doyle, Laura, and Laura Winkiel, eds. *Geomodernisms: Race, Modernism, Modernity*. Bloomington: Indiana University Press, 2005.

Dubrow, Jennifer. *Cosmopolitan Dreams: The Making of Modern Urdu Literary Culture in Colonial South Asia*. Honolulu: University of Hawaii Press, 2018.

Dwivedi, Mahavir Prasad. "Nāyikā Bhed." In *Mahāvīrprasād Dvivedī Racanāvalī, Vol. 2*, edited by Bharat Yayavar, 55–58. New Delhi: Kitabghar, 1995. First published 1901.

Ebeling, Sascha. *Colonizing the Realm of Words: The Transformation of Tamil Literature in Nineteenth-Century South India*. Albany: State University of New York Press, 2010.

Esty, Jed, and Colleen Lye. "Peripheral Realisms Now." *Modern Language Quarterly* 73, no. 3 (2012): 270–87.

Fernandes, Leela. *India's New Middle Class: Democratic Politics in an Era of Economic Reform*. Minneapolis: University of Minnesota, 2006.

Forbes, Geraldine. *Women in Modern India*. Cambridge: Cambridge University Press, 1996.

Forrester, Duncan. "The Madras Anti-Hindi Agitation, 1965: Political Protests and Its Effects on Language Policy in India." *Pacific Affairs* 39, no. 1/2 (1966): 19–36.

Forster, E. M. *Aspects of the Novel*. New York: Harcourt, Brace, 1927.

Foucault, Michel. "What Is an Author?" In *Language, Counter-Memory, Practice: Selected Essays and Interviews*, edited by Donald Bouchard, 113–38. Translated by Donald Bouchard and Sherry Simon. Ithaca, NY: Cornell University Press, 1977. Originally published 1969 in French.

Friedman, Susan Stanford. "Definitional Excursions: The Meanings of Modern/Modernity/Modernism." *Modernism/modernity* 8, no. 3 (2001): 493–513.

———. "Periodizing Modernism: Postcolonial Modernities and the Space/Time Borders of Modernist Studies." *Modernism/modernity* 13, no. 3 (2006): 425–43.

———. "Planetarity: Musing Modernist Studies." *Modernism/modernity* 17, no. 3 (2010): 471–99.

Frye, Northrop. *Anatomy of Criticism*. Princeton, NJ: Princeton University Press, 1957.

Fuller, C. J., and Haripriya Narasimhan. *Tamil Brahmins: The Making of a Middle-Class Caste*. Chicago: University of Chicago Press, 2014.

Gajarawala, Toral. "The Casteized Consciousness: Literary Realism and the Politics of Particularism." *Modern Language Quarterly* 73, no. 3 (2012): 329–49.

———. "Mother Russia, Dalit Internationalism and the Geography of Postcolonial Citation." *Interventions: International Journal of Postcolonial Studies* 22, no. 3 (2020): 329–45.

———. *Untouchable Fictions: Literary Realism and the Crisis of Caste*. New York: Fordham University Press, 2013.

Geetha, V. "History and the Caste Imagination: Some Notes on Contemporary Tamil Fiction." In *History and Imagination: Tamil Culture in the Global Context*, edited by R. Cheran, Darshan Ambalavanar, and C. Kanaganayakam, 76–89. Toronto: TSAR Publications, 2007.

Geetha, V., and S. V. Rajadurai. *Towards a Non-Brahmin Millennium: From Iyothee Thass to Periyar*. Calcutta: Samya, 1998.

Genette, Gérard. *The Architext: An Introduction*. Translated by Jane E. Lewin. Berkeley: University of California Press, 1992. Originally published 1979 in French.

———. *Narrative Discourse: An Essay in Method*. Translated by Jane E. Lewin. Ithaca, NY: Cornell University Press, 1980. Originally published 1972 in French.

———. *Paratexts: Thresholds of Interpretation*. Translated by Jane E. Lewin. Cambridge: Cambridge University Press, 1997. Originally published 1987 in French.

George, K. M., ed. *Comparative Indian Literature, Volume 1*. Thrissur, India: Kerala Sahitya Akademi, 1984.

———, ed. *Comparative Indian Literature, Volume 2*. Thrissur, India: Kerala Sahitya Akademi, 1985.

George, Rosemary Marangoly. *Indian English and the Fiction of National Literature*. Cambridge: Cambridge University Press, 2013.

Ghosh, Bishnupriya. "In Difference: The Vernacular Then and Now." *South Asian Review* 41, no. 2 (2020): 200–203.

Gide, André. "The Individual." *Left Review* 1, no. 11 (1935): 447–52.

Gikandi, Simon. "Realism, Romance, and the Problem of African Literary History." *Modern Language Quarterly* 73, no. 3 (2012): 309–28.

Gilbert, Sandra, and Susan Gubar. *The Madwoman in the Attic: The Woman Writer and the Nineteenth-Century Literary Imagination*. New Haven, CT: Yale University Press, 1979.

Goldstone, Andrew. *Fictions of Autonomy: Modernism from Wilde to de Man*. New York: Oxford University Press, 2013.

Gonda, Jan, ed. *A History of Indian Literature*. 10 vols. Wiesbaden, Germany: Harrassowitz, 1973.

Gopal, Priyamvada. *Literary Radicalism in India: Gender, Nation and the Transition to Independence*. London: Routledge, 2005.

Gorky, Maxim. "Soviet Literature." In *Soviet Writers' Congress, 1934: The Debate on Socialist Realism and Modernism in the Soviet Union*, edited by H. G. Scott, 25–69. Translated by H. G. Scott. London: Lawrence and Wishart, 1977. First published 1934 in Russian.

Gupta, Charu. "Portrayal of Women in Premchand's Stories: A Critique." *Social Scientist* 19, no. 5/6 (1991): 88–113.

———. *Sexuality, Obscenity, Community: Women, Muslims, and the Hindu Public in Colonial India*. Basingstoke, UK: Palgrave Macmillan, 2002.

Gupta, Charu, Laura Brueck, Hans Harder, and Shobna Nijhawan. "Literary Sentiments in the Vernacular: Gender and Genre in Modern South Asia." *South Asia: Journal of South Asian Studies* 43, no. 5 (2020): 803–16.

Guy, Randor. "An Icon in Her Time." *The Hindu*, January 10, 2002. https://www.thehindu.com/todays-paper/tp-miscellaneous/tp-others/an-icon-in-her-time/article28367907.ece.

Hammond, Meghan Marie, and Sue J. Kim, eds. *Rethinking Empathy through Literature*. New York: Routledge, 2014.

Hawley, John Stratton. *A Storm of Songs: India and the Idea of the Bhakti Movement*. Cambridge, MA: Harvard University Press, 2015.

Hayot, Eric. *On Literary Worlds*. Oxford: Oxford University Press, 2012.

Head, Dominic. *The Modernist Short Story: A Study in Theory and Practice*. Cambridge: Cambridge University Press, 1992.

Heidegger, Martin. "The Origin of the Work of Art." In *Off the Beaten Track*, edited by Julian Young and Kenneth Haynes, 1–56. Translated by Julian Young.

Cambridge: Cambridge University Press, 2002. Originally published 1936 in German.

Holmstrom, Lakshmi. "Making It New: Pudumaippittan and the Tamil Short Story, 1934–1948." In *Pudumaippittan: Fictions*, edited by Lakshmi Holmstrom, 230–51. Delhi: Katha Books, 2002.

Hunter, Adrian. *The Cambridge Introduction to the Short Story in English*. Cambridge: Cambridge University Press, 2007.

Hutcheon, Linda. *A Theory of Parody: The Teachings of Twentieth-Century Art Forms*. Urbana: University of Illinois Press, 2000. First published 1985.

Irigaray, Luce. *This Sex Which Is Not One*. Translated by Catherine Porter and Carolyn Burke. Ithaca, NY: Cornell University Press, 1985. Originally published 1977 in French.

Isenburg, Artur. "Modern Indian Literature: Regional Private Limited or Wealth of a Nation?" *Indian Literature* 6, no. 1 (1963): 51–65.

Jacobus, Mary. "Is There a Woman in This Text?" In *Reading Woman: Essays in Feminist Criticism*, 83–109. New York: Columbia University Press, 1986.

Jain, Nirmala. *Kathā-Samay meṃ Tīn Hamsafar* [Three co-travelers in the era of the short story]. New Delhi: Rajkamal Prakashan, 2011.

Jakobson, Roman. "On Realism in Art." In *Language in Literature*, edited by Krystyna Pomorska and Stephen Rudy, 19–27. Translated by Karol Magassy. Cambridge, MA: Belknap Press, 1987. Originally published 1921 in Czech.

Jalil, Rakhshanda. *Liking Progress, Loving Change: A Literary History of the Progressive Writers' Movement in Urdu*. New Delhi: Oxford University Press, 2014.

Jameson, Fredric. *The Antinomies of Realism*. London: Verso, 2013.

———. "Antinomies of the Realism-Modernism Debate." *Modern Language Quarterly* 73, no. 3 (2012): 475–85.

———. *The Political Unconscious: Narrative as a Socially Symbolic Act*. London: Routledge, 1983. First published 1981.

Jayakanthan, D. "Akkiṉip Piravēcam" [Trial by fire]. In *Jeyakāntaṉ: Oru Pārvai*, 97–109. First published 1966.

———. "D. Jayakanthan in Conversation with K. S. Subramanian." *Indian Literature*, 50, no. 3 (2006): 158–65.

———. "Enfant Terrible." In *Jeyakāntaṉ: Oru Pārvai*, 170. First published 1972.

———. "Etaṟkāka Eḻutukiṟēṉ?" [Why do I write?]. In *Etaṟkāka Eḻutukiṟēṉ?*, edited by K. Naa. Subramanyam, 10–16. Chennai: Eluttu Prachuram, 1972. First published 1962.

———. *Jeyakāntaṉ: Oru Pārvai* [Jayakanthan: A perspective]. Edited by K. S. Subramanian. Chennai: Kavitha Publications, 2000.

———. "Katāpāttirattiṉ Āḷumaiyaik Kākkum Tāymaikkural" [A motherly voice protects the character's personality]. In *Jeyakāntaṉ: Oru Pārvai*, 187–90. First published 1967.

———. "Muṟpōkku—Varaiyaṟai Cārnta Kaṇṇōṭṭam" [Progressivism: My perspectives toward a definition]. In *Jeyakāntaṉ: Oru Pārvai*, 183–85. First published 1963.

———. "Nāṉ Jaṉṉalarukē Uṭkārntirukkiṟēṉ" [I sit by the window]. In *Jeyakāntaṉ Ciṟukataikaḷ: Iranṭām Tokuti* [The short stories of Jayakanthan: Volume two], 474–87. Chennai: Kavitha Publications, 2001. First published 1968.

———. *Ōr Ilakkiyavātiyiṉ Araciyal Aṉupavaṅkaḷ* [A literary man's experiences in politics]. Chennai: Meenakshi Puthaka Nilaiyam, 1974.

———. *Pirammōpatēcam* [The initiation of the Brahmin]. Madurai: Minatci Puttaka Nilaiyam, 1963.

———. "Tamiḻum Taṉittamiḻum" [Tamil and pure Tamil]. In *Jeyakāntaṉ: Oru Pārvai*, 158–60. First published 1964.

John, Mary. "Gender, Development and the Women's Movement: Problems for a History of the Present." In *Signposts: Gender Issues in Post-Independence India*, edited by Rajeswari Sunder Rajan, 101–23. New Delhi: Kali for Women, 1999.

Johnson, Rebecca. "Archive of Errors: Aḥnad Fāris Al-Shidyāq, Literature, and the World." *Middle Eastern Literatures* 20, no. 1 (2017): 31–50.

Joshi, Umashankar. "Modernism and Indian Literature." *Indian Literature* 1, no. 2 (1958): 19–30.

Jussawalla, Feroza, and Reed Way Dasenbrock. "Anita Desai." In *Interviews with Writers of the Post-Colonial World*, 156–79. Jackson: University of Mississippi Press, 1992.

Kadir, Djelal. "To World, to Globalize: Comparative Literature's Crossroads." *Comparative Literature Studies* 41, no. 1 (2004): 2–9.

Kailasapathy, K. *Tamiḻ Nāval Ilakkiyam* [Studies in the Tamil novel]. Chennai: Pari Nilayam, 1968.

Kalliney, Peter. "Modernism, African Literature, and the Cold War." *Modern Language Quarterly* 76, no. 3 (2015): 333–68.

Kamleshwar. "Aura Kitne Pākistān" [How many more Pakistans?]. In *Samagra Kahāniyāṁ: Kamaleśvara* [The complete stories of Kamleshwar], 603–15. Delhi: Rajpal and Sons, 2001. First published 1969.

———. "Bhūmikā se Pahale" [Preface]. In *Koharā* [Fog], 5–6. Delhi: Rajpal and Sons, 1994.

———. *Nayī Kahānī kī Bhūmikā* [Introduction to the new story]. New Delhi: Akshar Prakashan, 1966.

Kapur, Geeta. "Mythic Material in Indian Cinema." *Journal of Arts and Ideas*, no. 14/15 (1987): 79–107.

———. *When Was Modernism: Essays on Contemporary Cultural Practice in India*. New Delhi: Tulika Books, 2000.

Kaviraj, Sudipta. *The Imaginary Institution of India: Politics and Ideas*. New York: Columbia University Press, 2010.

———. "On State, Society and Discourse in India." In *Rethinking Third World Politics*, edited by James Manor, 72–99. London: Longman, 1991.

———. "The Two Histories of Literary Culture in Bengal." In Pollock, *Literary Cultures in History*, 503–66.

Keen, Suzanne. *Empathy and the Novel*. Oxford: Oxford University Press, 2007.

———. "Narrative Empathy." In *The Living Handbook of Narratology*, edited by Peter Hühn, Jan Christoph Meister, John Pier, and Wolf Schmid. Hamburg: Hamburg University, 2013. http://www.lhn.uni-hamburg.de/article/narrative-empathy.

———. "A Theory of Narrative Empathy." *Narrative* 14, no. 3 (2006): 207–36.

Kennedy, Richard. "A Comparison of Two Tamil Literary Renaissances in Madras." *Journal of South Asian Literature* 25, no. 1 (1990): 33–54.

———. "Public Voices, Private Voices: Manikkoti, Nationalism, and the Development of the Tamil Short Story, 1914–1947." PhD diss., University of California, Berkeley, 1980.

Khilnani, Sunil. "Gandhi and Nehru: The Uses of English." In *A History of Indian Literature in English*, edited by Arvind Krishna Mehrotra, 135–56. New York: Columbia University Press, 2003.

———. *The Idea of India*. New York: Farrar Straus Giroux, 1997.

King, Christopher. *One Language, Two Scripts: The Hindi Movement in Nineteenth Century North India*. Bombay: Oxford University Press, 1994.

King, Robert. *Nehru and the Language Politics of India*. Delhi: Oxford University Press, 1997.

Kosambi, Meera. *Women Writing Gender: Marathi Fiction before Independence*. Ranikhet, India: Permanent Black, 2012.

Kothari, Rita, ed. *A Multilingual Nation: Translation and Language Dynamic in India*. New Delhi: Oxford University Press, 2018.

Krishnan, Sanjay. "V. S. Naipaul and Historical Derangement." *Modern Language Quarterly* 73, no. 3 (2012): 433–51.

Kristeva, Julia. *The Kristeva Reader*. Edited by Toril Moi. New York: Columbia University Press, 1986.

Kuchedkar, Shirin. Introduction to *Whom Can I Tell? How Can I Explain?: Selected Stories*, by Saroj Pathak, x–xxvi. Kolkata: Stree, 2002.

Kumar, Dilip, ed. *Nākaliṅka Maram: Ār. Cūtāmaṇi, Tērnteṭukkappaṭṭa Kataikaḷ* [The Nagalinga tree: R. Chudamani, selected stories]. Puthanatham, India: Adaiyaalam, 2010.

Kumar, Dilip. "Tokuppurai" [Preface to the collection]. In Kumar, *Nākaliṅka Maram*, 7–12.

Kumar, Jainendra. *Premacanda: Ek Kṛtī Vyaktitva* [Premchand: A successful personality]. Delhi: Purvodya Prakasan, 1967.

Kumar, Radha. *The History of Doing: An Illustrated Account of Movements for Women's Rights and Feminism in India, 1800–1990*. London: Verso, 1993.

Kumar, Sukrita Paul, and Sadique. *Ismat: Her Life, Her Times*. New Delhi: Katha, 2000.

Lakshmi, C. S. *The Face Behind the Mask: Women in Tamil Literature*. New Delhi: Vikas, 1984.

———. "Landscapes of the Body." *The Hindu*, December 7, 2003. https://www.thehindu.com/todays-paper/tp-features/tp-literaryreview/landscapes-of-the-body/article28498998.ece.

———. "Loss of a Crest Jewel." *The Hindu*, October 2, 2010. https://www.thehindu.com/books/Loss-of-a-crest-jewel/article15766447.ece.

———. "Maṉattukkiṉiya Oru Tōḻi" [A friend close to my heart]. In Kumar, *Nākaliṅka Maram*, 322–25.

———. "Maṉattukkiṉiyavaḷum Maraṇamum" [Death and the woman close to my heart]. *Kālaccuvaṭu*, no. 131 (November 2010): n.p.

Lazarus, Neil. *The Postcolonial Unconscious*. Cambridge: Cambridge University Press, 2011.

Lewis, Pericles. *The Cambridge Introduction to Modernism*. Cambridge: Cambridge University Press, 2007.

Lindhé, Anna. "The Paradox of Narrative Empathy and the Form of the Novel, or What George Eliot Knew." *Studies in the Novel* 48, no. 1 (2016): 19–42.

Lotz, Barbara. "Rāhoṃ ke Anveṣī: The Editor of the Saptak Anthologies and His Poets." In *Hindi Modernism: Rethinking Agyeya and His Times*, edited by Vasudha Dalmia, 125–46. Berkeley: Center for South Asian Studies, University of California, Berkeley, 2012.

Lukács, Georg. *The Historical Novel*. Translated by Hannah and Stanley Mitchell. Lincoln: University of Nebraska Press, 1962. Originally published 1937 in German.

———. *The Meaning of Contemporary Realism*. Translated by John and Necke Mander. London: Merlin Press, 1963. Originally published 1957 in German.

———. "Narrate or Describe?" In *Writer and Critic, and Other Essays*, 110–48. Translated by Arthur Kahn. London: Merlin Press, 2007. Originally published 1936 in German.

———. *The Theory of the Novel: A Historico-Philosophical Essay on the Forms of Great Epic Literature*. Translated by Anna Bostock. Cambridge, MA: MIT Press, 1994. Originally published 1920 in German.

Macaulay, Thomas Babbington. "Minute on Indian Education." In *Archives of Empire: Volume I: From the East India Company to the Suez Canal*, edited by Mia Carter and Barbara Harlow, 227–38. Durham, NC: Duke University Press, 2003. First published 1835.

Machwe, Prabhakar. "The Problem of Translation from and into Hindi." *Indian Literature* 10, no. 1 (1967): 68–81.

Madhuresh. *Hindī Kahānī kā Vikās* [The development of the Hindi short story]. Allahabad: Lok Bharati Prakashan, 1996.

Mahmud, Shabana. "Angāre and the Founding of the Progressive Writers' Association." *Modern Asian Studies* 30, no. 2 (1996): 447–67.

Majumdar, Rochona. *Marriage and Modernity: Family Values in Colonial Bengal*. Durham, NC: Duke University Press, 2009.

———. "'Self-Sacrifice' Versus 'Self-Interest': A Non-Historicist Reading of the History of Women's Rights in India." *Comparative Studies of South Asia, Africa and the Middle East* 22, no. 1/2 (2002): 20–35.

Mani, Preetha. "Literary and Popular Fiction in Late Colonial Tamil Nadu." In *Indian Genre Fictions: Pasts and Future Histories*, edited by Bodhisattva Chattopadhyay, Aakriti Mandhwani, and Anwesha Maity, 17–37. London: Routledge, 2019.

———. "What Was So New about the New Story? Modernist Realism in the Hindi Nayī Kahānī." *Comparative Literature* 73, no. 1 (2019): 226–51.

March-Russell, Paul. *The Short Story: An Introduction*. Edinburgh: Edinburgh University Press, 2009.

May, Charles E. *"I Am Your Brother": Short Story Studies*. CreateSpace Independent Publishing, 2013.

———, ed. *The New Short Story Theories*. Athens: Ohio University Press, 1994.

———. "Reality in the Short Story." *Style* 27, no. 3 (1993): 369–80.

———, ed. *Short Story Theories*. Athens: Ohio University Press, 1976.

———. *The Short Story: The Reality of Artifice*. New York: Twayne Publishers, 1995.

Menon, Dilip. *The Blindness of Insight*. New Delhi: Navayana, 2006.

Menon, Nitya. "When the National Poet Spoke up for Tamil." *The Hindu*, May 13, 2015. https://www.thehindu.com/news/cities/chennai/when-the-national-poet-spoke-up-for-tamil/article7200244.ece.

Merrill, Christi. *Riddles of Belonging: India in Translation and Other Tales of Possession*. New York: Fordham University Press, 2009.

———. "Translations from South Asia: The Power of Babel." In *Literature in Translation: Teaching Issues and Reading Practices*, edited by Carol Maier and Françoise Massardier-Kenney, 167–75. Kent, OH: Kent State University Press, 2010.

Minault, Gail. "Urdu Women's Magazines in the Early Twentieth Century." *Manushi*, no. 48 (September–October 1988): 2–9.

Minh-ha, Trinh T. *Woman, Native, Other: Writing Postcoloniality and Feminism*. Bloomington: Indiana University Press, 1989.

Mir, Farina. *The Social Space of Language: Vernacular Culture in British Colonial Punjab*. Berkeley: University of California Press, 2010.

Mitchell, Lisa. *Language, Emotion, and Politics in South India: The Making of a Mother Tongue*. Bloomington: Indiana University Press, 2009.

Mody, Sujata. *The Making of Modern Hindi: Literary Authority in Colonial North India*. New Delhi: Oxford University Press, 2018.

Moers, Ellen. *Literary Women: The Great Writers*. Garden City, NY: Doubleday, 1976.

Mohanty, Chandra Talpade, and Satya P. Mohanty, eds. *The Slate of Life: More Contemporary Stories by Women Writers of India*. New York: Feminist Press at the City University of New York, 1990.

Moi, Toril. "I Am Not a Woman Writer: About Women, Literature and Feminist Theory Today." *Eurozine*, June 12, 2009. https://www.eurozine.com/i-am-not-a-woman-writer/.

———. *Sexual/Textual Politics: Feminist Literary Theory*. London: Routledge, 2002.

Moretti, Franco. "Conjectures on World Literature." *New Left Review* 1 (2000): 54–68.

———. "Evolution, World-Systems, *Weltliteratur*." In *Studying Transcultural Literary History*, edited by Gunilla Lindberg-Wada, 113–21. Berlin: W. de Gruyter, 2006.

———. "More Conjectures." *New Left Review* 20 (2003): 73–81.

———. *Way of the World: The Bildungsroman in European Culture*. Translated by Albert Sbragia. London: Verso, 1987.

Mufti, Aamir. *Enlightenment in the Colony: The Jewish Question and the Crisis of Postcolonial Culture*. Princeton, NJ: Princeton University Press, 2007.

———. *Forget English! Orientalisms and World Literature*. Cambridge, MA: Harvard University Press, 2016.

Mukherjee, Meenakshi, ed. *Early Novels in India*. New Delhi: Sahitya Akademi, 2002.

———. Introduction to *Early Novels in India*, edited by Meenakshi Mukherjee, vii–xix. New Delhi: Sahitya Akademi, 2002.

———. *The Perishable Empire: Essays on Indian Writing in English*. New Delhi: Oxford University Press, 2003.

———. *Realism and Reality: The Novel and Society in India*. Delhi: Oxford University Press, 1985.

Mukherjee, Sujit, ed. *The Idea of an Indian Literature: A Book of Readings.* Mysore, India: Central Institute of Indian Languages, 1981.

Mukherjee, Sujit. Preface to Mukherjee, *The Idea of an Indian Literature,* vi–vii.

———. *Towards a Literary History of India.* Simla: Indian Instutite of Advanced Study, 1975.

Nambi Arooran, K. *Tamil Renaissance and Dravidian Nationalism, 1905–1944.* Madurai: Koodal Publishers, 1980.

Narayanan, Padma and Prema Seetharam. "Narratives That Linger: A Profile of the Tamil Writer R. Chudamani." *The Hindu,* October 2, 2005. https://www.thehindu.com/todays-paper/tp-features/tp-literaryreview/narratives-that-linger/article28500257.ece.

Nehru, Jawaharlal. "Creative Writing in the Present Crisis." *Indian Literature* 6, no. 1 (1963): 66–69.

———. Foreword to *History of Bengali Literature,* edited by Sukumar Sen, v–viii. New Delhi: Sahitya Akademi, 1960.

———. "The Question of Language." In *The Unity of India: Collected Writings 1937–1940,* edited by V. K. Krishna Menon, 241–67. London: Lindsay Drummond, 1941.

Nerlekar, Anjali. *Bombay Modern: Arun Kolatkar and Bilingual Literary Culture.* Evanston, IL: Northwestern University Press, 2016.

Nijhawan, Shobna. *Women and Girls in the Hindi Public Sphere: Periodical Literature in Colonial North India.* New Delhi: Oxford University Press, 2012.

Novetzke, Christian. *The Quotidian Revolution: Vernacularization, Religion, and the Premodern Public Sphere in India.* New York: Columbia University Press, 2016.

Oldenburg, Veena Talwar. "Lifestyle as Resistance: The Case of the Courtesans of Lucknow, India." *Feminist Studies* 16, no. 2 (1990): 259–87.

Orsini, Francesca. "Domesticity and Beyond: Hindi Women's Journals in the Early Twentieth Century." *South Asia Research* 19, no. 2 (1999): 137–60.

———. *The Hindi Public Sphere: Language and Literature in the Age of Nationalism.* New Delhi: Oxford University Press, 2002.

———. "How to Do a Multilingual Literary History? Lessons from Fifteenth- and Sixteenth-Century North India." *Indian Economic and Social History Review* 49, no. 2 (2012): 225–46.

———. Introduction to *The Oxford India Premchand,* by Premchand, vii–xxvi. New Delhi: Oxford University Press, 2004.

———. "The Multilingual Local in World Literature." *Comparative Literature* 67, no. 4 (2015): 345–74.

———. "Present Absence: Book Circulation, Indian Vernaculars and World Literature in the Nineteenth Century." *Interventions: International Journal of Postcolonial Studies* 22, no. 3 (2019): 310–28.

———. *Print and Pleasure: Popular Literature and Entertaining Fictions in Colonial North India.* Ranikhet, India: Permanent Black, 2009.

———. "The Short Story as an *Aide À Penser*: Ajñeya's Stories." In *Hindi Modernism: Rethinking Agyeya and His Times,* edited by Vasudha Dalmia, 103–23. Berkeley: Center for South Asian Studies, University of Calfiornia, Berkeley, 2012.

———. "Vernacular: Flawed but Necessary?" *South Asian Review* 41, no. 2 (2020): 204–6.

Padikkal, Shivarama. "Inventing Modernity: The Emergence of the Novel in India." In *Interrogating Modernity: Culture and Colonialism in India*, edited by Tejaswini Niranjana, P. Sudhir, and Vivek Dhareshwar, 220–41. Calcutta: Seagull, 1993.

Padmanabhan, V. K. "Communist Parties in Tamil Nadu." *Indian Journal of Political Science* 48, no. 2 (1987): 225–50.

Pandey, Geetanjali. "How Equal? Women in Premchand's Writings." *Economic and Political Weekly* 21, no. 50 (1986): 2183–87.

Pandian, M. S. S. *Brahmin and Non-Brahmin: Genealogies of the Tamil Political Present*. Ranikhet, India: Permanent Black, 2007.

———. "Notes on the Transformation of 'Dravidian' Ideology: Tamilnadu, C. 1900–1940." *Social Scientist* 22, no. 5/6 (1994): 84–104.

———. "One Step Outside Modernity: Caste, Identity Politics and Public Sphere." *Economic and Political Weekly* 37, no. 18 (2002): 1735–41.

Parameswaran, Uma. *Lady Lokasundari Raman: Reflections of Her Early Life and Times*. Manipal, India: Manipal University Press, 2013.

Parashar, Archana. *Women and Family Law Reform in India: Uniform Civil Code and Gender Equality*. New Delhi: Sage, 1992.

Parry, Benita. "Aspects of Peripheral Modernism." *ARIEL* 40, no. 1 (2009): 27–55.

Parts, Lyudmila, ed. *The Russian Twentieth-Century Short Story: A Critical Companion*. Boston: Academic Studies Press, 2009.

Patel, Geeta. "Vernacular Missing: Miraji on Sappho, Gender, and Governance." *Comparative Literature* 70, no. 2 (2018): 132–44.

Pernau, Magrit. *Emotion and Modernity in Colonial India: From Balance to Fervor*. New Delhi: Oxford University Press, 2019.

———. "Love and Compassion for the Community: Emotions and Practices among North Indian Muslims, c. 1870–1930." *Indian Economic and Social History Review* 54, no. 1 (2017): 21–42.

Piccamurti, Na. "Taṟkālat Tamiḻk Kavikaḷ" [Contemporary Tamil poets]. In *Na. Piccamūrtti Kaṭṭuraikaḷ* [Essays of Na. Piccamurti], edited by Munaivar W. Manikantan, 45–58. Chennai: Sandhya Patippakam, 2012. First published 1936.

Pollock, Sheldon. "Introduction: An Intellectual History of Rasa." In *A Rasa Reader: Classical Indian Aesthetics*, edited by Sheldon Pollock, 1–45. New York: Columbia University Press, 2016.

———. "The Cosmopolitan Vernacular." *Journal of Asian Studies* 57, no. 1 (1998): 6–37.

———. *The Language of the Gods in the World of Men*. Berkeley: University of California Press, 2006.

———, ed. *Literary Cultures in History: Reconstructions from South Asia*. New Delhi: Oxford University Press, 2003.

Pradhan, Sudhi. *Marxist Cultural Movement in India: Chronicles and Documents (1936–47)*. Calcutta: National Book Agency, 1979.

Prasad, M. Madhava. "The State In/Of Cinema." In *Wages of Freedom: Fifty Years of the Indian Nation State*, edited by Partha Chatterjee, 123–46. Delhi: Oxford University Press, 1998.

Pratt, Mary Louise. "The Short Story: The Long and the Short of It." In *The New Short Story Theories*, edited by Charles E. May, 91–113. Athens: Ohio University Press, 1994.

Premchand. "Abhilāshā" [Desire]. In *Mānasarovar*, 4:63–67. First published 1928.

———. "Adab kī Gharaz-o-Ghāyat" [The purpose and purview of literature]. In *Mazāmīn-e-Premacanda* [Essays of Premchand], edited by Qamar Rais, 234–53. Hyderabad: Yuniv Publications, 1960. First published 1941.

———. "Antarprāntīya Sāhityak Ādān-Pradān ke Liye" [On intranational literary exchanges]. In *Sāhitya kā Uddeśya*, 217–39.

———. "Bhāratīya Sāhitya aura Paṇḍit Javāharlāl Nehrū" [Indian literature and Pandit Jawaharlal Nehru]. In *Vividh Prasaṅg*, 3:105–8. First published 1935.

———. "Bhāratīya Sāhitya Parishad" [The All-India Literary Society]. In *Vividh Prasaṅg*, 3:117–18. First published 1936.

———. "Dakshiṇ meṃ Hindī Pracār" [The propagation of Hindi in the South]. In *Vividh Prasaṅg*, 3:277–78. First published 1932.

———. "Galpāṅk kā Prastāv" [Introduction to the short story issue]. In *Vividh Prasaṅg*, 3:39–48. First published 1926.

———. *Godān* [The gift of a cow]. Varanasi: Prakashan Sansthan, 2003. First published 1936.

———. "Hindī Galp-Kalā kā Vikās" [The development of Hindi short story writing]. In *Premcanda kā Aprāpya Sāhitya: Khaṇḍ Do* [Premchand's unpublished writings: volume two], edited by Kamalkishore Goyanka, 551–57. New Delhi: Bharatiya Gyanpit, 1988. First published 1934.

———. "Jīvan aura Sāhitya meṃ Ghṙṇā kā Sthān" [The place of hatred in life and literature]. In *Vividh Prasaṅg*, vol. 3:54–59. First published 1933.

———. "Jīvan meṃ Sāhitya kā Sthān" [The place of literature in life]. In *Kuch Vicār*, 90–100.

———. "Kahānī Kalā 1" [The art of the story 1]. In *Kuch Vicār*, 26–30. First published in 1934.

———. "Kahānī Kalā 2" [The art of the story 2]. In *Kuch Vicār*, 31–39. First published 1934.

———. "Kahānī Kalā 3" [The art of the story 3]. In *Kuch Vicār*, 40–46. First published 1934.

———. *Kuch Vicār* [Some thoughts]. Allahabad: Saraswati Press, 1985.

———. "Landan meṃ Bhāratīya Sāhityakāroṃ kī Ek Nayī Saṃsthā" [A new society of Indian writers in London]. *Haṃs*, January 1936, 117–18.

———. *Mānasarovar* [The lake of intelligence]. 7 vols. Patna: Anupam Prakashan, 2011.

———. "Mis Padmā" [Miss Padma]. In *Mānasarovar*, 2:58–62. First published 1936.

———. "Miss Padma." In *Premchand: The Complete Short Stories*, 4: 587–99. Translated by Fatima Rizvi. First published 1936.

———. "Premcanda kī Prem-Līlā kā Uttar" [A response to Premchand's game of love]. In *Vividh Prasaṅg*, 3:70–72. First published 1926.

———. *Premchand: The Complete Short Stories*. Edited by M. Asaduddin. 4 vols. London: Penguin Books, 2017.

———. "Rāshṭrabhāshā Hindī aura Uskī Samasyāeṁ" [The national language Hindi and its problems]. In *Sāhitya kā Uddeśya*, 149–69. First published 1934.

———. "Rāshṭrabhāshā Kaise Samṙddh Ho" [How the national language can thrive]. In *Vividh Prasaṅg*, 3:108–10. First published 1935.

———. "Sāhitya kā Ādhār" [The basis of literature]. In *Sāhitya kā Uddeśya* [The aim of literature], 30–34. Allahabad: Hams Prakashan, 1954.
———. "Sāhitya kā Uddeśya" [The aim of literature]. In *Kuch Vicār*, 5–25. First published 1936.
———. *Sāhitya kā Uddeśya* [The aim of literature]. Allahabad: Hams Prakashan, 1954.
———. "Sāhitya kī Pragati" [The progress of literature]. In *Vividh Prasaṅg*, 3:48–55. First published 1933.
———. "Sāhityik Kluboṃ kī Āvaśyakatā" [The necessity of literary clubs]. In *Vividh Prasaṅg*, 3:113. First published 1931.
———. "Upanyās" [The novel]. In *Vividh Prasaṅg*, 3:33–38.
———. *Vividh Prasaṅg* [Various matters]. Edited by Amrit Rai. Vol. 3. Allahabad: Hams Prakashan, 1962.
———. *Zād-e-Rāh* [Provisions for the Journey]. Lahore: Ishrat Publishing House, n.d. First published 1936.
Pudumaippittan. "Akalyai" [Ahalya]. In *Putumaippittaṉ Kataikaḷ*, 131– 35. First published 1934.
———. "Cāpa Vimōcaṉam" [Deliverance from the curse]. In *Putumaippittaṉ Kataikaḷ*, 535–48. First published 1943.
———. "Cellammāḷ" [Chellammal]. In *Putumaippittaṉ Kataikaḷ*, 517–34. First published 1943.
———. "Ciṉṉa Viṣayam" [A small matter]. In *Putumaippittaṉ Kaṭṭuraikaḷ*, 109–11. First published 1934.
———. "Ciṟpiyiṉ Narakam" [The sculptor's hell]. In *Putumaippittaṉ Kataikaḷ*, 325–30. First published 1935.
———. "Ciṟukatai" [The short story]. In *Putumaippittaṉ Kaṭṭuraikaḷ*, 142–45. First published 1935.
———. "Ciṟukatai: Maṟumalarccik Kālam" [The short story: the era of renaissance]. In *Putumaippittaṉ Kaṭṭuraikaḷ*, 234–38. First published 1946.
———. "Eccarikkai!" [Warning!]. In *Putumaippittaṉ Kataikaḷ*, 777–80. First published 1943.
———. "Eṉ Kataikaḷum Nāṉum" [My stories and I]. In *Putumaippittaṉ Kaṭṭuraikaḷ*, 172–78. First published 1942.
———. "Ilakkiyattiṉ Irakaciyam" [The secret of literature]. In *Putumaippittaṉ Kaṭṭuraikaḷ*, 118–19. First published 1934.
———. "Ilakkiyattiṉ Uṭpirivukaḷ" [Literary genres]. In *Putumaippittaṉ Kaṭṭuraikaḷ*, 122–24. First published 1934.
———. "Kāñcaṉai" [Kanchanai]. In *Putumaippittaṉ Kataikaḷ*, 507–16. First published 1943.
———. "Kataikaḷ" [Short stories]. In *Putumaippittaṉ Kaṭṭuraikal*, 112–14. First published 1934.
———. "Poṉṉakaram" [The golden city]. In *Putumaippittaṉ Kataikaḷ*, 66–68. First published 1934.
———. *Putumaippittaṉ Kataikaḷ* [The complete short stories of Pudumaippittan]. Edited by A. R. Venkatachalapathy. Nagarcoil: Kalachuvadu, 2000.
———. *Putumaippittaṉ Kaṭṭuraikaḷ* [The complete essays of Pudumaippittan]. Edited by A. R. Venkatachalapathy. Nagarcoil: Kalachuvadu, 2002.

———. "Tamiḻaip paṟṟi" [About Tamil]. In *Putumaippittaṉ Kaṭṭuraikaḷ*, 84–87. First published 1934.

———. "Taṉimai" [Loneliness]. In *Putumaippittaṉ Kaṭṭuraikal*, 60–61. First published 1933.

———. "Uṇarcci Vēkamum Naṭai Nayamum" [The rush of emotions and the subtlety of style]. In *Putumaippittaṉ Kaṭṭuraikaḷ*, 128–31. First published 1934.

———. "Uṅkaḷ Katai" [Your story]. In *Putumaippittaṉ Kaṭṭuraikaḷ*, 222–29. First published 1946.

———. "Yātrā Mārkkam" [The journey's path]. *Maṇikkoṭi* 5, no. 2 (1937): 74–77.

———. "Yātrā Mārkkam: Cantēkat Teḷivu" [The journey's path: A clarification of doubt]. *Maṇikkoṭi* 5, no. 8 (1937): 52–56.

———. "Yātrā Mārkkam: Taḻuvalum Moḻi Peyarppum" [The journey's path: Adaptation and translation]. *Maṇikkoṭi* 5, no. 7 (1937): 69–72.

Pullin, Eric D. "'Money Does Not Make Any Difference to the Opinions That We Hold': India, the C.I.A., and the Congress for Cultural Freedom, 1951–58." *Intelligence and National Security* 26, no. 2/3 (2011): 377–98.

Radek, Karl. "Contemporary World Literature and the Tasks of Proletarian Art." In *Soviet Writers' Congress, 1934: The Debate on Socialist Realism and Modernism in the Soviet Union*, edited by H. G. Scott, 72–182. Translated by H. G. Scott. London: Lawrence and Wishart, 1977. Originally published 1934 in Russian.

Radhakrishnan, R. "A Writer's Role in National Integration: Inaugural Address." *Indian Literature* 5, no. 1 (1962): 25–29.

Radhakrishnan, S. "Editorial Note." *Indian Literature* 1, no. 1 (1957): 1–3.

———. Foreword to *Contemporary Indian Literature*, v. New Delhi: Sahitya Akademi, 1957.

———. "A Key-Note of Great Indian Literature." *Indian Literature* 5, no. 1 (1962): 1–3.

———. "Speech at Inaugural Ceremony." In *Sahitya Akademi: National Academy of Letters, Annual Report 1954–1957*, 1–25. New Delhi: Sahitya Akademi, 1957.

Raghavan, V. "Sanksrit." In *Contemporary Indian Literature*, 201–52. New Delhi: Sahitya Akademi, 1957.

Rai, Alok. *Hindi Nationalism*. Hyderabad: Orient Longman, 2001.

———. "A Kind of Crisis: Godan and the Last Writings of Munshi Premchand." *Journal of the School of Languages, Jawaharlal Nehru University* 2, no. 1 (1974): 1–13.

Rai, Gopal. *Hindi Kahānī kā Itihās* [The history of the Hindi short story]. New Delhi: Rajkamal Prakashan, 2011.

———. *Hindī Upanyās kā Itihās* [The history of the Hindi novel]. New Delhi: Rajkamal Prakashan, 2002.

Rajamarttandan. "Ci. Cu. Cellappāvum *'Eḻuttu'*m" [C. S. Chellappa and *Eḻuttu*]. In *Ci. Cu. Cellappā Ilakkiyattaṭam* [C. S. Chellappa's literary path], edited by S. Shanmukasundaram, 88–96. Chennai: Kavya, 2001.

———. "Kaṉavukaḷum Yatārttamum: *'Eḻuttu'* Mutal *'Kollippāvai'* Varai" [Dreams and reality: from the journal *Eḻuttu* to the journal *Kollipāvai*]. *Kālaccuvaṭu*, no. 100 (2008): 62–70.

Rakesh, Mohan. "Ādmī aura Dīvār" [The man and the wall]. In *Mohan Rākeś kī Sampūrṇ Kahāniyāṁ*, 163–72. First published 1960.

———. "Bakalam Khud: Prem-Tikon, Andar kī Uphanatī Huī Duniyā, Satah ke Bulbule" [Just me and a pen: love triangle, a world boiling within, bubbles on the surface]. *Naī Kahāniyāṁ* 1, no. 3 (1960): 75–79.

———. "Bakalam Khud: Udās-Dhaṛkaneṃ aura Kālatīt Kshaṇ . . . Ek Viśesh Manaḥsthiti" [Just me and a pen: thobs of sadness and a timeless moment . . . a special state of mind]. *Naī Kahāniyāṁ* 1, no. 5 (1960): 75–78.

———. "Ek Aura Zindagī" [Another life]. In *Ek Aura Zindagī* [Another life], 157–200. Delhi: Rajpal and Sons, 1961.

———. "Interview with Mohan Rakesh." *Journal of South Asian Literature* 9, no. 2/3 (1968): 15–45.

———. "Klem" [The claim]. In *Mohan Rākeś kī Sampūrṇ Kahāniyāṁ*, 108–13. First published 1958.

———. "Malbe kā Mālik" [The owner of rubble]. In *Mohan Rākeś kī Sampūrṇ Kahāniyāṁ*, 224–31. First published 1957.

———. "Mis Pāl" [Miss Pal]. In *Mohan Rākeś kī Sampūrṇ Kahāniyāṁ*, 9–27. First published 1961.

———. *Mohan Rākeś kī Ḍāyarī* [Mohan Rakesh's diary]. Delhi: Rajpal and Sons, 1994.

———. *Mohan Rākeś kī Sampūrṇ Kahāniyāṁ* [The complete stories of Mohan Rakesh]. Delhi: Rajpal and Sons, 2004.

———. "Paramātmā kā Kuttā" [God's dog]. In *Mohan Rākeś kī Sampūrṇ Kahāniyāṁ*, 322–26. First published 1958.

———. *Sāṁskṛtik aura Sāhityak Dṛshṭi* [Perspectives on literature and culture]. Delhi: Radhakrishnan Prakashan, 1975.

Ram, Harsha. "The Scale of Global Modernisms: Imperial, National, Regional, Local." *PMLA* 131, no. 5 (2016): 1372–85.

Ramaiah, B. S. *Maṇikkoṭi Kālam* [The era of *Manikkoti*]. Chennai: Meyyappan Pathipakam, 1980. First published 1969–71.

Ramamurthy, Priti. "The Modern Girl in India in the Interwar Years: Interracial Intimacies, International Competition, and Historical Eclipsing." *Women's Studies Quarterly* 34, no. 1/2 (2006): 197–226.

Raman, Bhavani. *Document Raj: Writing and Scribes in Early Colonial South India*. Chicago: University of Chicago Press, 2012.

Raman, Srilata. "The Face Behind the Mask: Ambai on Women." In *Narrative Strategies: Essays on South Asian Literature and Film*, edited by Vasudha Dalmia and Theo Damsteegt, 110–21. Leiden: Research School CNWS, 1998.

Ramanujan, A. K. "Three Hundred Ramayanas: Five Examples and Three Thoughts on Translation." In *The Collected Essays of A. K. Ramanujan*, edited by Vinay Dharwadker, 131–60. New Delhi: Oxford University Press, 1991.

Ramaswamy, Sumathi. *Passions of the Tongue: Language Devotion in Tamil India, 1891–1970*. Berkeley: University of California Press, 1997.

Ramaswamy, Sundara. "Kiṭāri" [Heifer]. In *Cuntara Rāmacāmi Ciṟukataikaḷ: Muḻuttokuppu* [The short stories of Sundara Ramaswamy: The complete volume], 156–75. Nagarcoil: Kalachuvadu, 2006. First published 1959.

Rancière, Jacques. "Contemporary Art and the Politics of Aesthetics." In *Communities of Sense: Rethinking Aesthetics and Politics*, edited by Beth Hinderliter, William Kaizen, Vared Maimon, Jaleh Mansoor, and Seth McCormick, 31–50. Durham, NC: Duke University Press, 2009.

Rao, D. S. *Five Decades: The National Academy of Letters, India: A Short History of the Sahitya Akademi*. New Delhi: Sahitya Akademi, 2004.

Raveendran, P. P. "Genealogies of Indian Literature." *Economic and Political Weekly* 41, no. 25 (2006) 2558–63.

Ritter, Valerie. *Kama's Flowers: Nature in Hindi Poetry and Criticism, 1885–1925*. Albany: State University of New York Press, 2011.

———. "The Proper Female Subject: Poetics and Erotics in Early-Twentieth-Century Hindi." *Journal of Women's History* 22, no. 1 (2010) 107–29.

Roadarmel, Gordon Charles. "The Theme of Alienation in the Modern Hindi Short Story." PhD diss., University of California, Berkeley,1969.

Rosenstein, Lucy. "Introduction." In *New Poetry in Hindi: Nayi Kavita: An Anthology*, edited by Lucy Rosenstein, 1–18. London: Anthem Press, 2004. First published 2002.

Roye, Susmita. "Politics of Sculpting the 'New' Indian Woman in Premchand's Stories: Everything the Mem Is Not." *South Asia Research* 36, no. 2 (2016) 229–40.

Sadana, Rashmi. *English Heart, Hindi Heartland: The Political Life of Literature in India*. Berkeley: University of California Press, 2012.

———. "Writing in English." In *The Cambridge Companion to Modern Indian Culture*, edited by Vasudha Dalmia and Rashmi Sadana, 124–41. Cambridge: Cambridge University Press, 2012.

Sahitya Akademi. *Sahitya Akademi Progress Report (1956–57)*. New Delhi: Sahitya Akademi, 1957.

———. *Sahitya Akademi: National Academy of Letters, Annual Report 1954–1957*. New Delhi: Sahitya Akademi, 1957.

Said, Edward. *Culture and Imperialism*. New York: Alfred A. Knopf, 1993.

Sakai, Naoki. *Translation and Subjectivity: On "Japan" and Cultural Nationalism*. Minneapolis: University of Minnesota Press, 1997.

Sangari, Kumkum. "Aesthetics of Circulation: Thinking between Regions." *Jadavpur Journal of Comparative Literature*, no. 50 (2014): 9–38.

———. "The Politics of the Possible." *Cultural Critique* 7 (Autumn 1987): 157–86.

———. "*Viraha*: A Trajectory in the Nehruvian Era." In *Poetics and Politics of Sufism and Bhakti in South Asia: Love, Loss and Liberation*, edited by Kavita Punjabi, 256–87. Hyderabad: Orient Blackswan, 2011.

Sangari, Kumkum, and Sudesh Vaid, eds. *Recasting Women: Essays in Colonial History*. New Brunswick: Rutgers University Press, 1989.

Sarkar, Tanika. *Hindu Wife, Hindu Nation: Community, Religion, and Cultural Nationalism*. Bloomington: Indiana University Press, 2001.

Sawhney, Simona. *The Modernity of Sanskrit*. Minneapolis: University of Minnesota Press, 2009.

Schomer, Karine. *Mahadevi Varma and the Chhayavad Age of Modern Hindi Poetry*. Delhi: Oxford University Press, 1998.

Schweig, Graham, and David Buchta. "*Rasa* theory." In *Brill's Encyclopedia of Hinduism Online*, edited by Knut A. Jacobsen, Helene Basu, Angelika Malinar, and Vasudha Narayanan. Brill, 2018. http://dx.doi.org/10.1163/2212-5019_BEH_COM_2040070.

Scofield, Martin. *The Cambridge Introduction to the American Short Story*. Cambridge: Cambridge University Press, 2007.

Selvamony, Nirmal. "Vernacular as Homoarchic Mode of Existence." *South Asian Review* 41, no. 2 (2020): 194–96.

Seth, Rajee. "Apne Viruddh" [Against myself]. In *Andhe Moṛ se Āge* [Beyond the blind alley], 70–79. Delhi: Rajpal and Sons, 1979.

Shankar, Subramanian. "Comparatism, Partition, and the Vernacular." *PMLA* 127, no. 3 (2012): 643–44.

———. *Flesh and Fish Blood: Postcolonialism, Translation, and the Vernacular.* Berkeley: University of California Press, 2012.

———. "Literatures of the World: An Inquiry." *PMLA* 131, no. 5 (2016): 1405–13.

———. "The Vernacular: An Introduction." *South Asian Review* 41, no. 2 (2020): 191–93.

Shingavi, Snehal. *The Mahatma Misunderstood: The Politics and Forms of Literary Nationalism in India.* London: Anthem Press, 2014.

———. "Premchand and Language: On Translation, Cultural Nationalism, and Irony." *The Annual of Urdu Studies*, no. 28 (2013): 149–64.

Showalter, Elaine. *A Literature of Their Own: English Women Novelists from Bronte to Lessing.* Princeton, NJ: Princeton University Press, 1977.

Shree, Geetanjali. "I'm Waiting to Write the Book Which Will Slip out of My Grasp." Interview by Manoj Nair. *Outlook*, April 20, 2001. http://www.outlookindia.com/website/story/im-waiting-to-write-the-book-which-will-slip-out-of-my-grasp/211369.

———. *Māī* [Mother]. Delhi: Raj Kamal Prakashan, 1993.

———. "My Language: Why and How Hindi?" Azim Premji University, May 10, 2018. https://www.youtube.com/watch?v=brCbmdSALhQ.

———. "The Past Is Ever Present." Interview by Preeti Verma Lal. Deep Blue Ink, n.d. http://deepblueink.com/writing/interviews/geetanjalishree.htm.

———. "Writing Is Translating Is Writing Is. . . ." In *India in Translation through Hindi Literature: A Plurality of Voices*, edited by Maya Burger and Nicola Pozza, 267–76. Bern, Switzerland: Peter Lang, 2010.

Shukla, Ramchandra. *Cintāmaṇi: Pahalā Bhāg* [Jewels of thought: Part one]. Allababad: Indian Press, 1969. First published 1939.

———. *Hindī Sāhitya kā Itihās* [History of Hindi literature]. Varanasi: Nagari Pracharini Sabha, 1929.

———. "Kavitā Kyā Hai?" [What is poetry?]. In *Pratinidhi Nibandha*, edited by Sudhakar Pandey, 65–76. New Delhi: Radhakrishna Prakashan, 1971. First published 1903.

Shulman, David. *Tamil: A Biography.* Cambridge, MA: Harvard University Press, 2016.

Singh, Avadhesh Kumar. "Interliterariness 'Still,' and 'Methodized,' Too: Literary Contactuality in India." *Comparative Studies of South Asia, Africa and the Middle East* 32, no. 3 (2012): 604–10.

———. "Premchand On/In Translation." In *Premchand in World Languages: Translation, Reception, and Cinematic Representations*, edited by M. Asaduddin, 129–43. Abingdon, England: Routledge, 2016.

Singh, Dinanath. *Hindī Kahānī ke Sau Varsh* [One hundred years of the Hindi short story]. Delhi: Meenakshi Prakashan, 2009.

Singh, Namvar. "Hindi." In *Indian Literature since Independence: A Symposium*, edited by R. K. Srinivasa Iyengar, 79–92. New Delhi: Sahitya Akademi, 1973.

———. *Kahānī: Nayī Kahānī* [Story: New story]. Allahabad: Lokbharati Prakashan, 1998. First published 1956–65.

———. *Kavitā ke Naye Pratimān* [A new model of poetry]. New Delhi: Rajkamal Prakasan, 1968.

Sinha, Arunava. "Why Aren't Translations the Big Story of Indian Publishing?" *Scroll.in*, 2015. https://scroll.in/article/698475/why-arent-translations-the-big-story-of-indian-publishing.

Sinha, Mrinalini. *Specters of Mother India: The Global Restructuring of an Empire.* Durham, NC: Duke University Press, 2006.

Sobti, Krishna. "Krishna Sobti: Author's Integrity Is Supreme." Interview by Ranavira Rangra. In *Women Writers: Literary Interviews*, by Ranavira Rangra, 63–82. Delhi: B. R. Publishing, 1998.

Sogani, Rajul. *The Hindu Widow in Indian Literature.* Oxford: Oxford University Press, 2002.

Söhnen-Thieme, Renate. "The Ahalyā Story through the Ages." In *Myth and Mythmaking: Continuous Evolution in the Indian Tradition*, edited by Julia Leslie, 39–62. Richmond, England: Curzon, 1996.

Spivak, Gayatri. *A Critique of Postcolonial Reason: Toward a History of the Vanishing Present.* Cambridge, MA: Harvard University Press, 1999.

———. "A Literary Representation of the Subaltern: A Woman's Text from the Third World." In *In Other Worlds: Essays in Cultural Politics*, 241–68. New York: Methuen, 1987.

———. "The Rani of Sirmur: An Essay in Reading the Archives." *History and Theory* 24, no. 3 (1985): 247–72.

———. "Three Women's Texts and a Critique of Imperialism." *Critical Inquiry* 12, no. 1 (1985): 243–61.

Sreenivas, Mytheli. "Emotion, Identity, and the Female Subject: Tamil Women's Magazines in Colonial India, 1890–1940." *Journal of Women's History* 14, no. 4 (2003): 59–82.

———. *Wives, Widows, Concubines: The Conjugal Family Ideal in Colonial India.* Bloomington: Indiana University Press, 2008.

Srivastava, Sanjay. "The Idea of Lata Mangheshkar: Hindu Sexuality, the Girl-Child, and Heterosexual Desire in the Time of the Five Year Plans." In *Passionate Modernity: Sexuality, Class, and Consumption in India*, 79–115. New Delhi: Routledge, 2007.

Subrahmanyam, Sanjay, David Shulman, A. R. Venkatachalapathy, Francesca Orsini, Aamir R. Mufti, and G. P. Deshpande. "A Review Symposium: Literary Cultures in History." *Indian Economic and Social History Review* 42, no. 3 (2005): 377–408.

Subramanian, N. Chidambara. "Yātrā Mārkkam: Abippirāya Pētam, Cantēkat Teḷivu" [The journey's path: A difference of opinion, a alarification of doubt]. *Maṇikkoṭi* 5, no. 8 (1937): 50–52.

Subramanyam, Ka. Naa. "Cāhitya Akāṭami Tamiḻ Paricu" [The Sahitya Akademi Tamil Award]. *Eḻuttu*, no. 1 (1959): 4.

———. "Ciṟanta Tamiḻc Ciṟukataikaḷ: Oru Tokuppukkāṉa Cila Kuṟippukaḷ" [Distinguished Tamil short stories: Some thoughts for a collection]. *Eḻuttu*, no. 1 (1959): 7–12.

———, ed. *Etar̲kāk El̲utukir̲ēn̲?* [Why do I write?]. Chennai: Eluttu Prachuram, 1972. First published 1962.

———. "Ilakkiyat Taram Uyara. . . ." [May literary quality advance . . .]. In *Ilakkiya Vaṭṭam Ital̲ttokuppu* [Selections from the journal *Ilakkiya Vaṭṭam*], 221–22. Chennai: Sandhya Patippakam, 2004. First published 1963.

———. "Ilakkiyattil Karuttum Urupamum: Oru Campāṣṇai" [Content and form in literature: a dialogue]. In *Ilakkiyattukku Oru Iyakkam*, 79–109. First published 1964–65.

———. *Ilakkiyattukku Oru Iyakkam: Ilakkiya Vaṭṭak Kaṭṭuraikaḷ* [A movement for literature: Essays from the journal *Ilakkiya Vaṭṭam*]. Chennai: Kavya, 1985.

———. *Ilakkiya Vimarcan̲aṅkaḷ: Ka. Nā. Cu. Kaṭṭuraikaḷ—2* [Literary criticism: essays by Ka. Naa. Subramanyam, volume 2]. Edited by Kavya Shanmugasundaram. Chennai: Kavya, 2005.

———. "In̲r̲aiyat Tamil̲ Ilakkiyam" [Contemporary Tamil literature]. In *Ilakkiyattukku Oru Iyakkam*, 65–78. First published 1959.

———. *Intiya Ilakkiyam* [Indian literature]. Chennai: Kalaignaan Pathipagam, 1984.

———. "Kavi Pāratiyār" [The poet Bharati]. In *Ilakkiyattukku Oru Iyakkam*, 43–54. First published 1964–65.

———. "Mūn̲r̲u Cir̲ukatāciriyarkaḷ: Lā. Ca. Rā., Ti. Jān̲kirāman̲, Cundara Rāmacāmi" [Three short story writers: Laa. Sa. Raa., Thi. Janakiraman, Sundara Ramaswamy]. In *Ilakkiya Vimarcan̲aṅkaḷ*, 270–74. First published 1964.

———. "Tamil Literature." *Indian Literature* 7, no. 2 (1964): 97–103.

———. "Tamil Literature." *Indian Literature* 3, no. 1 (1959–60): 102–5.

———. "Tamil̲c Cir̲ukataiyil Ver̲r̲i Kaṇṭavarkaḷ" [Succesful Tamil short story writers]. In *Intiya Ilakkiyam*, 62–77. First published 1966.

———. "Tamil̲il Cir̲ukatai" [The short story in Tamil]. In *Ilakkiyattukku Oru Iyakkam*, 177–81. First published 1963–65.

———. "Tamil̲il Puṭuk Kavitai" [New poetry in Tamil]. In *Intiya Ilakkiyam*, 78–87. First published 1959.

———. "Ulaka Ilakkiyam" [World literature]. In *Ilakkiyattukku Oru Iyakkam*, 110–22. First published 1964–65.

———. "Yātrā Mārkkam: Tal̲uvalum Mol̲i Peyarppum" [The journey's path: Adaptation and translation]. *Maṇikkoṭi* 5, no. 8 (1937): 62–66.

Sundararajan, P. G. "Chitti." "Cūṭāmaṇi Kataikaḷ" [Chudmani's stories]. *El̲uttu* 8, no. 3 (1960): 53–55.

Sundararajan, P. G. "Chitti" and Cho. Sivapathasundaram. *Tamil̲il Cir̲ukatai: Varalār̲um Vaḷarcciyum* [The Tamil short story: History and development]. Madras: Crea, 1989.

Tagore, Rabindranath. "Modernism in Literature." *Indian Literature* 6, no. 1 (1963): 1–5.

Tharu, Susie. "The Impossible Subject: Caste and the Gendered Body." *Economic and Political Weekly* 31, no. 22 (1996): 1311–15.

Tharu, Susie, and K. Lalita, eds. *Women Writing in India, Volume 1: 600 B.C. to the Early 20th Century*. New York: Feminist Press at the City University of New York, 1991.

———, eds. *Women Writing in India, Volume II: The Twentieth Century*. New York: Feminist Press at the City University of New York, 1993.

Todorov, Tzvetan. *Genres in Discourse*. Translated by Catherine Porter. Cambridge: Cambridge University Press, 1990. Originally published 1978 in French.

Trautmann, Thomas. *Languages and Nations: The Dravidian Proof in Colonial Madras*. Berkeley: University of California Press, 2006.

Trivedi, Harish. "The Urdu Premchand: The Hindi Premchand." *Jadavpur Journal of Comparative Literature* 22 (1984): 104–18.

Tyagi, Rajeshwari. "Nayī Kahānī ke Trikoṇ par Ek Ṭeḍī Nazar" [A sideways glance at the Nayī Kahānī Triumvirate]. *Dharmayuga* 15, no. 9 (1964): 39.

Uberoi, Patricia. *Freedom and Destiny: Gender, Family, and Culture in India*. New Delhi: Oxford University Press, 2006.

———. "When Is Marriage Not a Marriage? Sex, Sacrament and Contract in Hindu Marriage." In *Social Reform, Sexuality, and the State*, edited by Patricia Uberoi, 318–45. New Delhi: Sage, 1996.

Vaithees, V. Ravi. *Religion, Caste, and Nation in South India: Maraimalai Adigal, the Neo-Saivite Movement, and Tamil Nationalism, 1876–1950*. New Delhi: Oxford University Press, 2015.

Vaitheespara, Ravi, and Rajesh Venkatasubramanian. "Beyond the Politics of Identity: The Left and the Politics of Caste and Identity in Tamil Nadu, 1920–1963." *South Asia: Journal of South Asian Studies* 38, no. 4 (2015): 543–57.

Vallikkannan. *Carasvati Kālam*: Maṇikkoṭi *Mutal* Carasvati *Varaiyilum* [The era of Saraswati: From the journal *Maṇikkoṭi* to the journal *Carasvati*]. Palaiyankottai: Ilakiya Tedal Veliyeedu, 1982.

———. *Tamiḻil Ciṟu Pattirikkaikaḷ* [Small magazines in Tamil]. Chennai: Manivasakar Patippakam, 2004.

Varma, Archana. "Behada" [Without boundaries]. In *Sthagita* [Delayed], 143–56. Delhi: Rajkamal Prakashan, 1981. First published in 1979.

———. "A 'Grand Celebration' of Feminist Discourse." Translated by Simona Sawhney and Ruth Vanita. *Seminar* 616 (2010): 73–77.

Venkatachalapathy, A. R. "From *Pulavar* to Professor: Politics and the Professionalization of Tamil Pandits." Working Paper Series 11, TRG Poverty & Education, Max Weber Foundation, 2018. https://perspectivia.net/receive/ploneimport_mods_00011890.

———. *In Those Days There Was No Coffee: Writings in Cultural History*. New Delhi: Yoda Press, 2006.

———. *The Province of the Book: Scholars, Scribes, and Scribblers in Colonial Tamilnadu*. Ranikhet, India: Permanent Black, 2012.

Verma, Nirmal. *Hara Bāriś meṃ* [During each rain]. Delhi: Radhakrishna Prakasan, 1970.

———. "Nayī Kahānī: Lekhak ke Bahī Khāte se" [The new story: From a writer's ledger]. *Dharmayuga* 15, no. 3 (1964): 18–19.

Vyasan. "Yātrā Mārkkam" [The journey's path]. *Maṇikkoṭi* 5, no. 4 (1937): 54–57.

———. "Yātrā Mārkkam: Taḻuvalum Moḻi Peyarppum" [The journey's path: Adaptation and translation]. *Maṇikkoṭi* 5, no. 8 (1937): 67–72.

Wakankar, Milind. "The Moment of Criticism in Indian Nationalist Thought: Ramchandra Shukla and the Poetics of a Hindi Responsiblility." *South Atlantic Quarterly* 101, no. 4 (2002): 987–1014.

Warwick Research Collective (WReC). *Combined and Uneven Development: Towards a New Theory of World Literature*. Liverpool: Liverpool University Press, 2015.

Watt, Ian. *The Rise of the Novel: Studies in Defoe, Richardson and Fielding*. London: Hogarth Press, 1987. First published 1957.

Weber, Albrecht. "The Name 'Indian Literature.'" In Mukherjee, *The Idea of an Indian Literature*, 1–8.

Weinbaum, Alys Eve, Lynn M. Thomas, Priti Ramamurthy, Uta G. Poiger, Madeleine Y. Dong, and Tani E. Barlow. "The Modern Girl as a Heuristic Device: Collaboration, Connective Comparison, Multidirectional Citation." In *The Modern Girl around the World: Consumption, Modernity, and Globalization*, edited by Alys Eve Weinbaum, Lynn M. Thomas, Priti Ramamurthy, Uta G. Poiger, Madeleine Y. Dong, and Tani E. Barlow, 1–24. Durham, NC: Duke University Press, 2008.

Wellek, René, and Austin Warren. *Theory of Literature*. New York: Harcourt, Brace, 1948.

Yadav, Rajendra. "Ek Duniyā Samānāntar" [A parallel world]. In *Ek Duniyā Samānāntar* [A parallel world], edited by Rajendra Yadav, 17–75. New Delhi: Akshar Prakashan, 1966.

———. "Ek Kamzor Laṛki kī Kahānī" [The story of a weak girl]. In *Jahāṁ Lakshmī Qaid Hai* [Where Lakshmi is imprisoned], 15–33. New Delhi: Radhakrishna Prakashan, 2001. First published 1957.

———. "Kahānī: Naī Kahānī Tak" [From the story to the new story]. In *Kathā Yātrā* [The journey of the story], edited by Rajendra Yadav, 1–28. New Delhi: Akshar Prakashan, 1965.

———. *Kahānī: Svarūp aura Saṃvedanā* [The short story: Form and sensibility]. New Delhi: National Publishing House, 1968.

———. *Muṛ-Muṛke Dekhtā Huṁ: Lagabhaga Ātmakathya* [I look back continually: An approximate autobiography]. Delhi: Rajkamal Prakashan, 2001.

———. *Premacanda kī Virāsata aura Anya Nibandha* [Premchand's heritage and other essays]. New Delhi: Akshar Prakashan, 1978.

———. "Sunie Rajendra Yādav kā 93 Minaṭ Inṭarvyū" [Listen to a 93-minute interview with Rajendra Yadav]. *Baiṭhak Vicāroṁ kī* [Forum of ideas], edited by Anand Prakash, March 16, 2010. http://baithak.hindyugm.com/2010/03/listen-rajendra-yadav-long-interview.html.

Yashaschandra, Sitamshu. "From Hemacandra to *Hind Swarāj*: Region and Power in Gujurati Literary Culture." In Pollock, *Literary Cultures in History*, 567–611.

Yildiz, Yasemin. *Beyond the Mother Tongue: The Postmonolingual Condition*. New York: Fordham University Press, 2012.

Young, Robert J. C. "The Postcolonial Comparative." *PMLA* 128, no. 3 (201): 683–89.

———. "That Which Is Casually Called a Language." *PMLA* 131, no. 5 (2016): 1207–21.

Zaheer, Sajjad. *The Light: A History of the Movement for Progressive Literature in the Indo-Pakistan Subcontinent*. Translated by Amina Azfar. Karachi: Oxford University Press, 2006. Originally published 1954 in Urdu.

———. "Reminiscences." In Pradhan, *Marxist Cultural Movement in India*, 33–47.

Zhdanov, A. A. "Soviet Literature: The Richest in Ideas, the Most Advanced Literature." In *Soviet Writers' Congress, 1934: The Debate on Socialist Realism and Modernism in the Soviet Union*, edited by H. G. Scott, 25–69. Translated by H. G. Scott. London: Lawrence and Wishart, 1977. Originally published 1934 in Russian.

Zvelebil, Kamil. *The Smile of Murugan on Tamil Literature of South India*. Leiden: Brill, 1973.

Index

FLASHPOINTS

1. *On Pain of Speech: Fantasies of the First Order and the Literary Rant*, Dina Al-Kassim
2. *Moses and Multiculturalism*, Barbara Johnson, with a foreword by Barbara Rietveld
3. *The Cosmic Time of Empire: Modern Britain and World Literature*, Adam Barrows
4. *Poetry in Pieces: César Vallejo and Lyric Modernity*, Michelle Clayton
5. *Disarming Words: Empire and the Seductions of Translation in Egypt*, Shaden M. Tageldin
6. *Wings for Our Courage: Gender, Erudition, and Republican Thought*, Stephanie H. Jed
7. *The Cultural Return*, Susan Hegeman
8. *English Heart, Hindi Heartland: The Political Life of Literature in India*, Rashmi Sadana
9. *The Cylinder: Kinematics of the Nineteenth Century*, Helmut Müller-Sievers
10. *Polymorphous Domesticities: Pets, Bodies, and Desire in Four Modern Writers*, Juliana Schiesari
11. *Flesh and Fish Blood: Postcolonialism, Translation, and the Vernacular*, S. Shankar
12. *The Fear of French Negroes: Transcolonial Collaboration in the Revolutionary Americas*, Sara E. Johnson
13. *Figurative Inquisitions: Conversion, Torture, and Truth in the Luso-Hispanic Atlantic*, Erin Graff Zivin
14. *Cosmopolitan Desires: Global Modernity and World Literature in Latin America*, Mariano Siskind
15. *Fiction Beyond Secularism*, Justin Neuman
16. *Periodizing Jameson: Dialectics, the University, and the Desire for Narrative*, Phillip E. Wegner
17. *The Practical Past*, Hayden White
18. *The Powers of the False: Reading, Writing, Thinking Beyond Truth and Fiction*, Doro Wiese
19. *The Object of the Atlantic: Concrete Aesthetics in Cuba, Brazil, and Spain, 1868–1968*, Rachel Price
20. *Epic and Exile: Novels of the German Popular Front 1933–1945*, Hunter Bivens
21. *An Innocent Abroad: Lectures in China*, J. Hillis Miller
22. *Form and Instability: East Europe, Literature, Postimperial Difference*, Anita Starosta
23. *Bombay Modern: Arun Kolatkar and Bilingual Literary Culture*, Anjali Nerlekar
24. *Intimate Relations: Social Reform and the Late Nineteenth-Century South Asian Novel*, Krupa Shandilya
25. *Media Laboratories: Late Modernist Authorship in South America*, Sarah Ann Wells
26. *Acoustic Properties: Radio, Narrative, and the New Neighborhood of the Americas*, Tom McEnaney

27. *The New Woman: Literary Modernism, Queer Theory, and the Trans Feminine Allegory*, Emma Heaney
28. *Civilizing War: Imperial Politics and the Poetics of National Rupture*, Nasser Mufti
29. *Late Colonial Sublime: Neo-Epics and the End of Romanticism*, G. S. Sahota
30. *Globalizing Race: Anti-Semitism, Empire, and the Politics of Scale in Modern French and European Culture*, Dorian Bell
31. *Domestications: American Empire, Literary Culture, and the Postcolonial Lens*, Hosam Mohamed Aboul-Ela
32. *Behold an Animal: Four Exorbitant Readings*, Thangam Ravindranathan
33. *Capital Letters: Hugo, Baudelaire, Camus, and the Death Penalty*, Ève Morisi
34. *Immaterial Archives: An African Diaspora Poetics of Loss*, Jenny Sharpe
35. *Figures of the World: The Naturalist Novel and Transnational Form*, Christopher Laing Hill
36. *Imperfect Solidarities: Tagore, Gandhi, Du Bois, and the Forging of the Global Anglophone*, Madhumita Lahiri
37. *Fictional Environments: Mimesis, Deforestation, and Development in Latin America*, Victoria Saramago
38. *How to Read a Moment: The American Novel and the Crisis of the Present*, Mathias Nilges
39. *Secondhand China: Spain, the East, and the Politics of Translation*, Carles Prado-Fonts
40. *New World Maker: Radical Poetics, Black Internationalism, and the Translations of Langston Hughes*, Ryan James Kernan